3rd edition

AQA Business Studies for AS

**Malcolm Surridge
and Andrew Gillespie**

**HODDER
EDUCATION**

AN HACHETTE UK COMPANY

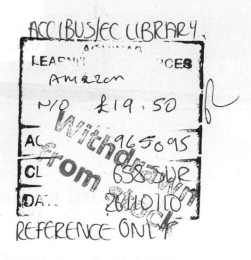
Orders: please contact Bookpoint Ltd, 130 Milton Park, Abingdon, Oxon OX14 4SB. Telephone: (44) 01235 827720. Fax: (44) 01235 400454. Lines are open from 9.00 – 5.00, Monday to Saturday, with a 24-hour message answering service. You can also order through our website www.hoddereducation.co.uk.

British Library Cataloguing in Publication Data
A catalogue record for this title is available from the British Library

ISBN: 978 0340 957172

First Published 2000
Second edition 2004
Third edition 2008
Impression number   10 9 8 7 6 5
Year   2014 2013 2012 2011 2010

Cover photo © Gregor Schuster/zefa/Corbis.
Typeset by Pantek Arts Ltd, Maidstone, Kent.
Illustration on page 32 by Barking Dog Arts
Printed in Italy for Hodder Education, an Hachette UK company, 338 Euston Road, London NW1 3BH

Contents

How to use this book

This book provides a thorough coverage of the AQA AS specification. By the end of this book we hope you will have developed a real interest in the stimulating world of business as well as being in a strong position for your exams. We aim to help you to understand the key issues in each topic and also learn how to use your knowledge and develop the right skills for exam success.

The book is divided into chapters that match exactly the contents and structure of the AQA specification. This means you should be able to see exactly where you are in terms of covering the exam material.

At the start of each chapter there we give an overview of the issues that will be covered and give you a list of the topics that you need to make sure you have understood by the end of the chapter.

Within each chapter there are also several features to help you understand the material. These are:

- Business in focus: this feature highlights the type of question that might be asked in the exam and the issues you should think about when revising. What do you think? This feature should help to bring a topic to life by showing it in action in a real business. We hope to show you how the various theories and models can be applied to real business decisions
- Examiner's advice: this feature is to help you reflect on what has just been covered in the book. How does it relate to other topics or your own experiences? What would you do in a given situation?
- Key terms: this feature will give you definitions for key terms
- Web links: these will give you links to website where you can get more information on a particular story so you can follow it up and do more research.

At the end of each chapter we provide:

- A summary of the key points covered. If you want to get a quick idea of what a chapter is looking at then the summary is quite a good place to start.
- Quick questions. These are short questions to help you check whether you have understood the key points
- Issues for analysis and evaluation. These sections highlight the possible connections between the theory covered in the chapter as well as issues that may involved judgements and are therefore evaluative issues. These features are there to help you pick out the key points in the chapter.
- Analysis and evaluation. These quesions will help you to develop your examination skills. By practising these you can practice key skills such as applying your answers and evaluating the key points in your argument. Suggested answers are available on the CD that accompanies this book.
- A case study. This helps you develop your examination technique even further by providing a series of questions that are similar to the type of data question you might get in the exam. Again this provides excellent practice for you. Suggested answers to these questions again are provided on the CD that accompanies this book.
- One step further. This provides extension material that is useful if you want to go beyond the specification or add further to your understanding of a topic.

Overall, we hope this book provides an interesting read and that you feel it provides a good coverage of the AQA specification and helps prepare you effectively for your exams. If you have any suggestions how we can improve the book in future editions do not hesitate to contact us on wattgill@aol.com

What does 'the expert choice' mean for you?

We work with more examiners and experts than any other publisher

- Because we work with more experts and examiners than any other publisher, the very latest curriculum requirements are built into this course and there is a perfect match between your course and the resources that you need to succeed. We make it easier for you to gain the skills and knowledge that you need for the best results.

- We have chosen the best team of experts – including the people that mark the exams – to give you the very best chance of success; look out for their advice throughout this book: this is content that you can trust.

Welcome to Dynamic Learning

Dynamic Learning is a simple and powerful way of integrating this text with digital resources to help you succeed, by bringing learning to life. Whatever your learning style, Dynamic Learning will help boost your understanding.

- Boost your understanding through interactive activities, and quizzes available on both Student Online and Network editions

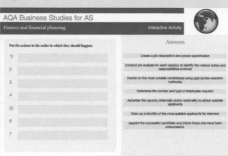

More direct contact with teachers and students than any other publisher

- We talk with more than 100 000 students every year through our student conferences, run by Philip Allan Updates. We hear at first hand what you need to make a success of you're A-level studies and build what we learn into every new course. Learn more about our conferences at **www.philipallan.co.uk**

- Our new materials are trialled in classrooms as we develop them, and the feedback built into every new book or resource that we publish. You can be part of that. If you have comments that you would like to make about this book, please email us at: **feedback@hodder.co.uk**

More collaboration with Subject Associations than any other publisher

- Subject Associations sit at the heart of education. We work closely with more Associations than any other publisher. This means that our resources support the most creative teaching and learning, using the skills of the best teachers in their field to create resources for you.

More opportunities for your teachers to stay ahead than with any other publisher

- Through our Philip Allan Updates Conferences, we offer teachers access to Continuing Professional Development. Our focused and practical conferences ensure that your teachers have access to the best presenters, teaching materials and training resources. Our presenters include experienced teachers, Chief and Principal Examiners, leading educationalists, authors and consultants. This course is built on all of this expertise.

Dynamic Learning Network Edition

- Network Edition gives easy access to the book's key photographs, charts and diagrams so that you can use them in your studies

- Key business concepts are illustrated in 20 video clips with exciting young entrepreneur Fraser Doherty in the Network Edition

- Hear examiners talk you through exam-style questions and answers in detail using our unique 'Personal Tutor' software. You will see them build the answer that gets the best-possible marks and highlight common problems and errors

- Network Edition gives access to easy-to-use PowerPoint presentations which show you what each chapter is going to deliver for you, and help you to check your understanding once you have worked through the section

This book is supported by a free website at **www.dynamic-learning-student.co.uk**. To access this website refer to the instructions printed on the inside front cover.

Copyright restrictions mean that some materials may not be accessible from within the Student Online edition.

You can find out more at www.dynamic-learning.co.uk

Acknowledgements

For Alex with much love from Malcolm
Malcolm Surridge

All my love to my beautiful wife, my fantastic daughters, and our baby boy, Seth.
Andrew Gillespie

The authors would like to thank everyone at Hodder Education for all their help.
Every effort has been made to trace and acknowledge ownership of copyright. The publishers will be glad to make suitable arrangements with any copyright holder whom it has not been possible to contact. The authors and publishers would like to thank the following for the use of photographs in this volume:

Courtesy of Beautiful Vending, p5; Action Press/Rex Features, p6 (Figure 1.2a); TopFoto.co.uk. p6 (Figure 1.2b); Kevin Winter/Getty Images for GQ, p6 (Figure 1.2c); © Content Mine International/Alamy, p8; Jez Gunnall, courtesy of Mamas & Papas, p14; © & ® Meccano SA, p15; John Dee/Rex Features, p16; © Lew Robertson/Corbis, p17; Tenza Technologies Ltd, p18; Courtesy of Toni&Guy Media, p22; Gecko Head Gear, p35; Anti Aimo-Koivisto/Rex Features, p39; Nils Jorgensen/Rex Features, p43; Rex Features, p52; David Paul Morris/Getty Images, p62; Nils Jorgensen/Rex Features, p63; Pauline Clifford StarSparkles, p77; Trevor Palin, courtesy of SpinVox Ltd, p95; Nick Randall/Rex Features, p109; © Jack Carey/Alamy, p111; Liz Steketee/Getty Images, p117; The White Company, p124; © Carlos Lumiere, courtesy of Hannah Marshall, p126; © Steven May/Alamy, p139; CenterParcs, p158; Special Collections Department, J. Willard Marriott Library, University of Utah, p170; Paul Dawson, p178; © mediablitzimages (uk) Limited/Alamy, p187; © Ferruccio/Alamy, p191; Lakeland, p221; Courtesy of Dell Inc., p222; Geoff Robinson/Rex Features, p227; UPPA/Photoshot, p228 (top left); ©2004 Credit:TopFoto/UPPA, p228 (torch); By kind permission of the Conservative Party, p228 (tree); © vario images GmbH & Co.KG/Alamy, p229; Dualit, p237; © David R. Frazier Photolibrary, Inc./Alamy, p262; Richard Jones/Rex Features, p272.

unit one

THE AQA STORY...

There is a story that runs through AQA AS Business Studies and on into the A2 specification. It is important that you understand this story because it sets out the philosophy of the specification and the extent of each part of the specification. It will help to guide you through your studies as well as assisting in preparing you for the AS and A2 examinations.

Unit 1: Planning and financing a business

The AQA story starts with an entrepreneur planning a business. Therefore this part of the specification focuses on *small* businesses. These can be businesses operating in any part of the economy (for example, services, manufacturing, construction, or the primary sector). It will help you to think about and study diverse small businesses. These businesses do not sell their products in international markets. Instead, they sell their goods and services in local or regional markets, or perhaps throughout the UK.

The major emphasis in Unit 1 is on the business *before* it starts trading. So we are looking at a business from the germ of the idea through the research and planning stages and up to the start of trading. This encompasses a lot of different types of business activities and is intended to introduce you to the breadth of business studies.

The Unit 1 story does take you a little further, however. It invites you to look back at a business after it has been trading for a short period of time and to think about how well the entrepreneur planned the business. This will give you a chance to assess the quality of the entrepreneur's planning and the importance of the planning process to the success (or otherwise) of a specific business.

Unit 1 provides a foundation on which Unit 2 and the A2 units will build.

When studying this unit you will cover such topics as:

- how to generate and perfect business ideas
- deciding how to raise the finance to get you started
- assessing the profitability of a business
- choosing the best legal structure
- researching the market
- deciding whether or not to employ others
- deciding how and where to produce your product
- planning your cash and spending

These are all vital topics when you are thinking about starting a business. This unit will therefore help you to understand the key issues involved in a start-up and help you to solve some of the problems that entrepreneurs face.

> **The skills assessed in this unit are:**
> **Content:** This assesses your understanding of a concept. It is very useful to define terms to gain these marks.
> **Application:** This assesses your ability to relate to the given content. You need to make sure your answers relate to the actual case you have been given.
> **Analysis:** This assesses your ability to develop an argument. You need to show a chain of reasoning for this and using theory helps.
> **Evaluation:** This assesses your ability to show judgement, for example, to decide on the most important factor or key issue in an answer. Weighing up issues and prioritising are very important evaluation skills.

The Unit One Examination

This examination is based on a short case study following the planning process of a new business. It may include numerical data relating to marketing or financial planning, and calculation questions will be a regular part of this examination. The questions will be in two sections. Section A will comprise short questions ranging from definitions to explanations and calculations. Section B will include longer, higher mark questions calling for analysis and evaluation.

The majority of the marks in the Unit One examination are for content (or knowledge) and application as shown in the table below.

THE UNIT ONE EXAMINATION	
SKILL	PERCENTAGE OF MARKS
Content (or knowledge)	35
Application	28
Analysis	20
Evaluation	18

Section 1: Starting a business

1

Entrepreneurs and Enterprise

Have you ever had an idea for a new business? Have you thought about a product or service you think would do well? Most of us have had an idea we think might make our fortunes at some time in our lives. However, having an idea is one thing. Actually going out and setting up your business is another. To start a business and make it work takes particular skills and usually involves a great deal of hard work. In this chapter we consider what is meant by the terms 'enterprise' and 'entrepreneur', what skills or qualities you may need to be an entrepreneur and how entrepreneurs get their ideas. What you need to know by the end of this chapter:

- the meaning of 'enterprise' and 'entrepreneur'
- the importance of risk and rewards and opportunity cost
- the motives for becoming an entrepreneur
- government support for enterprise and entrepreneurs.

Entrepreneurs

An entrepreneur is someone who is willing to take a risk to start a new project or a new business. 'Enterprise' refers to the skills needed to do this. An entrepreneur has an idea and then tries to make it work. Entrepreneurs see the resources that are available and the possibilities of combining them in a particular way to provide a product or service. Entrepreneurs create new businesses and in so doing provide new products and services. Some entrepreneurs, such as Richard Branson of Virgin and Stelios Haji-Ioannou of easyGroup, continually have ideas for new businesses and set up many different ones during their careers. Such people are called 'serial entrepreneurs'.

Key terms
Entrepreneurs are individuals who take the risk to create or start a new business or project.
Enterprise is the skill needed to make a new idea work.

Entrepreneurs create change and challenge the way things are done. They find and create new markets, generate income and employment and bring about innovation. They are extremely important to the growth of an economy and to improving the quality and range of goods and services on offer.

Enterprise (or entrepreneurship) involves discovering, evaluating, and exploiting business opportunities.

Risk and reward

Entrepreneurs are prepared to take risks. They are investing time, money and effort into a new project that may or may not work. The danger is that it will not work and all their investment will be lost. Many new businesses fail. Look at the high street in your nearest village or town. How long have the shops been there? Have some opened up recently? Have some closed down in the last year? The landscape of the centre of most villages and towns is changing all the time as some business ideas fail and others rise to take their place. The real risk to entrepreneurs is that they will lose much or even everything they have put into a project because the business idea ends up failing.

Some of the causes of risk are external. For example, there could be a change in the economy, meaning people have less money to spend than entrepreneurs had expected (and so demand for their products is lower than they hoped), or competitors may have changed their behaviour, making it more difficult for similar businesses to survive.

Alternatively, the causes of risk could be internal. It may be that an entrepreneur's understanding of the market is not as good as he had thought and he makes some bad pricing decisions. It may be that his judgement of people is poor and he hires the wrong people, with the result that the quality of service is not as good as he had hoped.

Entrepreneurs may sometimes undertake a project 'because it is there to be done'. They may be driven by a desire to do something new. This in itself may be a reward in terms of self satisfaction: they can hopefully look back on their careers and be proud of what they have achieved. However, they may also be interested in other rewards from setting up, such as the financial gain from owning their own business. These rewards can be high! For example, YouTube was set up in February 2005 by Chad Hurley, Steve Chen, and Jawed Karim. The website includes music videos and movie and TV clips, as well as material posted by the general public. In 2006 the founders of YouTube sold their business to Google for $1.65 billion! Not a bad return in less than two years.

To go ahead with any venture, the expected rewards must justify the risk involved. In an ideal world a project would have a high reward and low risk, but typically new ventures are very risky because there are so many things that can go wrong. In fact, many ideas do not even end up being launched. Entrepreneurs hit so many setbacks or face so many difficulties that the project does not go ahead.

Table 1.1 Risk – reward matrix

		Risk	
		Low	High
Reward	Low	These are safe projects but do not generate high returns	These projects are not of interest because of the high risk relative to the low rewards
	High	These projects are ideal: low risk but high rewards. However it may not be easy to find projects like this!	These projects are of interest but risky. To go ahead entrepreneurs must believe the rewards outweigh the risks.

Business in Focus

A survey for Learndirect Business found that first-time entrepreneurs were willing to pay a high price to fulfil their dreams. Eleven per cent of entrepreneurs said they were willing to risk their relationship with their partner, 26 per cent were prepared to go into heavy debt, 30 per cent were prepared to lose their savings and four per cent were even willing to sacrifice their health for the sake of the business!

Beautiful Vending

Neil Mackay and Richard Starrett met while studying at Glasgow's Strathclyde University. One day in 2004, they were talking about the problems that young women have with 'frizzy hair' when out clubbing. They came up with a great product idea – a vending machine that helps women to straighten their hair quickly on arrival at their destination. They took over a year to develop the idea, and over £100,000 was invested into manufacture, design, marketing and legal costs. The product – originally called the 'Straight Up' styler (now called Beautiful Vending Style) – was first released in Scotland in 2005 and the machines are now available nationally in 900 nightclubs, four gym chains and two shopping centres as well as being available in 500 locations internationally. This is the third successful business that Neil and Richard have established together. Their company, Beautiful Vending, is based in Hamilton and is the only company in the world to make and distribute the styling machines.

Figure 1.1 The 'Straight-Up' styler

Why become an entrepreneur?

More than three million people, or 12 per cent of the UK population, have already set up in business on their own. Research by Vodafone indicates that a further 6 per cent of UK adults are in the process of setting up their own business and nearly a third of all people are considering doing so. So what drives people to set up their own business?

There are many attractions to being an entrepreneur:

- You will experience a great feeling of satisfaction if your idea is successful. Imagine being able to look at a large business and know that you created it and helped it to grow.

- You will be your own boss. Fed up being told what to do? Dislike orders? Then being an entrepreneur may be the way forward. Setting up on your own means it is your business, to do with as you wish. This can be challenging and demanding but it does mean you are more in control of your own destiny. Some people prefer this to working for others: they like their independence.

- You keep the rewards. If you work in a business for someone else then the rewards belong to them. You may work very hard and very successfully and get a bonus, but the major rewards will usually go to the owners. If you are an entrepreneur, you are the owner and so any rewards there

Luke Johnson

Luke Johnson is a serial entrepreneur who, among other ventures, transformed PizzaExpress and set up the Belgo restaurants. He then went on to become chairman of the television station, Channel 4, as well as writing a book called *The Maverick*.

His book includes the top 14 reasons to be an entrepreneur:

1 Building your own company is the best fun you can have with your clothes on.
2 It's still the best way to get rich .

3 Working for yourself is not just about becoming rich – it's also about making things happen and making a difference.

4 If you work for yourself you control your destiny.

5 Jobs for life and final salary pension schemes don't exist any more.

6 If you're the boss, you make the rules.

7 Thanks to the internet, it's never been easier to set up business in focus.

8 As an entrepreneur, you get the rewards for your efforts.

9 Entrepreneurs are the main source of new jobs and growth.

10 Being an entrepreneur can be a highly creative endeavour.

11 Entrepreneurs are cool – look at the success of TV shows like *Dragons' Den* and *Make Me a Million*.

12 There is no hierarchy in your own firm – anything is possible.

13 Building a team and developing talent is really satisfying.

14 Because you don't want to wake up one day when you're too old and say 'I wish I had gone for it with that idea I had…'

are belong to you. The downside is that if anything goes wrong the losses are yours as well.

- You have more control of what you do and when you do it compared to working for someone else. A survey by Yorkshire Bank found that almost three in five small-business owners first decided to become self-employed because of a desire for more flexible working and an improved balance between work and their social lives Two in five did so for greater financial control.

What do you think?

Do you recognise any of the following entrepreneurs?

Figure 1.2a

Figure 1.2b

Figure 1.2c

Answers:
Figure 1.2a Pierre Omidya, founder of eBay
Figure 1.2b James Palumbo, founder of Ministry of Sound
Figure 1.2c Chad Hurley and Steve Chen founders of YouTube

Real-life Business

League of Adventurists

The winners of the 2007 Shell LiveWIRE Young Entrepreneurs of the year were Tom Morgan, Dan Wedgwood and Lamorna Trahair. These three entrepreneurs have set up a company called the League of Adventurists International. They believe that:

'Travelling is for wimps, where is the fun in lounging on a beach surrounded by guitar wielding chumps? What's the point of going to a country if you've bought a guide book – you know what's going to happen before it docs. The phrase 'adventure travel' conjures images of guided tours for pensioners to Everest base camp. We want real adventure, not a sterilised imitation. We want to be stuck up to our armpits in mud fighting a giant snake or thundering across a desert miles from civilisation.'

To this end the company offers 'real' adventures. 'These things aren't safe. We can't guarantee you will be able to complete them or even come out the other end unscathed. We can guarantee you will have a good old-fashioned adventure. Proper adventure, not flimsy half wit adventure with a guide and an itinerary.' The adventures include the Mongol rally where you 'travel a third of the way around the earth, from London to Mongolia via a plethora of countries most people haven't heard of in any old car that has an engine with no more than 1 litre of power.

Starting from London, the rally finishes in the Mongolian capital Ulaanbaatar around three weeks and a whole heap of adventure later. It's between about 8 and 10,000 miles depending on the route you choose. To get to the end teams have gone as far north as the Arctic Circle and as far south as Afghanistan. What happens to you between London, the deserts, mountains, bandits and wilderness is anyone's guess. In a normal year just over half the teams make the finish line in one piece.' Last year the race raised over £200,000 for charity.

Web link

For more information, visit www.theadventurists.com

Opportunity cost

The opportunity cost of starting a business venture refers to the benefits that could have been gained from an alternative project. If an entrepreneur invests her money and time into setting up a fashion business rather than a café, the opportunity cost is the rewards that could have been gained from the café.

Any decision to set up a business will involve an opportunity cost. For example, an individual may give up a full-time job working for a large business to go and set up on her own. The opportunity cost will refer to the salary and benefits given up by choosing to be an entrepreneur.

When choosing to start up you should be careful to consider what you are sacrificing. You need to be sure that you think it is really worth it.

Key terms
Opportunity cost is the benefit from the next best alternative that has been given up.

Examiner's advice

The concept of opportunity cost is a very powerful one. Whenever you make a decision you should think of what you are *not* doing as a result – is it worth the sacrifice?

What skills do you need to be a successful entrepreneur?

There is no single set of qualities that has been identified that will definitely make someone a successful entrepreneur. Entrepreneurs can differ enormously in terms of their backgrounds, skills, interests and personalities.

However, it is likely that a successful entrepreneur is someone who:

- is prepared to work very hard, especially in the initial stages of setting up the business. This means you need determination and the ability to cope with stress and setbacks
- has a vision. Many entrepreneurs have stories about the various problems they encountered when they first started up. Problems with money, suppliers, equipment and so on are all fairly common. It is also quite usual for others around you to be more cautious and less certain that your project will work than you are. To be successful you need faith in your idea and a belief in your own vision even when there are initial problems.
- is willing to take a risk. It takes a lot of nerve to give up your existing job and start out on your own and yet this is what many people do. You may have to give up the salary, the company car, the support from head office and the pension just to pursue your dream. You may also have to go through quite a long period of time with relatively low rewards before you make it a success (if you ever do!).

According to the Royal Bank of Scotland (RBS) a successful entrepreneur is usually:

- well-rounded: someone who can make the product, promote it, sell it and count the money
- able to bounce back: a person who can cope with mistakes and have the confidence to try again
- innovative: not an 'inventor' in the traditional sense but a person who is able to carve out a new niche in the market, often a niche that is invisible to others
- results-orientated: to make a business successful requires a drive that only comes from setting goals and targets and getting pleasure from achieving them
- a professional risk-taker: to succeed means taking measured risks. Often, successful entrepreneurs use a step-by-step approach to risk-taking, at each stage

exposing themselves to only a measured amount of personal risk and moving from one stage to the next only as each decision is proved correct.

- totally committed: hard work, energy and single-mindedness are essential elements in the entrepreneurial profile.

Real-life Business

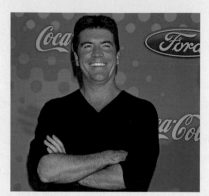

Figure 1.3 Simon Cowell

Simon Cowell

Simon Cowell was born on 7 October 1959. Although not hugely successful at school, he has gone on to become a multi-millionaire in the media business. He claims that he is a serial entrepreneur. He started work in the music business at EMI Music Publishing in London in 1979, where he identified a number of pop stars. He then set up several record labels and a TV production company, although not all of his ventures at this stage were successful. In 1989 he was hired by BMG, a music group, and signed several groups that went on to major stardom such as Westlife and Robson & Jerome

In 2001, Cowell hosted the TV singing competition *Pop Idol* in the UK and later did the same in America. He became very popular, due to his excellent insight into the ability of artists but also his outspoken nature. *Pop Idol* attracted over 10 million viewers and *American Idol* attracted over 22 million. Around this time Cowell set up another label called S Records: this signed the 2002 *Pop Idol* winner Will Young, who sold 1.8 million records with his first release. Cowell has also launched the operatic pop group Il Divo, which is made up of four singers from around the world. His next idea in America was *American Inventor* in which entrepreneurs compete to see who can come up with the best new product concept. The winner receives $1 million and the opportunity to develop the idea into a business.

In an interview with *Business Week* magazine Cowell said, 'I've always treated the music business as a business. Whether I'm making TV shows or signing artists, you have to do it by the head and not the heart – and I run my businesses that way.' To be a successful entrepreneur, he says, it is important to, 'Work hard, be patient, and be a sponge while learning your business. Learn how to take criticism. Follow your gut instincts and don't compromise.'

What do you think?

Imagine you were going to the bank and aiming to convince them to lend you money to start up your business. What could you say about yourself to show them that you had the right qualities to be a successful entrepreneur?

Web link

Stelios Haji-Ioannou is still looking for ideas for new businesses. If you have one, you can contact his business on www.easygroup.com. However, be warned: if you send an idea, it becomes his, so he might end up becoming wealthier, not you!

Why do governments like entrepreneurs?

Governments like entrepreneurs because they set up new businesses in an economy. This means that entrepreneurs:

- create jobs and help keep unemployment low in the economy
- earn money and pay taxes
- create competition for the existing providers in markets and provide new products and services. This is good for customers, who get more choice, and this is likely to lead to better service

Given the benefits of entrepreneurship, many governments are willing to help entrepreneurs to start up and grow their businesses.

What do governments do to help entrepreneurs?

They are many ways in which governments can help entrepreneurs. They can provide:

- access to advice and useful information to help them get started. For example, a new entrepreneur may have little experience of financial matters and appreciate some advice in this area.
- funding such as grants to help with the initial start-up costs
- legal protection for new ideas. For example, a patent provides legal protection for an invention. This means that inventors can make profits without their ideas being 'stolen' by others (see Chapter 2).

What do you think?

If you were thinking of starting up your own business, what do you think the government could or should do to help you, apart from the ideas listed above?

The entrepreneurial culture

If a country is said to have an entrepreneurial culture this means that entrepreneurs are highly valued and respected and that the business environment encourages and helps people to set up on their own. In America, for example, millions of people start their own business every year. It is generally accepted that some of these will fail, so if you have started a business and it has gone wrong, it is not seen as being particularly unusual. In other countries, if you have failed the tendency is for people to be suspicious about your business skills and you can find it very difficult to start up again: for example, you may find it almost impossible to borrow money again. This type of culture would not encourage others to try and start up their own businesses because of the fear of failure.

The number of regulations in a country can also have a significant impact on the willingness and ability of people to start up in business. If there are many forms to fill in, and many restrictions on what can and cannot be done. it can make it difficult and expensive for entrepreneurs to set up. This can reduce the incentive to start up on your own.

Business in Focus

UK entrepreneurs

A study by the London School of Economics found that, in the early 2000s, the UK is a much more entrepreneurial country than it was in the 1980s. It found that:

- entrepreneurs feel more respected now than at any time during the past 25 years

- profit is no longer of utmost importance for entrepreneurs – only 50 per cent of entrepreneurs surveyed said making money was their number one priority. In the early twenty-first century, entrepreneurs' main motivation is to create fun and dynamic teams, cultures and lifestyles
- entrepreneurs' role-models are those renowned for social consciousness and style – the founders

of Innocent Drinks, Richard Branson and dot-com success stories are frequently mentioned as the heroes of today's entrepreneurs. When asked which entrepreneur they preferred – Richard Branson or Alan Sugar – 84 per cent voted for Branson.

	Enterprise culture of the 1980s:	New economy of the 2000s:
View of entrepreneurs	Anti-establishment, maverick.	Respectable business or lifestyle choice.
View of entrepreneurship	Identify with entrepreneurial personality: risk-taking, growth and money-oriented.	Entrepreneurship seen as creative and enjoyable.
Entrepreneurial goals	Unlimited ambition and growth seen as important goals.	Aiming to achieve a certain size that will support their lifestyle or a particular way of life.
Entrepreneurial skills	Trading, dealing, negotiating.	Making something new.

One step further

Given the importance of entrepreneurship, it is not surprising that there have been many studies to try and find out what makes someone want to be an entrepreneur. The findings of the studies are varied, as highlighted below:

- David McClelland (1961) stated that entrepreneurs are mainly motivated by an overwhelming need for achievement and a strong desire to build something for themselves.
- Collins and Moore (1970) studied 150 entrepreneurs and concluded that they are tough, pragmatic people who are driven by the need to be independent and achieve: they do not like to submit to authority.
- Bird (1992) states that entrepreneurs are capable of great insight, good at brainstorming, capable of deception, ingenuity and resourcefulness. They are cunning, opportunistic, creative, and unsentimental.
- 'If you look at their distinct characteristics, they are definitely more positive about their skills and opportunities,' according to the Global Entrepreneurship Monitor (GEM). 'But just because you're not born with that natural optimism doesn't mean you can't become an entrepreneur. You learn to do it by watching other people and by seeing issues that you want to solve.'
- Professor Andrew Burke, director of the Bettany Centre for Entrepreneurial Performance and Economics at the Cranfield University School of Management, says there are no personality traits unique to entrepreneurs: instead there are personality traits unique to specific enterprises. 'If you take Dell, Microsoft or Apple, it is important to have individuals who are idea-driven, a bit of a butterfly moving from one thing to another,' he says. 'But if you switch to a different type of business, such as Virgin, the key thing is being in tune with the consumer.'

Summary

Being an entrepreneur brings with it many risks but also many rewards, not least the satisfaction of having set up a business for yourself. Entrepreneurs create jobs and bring more choice to consumers. This is why governments tend to be eager to encourage people to start up on their own.

Having studied this chapter, you should be able to discuss the reasons why people want to be entrepreneurs and the features that successful entrepreneurs tend to have.

Web link

GEM is the Global Entrepreneurship Monitor. This organisation produces surveys about attitudes and levels of entrepreneurship in different countries. To find out more, visit www.gemconsortium.org/

Quick questions

1 Who in business today do you admire?
2 State two reasons why people may want to set up in business on their own.
3 State two reasons why governments might want to help people to set up on their own.
4 What is the opportunity cost of you studying for your A levels?
5 Identify two problems that individuals might experience when setting up a business for themselves.
6 Identify two ways in which a government might encourage entrepreneurs to set up a business.
7 Outline two possible characteristics of a successful entrepreneur.
8 What does it mean if a country is said to have an 'entrepreneurial culture'?
9 As an entrepreneur, should you aim to take more, or less risk?

Issues for analysis:

- Choosing a project involves an opportunity cost.
- Entrepreneurs increase customer choice and create jobs.
- Entrepreneurs increase growth in the economy.

Issues for evaluation:

- How important is luck in determining the success of entrepreneurs?
- How much risk should entrepreneurs take?

Analysis and evaluation questions

1 Fed up with the quality of the burgers in his home town, George Salter set up his own Prime Burger store, selling top-of-the-range fast food. He uses only organic products and aims to provide healthy burgers that are significantly tastier than those found in typical fast-food stores. His products seem to fit with the trend for better, healthier food. Within five years his business has been so successful that he now has 15 shops around the region and is looking to expand further.

a Analyse the benefits that successful entrepreneurs such as George bring to their communities and the economy.
b George's products happened to fit with market trends. To what extent is the success of his business likely to have been due to luck?

2 Sami is a highly talented, self-taught computer programmer and designer. He has a place at university but has decided to start his own online social networking website ('like Facebook' he says, 'but better!'), rather than go on to further studies. He believes that the rewards from starting his business are worth pursuing now, rather than waiting a few years.

a Examine the meaning of opportunity cost in the context of Sami's venture.
b To what extent do you think Sami is right to set up his business now, rather than going to university?

Assessment

The Friends Reunited website was created by Steve and Julie Pankhurst of Barnet, Hertfordshire in 1999. Julie was curious about what her old school friends were up to. Did they all have families of their own? Did they still live in the same area? Were they married, divorced, still alive?! At the same time Steve, along with his business partner, Jason, was looking at ideas to develop an internet business. They realised that the internet was an ideal medium to get back in touch with old friends. The site was born in the back bedroom of the house and Friends Reunited was officially launched in July 2000. By the end of the year it had 3,000 registered members. They then redesigned the site and created a new logo, which is still used today. The aim was to make the site really simple to use and quick to download. The people shown in the logo are Steve's mum and dad and two of his friends.

The site went from success to success and expanded into other areas. For example, further sites were launched in Australia, South Africa and New Zealand. They later set up Genes Reunited to help people trace their ancestors. The site now has 12 million people registered (about half of all UK households with internet access). This growth has been helped by the fact that the Pankhursts brought in a new partner with more business experience to be Chief Executive in 2003.

In 2005, Friends Reunited was sold to ITV for £120 million and the Pankhursts stood down from the day-to-day running of the business.

Questions

(30 marks, 40 minutes)

1 Explain two possible factors for the success of Friends Reunited. (6 marks)
2 Analyse two possible reasons the Pankhursts sold the business. (9 marks)
3 Evaluate the factors that you think will determine the future success of the business. (15 marks)

2 Generating and protecting business ideas

The starting point for most entrepreneurs is their business idea. They see a business opportunity and are willing to take the risks necessary to try and achieve the desired rewards. In this chapter we consider how ideas for new businesses are generated and how entrepreneurs can protect these ideas against competitors.

What you need to know by the end of this chapter:
• how entrepreneurs identify a new product idea or market niche
• the advantages and disadvantages of franchising
• ways of protecting your business idea, such as patents and copyrights.

Where do entrepreneurs get their ideas from?

Entrepreneurs identify business opportunities. For example, they see that there is room in the market for a new product – something that they think would be in demand and that they could provide, that is not already being offered. Therefore, they see a business opportunity and seize the chance.

The product may be a completely new item, or a new way of doing things. It may be something that exists already but that could be aimed at a new market, or at a part of a market (known as a 'market niche').

> **Key terms**
> A market niche is a small segment within a market.

In many cases, a business idea will be linked to an entrepreneur's own experience or expertise, either at work or in their personal lives. For example, they may have been working in a particular industry and see an opportunity for a new product, or they may have a hobby and can see how to turn it into a business. In other cases entrepreneurs see something offered elsewhere (perhaps in another country) and decide to imitate it. They may have been looking for a particular product themselves, and when they found it was not readily available, saw this as a

market opportunity. An entrepreneur may also buy the rights to sell an existing product. This is called a franchise. (Franchises are examined in more detail in Chapter 3.)

Usually, the idea for an enterprise will come first and then the people concerned have to decide whether to set up in business or not. However, sometimes individuals know that they want to be entrepreneurs even if they are not sure what they actually want to do! In this case, they may ask friends or brainstorm to find the 'right' idea. This is what the founders of Innocent Drinks did. Richard Reed, Adam Balon and Jon Wright met at university and got on well. They knew they wanted to work together and set up their own business, but were not sure exactly what they wanted to do. They tried out a number of ideas (including a device to alert people that their bath was overflowing) before eventually deciding on the idea of healthy drinks.

> **Web link**
>
> For more information on Innocent Drinks, visit www.innocent.co.uk

So, some ideas are genuinely new. Others adapt something that already exists: in the case of a franchise, the entrepreneur uses the approach and products of an existing business.

> **Key term**
> **Brainstorming** is a problem-solving and idea-generating technique in which individuals are asked to come up with as many ideas as possible. Everyone is encouraged to talk, then after a given amount of time the ideas are analysed in more detail.

Some ideas will be the entrepreneur's own. Some entrepreneur's have a conviction that their ideas will work and are determined to go ahead. This is known as a product-led approach. Other ideas come from an analysis of the market. This is a market-led approach.

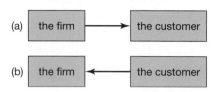

Figure 2.1 (a) Product-led and (b) market-led approach

Why protect your idea?

Obviously, if someone sets up on their own, they want their business to be successful over a period of time. They don't want someone else stealing their idea and benefiting from all their initial work. There are ways of protecting a business idea so that others cannot imitate it without the permission of the owner. If someone has ownership of a particular product or a unique way of doing business and others cannot copy it, it means that they may:

- have more customers because there won't be any substitutes
- be able to charge more because customers won't be able to switch to something similar
- be able to earn money letting others use their idea (for example, see Chapter 3 on franchises).

Real-life Business

Luisa Scacchetti, founder of Mamas & Papas

Figure 2.2 Luisa Scacchetti

When she was eleven years old, Luisa Scacchetti moved with her family from Italy to England so her father could work in the family's wholesale business.

She left school at 18 and took a secretarial and accounting course before joining the family firm. She carried on working there until she was 27, when she was expecting her first baby. It was when looking around for baby products that she got the idea of setting up on her own. She travelled regularly to Italy and was disappointed with the range of choice available in the UK by comparison. She bought her own pushchair and prams in Italy and when she started using them, lots of people approached her to find out where she got them. So, in 1981 she opened a shop in Huddersfield called Mamas & Papas, selling prams and other baby items imported from Italy. All purchased products were gift wrapped. Over time, Luisa also supplied other businesses with prams and baby products from Italy and eventually decided to close the shop and just focus on wholesale. However, in 1998 she opened a store again: this time she was more involved in the design of many of the products such as clothes and bedding. The company now has over 30 stores. The Scacchettis still own 100 per cent of the company.

How to protect a business idea

Ways of protecting a business idea include:

- patents
- trademarks
- copyright.

Patents

If you have a new invention you can patent it. A patent can protect many different aspects of a new product such as how it works, what it does, what it is made of and how it is made.

To gain a patent, your product must:

- be a new invention
- have an inventive step that is not obvious to some-one with knowledge and experience in the subject
- be capable of being made or used in some kind of industry.

A patent provides legal protection for up to 20 years (although must be reviewed every fifth year). If other individuals or firms want to use the invention they must pay you for the right to do so. If they do not have this right but go ahead and copy your invention you can sue them and gain compensation. The only problem with this is that it relies on you taking them to court: this can be time consuming and expensive, particularly if you are required to sue them in different countries.

Famous patents that have been taken out by UK inventors include:

- Meccano. This was invented by Frank Hornby as a way of keeping his sons entertained.
- The collapsible pushchair patented by Owen Maclaren when his daughter and grandson were struggling to get around.
- The wind-up radio invented by Trevor Baylis in his home workshop.

Figure 2.3 Meccano

Trademarks

Entrepreneurs can also protect their business by registering a trademark. A trademark protects any sign or symbol that distinguishes what you offer from your competitors. You can register a name, logo, slogan, domain name, a shape, a colour or a sound. If you look at the packaging on products, you will often see a symbol that shows it has a registered trademark. Think of the instantly recognisable CocaCola symbol, Apple logo, Google logo and Nike 'swoosh', and the value of a brand, and why the owner might want to protect it, becomes clear.

To be registered, a trade mark must be:

- distinctive
- not deceptive, illegal or immoral.

A registered trade mark must be renewed every ten years to keep it in force.

Copyright

A copyright protects creative or artistic works such as:

- literature, including novels, instruction manuals, computer programs, song lyrics, newspaper articles and website content
- music compositions and recordings
- art, including paintings, engravings, photographs, sculptures, collages, – recordings of a work, including sound and film
- broadcasts of a work.

You automatically have a copyright when you create something. Others have to pay for the right to use your work. For example, when music is played on the radio, a copyright fee is paid to the artists who wrote it: if you photocopy large sections of this book you also should pay a copyright!

Various forms of protection are available to an entrepreneur. However, in many cases an entrepreneur will not be able to protect her idea. This means that if you come up with an idea for a busness you may find that if it is successful others will soon be imitating you. While imitation may be the sincerest form of flattery, it is not good for sales or for your business's success.

> **Web link**
>
> To find out more about copyrights, patents and trademarks, visit the UK Patent Office at www.ipo.gov.uk/

Real-life Business

Figure 2.4 Trevor Baylis

Trevor Baylis was born in Kilburn, London, in 1937 and brought up in Southall. At the age of 16 he joined the Soil Mechanics Laboratory in Southall where part-time day-release enabled him to study mechanical and structural engineering at the local technical college. He then went into the army, after which he joined Purley Pools as a salesman. However, Trevor soon became involved in researching and developing new products. He went on to start his own swimming-pool company (as well as working as a stuntman on various TV shows!).

In 1991, after seeing a programme about the spread of Aids in Africa, Trevor set about developing a wind-up radio. His first working prototype ran for 14 minutes and in 1994 was featured on the television programme *Tomorrow's World*. The product's potential was immediately recognised by financial expert Christopher Staines and South African entrepreneur Rory Stear, who together acquired funding and, the following year, set up BayGen Power Industries in Cape Town, employing disabled workers to manufacture the Freeplay® wind-up radio.

The BBC filmed and broadcast an award-winning documentary about Trevor's development of the radio and in June 1996 the Freeplay® radio was awarded the BBC Design Award for Best Product and Best Design. Trevor was also awarded the Order of the British Empire (OBE).

Key terms
Patent: legal protection for a new invention
Copyright: legal protection for artistic or creative works
Trademark: legal protection for signs and symbols

What do you think?

Could you draw the trademarks of: Ministry of Sound? Nike? Adidas? Gucci? Google? Radley handbags? What do you think are the advantages of having such a well-known logo? Many entrepreneurs hope that one day their name and logo will be as famous as these.

Examiner's advice

By the end of this chapter you need to know the different ways in which entrepreneurs can protect their businesses. You also need to be able to decide whether a particular idea is a good one or not.

What makes a good idea?

A business idea is only good if it is possible to provide it and if it meets the needs of customers and the firm itself. For example, will it be perceived as value for money by customers and can the business make a profit? It can be quite easy to have ideas – what about a kettle that plays music as it boils? Or home-delivery breakfasts? However, for these ideas to be worth pursuing you must consider the following questions:

- **Do you have the facilities and expertise to provide such a service efficiently?** Do you have the necessary funds to get it started and pay for all the start-up costs? Do you know how to make it a success?. There are many property developers who have bought houses and decorated them only to find they have not done it very well or that the housing market has changed and the house is difficult to sell. A good property developer understands the market and has the skills necessary to improve properties successfully.

Post-it® notes

Figure 2.5 Post-it® notes

Some ideas may not immediately seem 'good' or likely to succeed. Would you have invested in a non-stick adhesive? Probably not, but this idea eventually became Post-it® notes. Interestingly, this was not a planned product. Spencer Silver, a researcher at the company 3M, was working on a strong adhesive but the one he developed was so weak you could easily lift if off objects. Instead of developing a super-strong adhesive he had produced a super-weak one! No one knew what to do with it, but Silver kept asking people for ideas. Four years later another researcher, Arthur Fry, was singing in his church choir and using markers in the hymn book to show what hymns were to be sung. The markers kept falling out and so he tried paper with the weak adhesive on it. This worked well and eventually the Post-it® concept was developed and launched, ten years after Silver first produced it!

Question:
Was the success of Post-it® notes due to luck?

- **Is there a demand for it?** Buying a house, converting it into several small rooms and offering it as shared accommodation for six people may work well in a city where there are a lot of students, but would be more difficult to sell elsewhere. An online financial information service may be of interest to a City stockbroker but of less interest to a 12-year-old football fanatic. As we will see later (in Chapter 6) a business only survives if it has customers. This means that the business idea must meet their needs. Sometimes, of course, people do not know their needs until you introduce your product (think of the many hit films that you would not necessarily have predicted were going to be successful in advance, or the latest fashion craze that seemed to come from nowhere). In this case, entrepreneurs have to anticipate the market needs or even create demand.
- **Can you benefit from providing it?** Ultimately, a business needs to meet its own objectives or it is not worth carrying on producing. If these objectives are to make a profit, for example, then the money earned from selling the product must be greater than the cost of making it. Many entrepreneurs fail because they have what seems like a good idea, but when they try to sell it they realise the costs of providing it are too great compared to what they can sell it for.

Summary

Entrepreneurs can get their ideas from many sources such as customers, competitors or their own inspiration. When they can, they should protect these ideas. This may be possible through patents, trademarks or copyrights. Of course, not every idea is viable, so entrepreneurs should consider their own strengths, their ability to produce the product and whether or not it is likely to be demanded in sufficient quantities to be profitable.

Quick questions

1. A new product is automatically patented. True or false?
2. A copyright applies to written work and music. True or false?
3. A trademark protects a new invention. True or false?
4. State two possible sources of new business ideas.
5. State two factors that can determine the success of a new business idea.
6. Outline one benefit to a business of having a patent.

7 What is meant by a market niche?

8 What is meant by brainstorming?

Issues for analysis

- The value of protecting a new business idea.
- Protection for new ideas encourages more entrepreneurs.
- The link between the success of a new business and the skills of the entrepreneur.

Issues for evaluation

- Where is the best place to get a new business idea from?
- How important is a patent to the success of a new business?
- What are the key elements of a good business idea?

Analysis and evaluation questions

1 JoJo French recently set up a mail order business selling baby products. When her own daughter was young she wanted a site where she could get information and order products easily. As her child grew up, she still couldn't find one, so she decided to set up a site herself. ' I knew it would work because I would buy from it. If I would buy from it, so would my friends, and that means there is a market'.

a Analyse the skills that might be necessary to make JoJo's business a success.

b To what extent is your own interest in a business idea a guarantee that it will be successful if you go ahead and set it up?

2 'If it had not been for my patent I would never have been able to grow my business', said Jack Coogan. Jack developed a device to lock front and back doors based on fingerprints. The device was relatively cheap and very secure: it sold extremely well once launched.

a Analyse the possible benefits of a patent to Jack Coogan.

b To what extent does a patent guarantee the success of a product such as Jack's?

Assessment

Figure 2.6 The Reuzip

Tenzip® images on this page may not be reproduced without full consent from Tenza Technologies Ltd

Case study

In 1996 Heather Kitching invented Reuzip, the world's first polyethylene weldable zip fastener with teeth, which doesn't break under repeated use like some 'tramline'-type zips. At first the idea seemed so simple that she nearly discounted it, but it soon became clear that it had potentially successful commercial possibilities – and that she would need patent protection to make the most of these possibilities.

The first step to getting a patent was to draw up a specification for the idea from which she could finalise her application. She spent a lot of time and money getting this right and got professional advice to get her conceptual drawings spot-on. She was then ready to submit the first part of her patent application, known as the 'abstract'. Essentially, an abstract outlines how an idea solves a problem. The second part of the application was to prepare her 'claims'. These explain in simple terms what your idea actually is. While all of this was being done she carried out searches at the UK Intellectual Property Office to check that her idea had not been registered before. Once this was done, she submitted her complete patent application.

'Patent applications take a few years to be approved so during this time I turned my attention to developing the idea and finding companies that could turn the idea into commercial products. Eventually the patent was approved and, armed with proto-types. I licensed the technology to a major packaging company. Unfortunately, this venture was unsuccess-ful after the licensee was found in breach of the agreement. Having secured the patent, it was easier for me to get the licensee to stop using the idea.'

(Adapted from www.businesslink.gov.uk)

Questions

(30 marks, 40 minutes)

1 Outline the different stages involved in gaining a patent. (6 marks)

2 Analyse the possible benefits of having a patent to a business such as Reuzip. (9 marks)

3 Discuss whether having a patent guarantees the success of a business idea such as Reuzip. (15 marks)

3 Franchises

One possible source of a business idea is a franchise. Rather than think of your own business idea, you might prefer to pay someone to allow you to use theirs: this is what happens in a franchise agreement. In this chapter we consider the case for and against franchise agreements.

What you need to know by the end of this chapter:
- what is meant by a franchise
- the advantages and disadvantages of buying and selling a franchise.

What is a franchise?

A franchise occurs when one business (the franchisor) sells the right to use and sell its products and/or services to another business (the franchisee). Imagine you were interested in setting up a fast-food business. You could sit down and develop your own idea from scratch. However, it could prove to be difficult to come up with something that would capture demand and then decide on a brand image, a way of producing the food, a menu and décor for your stores. An alternative would be to buy the rights to sell McDonald's products in a given area. In this case, you would be buying a McDonald's franchise.

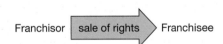

Figure 3.1 Franchisor selling to franchisee

How do franchises work?

There are many different forms of franchise, but the basic elements of a franchise agreement are:

- The franchisor sells the right to the product in return for an initial fee and a percentage of the franchisee's turnover.
- The franchisee receives the right to the name and the systems used by the franchisor. This may include access to materials and training methods.

In the case of McDonald's, for example, the company wants to keep close control over its brand name, products and reputation. Therefore if you buy a McDonald's franchise you have to follow very close rules in terms of what you sell, how you sell it,

the pricing, the way the food is cooked, where it is bought, how you use the logo, and so on.

Franchises include:

- Ben and Jerry's ice cream
- Domino's Pizza
- Threshers off-licence
- Riverford Organic Vegetables.

> **Key term**
> A **franchise** occurs when a franchisor sells the rights to use or sell his or her products to a franchisee

Buying a franchise

If you buy a franchise you are buying a product that has already been on sale and therefore has a track record. This means you can see whether it works. You can also learn from other franchisees who are already established, and benefit from their experience.

Advantages of buying a franchise include the following:

- You have the support of the franchisor and this can help you with decisions such as pricing, choosing suppliers and planning ahead. This should reduce the risk of it going wrong because there is more experience, joint power and support than if you were setting up alone.
- Buying a franchise may be less risky than setting up completely on your own. This is because there is past data for you to analyse before deciding whether to go ahead with the idea or not. At the same time it will be your own business and so there is still the incentive to make it successful, as you will benefit directly.

- Because you are likely to be joining other franchisees, then as a group you may have more bargaining power than you would have on your own. This may mean you get better deals with suppliers or when buying advertising space. Franchisees will often pool money to promote the brand on a national or regional scale. Any advert for the brand helps all the franchisees.

The problems of buying a franchise

The most obvious problem with buying a franchise is that it costs you money! This reduces the profits you make. However, you obviously hope that by buying a franchise you will do better than you would have done on your own. Whether you are better off with a franchise therefore depends on its success and the terms and conditions of the contract.

Although one of the main benefits of buying a franchise is that you are linked to other franchisees, this can also be a problem. If, for example, the quality of service in other franchisees falls, it may damage the overall brand and hit your sales as well. You become dependent on others and vulnerable if there are problems elsewhere.

How much should you pay for a franchise?

Usually, there are several different types of payments involved in buying a franchise. For example, there may be an initial purchase fee plus a percentage of turnover each year. On top of this there may be money you have to invest each year to cover marketing and management expenses. The amount you pay will depend on:

- the likely turnover of the business
- the typical profit margin
- whether you have the exclusive rights to a particular geographical area and if so how big and attractive this area is
- the amount of training and support provided.

Business in Focus

Barking Mad

The philosophy at Barking Mad is simple: if you love dogs, don't want to leave them in a kennel or impose on family, friends or neighbours then it has the 'perfect home from home pet care solution'. Barking Mad arranges accommodation with carefully selected host families who maintain pets' home life routine for exercise and feeding, and whose home environment is similar to the owners' own. Pets are matched with the most appropriate host family. The service includes collection and delivery, ensuring that parting is less stressful for both the owners and the pets.

Franchising

Since 2002, franchising has given Barking Mad the opportunity to meet customer demand. The operation is 'cash flow positive'. Customers make payment in advance, and so the problem of waiting for money to come in after the sale has been made, an issue that many business people have to contend with, is avoided entirely.

As with all franchises, brand and image are exceedingly important, so franchisees' vehicles are liveried to display the distinctive Barking Mad logo, local telephone number and website address. Training is also provided:

'We provide a five-day training programme at Head Office, where our unique Barking Mad systems and procedures are explained. The training programme has been designed to address all aspects of the business dealing with office systems and procedures, day to day operations, sales and marketing, accounts and pet behaviour.

Once training is complete, return to own area with a local sales and marketing activity plan detailing activities you will carry out which aim to get you known quickly. We will contact the local media with your Barking Mad story, including newspapers, radio and TV stations.

As a Barking Mad franchisee, you will have access to our on-line franchise forum, receive regular weekly correspondence from HQ, and attend regional meetings and training seminars.'

(Adapted from: www.barkingmad.uk.com)

Question:

Would you be interested in a Barking Mad franchise? Why? Why not? What else would you want to know before agreeing to buy one?

What do you think?

Do you think the qualities required to be a successful entrepreneur and a successful franchisee are the same, or not?

Selling a franchise

One benefit of being a franchisor is that you benefit from the income generated from the franchisees. They will pay a fee to buy the franchise and a percentage of turnover. This generates earnings for the franchisor.

Franchising is also a way of growing fast. If you were trying to grow a business on your own, you would have to fund it all yourself. For example, you would have to find the funds to buy more premises and refurbish more outlets. If you sell franchises, then the costs of opening a particular outlet falls to the franchisee. This may make fast growth much more feasible because individual franchisees are all funding their own enterprises. Domino's Pizza, for example, was founded in 1960 by Tom Monaghan. His ambition was to grow the business to three stores – that's why there are three dots on the company logo. However, through franchising the business has grown to become the world leader in pizza delivery. The company now has more than 8,000 stores in over 50 international markets.

Another benefit of being a franchisor is that it may lead to more motivated managers because they are running their 'own' stores or businesses, rather than just being employees of a bigger business. This may help the business as a whole be more successful.

Web link

To find out more about franchising in the UK, visit www.thebfa.org/

Real-life Business

Toni&Guy

Figure 3.3 Toni Mascolo

The Toni&Guy hairdressing business is a global brand with over 400 salons all over the world including stores in Qatar, Kazakhstan, Japan and New Zealand. Toni Mascolo, who set up the business, is now in his sixties, but still cuts hair in his West End salons. The business has grown via franchising.

Toni had originally thought of becoming a lawyer but that changed when his father moved the family to London. Toni, aged 14, and known then by his real name of Giuseppe, spoke no English, so despite excelling at school back in Italy he had little choice but to start working in his father's hairdressing business.

Toni&Guy got off the ground in 1963 when Toni and his brother Gaetano – who changed his name to Guy – decided to open their own salon in Clapham. Other business interests apart from the salons themselves now include:

- the production and distribution of products used and sold in the salons
- the Toni&Guy branded products, which have been developed with Alliance Boots
- another hairdressing chain called essensuals
- hairdressing training academies
- a business which supplies the salons with fixtures and fittings
- an IT business
- an in-house media agency.

(Adapted from *The Independent*, 15 October 2006)

Question:

Do you think the business model adopted by Toni Mascolo would be easy for other hairdressers to adopt?

Examiner's advice

When studying franchises you need to compare this way of starting up your own business with the alternatives. What are its advantages and disadvantages compared to other ways of starting up? What would determine whether an individual did this, rather than 'going it alone'?

Summary

If an entrepreneur is looking to start up in business one option is to buy a franchise. This has various advantages – for example, you can examine the track record of the product idea before investing – but it also involves a cost and some loss of control. Also, the rewards have to be shared. If you are thinking about setting up in business you have to consider whether the benefits of buying an established idea, along with the support and training, outweigh the costs.

Quick questions

1 A franchisee sells a franchise to a franchisor. True or False?

2 A franchisee usually pays a percentage of turnover to the franchisor. True or false?

3 Selling a franchise is likely to enable a franchisor to grow more quickly than a business could otherwise grow. True or false?

4 All the rewards of a franchisee belong to the franchisor. True or false?

5 State two benefits to a franchisor of selling a franchise.

6 State two benefits to a franchisee of buying a franchise.

7 State two disadvantages to a franchisee of buying a franchise

8 What factors might determine how much a franchisee pays for a franchise?

Issues for analysis

- The reasons for selling a franchise.
- The reasons for buying a franchise.
- The skills required to be a successful franchisee.

Issues for evaluation

- What determines how much you should pay for a franchise?
- Is it better to buy a franchise or set up on your own?
- What are the advantages and disadvantages of buying a franchise.

Analysis and evaluation questions

1 Ali Watts had always wanted a business of her own but was not sure exactly what sort of business to set up. She had only ever worked for others and lacked the confidence to set up alone. Then one day she saw an advert in a newspaper for a conference on franchises, went along and ended up buying a franchise for a cosmetics shop.

a Analyse the disadvantages to Ali of buying a franchise.

b To what extent is a franchise a better option than setting up on her own?

2 Ashok Sarper had built up a successful hairdressing salon and now wanted to grow the business by selling franchises.

a Analyse the potential disadvantages to Ashok of selling franchises.

b To what extent is franchising a better way for Ashok to grow his business than setting up more salons himself?

Assessment

MOLLY MAID is one of the world's largest and longest-established domestic cleaning franchise companies. It carefully selects its franchisee partners who manage teams of maids offering high quality, domestic cleaning.

We provide on-going support for the life of the franchise – so you're never out there on your own.

What you get for your investment

- An exclusive area, meaning one in which there will be no other MOLLY MAID franchises, ranging in size from 12,000 to 24,000 potential customers.
- The right to use the MOLLY MAID mark, the most recognised and highly respected brand name in the UK domestic cleaning market.
- Our 'Right Start' marketing, staff recruitment and support programme, designed to help build your business, attract new staff and overcome the challenges that you will face in your launch phase.
- One full week comprehensive training on the MOLLY MAID System before you start-up.
- 3 days on-site support the week your business is launched and continued support for as long as you are a MOLLY MAID Franchise Owner – your success is our primary goal.
- A start-up package which includes cleaning equipment and supplies, uniforms, stationery, literature and publicity material, all custom-designed to complement the MOLLY MAID System.

Investment level

- The investment level for a MOLLY MAID franchise ranges from approximately £16,975 to £22,975. This is the initial amount that has to be spent to buy the franchise.
- The royalty rate starts at 8 per cent and declines to as low as 5.5 per cent as sales increase. This is the percentage of turnover paid by the franchisee to the franchisor.

Have you got what it takes to be a successful Molly Maid franchisee?

If you can manage a small office, you could successfully manage a MOLLY MAID franchise. The qualities pinpointed as most appropriate weren't those associated with 'big' business: rather they were human attributes such as common sense, ability to get on with people and a willingness to work hard.

(Source: Adapted from www.mollymaid.co.uk)

Questions

(30 marks, 40 minutes)

1. Explain two factors you might consider when deciding whether to buy a MOLLY MAID franchise. (6 marks)
2. Analyse the reasons why MOLLY MAID might sell a franchise (9 marks)
3. Discuss the advantages and disadvantages of buying a MOLLY MAID franchise rather than starting up a cleaning business on your own. (15 marks)

4 Business plans

When setting up a business, it is often useful to have a plan of what you are trying to do, what needs to be done when, and what you hope to achieve by a given date. This information is usually contained in a business plan. This chapter examines the benefits of developing a business plan. What you need to know by the end of this chapter:

• the purpose and contents of a business plan
• the benefits and problems of a business plan
• sources of information and guidance used for a business plan.

The purpose and contents of a business plan

When an entrepreneur is thinking about setting up in business it is important to think carefully about what is needed to make the idea a success, how the business will compete against other firms and how much money is needed to run it. These items would usually be included in a business plan.

A business plan is a document that sets out information on:

• the nature of business, its history and its legal structure (see Chapter 8)
• the product it offers, what makes it different from anyone else, why customers would buy it and how it is protected from the competition
• the nature of the market and the firm's customer base
• the objectives of the business. This means the business plan would usually set out the targets the entrepreneur would like to achieve. These are usually in terms of sales and/or profits. For example, the objective might be to achieve profits of £30,000 a year by the second year. Having an objective provides a focus and a clear definition of success.
• the strategy. This sets out how the objective is going to be achieved. For example, an entrepreneur might decide to target busy business people in the city centre in their lunch hour with freshly made sandwiches.
• the approach to marketing (e.g. how the business intends to market the product and how it will position itself against rivals)

• the founders and employees (e.g. who they are and their experience and skills)
• the firm's operations (e.g. where it is based, the production facilities it requires, the capacity it has)
• a forecast of sales over a period in the future – this will be important to calculate revenues, costs and profits and work out how many staff and what equipment and premises are needed.

Web link

For information on business plans, visit the government's Business Link at www.businesslink.gov.uk/bdotg/action/layer?topicId=1073858944

Key term

A **business plan** is a document setting out the strengths, aims and strategies of a business.

Who needs a business plan?

Producing a business plan is a very useful exercise for anyone who is setting up in business, because it makes them think carefully about what they are doing. Too many people rush into setting up a business without thinking through their idea. Planning makes you look in some detail at the different aspects of the idea and consider some of the potential problems. This can help you to work out how to overcome these difficulties.

A business plan can help the entrepreneur to clarify what needs to be done and when it needs to be done. Simply by writing out the different elements of the plan can help an entrepreneur to see what will and will not work. The plan can then be shown to other employees in the organisation and help them to understand what the firm is trying to achieve and how it intends to do this. This can help to coordinate actions and build more of a team spirit.

A business plan can also be useful:

- as a benchmark: the firm can measure its success against what it set out to do.
- to show to potential investors or lenders (such as a bank). They will see what the firm hopes to achieve and can test the logic of its assumptions and forecasts. By looking at the financial projections, for example, lenders can assess whether the business will be able to repay the loans or not.

Although business plans are most commonly drawn up when an entrepreneur is setting up for the first time, they should be revisited and updated so that the business always has an idea of where it is going and how it intends to get there. The business environment is continually changing, with new laws, changes in the economy, new competitors and changing tastes of customers. This means that plans need to be updated regularly to continue to be relevant.

Where do you get the information for a business plan?

A business plan has several different elements and information is needed from a range of sources. A starting point will be your own market research. This could come from asking friends or potential customers or watching competitors (this is called primary research – see Chapter 5) or you might look at government statistics or newspaper surveys (secondary research – also in Chapter 5). Given that you are starting out, your research may be limited because you may be constrained in terms of time and money. There is also the danger of the research being biased because you conduct it in a way to get the results you want. For example, if you ask friends 'How successful do you think my business will be? a. very successful, or b. extremely successful', then you are not giving them the opportunity to say if they think it will fail! You need to try and make sure that your research is reliable and unbiased.

You may also seek the opinion and advice of experts. These may be other more experienced entrepreneurs in the same area, professional consultants or government advisers. Advice may be needed on the whole business idea, or just one aspect of it, such

Business in Focus

David Harber

David Harber recently beat 17 other companies to win the Small Business of the Year award at the Henley Business Awards.

The criteria for the award were:

- profitable growth of the existing business
- a written business plan with a strategy and vision for the next 3–5 years
- management with the ability to drive the business forward

David Harber's business produces stylishly designed sundials and water features. It has earned an international reputation for creating innovative, contemporary designs. The business has grown rapidly in recent years.

Web link

For more information on David Harber's business, visit www.davidharbersundials.co.uk

Questions:

- Outline the different individuals or groups that might want to examine the business plan of a firm such as David Harber's.
- To what extent might producing a business plan for the next three to five years help a business such as David Harber's?

as the marketing. You may also seek advice from your local bank (most of whom have small business advisers). The bank may help you to identify how much money may be required for your business, your cashflow needs and how to decide on the best way of raising the finance you may need. Equally, accountants are able to give expert financial advice.

Of course, outside advice usually costs money, but the benefits of such advice can outweigh the expense if you choose the right source.

Business in Focus

Business Link

Business Link is a government service providing advice and information for new and small businesses.

Web link

For more information on Business Link, visit www.businesslink.gov.uk

This website has many useful resources for entrepreneurs and for people who are studying entrepreneurs.

The limitations of a business plan

One of the main issues to remember when producing a business plan is that it is forward-looking and therefore cannot be absolutely guaranteed. Due to limited market research many of the projections, such as sales and profits, may be inaccurate. Also, there are many changes that can occur, such as new competitors starting up or changes in the economy, that can affect market conditions significantly. Entrepreneurs must therefore appreciate the possible limitations of any business plan. This does not mean that planning is a waste of time – it can still highlight key issues and potential problems and show the likely scale of profits and losses. But some degree of caution is advisable. There are, of course, steps that entrepreneurs can take to make the plan as accurate as possible. For example, they can:

- use whatever relevant secondary data exists and undertake primary research where it would be useful and cost effective
- use expert advice such as government agencies and the bank
- talk to others in the industry
- look at how similar products or businesses have done and learn from this

Having said this, entrepreneurs must not spend so long planning that they miss the opportunity and let someone else seize it, stealing the market from them. Too much planning may slow down decision-making and halt progress.

What do you think?

A friend of yours comes to you with an idea of setting up a hotel for pets. He wants you to invest £15,000 in the idea to help him set it up. What would you want to know before agreeing to this?

Examiner's advice

When studying a business plan you need to think about:

- the benefits of producing one
- the problems of producing one.

Overall, you will need to be able to discuss the value of having a business plan and the things that determine how useful it is.

Summary

A business plan is an important planning tool in business. It helps an entrepreneur to analyse the factors that are likely to determine the success of his or her idea. It can highlight potential problems, which can help the entrepreneur to anticipate and plan for these, rather than having to react to an unexpected difficulty.

Quick questions

1 A business plan guarantees a firm success. True or false?
2 A business plan should only be produced when a business starts up. True or false?
3 A business plan would usually include a sales forecast. True or false?
4 Outline two important elements of a business plan.
5 Outline two groups that might be interested in looking at a firm's business plan.
6 Where might an entrepreneur gather the information required for a business plan?
7 State two benefits of drawing up a business plan.
8 State two difficulties of drawing up a business plan.

Issues for analysis

- The elements of the business plan.
- The internal uses of a business plan.
- The external uses of a business plan.

Issues for evaluation

- What is the value of a business plan?
- What are the limitations of a business plan?
- To what extent does a business plan guarantee success?

Analysis and evaluation questions

1 Nyeleti Camron has an idea to set up an exclusive hat shop in her local village. She feels that there is a lack of good hat shops in the region and that she will be able to draw people from a wide area who are looking for a hat for a special occasion. She has money that she has saved from her present job in insurance and is determined to go ahead with the idea. Friends have told her to produce a business plan because it would help her understand the market, but she does not see the point.

a Analyse the factors that Nyeleti may need to understand about the hat market before setting up her business.
b To what extent would producing a business plan help Nyeleti's business to be successful?

2 'We regularly update our business plan and it helps us keep ahead of our competitors'. So says Annie Hall, who runs a recruitment agency specialising in the healthcare sector. The business was set up five years ago and now has three offices, 25 staff and has seen turnover grow 20 per cent last year. 'The plan is incredibly useful for us internally as well as showing potential investors.'

a Analyse the possible elements that Annie Hall might include in her business plan.
b Discuss the ways in which producing a business plan might benefit Annie Hall's business.

Assessment

Case study

Darren Jones launched his care business, AKC Home Support Services, in 1991 with his wife Sharron.

'When we started the firm I knew we needed a business plan but saw it more as a document for everyone else than something to help us. If I started another business tomorrow I would write one much more willingly as it brings a number of benefits – from helping you secure finance to keeping you focused on your goals.'

'We used our business plan to set out the financial and strategic goals we wanted to achieve in the short and long-term. We review it annually now unless there's a significant shift in our market and then we use it to immediately re-evaluate our goals.

Our business plan has also helped us to avoid expanding too quickly. Early on, we were offered work in another county. This seemed great but when we looked at our business plan – and particularly our cashflow forecasts – we realised it was important to establish a firm base in one county before taking on work in another otherwise we would overstretch ourselves.'

'We purchased a residential unit four years ago and our business plan definitely helped us demonstrate why the bank should lend us the money. Without it being put down on paper I don't think it would have sounded like a very viable suggestion.'

'Our plan also helped us to get support from Shell LiveWIRE – the organisation that assists 16- to 30-year-olds to start and develop businesses – as you must have a business plan to enter its competitions. We were awarded prizes twice – not only bringing in extra money but publicity too.'

(Source: www.businesslink.gov.uk)

Questions

(30 marks: 40 minutes)

1 Identify two groups that might be interested in AKC's business. Explain why they might be interested. (6 marks)

2 Analyse the benefits to AKC of having a business plan. (9 marks)

3 To what extent did having a business plan guarantee the success of AKC? (15 marks)

5 Conducting start-up market research

As we saw in Chapter 2, one way of identifying a business opportunity and generating business ideas is through market research. This means that you examine the market and try to identify a gap that you think you could satisfy profitably. By gathering information, you should reduce the risks of failure. Market research is also invaluable when it comes to producing a business plan (as shown in this chapter). In this chapter we examine the advantages and possible problems of market research undertaken by people starting their own businesses.

What you need to know by the end of this chapter:
- different methods of primary and secondary market research
- what is meant by qualitative and quantitative research
- what is meant by sampling, and the different types of sample.

What is market research?

Market research involves the gathering and analysis of data that is relevant to your marketing. For example, you might want to know:

- the size of the market: this can be measured in terms of the number of pounds spent in it (the value of the market) or the number of items purchased (the volume of the market)
- key market trends, for example whether the market as a whole is growing, or whether particular types of products are increasing in popularity
- what customers value about the product, how much they are prepared to pay for it, and what your product can do better than other products on the market.

Market research provides an entrepreneur with information. This is important for effective decision-making. Imagine you are wandering around a house at midnight and none of the lights are on. You stumble, move slowly and make mistakes getting around: market research can provide the lighting in the room that enables you to move quickly, efficiently and effectively, to get to where you want.

By undertaking market research, entrepreneurs should have a better idea of what people want and how they behave. This should mean that the firm can meet their needs more effectively and avoid wasteful

marketing activities. Imagine that you are considering launching a new product. If you can find out who your target market is, what they like, what they read, where they shop, what they watch and listen to, then your marketing can be much more effective. For example, there is no point in spending money on a big Saturday evening television campaign if your target audience is likely to be at a nightclub.

Market research may be undertaken before the business is set up, to decide whether it is viable or not. It can also be undertaken once the business is up and running to decide what to do next – for example, whether to change the price of a product or launch a new brand.

Figure 5.1 Uses of market research

Typically, market research is used to:

- identify market opportunities
- assess the alternative options open to the business to meet customer needs
- assess the effectiveness of different marketing actions.

> **Key terms**
> **Market research** is the process of gathering, analysing and producing data relevant to the marketing process.

Secondary market research

Given that the amount of money you have available to spend when starting up a business is likely to be limited, you will probably have to carry out most of your market research yourself rather than use specialist companies to do it for you. The cheapest and quickest way of doing this is to see what information about the market already exists. What data has been collected and published? A tremendous amount of information is available on the internet, in libraries and in newspapers, as well as from other sources. For example:

- www.statistics.gov.uk, the Office of National Statistics online, has lots of government data on the UK economy, the labour market, transport and society
- www.guardianunlimited.co.uk allows you to look through past copies of *The Guardian* newspaper
- at www.upmystreet.co.uk you can search for any given postcode area and look at data on house prices, the type of people living in that region and their lifestyle habits (such as whether they are likely to have been to university, have satellite TV or have children).

Using data that already exists is called 'secondary market research'. It is particularly useful for general information on the economy, the market and on competitors.

While secondary data is usually quite quick to get hold of, it is not always in the right format for your needs, or up to date. The research may have been done in the previous year, when what you want is this year's figure. It may organise sales data according to the sales per country, when what you need is data focusing on a particular city. Nevertheless, secondary research is usually a good starting point. Once you have looked at secondary sources you can identify what else you need to know and what information needs to be gathered for the first time.

Primary market research

In some cases, you may have to gather new data. This is called primary market research. For example, you may want to discover what people in your local area think of your specific idea, whether they are likely to use your particular service or what they think of your business name. This sort of information will not exist already, so you will need to undertake new research.

Primary research can be tailored precisely to your own needs but can be quite expensive and time consuming, compared with using information already collected. The danger is that because of cost constraints or because you are inexperienced you only ask a relatively small number of people, or a specific group that do not really represent the population as a whole. This means that your results may be biased and misleading. If you ask your friends, for example, they may well tell you it is a great idea even if isn't because they do not want to upset you!

If you are going to undertake primary research you need to make sure that you:

- don't lead people into giving you the answer you want (e.g. 'Why do you think my idea is so good?' is a leading question)
- ask a representative group of people (i.e. that you hope will represent your target group)
- ask enough people for the findings to be significant. One person's opinion may not necessarily reflect the views of the population as a whole.

Primary data can be gathered:

- by observation – for example, you may watch what is happening in the stores of your possible competitors or count how many people walk by a possible location for your shop on a typical day to calculate the 'footfall'. (The footfall is an important indicator in retailing of the likely number of customers. The more people that walk past the more customers you may get.)
- through surveys – you may have been stopped in the street and asked your opinion of something: this is a face-to-face survey and is one way of finding out what people think. Firms also use telephone, mail or online surveys to find out the views of potential customers. Surveys may give you an idea of what people think of your idea and help you decide whether to go ahead.

Business in Focus

Innocent Drinks

In 1998, after six months of trying out recipes on friends, the three founders of Innocent Drinks spent £500 on fruit, turned it into smoothies, and sold them at a small music festival in London.

Figure 5.2 An easy decision?

'We put up a big sign saying, 'Do you think we should give up our jobs to make these smoothies?' and put out a bin saying 'YES' and a bin saying 'NO' and asked people to put the empty bottle in the right bin.'

'At the end of the weekend the 'YES' bin was full so we went in the next day and resigned.'

(Adapted from: www.innocentdrinks.co.uk)

Questions:

- Do you think this was a good way of researching the market?
- Do you think secondary research would have been useful? If so, what secondary research would you have done?

> **Key terms**
> **Primary market research** gathers data for the first time.
> **Secondary market research** uses data that already exists.

Sampling

If you decide to undertake a survey, the total number of people who you are interested in is known as your 'target population'. For example, if you have an idea for a website dedicated to your favourite football team, your target population would be all the fans of the club around the world. In most cases it will not be possible to interview all of the people in your target group. It may be too expensive or would simply take too long to talk to everyone. Imagine your website was aimed at the fans of a big club like Manchester United or Chelsea. There are hundreds of thousands of fans all over the world. Even if you managed to identify them somehow, all the cost and time involved in trying to talk to them would make it unrealistic, especially if you are a new business and therefore likely to have limited funds.

Instead of interviewing everyone in the target population, the firm might decide to take a sample. A sample is a group of people that is intended to represent the overall target population. By interviewing, say, 500 fans you would hope to get an impression of what all the others think.

Obviously, the results will not be 100 per cent reliable, because you have not asked everyone in the target population, you have only asked some of them. This means that you cannot be totally confident of the results. So it is important to choose your sample carefully, and ensure that it is big enough to be representative of the whole market. The findings from a sample that is too small may not be very reliable.

> **Key term**
> A **sample** is a group of people or items selected to represent the population as a whole.

Types of sample

There are three main ways of selecting a sample:

Random sample

With this type of sample, all the members of the target population have an equal chance of selection. If you wanted a random sample of 30 students at your school, you could take a list of names of all the pupils then pick 30 names at random. You would then have to find them to interview. This approach has the advantage that anyone could be asked. However, it can be quite time consuming because once the names are selected you then have to go and find those people. If they were not in school in that day you would have to wait until they were, slowing up the whole process.

Quota sample (or convenience sample)

This occurs when interviewers select people within the target population who meet set criteria (e.g. age, income, gender). For example, to represent the characteristics of your target population you may want a sample that comprises adults aged 25 to 35 and is made up of 70% male and 30% female respondents. You then choose a sample size (e.g. 30 people) and select the first 21 males aged 25 to 35 (i.e. 70% of your sample) and the first 9 women aged 25 to 35 (i.e. 30% of the sample) that you can find. This kind of sample is often done via in the street interviews.

With this approach you do not pick out the names of people and then find them (which you do with a random sample); you go and approach people and see if they match the set criteria.

A quota sample is easier and quicker to complete than a random sample (as you do not need to know all the members of the population), but it is not random because members of the population do not have an equal chance of selection. To find 30 adults of a certain age you might go and interview people in a particular shop on a particular day. This means only the people who happen to be there at that moment could be asked; anyone at home at that moment would not be included in your sample; this may give a distorted view of what the target population actually thinks.

Imagine you were doing a survey on the dangers of drinking and to interview the 20 adults needed for you quota you went to a pub; you would probably get a biased viewpoint.

Stratified sample

This type of sample is based on particular proportions (such as 60 per cent males, 40 per cent females; or 20 per cent aged 16–35 and 80 per cent aged over 35. This type of sample is used when the target population has particular characteristics that you want reflected in your sample. Most buyers of computer games, for example, are male and you might want this reflected in your sample.

Choosing a sampling method

The choice of sampling method will depend on factors such as:

- the time available. If time is limited a quota is likely to be used because it is relatively quick to do
- your knowledge of the target population. To select people randomly you must have details of the target population. If you were selecting from a list of cardholders or club members this would be feasible. However, if you were interested in potential buyers of your product you would not necessarily know who they were and so could not select from this group randomly.

- the extent to which the target population has clearly differentiated groups of buyers. If the buyers can be differentiated clearly (e.g. 70 per cent male, 30 per cent female) then you would want to use a stratified sample.

What do you think?

Which of the following pieces of information do you think it would be suitable to gather using secondary rather than primary research data?

- UK population size
- customers' thoughts about a new product
- the weather in your region next week
- typical house prices in your area
- what customers think of your new logo
- whether customers would be willing to pay an extra £5 for home delivery

Quantitative and qualitative market research

Quantitative and qualitative market research are two different approaches to market research.

Qualitative research is based on the opinions of a small focus group or in-depth one-to-one interviews. This type of research aims to understand why customers behave in certain ways or find out what they think of a product. It examines why customers do what they do. For example, a focus group might be used to discuss consumers' views of a brand to understand their shopping habits. This often helps marketing managers understand what customers think of their product compared to another and is often a starting point in the research process. Focus groups may highlight particular issues or a reaction to an business idea that can be examined in more detail. Given that qualitative research involves small groups, it means that the findings are not statistically reliable: this is why more extensive research is often used as a follow up. Qualitative research may highlight key issues that can be explored further in quantitative research.

Quantitative market research is based on relatively large samples and is therefore statistically valid. This sort of research is often used to show what has happened in a market and its findings can be expressed in numerical terms (for example, sales of Brand X have increased by 45 per cent; 12 million people watched Eastenders last week; the market for soft drinks is worth over £4 billion). Quantitative market research is used to explain what has happened.

Key term
A **focus group** is a small number of people gathered together to talk about a particular issue in open discussion.

Start-up market research

When thinking about starting up a business you naturally want to know if your idea will work and market research can therefore be very useful. You obviously don't want to invest time and effort in a project that then fails. However, there can be a number of problems with start-up market research:

- You are likely to have relatively little money available. This can limit the amount of market research you will be able to do. As a result your findings may not be particularly accurate. To save time and money, for example, you may rely purely on secondary data, so the information may not be completely up to date.
- You may not be able to afford market research experts. This means you may carry out the research yourself. This can lead to unreliable findings. For example, if you conduct interviews yourself you may tend to encourage people to give you the answers you want to hear, rather than the 'truth'.
- While it may seem obvious to say that you need to research the market, some entrepreneurs prefer to use the limited money that they do have to develop the product, rather than finding out what customers actually want. However foolish this may seem, entrepreneurs are often so eager to get on with starting up that they think market research is a waste of valuable time and money. In the long run this can prove costly.

Given the costs and difficulties of market research, entrepreneurs need to think carefully before undertaking it. They need to decide:

- what they want to know
- how much they want to spend
- how long they want to take to gather the information.
- the best way of gathering the information.

If they do not undertake effective market research, entrepreneurs will be relying on their intuition and 'gut feeling'. This can be very risky. When setting up in business it is important to remember that your potential customers may not like the same things you do, or think the way you do. If you can, you need to get reliable evidence of what they really want, rather than what you think they want.

Examiner's advice

When studying start-up market research you need to consider:

- whether market research is useful or not
- the most appropriate type of market research for a given problem
- the particular problems for entrepreneurs of undertaking market research.

One step further: confidence levels

When undertaking a survey, the reliability of the findings will vary according to factors such as the size of the sample used and how the sample has been selected. The reliability of a sample can be expressed in terms of a confidence level.

If the confidence level is 95 per cent, this means that 95 per cent of the time (i.e. 19 times out of 20) the results from the sample will represent the views of the overall target population. If the confidence level is 98 per cent, the sample results should represent the overall population 98 per cent of the time.

The bigger the sample the more likely it is that the findings will represent the target population and the greater the degree of confidence.

Managers must take account of the confidence level when using information to make a decision because it is an indicator of reliability. If the confidence level was only 50 per cent, then basing a decision on it would be fairly risky: the findings from the sample would only represent the target population half of the time.

Summary

Market research provides the information that entrepreneurs need to make decisions about a whole range of issues, such as what to produce, what everyone else is doing and whether their idea will be a success. There are different ways of undertaking market research – primary research uses new data, while secondary research uses existing information. When using primary research, a firm may sample the target population. There are various ways of sampling, each of which has advantages and disadvantages that must be considered before choosing the most appropriate method.

Quick questions

1 If every member of the target population has an equal chance of selection, is this a random or quota sample?

2 A focus group is an example of qualitative research. True or false?

3 The findings of a focus group are statistically reliable. True or false?

4 State one reason why an entrepreneur might want to undertake market research.

5 Outline the difference between primary and secondary market research.

6 What is meant by a stratified sample?

7 Outline one limitation on a start-up business when conducting market research

8 Outline one factor that might influence the type of sample a business chooses for its market research.

Issues for analysis

- The reasons for undertaking market research.
- The benefits of different types of market research.
- The links between market research and other business functions.

Issues for evaluation

- How much market research to undertake.
- What type of market research to undertake.
- The reliability and usefulness of market research.

Analysis and evaluation questions

1 'I know I am very good at helping people to organise their lives and achieve their goals. What I don't know is whether this is a viable business opportunity,' says Jacob Greaves. Jacob works in Human Resource Management for a major multinational insurance company and is thinking of setting up his own business.

a Analyse the information that Jacob might want to find out through market research to help him decide whether to set up in business or not.

b To what extent would undertaking market research guarantee the success of Jacob's business if he sets it up?

2 After ten years in the travel industry, Alex Pascale wants to create a new business offering highly personalised tours to France (where he was born and lived until he was 25). He would organise a tailor-made holiday for his clients and provide an escort for small groups of tourists to be there to organise everything for them.

a Analyse the benefits to Alex of undertaking market research.

b Discuss whether primary or secondary market research is more useful to Alex.

Assessment

Figure 5.3 Gecko headgear

Case study

Based in Cornwall, Gecko Headgear Ltd is a designer and manufacturer of marine safety helmets. Founded in 1993 by Jeff Sacrée, the company now employs seven people and started out as a surfboard business. Jeff says:

'As a surfer, I could see the potential for a helmet that was both lightweight and heat-retaining. I was also looking for ways to diversify my product offering, since selling surfboards is highly seasonal. I designed and made the first helmet for myself but the idea soon caught on with other surfers.

However, surfing is a relatively small market so I researched other potential users and a conversation with a lifeboatman led me to approach the Royal National Lifeboat Institution (RNLI), who were immediately interested in using a version of the helmet. Although I was already making helmets, working with the RNLI was a different ballgame. The helmet they wanted had to be adapted, tested and certified before I could start selling it. I also needed to take on staff, which meant the company needed investment. I got a bank loan on the back of the RNLI's involvement. A good relationship with the bank is crucial when you're trying to bring an innovative product to market. In our case the product development process took three years – far longer than we initially expected.

To date, we've gone through ten different versions of the safety helmet, refining it in line with customer feedback each time. The helmet can now accept a range of add-ons, such as cameras, torches and communications equipment, according to customer requirements. We've also developed a new full-face helmet for watercraft racing and a range designed to capitalise on the current boom in extreme sports.

Partnerships with suppliers have been another key to success. For example, we've worked with a manufacturer to develop a new adhesive that can withstand saltwater use. We've also partnered with The Welding Institute to find better ways of welding sections of the helmet together. This has helped us innovate and keep ahead of competitors.'

Questions

(30 marks, 40 minutes)

a Explain the problems you think might be caused for a business by operating in a highly seasonal market such as surfboards. (6 marks)

b Analyse the potential benefits to Gecko Headgear of undertaking market research before targeting the RNLI market. (9 marks)

c To what extent is the success of Gecko Headgear likely to have been due to luck? (15 marks)

6 Understanding markets

Businesses rely on customers. Businesses exist to meet customer needs. To meet these needs effectively, managers must understand the type of market in which they operate and the requirements of different groups of customers within this. In this chapter we examine the different types of markets that exist, the groups of different needs within this and issues such as the growth of the market.

What you need to know by the end of this chapter:
- the nature and types of markets
- the importance of demand
- the meaning of market size, growth and share.

Markets

A market exists whenever there is an exchange between suppliers and buyers. The buyers want to purchase the product so they provide the demand. Businesses want to provide the good or service so they are supplying it. The market involves the market forces of demand and supply interacting and enabling a transaction to take place. In many markets the price adjusts until supply and demand are equal. Consider eBay. Individuals and firms advertise that they have something to sell – this is the supply. Buyers search and decide to buy or make a bid for the item – this is demand. Buyers and sellers interact and a sale is made

Markets can be small, local markets with a specified location, such as a weekly farmers' market in a town where farmers sell their products. Other markets are national or international – for example, there is a world-wide market for oil. The suppliers in this market are from all over the world and demand is also global. This is why oil is shipped all over the globe in huge tankers and there is a 'world' price.

> **Key term**
> A **market** exists where buyers and sellers combine to exchange goods and services

Who are the customers and consumers in a market?

The person or business that buys a product is known as the customer. When you go into a shop and buy a magazine or a mobile phone, you are the customer. The consumer is the person who uses the product. For example, if you buy a birthday present for a friend, you are the customer and they are the consumer: similarly, if your parents buy you a car they are the customers and you are the consumer.

When trying to develop and sell their products, firms must consider the needs of both the customers and the consumers i.e. the needs of the buyer and the user. Children's magazines and toys, for example, may be aimed both at parents who buy the products and at the children who want them and often pester their parents to buy them. These groups may want different things, which can make marketing quite complicated!

Business-to-business and business-to-consumer markets

Business-to-business (B2B) marketing is when one firm sells to another. For example, one business may sell computers, photocopiers, office equipment or stationery to another business. Many organisations have a purchasing department that oversees all its buying (i.e. the customer in this case is a professional buyer). This type of buyer analyses the needs of the user and then looks for the best deal in terms of factors such as price, quality, service, reliability and after-sales service. When dealing directly with other businesses it is common to rely heavily on a salesforce. A salesforce may visit other businesses to explain the benefits of the company's products.

Business-to-consumer (B2C) markets exist when a firm sells to the final buyer. For example, Tesco sells its products to shoppers. In many cases in B2C markets the customer is also the consumer. In B2C markets the buyer is not a professional buyer and may therefore be influenced by factors such as the look of an item, the packaging or the brand name, rather than considering all the technical data on performance. When you bought your mobile phone, how much research did you do? Were you very logical about it or did you buy one because it looked good? B2C markets may involve millions of potential customers, so extensive advertising becomes more feasible as a way of attracting customers.

Influences on demand

Businesses are naturally eager to understand the factors that influence the demand for their products. This is because they will want to anticipate how it might change in the future and because they will want to try and influence demand themselves.

The demand for a product is likely to depend on many different factors.

Customers' level of income

With more income, customers may demand more products. For example, as their incomes rise, customers may go on holiday more often, join a health club, eat out more regularly and spend more on clothes. However, this is not true for all products. With more income, customers may buy less of some goods and services: for example, as incomes rise customers may buy less at bargain discount stores.

The reverse is also true. With less income, demand for most products will fall but sales of some products may rise. Customers may be forced to buy more own-brand items and to catch the bus or walk rather than travel by car. The impact of more or less income therefore depends on the nature of the product.

Competitors

The demand for a product will depend on what else is available. You may be attracted by the offer of O2

until you see the deal that T-Mobile is offering, or vice versa. This may make you switch from one to the other. When considering potential competitors you need to think broadly. Customers may well be choosing between two different types of products: should they buy a new carpet, or use the money to put towards a holiday? In this case the holiday and carpet are both competing for the customer's purchasing power even though they are very different products. With the growth of the internet, customers can now search more quickly to see what is the best deal at any moment and what else is on offer. This can make demand more vulnerable to change as people switch to competitors.

Seasonality

The demand for many products is seasonal. In the summer we expect a rise in demand for products such as barbecues, ice creams, sun cream, tennis raquets and sunglasses. In late August there is a rush for school clothes, calculators and pens as stores promote their 'Back to school' offers. In the winter, demand for fuel, skis, jumpers and cold remedies rise. Other products such as Christmas trees, fireworks, Easter eggs and Valentines cards are all highly seasonal. This has implications for production and employment because of the sudden surges in demand. For example, the business may have to produce and stockpile through the year. Alternatively, managers may try to stabilise demand and make it less seasonal. For example, turkeys have traditionally been eaten in the UK at Christmas. Turkey producers such as Bernard Matthews have tried to promote the appeal of this product as an all-year-round food to make demand less seasonal.

Business in Focus

Magners

The bad weather in June and July 2007 led to a fall in sales of Magners cider. These two months are key for sales of cider and the poor performance meant the company had to announce a cut in the profits forecasted for the year. Sales of barbecue sets, garden furniture and parasols also fell dramatically.

Question:

What businesses might gain from bad weather?

Customer tastes

The demand for a product will depend on what customers actually want and what they can afford. Over time, customer tastes can change, which alters the level of demand for different products. For example, in recent years there has been more interest in organic food and environmentally friendly products, which has increased the size of these markets. There has been less interest in cabbages, sherry and CDs.

Business in Focus

Crocs

Figure 6.1 Croc shoes

It all started when the three founders, based in Boulder, Colorado, decided to develop and market an innovative type of footwear called Croc Shoes. They were originally intended for boating and outdoor use because of the slip-resistant, non-marking sole. By 2003, Croc had become a fashion phenomenon, universally accepted (and much imitated) as an all-purpose shoe for comfort and fashion. The company says: 'We are committed to making a lightweight, comfortable, slip-resistant, fashionable and functional shoe, which can be produced quickly and at an affordable price to our customers.'
   (Adapted from www.crocs.com)

Company marketing

The way a business prices its products, the way it promotes them and the way it distributes them will all affect sales. A strong brand image, a good distribution system and good value for money will boost demand. This is explored in more detail in Section 5.

Market size

The demand for a product determines the size of the market. The size of a market can be measured in terms of the number of items sold (the volume of sales) or the amount of spending (the value of sales). For example, the volume of sales of an item may be 5 million units a year: if the average price is £4 a unit, then the value of sales would be £20 million a year.

   In many cases the volume and value of sales will move in the same direction. More units sold at the same price will increase the value of sales. However, it is possible for the volume of sales in a market to increase but the value to fall if the price is reduced enough.

   For example:

- Sales volume 5 million units, price £4: sales value £20 million.
- Sales volume 6 million units, price £3: sales value £18million.

As we can see, the volume has increased but the sales value has fallen because the price has been cut so much.

Market growth

Market growth occurs when the size of a market increases. For example, if a market is worth £20 million and then increases to £22 million, it has grown in size.

$$\text{Market growth rate} = \frac{\text{change in size}}{\text{original market size}} \times 100$$

$$= \frac{£2 \text{ million}}{£20 \text{ million}} \times 100$$

$$= 10 \text{ per cent.}$$

If a market is growing this may mean there are more sales opportunities. All firms may be able to sell more because demand is getting bigger.

   If, on the other hand, a market was worth £20 million one year and only £16 million later on then it has shrunk in size.

   The growth rate here is negative because the market has got smaller.

$$\text{Market growth rate} = \frac{\text{change in size}}{\text{original market size}} \times 100$$

$$= \frac{-£4 \text{ million}}{£20 \text{ million}} \times 100$$

$$= -20 \text{ per cent.}$$

In a shrinking market, the firms within the market may have to fight harder to maintain their sales. If there is less demand in total, firms may have to become more aggressive to prevent their own sales falling.

Within any given market, demand for some products may be increasing and demand for others falling. For example:

- demand for more environmentally friendly cars is growing, whereas sales of the large Sports Utility Vehicles is falling
- demand for chocolate confectionery is increasing slowly in the UK; demand for boxed chocolates is falling
- demand for CDs is falling; demand for downloaded music is increasing.

Market share

A firm's market share measures its sales as a percentage of the total market sales. If a firm sells products worth £1 million in a market worth £20 million then:

$$\text{Market share} = \frac{\text{the product's sales}}{\text{total market sales}} \times 100$$

$$= \frac{\text{£1 million}}{\text{£20 million}} \times 100$$

$$= 5 \text{ per cent.}$$

If the total sales in a market remain the same but a firm increases its own sales, then its market share will increase. For example, if the firm's sales are £2 million, and the total market sales are £20 million, then the market share is (£2 million/£20 million) x 100 = 10 per cent.

If a firm maintains the same level of sales when a market grows its share will fall. For example: if the firm's sales are £2 million and the total market sales are £20 million, then the market share is 10 per cent. However, if the firm's sales are £2 million and the total market sales are £40 million, then the market share is 5 per cent.

Market share is an important measure of performance when it comes to marketing and is often a marketing objective that a business will set for itself. By increasing its market share, a firm will be performing better relative to its competitors. With more market share a firm will have more power in a market: for example, it may have more bargaining power over its suppliers and may be able to negotiate better rates when advertising because it is such an important client. Customers should also have more awareness of its brand name, which could pro-

mote more sales in the future. Customers sometimes rely on a familiar name when deciding what to buy. Imagine you are looking for a television or laptop – you may decide to stick with a brand you know and that has worked well for you in the past.

Examiner's advice

In the exam you will be expected to understand and calculate market share, market size and market growth, so practise these calculations.

Summary

Businesses can only exist if there is a demand for their products. Demand can be affected by various factors, such as a firm's marketing, customers' income levels, competitors' actions and the season. The level of demand determines the size of the market: if demand increases the market may grow.

Quick questions

1 What is the difference between a customer and a consumer?
2 What is meant by a 'market'?
3 If a firm sells £2 million worth of goods in a market worth £40 million, what is its market share?
4 If a firm has 20 per cent of a market worth £300,000, what is its level of sales?
5 What does B2B mean?
6 A market that was worth £2 million grows by 15 per cent. What is the new total level of sales in the market?
7 State two factors that might affect the demand for a product.
8 State how the volume of sales might fall in a market but the value might increase.

Issues for analysis

- The differences between market size, market share and market growth.
- The significance of market growth.
- The benefits of increasing market share.

Issues for evaluation

- What are the main influences on demand for a product?
- Does increasing market share matter?
- What is the importance of market growth?

Analysis and evaluation questions

1 Bruno Frederico set up his fresh flowers business, Blooming Marvellous, in 2005. Over the last few years he has noticed that while the local demand for fresh flowers seems to be fairly constant, his share of the market is falling.

a Analyse the possible consequences for Bruno of a falling market share.
b Discuss the factors that determine the demand for a fresh flowers business such as Bruno's.

2 Mike Williams sells computers directly to businesses.

a Analyse the factors that might influence demand for his computers.
b Discuss the ways in which selling computers to businesses may differ from selling computers to individual buyers.

Assessment

Go back to Chapter 5, page 36 and read the case study on Gecko Headgear again.

Case study

Questions

(30 marks, 40 minutes)
1 Explain the factors that might determine demand for headgear by the RNLI (6 marks).
2 Analyse the factors that might determine the demand for surf headgear. (9 marks)
3 Discuss the possible benefits to Gecko of gaining a large share of the headgear market that it has targeted. (15 marks)

7

Transforming resources into goods and services

All businesses are involved in some form of transformation process: they take resources (inputs) and turn them into outputs designed to meet customer needs. In this chapter we examine the nature of the transformation process and how it can add value for customers.

What you need to know by the end of this chapter:
- the meaning and significance of inputs and outputs
- how the transformation process works
- what is meant by 'adding value'.

Inputs and outputs

Once entrepreneurs are convinced that a market exists for their goods or services, they must work out how best to provide them. They must decide what resources (inputs) are needed to do this and the best ways of transforming them into outputs (goods or services).

The transformation process is subject to change as entrepreneurs find new products to offer, new ways of producing them, and new inputs to use. Also, feedback from customers will influence the process. More demand from customers for organic food might lead a food shop to switch suppliers, for example.

Inputs

The inputs into a business include:

- people
- capital equipment
- materials and components
- finance
- entrepreneurship
- land.

Land

This involves choosing where to produce. For some businesses, such as a new shop or café, the main factors influencing the choice of location may be cost or ease of access for its customers. For others, such as farming, what will also matter is the quality of the land in terms of resources and the ability to grow different crops. The success of a farming business will be directly affected by changes to the quality of the land. High levels of rain in 2007 led to a lot of flooding in the UK, which ruined many crops. Tyrell's Potato Chips, the crisps manufacturer, grows potatoes on around 700 acres of land and lost around half of its crop. The significance of land as an input will be particularly high in the primary sector.

> **Key term**
> The **primary sector** is the first stage of production and includes extracting or growing resources. Farming, mining and fishing are all part of the primary sector.

Under the heading of land we also include premises. The amount of space available to a business can affect how much can be produced or how many customers can physically fit in the store: the nature

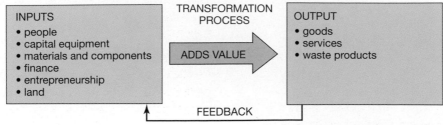

Figure 7.1 The transformation process

of the premises can also affect the working environment and employees' motivation.

Figure 7.2 Premises affect staff motivation

Labour

Organisations will need staff. The quality of employees in terms of their skills, their attitudes (e.g. to customers), their willingness to work, their creativity and their natural abilities will have an influence on the success of any business. What makes a film a blockbuster? The quality of the writing, the acting and the production – people play a key role in the success of any film. Many films therefore promote themselves on the basis of who the actors are. Universities promote their professors. Music labels promote their bands. Publishers promote their author list. So people can be a crucial element of the transformation process.

Capital

The word 'capital' has many meanings. In this instance, we mean the equipment used by businesses. The coffee machines in the coffee shop, the ovens in the fast food restaurants, the scanning equipment in shops are all examples of capital equipment. The amount and quality of equipment in a business can affect the service it provides. For example, the online retailer Amazon is admired for the efficiency with which it processes an order and is able to make suggestions to customers of what else they might like to buy.

Entrepreneurship

As we saw in Chapter 1, entrepreneurship involves taking risks to turn ideas into new businesses. This is a key skill in the transformation process. There are resources all around us: what makes them into a viable business idea is an entrepreneur – someone who has the idea, combines resources and turns them into a product or service that customers value. The ability of the entrepreneur to identify opportunities and take advantage of them effectively will determine the success of the business.

Materials and Components

The choice of inputs and who supplies them can affect:

- the costs of a business
- the quality of the final product (and therefore sales).

In recent years, customers have become increasingly interested in what resources have been used in a production process and where they came from. Firms may highlight the fact they use recycled materials or that their ingredients are 'natural' or 'organic'. Firms will also face the choice of whether to buy in some materials or produce them themselves.

Business in Focus

Vegetarian Shoes

Veggie Shoes first started in 1990. It was started by Robin Webb who, at that time, made all the shoes by hand. Originally he only made one style – a basic lace-up shoe. He had taught himself to make shoes four years earlier after leaving art college. He had heard that in parts of Africa, car tyres were recycled into shoe soles. This made him realise the possibilities when it came to making footwear and he was soon making shoes out of anything he could lay his hands on. However, being a vegetarian he didn't want to use leather. Then he found out about a material called Microfibre – a synthetic material used for yachting upholstery. It looked and felt like supple leather, but was 'breathable', unlike other plastics. Robin realised that this was what he had been looking for, and Vegetarian Shoes was born. The range of styles quickly grew – as well as shoes, he made boots, sandals and belts from this new fabric. Every thing was made to order and as the word spread he got busier and busier, to the point where he could not make things fast enough! So he took his material to a footwear factory to get them to make shoes for him. That enabled him to have a stock that he could mail-order to vegetarians all over the country.

How has the transformation process of Vegetarian Shoes changed over time as the business has grown?

Web link

To find out more about Vegetarian Shoes, visit www.vegetarian-shoes.co.uk

Outputs

The output of a business may be in the form of goods or services, or a combination of the two.

- A good (or a product) is a tangible item, such as a car or a laptop computer. A good is a physical item. Businesses can produce and stock them. This means that they can produce in advance of demand: for example, a store may stockpile new electrical goods before the Christmas rush.
- A service is intangible. Services include education, creating music, hairdressing and physiotherapy. Most businesses in the UK are in the service sector. Services cannot be stored: they have to be produced for customers as they are needed. This can create problems because if there is a rush of customers there are no products stockpiled and so queues form or waiting lists have to be introduced.

In many cases, a business provides a combination of goods and services. For example, you may choose a restaurant because of the food you can eat there (the goods) but also the waiters, the environment and the way you are treated (the service).

Most outputs are intended for sale. A firm produces goods and services to sell to customers. However, there may also be by-products from the transformation process: for example, a firm's production may create waste and pollution. Many customers pay attention to these issues and increasingly, firms are considering the effects of their production on other groups, such as the local community.

The transformation process

Every business undertakes a transformation process. It takes a range of inputs and transforms them into outputs that they hope customers want.

For most products there are series of stages in transformation processes involved in taking the initial materials and ending up with the final product. The author J.K. Rowling took her imagination, a computer and paper and turned this into magical manuscripts for her Harry Potter books. The publishing company worked with the author, designers, a marketing team, a printing business, a distribution business and turned the manuscripts into a series of books. Book stores such as Waterstones take a range of books and transform them into a retail experience for the customer. A series of transformations have gone to get the idea from the author's mind into a book and into the hands of the reader.

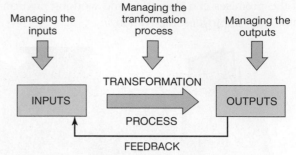

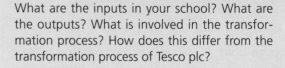

Figure 7.3 Chain of operations

What do you think?

What are the inputs in your school? What are the outputs? What is involved in the transformation process? How does this differ from the transformation process of Tesco plc?

When setting up in business you need to identify exactly what you want to provide in terms of the range and quality of the product. You then need to decide on the resources you will need to provide the product to the standard you want. There are a number of questions: How many people do you need? What skills will they need? How will you train them? What materials will you use? What equipment? And so on. You need to find a way of generating a product that customers value so much that they will pay more for it than it costs to produce it.

Business in Focus

Transformation processes

There are many different forms of transformation. These include:

- changing the characteristics of materials, information or customers. For example, manufacturers take components and build something new with it. Beauty salons and cosmetic surgeons take people and improve their appearance (we hope!). Doctors, dentists, physiotherapists, psychiatrists and teachers all help us to improve some aspect of ourselves. Accountants take our receipts and turn them into a set of accounts to show investors or government tax inspectors.

- changing the location of materials and information. Federal Express and Virgin Express move items or people around. Google helps you find something that is already there – it helps you to access information. An estate agent gives you information on houses that you might be interested in. This service saves time and money for the seller and helps the buyer to sell the property more quickly.
- changing the ownership of materials. Wholesalers buy in bulk from a number of producers. Retailers then buy from wholesalers because it is easier to deal with them than with every single producer: it reduces the number of transactions and makes the process simpler.

(Source: adapted from Open University material, at: http://openlearn.open.ac.uk/mod/resource/view.php?id=161703)

Can you think of any other types of transformation processes?

When designing a transformation process an entrepreneur must consider questions such as:

- What level of output will be provided? Are you aiming to produce hundreds, thousands or millions of units? How many customers do you want to be able to have?
- What quality of service will be provided? How many people will you have serving in your shop? Will you deliver your products to peoples' homes? What will your policy be if people want to return items?
- How will you provide the service? Will you provide it online or via shops? Will you use high staffing levels or invest in more equipment?
- What aspects of the process will the business undertake for itself and what elements will be outsourced to or bought in from other providers? You may decide to manage the shop yourself but get cleaners in to tidy up, employ accountants to do the finances and use specialists to design the décor. You may produce a range of clothes but simply do the design work yourself and get someone else to produce them: alternatively, you may manufacture them yourself. All these decisions will have an impact on the costs, flexibility and the complexity of running your business.

What do you think?

If you set up a fashion business would you want to produce the clothes yourself, or would you just want to design them? Why?

The transformation process may be:

- in the primary sector. This involves the first stage of production and includes extractive industries such as mining, farming, forestry and fishing. This sector is not very large in the UK.
- in the secondary sector. This represents manufacturing and construction industries.
- in the tertiary sector. This represents the service sector (e.g. tourism, accountancy and music). This is the biggest sector in the UK in terms of both employment and the value of the output.

Feedback

The transformation process is ongoing and dynamic and when you receive feedback (eg from your customers) you need to review what you do. If the output you produce is not acceptable or needs to be improved you will have to change the inputs and/or the way you produce. For example, you might change your menu, your opening hours, your prices, or your decor. You will then monitor the results and, if necessary, change again. Change may also be due to external factors. Increasing concern about the environment has influence over what is produced and how it is produced.

Adding value

Adding value occurs when outputs are produced that are worth more than the inputs used up to provide them.

For example, artists such as Andy Warhol, Vincent van Gogh, David Hockney and Rembrandt took their imagination, paint and canvas and produced amazing works of art that sell for millions of pounds: far more than the cost of the items used up in their production. They added value via the transformation process.

Jamie Oliver, the cook, takes standard ingredients: meat, herbs, vegetables, puts them together in a unique way and comes up with a fantastic meal. He takes ingredients that many others may use but transforms them in a way that appeals to customers, packs out his restaurant, sells books and attracts viewers for his TV series. Clearly, he has added value by using his talent, creativity and personality.

Adding value can be done in ways that may seem odd. Here are some examples:

- Some companies buy new jeans and then stretch them, batter them and fray them to make them look distressed while, at the same time more than doubling their price.
- A bottled water launched in 2007 for £5 a bottle comes from King Island, near Tasmania. It is called 'Cloud Juice' and is claimed to be the purest in the world. It is rain water collected from a plastic roof that has been bottled. It is supposed to be so pure because it comes from rain clouds that travel 7,000 miles from South America without passing over any land and therefore not encountering pollution.
- One of the most expensive coffees in the world is Luwak Coffee. This is made from coffee cherries that have been eaten and digested by common palm civets (a type of animal). The civets use their keen sense of smell to select the choicest and ripest beans. The beans are supposed to be much sweeter as a result of the digestion process and, having passed through the animal, they are hand-collected from the jungle floor.

Increasing added value

To increase its added value, a business might aim to:

- reduce the costs of producing it. This means cutting back on waste, ensuring the best price for the supplies and making sure that mistakes are not made. All activities that do not add value need to be examined to see if they are truly necessary. If time is wasted, jobs are being duplicated, materials are lost, errors are made, or equipment is sitting idle, the business is inefficient and the entrepreneur should look for ways to remove the inefficiency.
- increase the perceived benefit of the product in the eyes of the customer. This could be through building the brand, developing a unique selling proposition (USP) or differentiating it through the service provided. Faster delivery, better design, or improved customer service might all add value in this way.

Key term
A **unique selling point/proposition (USP)** is any aspect of a product that differentiates it from its competitors. For example, the USP of a product may be faster delivery, more features, a unique design or the fact that it is tailor-made.

What do you think?

A sandwich in a shop costs far more than it would to buy the ingredients and make it yourself. Why are we willing to pay so much for a sandwich in a shop?

Examiner's advice

In the exam you will need to think about how different firms add value. What can businesses do to add more value? Should they focus on the benefits they are providing, or try to control costs more effectively?

Summary

The transformation process is at the heart of all businesses. Inputs are transformed into outputs. The aim of business is to transform resources in a way that adds value. This means that the outputs are worth more than the inputs that are used up. Organisations are continually looking for ways of how to add more value for customers. They must regularly get feedback on the results of the transformation process to see how it can be improved further.

Quick questions

1. Identify three types of inputs that go into a business.
2. Outline two types of output produced by a business.
3. A product that offers good value for money always has a low price. True or false?
4. What is meant by adding value?
5. Distinguish between a good and a service.
6. What determines whether a product is good value?
7. To be competitive, a firm must always offer a lower price than its competitors. True or false?
8. How might a firm use its transformation process to add value?

Issues for analysis

- The importance of adding value.
- Choosing inputs and adding value.
- Choosing the transformation process and adding value.

Issues for evaluation

- What is the importance of price in terms of value for customers?
- What are the key factors that determine a firm's competitiveness?

Analysis and evaluation questions

1 Frank Freud set up on his own as an accountant last year. He concentrates on advising private individuals with high incomes.

a   Analyse the ways in which Frank might add value for his clients.
b   To what extent is the price of Frank's services likely to be a key factor in the success of his business?

2 Fran Bucknall runs a food shop in the centre of her local city.

a   Analyse the factors that determine which stores you choose to visit when shopping for food.
b   Discuss the ways in which the choice of supplies might determine the success of a food shop.

Assessment

Case study

Tyrrell's Potato Chips produces crisps from its own potatoes for selected stores and delicatessens. The owner, William Chase, decided to move out of just selling potatoes to producing hand-made crisps. So his company adds value to the basic potatoes by combining them with various flavourings, cooking them and branding them. He sells his crisps in stores such as Selfridges, Harvey Nichols and Waitrose.

Web link

To find out more, visit
www.tyrrellspotatochips.co.uk

Questions

(30 marks, 40 minutes)
1   Explain what is meant by adding value, and give examples. (6 marks)
2   Analyse the possible factors that determine how much customers are willing to pay to buy Tyrrell's crisps. (9 marks)
3   To what extent is price the key element of the marketing mix for Tyrell's crisps? (15 marks)

8 Choosing the right legal structure

When setting up in business, the founders must consider the most appropriate legal form for their enterprise. There are several different types of business organisation, each of which has its own legal structure. Owners can, of course, change the legal structure later in the life of a business, so the structure may change over time. In this chapter we consider four of the most common forms of business: sole traders, partnerships, private limited companies and public limited companies.

What you need to know by the end of this chapter:

• the advantages and disadvantages of being a sole trader, a partner, a private limited company and a public limited company
• the role of not-for-profit businesses.

Sole traders

When individuals set up in business on their own they are known as 'sole traders'. Plumbers, decorators, window cleaners and hairdressers are often sole traders. The people running these businesses work for themselves. In some cases, sole traders hire other people to help them out, but they remain responsible for the overall business and are actively involved in the running of it on a daily basis. There is no distinctions between them and their businesses.

What does it take to be a successful sole trader?

As a sole trader you need to be someone who is willing to work on your own, who has the confidence to take your own decisions and who can turn your hand to almost any aspect of your business. As a sole trader, you may have to serve customers, decide what equipment to buy, deal with suppliers and keep accurate and up-to-date business records. This requires a wide range of skills and an enormous degree of flexibility.

Sole traders have to be used to working hard: running your own business is no easy task. You must also be good at managing stress. All the decisions of the business are yours alone, so if you get it wrong the responsibilty is yours. On the other hand, if it is successful the sense of achievement and the rewards are yours, too!

Becoming a sole trader requires a high level of self-discipline because you are your own boss: there is no one to tell you what to do. This can be very exciting, because you decide what is going to happen. However, it also means that you have to motivate yourself to get things done. For example, you have to organise your day properly and use your time effectively.

The advantages of being a sole trader

One of the main advantages of being a sole trader is that it is so easy to start up in business. Unlike starting other types of organisation, you do not need to register with anyone or fill in any special forms: you can just start trading (provided you declare your profits to the tax authorities at the end of each financial year!). If you suddenly decide you want to be a gardener, web designer, an artist, an interior decorator or cleaner, you could start up in business tomorrow. It may be wise, however, to do some planning and get some training first!

Many sole traders also enjoy not having to take orders from other people. They like the freedom to make their own decisions, to decide when and where to work, what to do and how to do it. You can also make decisions quickly as you don't have to check with anyone to get permission to do something. It can be incredibly motivating to be your own boss.

Another important advantage of being a sole trader is that you keep all the rewards of the business. You don't have to share the profits with anyone else.

Many entrepreneurs begin as sole traders for these reasons.

The challenges of being a sole trader

While being a sole trader can be very fulfilling, it also brings with it many challenges. Making all the decisions can be exciting, but you carry all the responsibility if anything goes wrong. If you work for someone else and there is a real problem, you have someone to work with to solve it. Being a sole trader can be quite lonely: some people find it difficult to cope with the pressure. The hours may be quite demanding, too. This is particularly likely to be an issue in the early years when you are trying hard to build up enough business. Also, you may not be able to take much time off for holidays because you may not be able to afford to close the business and risk losing customers.

Another difficulty is raising finance to set up and expand. You generally have to rely on your own money or money from friends and family (plus the money from the business itself, once it is up and running). Of course, it is possible to borrow from a bank or other financial institution but they often charge smaller businesses quite high interest rates because they are worried about the risk of failure and want to cover their losses.

Being a sole trader is also quite risky if anything goes wrong. This is because sole traders have unlimited liability. The sole trader keeps any rewards the business makes, but is also personally responsible for any losses. If their businesses have problems, sole traders can lose their personal possessions.

> **Key term**
> **Unlimited liability** occurs when an individual or groups of individuals are personally responsible for all the actions of their business. With sole traders, there is no distinction in law between the individuals and the business and so they could lose their personal assets if the business has financial problems.

In many ways, working for other people in a large organisation is much easier because you are likely to:

- have other people to share ideas with
- receive a more regular income
- be able to call on experts to help you solve problems.

On the other hand, there is not quite the same sense of achievement and satisfaction of having created something for yourself.

Partnerships

If you join together with other people and set up together this is known as a partnership. This is common in professions such as accountancy and law. The benefits of forming a partnership over being a sole trader include:

- You have other people to share ideas with.
- There are more people to invest in the business and help finance it.
- You can benefit from each other's specialist skills: for example, if you have a legal practice you could have one partner specialising in tax law, another in marital law, another in company law and so on. This enables you to offer a wide service to customers.
- You can cover for each other if someone is ill or is on holiday.

Advantages	Disadvantages
Making your own decisions can be motivating.	Sources of finance are limited.
You can make decisions quickly and respond rapidly to changes in the market.	You rely heavily on your own ability to make decisions.
You have direct contact with the market.	You may work long hours and have limited holidays, leading to stress.
Setting up is easy.	You are subject to unlimited liability.

Table 7.1 Advantages and disadvantages of being a sole trader

However, a partnership can present challenges:

- You need to consult with others and there may be disagreements between the partners over the policies and direction of the business.
- You are dependent on the actions of others. If, for example, one of the partners makes a mistake or brings the partnership into disrepute, it will have an impact on all the partners. You are liable for your partners' actions, which can be risky.
- In most partnerships the partners have unlimited liability, which means that there is no distinction between the individuals and the business. If the business is sued, for example, the individuals may lose their personal possessions. This is a risk that some people may not be prepared to take.

To reduce some of the possible problems of a partnership, the individuals involved are advised to write a Deed of Partnership. This document sets out the 'rules' of the partnership: for example, it sets out:

- how the partnership would be dissolved if someone wanted to leave. It would set out how the partnership would be valued and therefore what the person leaving would receive
- how to resolve disputes if the number voting for and against an issue is equal
- how profits will be divided up: if this is not specified the profits are divided up equally.

What do you think?

Imagine you set up a partnership with your friends from school or college. Do you think you would work well as a team, or not?

Limited partnerships

In a 'limited partnership' there are:

- one or more persons called 'general partners', who are liable for all the debts and obligations of the firm, and
- one or more persons called 'limited partners' who contribute money to the partnership. Limited partners are not liable for the debts and obligations of the firm beyond the amount they have contributed. However, limited partners cannot draw out or receive back any part of their contribution to the partnership during its lifetime, nor can they take part in the management of the business.

Limited Liability Partnerships

A Limited Liability Partnership (LLP) is similar to a normal partnership, but it also offers reduced personal responsibility for business debts. Unlike the members of ordinary partnerships, the LLP itself is responsible for any debts that it runs up, not the individual partners.

At least two members of an LLP must be what is known as 'designated members' and the law places extra responsibilities on them.

Companies

To avoid some of the problems of being a sole trader or a partnership, you may decide to establish a company, instead. To set up a company, the owners have to complete various documents and register the business at Companies House. This process is known as incorporation.

A company is owned by shareholders. Each share in the business represents a part of the company. The more shares someone owns, the more of the company belongs to them.

A company has its own legal identity, separate from that of its owners. The company can own property, equipment and other goods in its own right and is responsible for its own debts. If the company fails, the shareholders can lose the money that they invested in the business when they bought shares, but they cannot lose more than this. This is because a company has limited liability. This means that a company is responsible for the money it owes but that the personal possessions of its owners are safe. This is different from a sole trader, who has unlimited liability and could lose everything if the business had financial problems.

Having limited liability is essential for companies to be able to raise money by selling shares. Without it, investors would be far less likely to buy shares because of the risk of losing their personal possessions. If you invested in a business with unlimited liability it would mean giving money to others and risking everything. With limited liability, you know what the maximum amount is that you could lose.

Having company status means that:

- the business must pay to have its accounts checked annually by independent accountants (called auditors)
- the company accounts must be made public, so that outsiders can see the revenue and profits of the business, as well as what it owns. This means that there is less privacy of affairs than if you were a sole trader.

Why become a shareholder?

By investing in a company, shareholders become the owners of the business. This means that, if the business is successful, the value of their shares should increase. Shareholders should also receive some of the profits that the company makes each year. The part of the profits paid out to shareholders is called the dividends. The more profit a firm makes, the bigger the dividends are likely to be. Each year the shareholders will decide on the amount of dividends to be paid per share: the more shares a person has, the more dividends they receive in total.

Shareholders can also influence the policy of the business. Most types of shares grant their owners voting rights. Each share is worth one vote. So, by buying more shares, people can get more votes and have a greater influence over what the firm actually does. If someone owns more than 51 per cent of the shares, they control the business and, therefore, can decide company policy.

All companies must have an Annual General Meeting (AGM) to which the shareholders are invited and every shareholder must receive a copy of the company's Annual Report. The Annual Report reviews the performance of the business over the last year. At the AGM, the directors and managers give an overview of the company's position and respond to any questions that shareholders might have.

In the UK, financial institutions such as banks, pension funds and insurance companies own most company shares. These organisations buy shares to make a profit through the dividends they receive and by selling the shares at a higher price later on. They can then pass their profits on to their own investors.

As you can see in Figure 8.1, individuals own less than 15 per cent of shares in the UK. Foreign investors own 40 per cent of shares in the UK.

Private limited companies

Private limited companies have 'ltd' after their names. They are owned by shareholders and the owners can place restrictions on who the shares are sold to in the future. For example, many (but not all) private limited companies are owned by families who limit the sale of shares to other members of the family: this makes sure that 'outsiders' do not become involved. Owners of shares in private limited companies cannot advertise their shares for sale: they have to sell them privately.

Public limited companies

Public limited companies have 'plc' after their names. Once again, they are owned by shareholders, but unlike private companies restrictions cannot be placed on the sale of these shares. Shareholders in public companies can sell their shares to whoever they like. This can cause problems if another firm starts to buy up shares in the business in an attempt to gain control of it. Some of the shareholders may want to resist this takeover, but they cannot stop fellow shareholders from selling their shares.

Another difference between plcs and ltd companies is that shares in plcs can be advertised in the media. This is why you can see the share prices of public companies listed in the newspapers, but not those of private companies. Most companies become public because they want to advertise their shares to the general public and raise relatively large sums of money. Most public companies are bigger than most private companies.

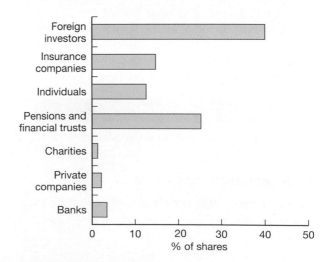

Figure 8.1 UK Share ownership data

(Source: National Statistics Website: **www.statistics.gov.uk** Crown copyright material is produced with the permission of the Controller of HMSO)

If the owners of a private company do not need to raise large sums via the sale of shares and want to maintain control over their company then they probably would not want to make it a public company.

What do you think?

You are thinking of buying shares in a company. What would you want to know before deciding which ones to buy?

Not-for-profit businesses

Not all enterprises are set up to make a profit. Local sports clubs, government organisations and charities, for example do not have profit as the main objective. They are set up for some other purpose.

Business in Focus

Wikipedia

Wikipedia was created in 2001. It is a multilingual, web-based, free-content encyclopedia project. It is written by volunteers all over the world. Its articles can be edited by anyone with internet access. It is now one of the largest online encyclopedias in the world. Articles are continually updated and improved by online contributors. The website was created by the not-for-profit Wikipedia Foundation.

Web link

To find out more, visit www.wikipedia.com

Question:

Why do you think people would contribute to Wikipedia?

Social enterprises, for example, are businesses that have social aims and trade in order to benefit the community or society in general. Examples of social aims are job creation and training, providing community services and 'Fair Trade' with developing countries.

Well-known social enterprises include Cafédirect, The Big Issue, The Co-operative Group, the Eden Project and Jamie Oliver's 'Fifteen' resturant, but there are many others (over 55,000) operating in a wide range of industries from farmers' markets and recycling companies to transport providers and childcare.

Web link

For more information on social enterprises, visit www.socialenterprise.org.uk

Real-life Business

Tom Hunter

Figure 8.2 Sir Tom Hunter

In 2007, Sir Tom Hunter, one of the richest men in Scotland, announced that he would give away at least £1bn to charity. Hunter is the ex-owner of the sports chain Sports Direct and is said to have a fortune of £1.05bn. The money will be transferred over several years but Hunter has already committed £100m to his charitable foundation to fight inequality in both Scotland and Africa.

In a recent interview Sir Tom said he was concerned about the growing gap in the UK between rich and poor, and that he wanted to boost opportunities for those at the bottom. He said: 'There is more great wealth in fewer hands than ever before in history. My own personal belief is that with great wealth comes great responsibility.'

Hunter grew up in the mining village of New Cumnock in Ayrshire, before attending the University of Strathclyde. He began his career by selling trainers from the back of a van and in 1984 founded the Sports Direct chain. The company was sold to retailer JJB Sports in 1998, making Sir Tom an estimated £250m.

Question:

Do you think business is good for society, or not?

What do you think?

If you had a personal fortune of £1bn, would you give any of it away to charity? Do you ever give money to charities at the moment? Why?

Examiner's advice

When studying this chapter you need to think about the advantages and disadvantages of the different forms of business. What determines the right structure for a business? What issues are involved in choosing a business format?

Summary

There are various forms of legal structure that a business can adopt: for example, you might set up as a sole trader, join with others to form a partnership or set up a company. Each of these forms of business has advantages and disadvantages. For example, a private limited company has limited liability, whereas a sole trader has unlimited liability: on the other hand, it is easier to set up as a sole trader.

Quick questions

1 A sole trader has unlimited liability. True or false?

2 A private limited company has plc after its name. True or false?

3 What is meant by 'limited liability'?

4 A private company can only be owned by family members. True or false?

5 What is meant by a Deed of Partnership?

6 State why an entrepreneur might try to find others to set up as a partnership rather than as a sole trader.

7 Outline two factors that individuals might consider when choosing an appropriate legal structure.

8 State one disadvantage of operating as a company rather than as a sole trader.

Business in Focus

The Big Issue

'The Big Issue is an international organisation that works with homeless people all over the world, from the United Kingdom to Africa, Asia and Australia. At the centre of its work is The Big Issue magazine, an award-winning entertainment and current affairs magazine, that is produced by professional journalists and sold on the streets by homeless people. In the UK, the homeless buy the magazine for 70 pence and sell it on for £1.50, keeping 80 pence for themselves. Although financial exclusion is one of the key reasons why people remain homeless- and one of the core aims of The Big Issue is to give people a legitimate way of making a living- there are other benefits of becoming a vendor.

Not only does beginning to sell the magazine provide an opportunity to access the services of The Big Issue Foundation, but also the act of having to organise themselves and their money, as well as committing to a sales pitch, teaches new skills and self reliance, which in turn builds self confidence and can be the key to moving on. The Big Issue offers social as well as financial inclusion. Editorially The Big Issue magazine is committed to giving homeless people a voice in the media and raising difficult issues that are overlooked in the mainstream press.'

(Source: www.bigissue.co.uk)

What other organisations can you think of that try to improve society rather than just make profit?

Issues for analysis

● The importance of limited liability.
● The importance of control.
● The motives for buying shares
● The role of shareholders

Issues for evaluation

● What should you consider when choosing a business structure?

Analysis and evaluation questions

1 When Bobby Charlton, a DJ for the last ten years, first thought about setting up a nightclub business his twin brother Jack, an accountant, asked if he could be a part of it.

a   Analyse the possible benefits for Bobby of taking on Jack as a partner.

b   Discuss the possible problems for Bobby setting up as a partnership with Jack rather than a sole trader.

2 Sally Ann Beckham has an idea for a series of hot-water bottles for children based on television characters and characters from children's' books. Unfortunately, she lacks the funds necessary to develop the idea further. She is considering creating a company and selling shares.

a   Analyse the factors that investors might take into account before buying shares in her company.

b   Discuss the possible advantages and disadvantages to Sally of setting up a company.

Assessment

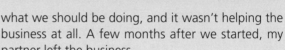

Case study

In 2001, after ten years as the general manager of an office supplies company, John Kerr decided that he wanted to run his own business.

'Originally I'd planned to take on my colleague as an employee. But he wanted to share in the management of the business, which seemed fair enough, so we talked to a solicitor about the choices. Setting up a partnership was the simplest option, and would avoid the extra costs of setting up and administering a company. The solicitor pointed out that we would both be personally liable for any business debts, but as we weren't planning to borrow this wasn't a big issue for us. The solicitor said that we needed a partnership agreement, and helped us draw one up. Preparing the agreement was a chance for us both to think about how we wanted to run the business and what our responsibilities would be.

Unfortunately, we soon realised that we didn't work together well. We each had our own ideas on what we should be doing, and it wasn't helping the business at all. A few months after we started, my partner left the business.

As it happened, there was someone else I wanted to bring into the business anyway. Turnover of our business has more than doubled in the last three years, so we must be doing something right!'

Source: Adapted from Business Link
www.businesslink.gov.uk

Case study questions

(30 marks, 40 minutes)
1 Outline the possible benefits to John Kerr of using a solicitor. (6 marks)
2 Analyse the possible benefits to John Kerr of setting up as a partnership. (9 marks)
3 To what extent do you think he would have been better setting up as a company? (15 marks)

9

Raising finance for a start-up

A big issue facing many new businesses is raising sufficient finance. There are several possible sources open to entrepreneurs, but it is not always easy to convince people to lend you money, even when you are convinced that you have a brilliant idea! In this chapter we outline the advantages and disadvantages of different forms of finance.

What you need to know by the end of this chapter:

• the sources of finance available to start-up businesses

• the advantages and disadvantages of alternative sources of finance.

Sources of finance

In theory there are several possible sources of funding available to an entrepreneur including funds from family, loans from a bank, or finance from outside investors. Each of these has advantages and disadvantages so there are various factors to consider before choosing the right source.

In reality, however, there may be relatively few feasible options and raising finance to start a business can be a major challenge.

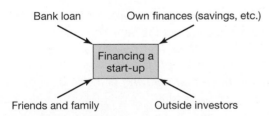

Figure 9.1 Sources of finance

Borrowing from family and friends

In many cases, people setting up in business have to borrow from family and friends. This has its advantages – they may be willing to wait for some time to be repaid because they like you and believe in you. If you have a difficult year, you may be able to convince them to wait a bit longer for their money.

On the other hand, you need to be careful of taking money from friends or family. You may feel worried about borrowing money from them in case you can't pay them back. You may also find that they

want to become more involved in the business than you would like. This can put a strain on your relationship and you may end up disagreeing and falling out.

Having said this, they may be willing to lend when others are not so eager. Some of the problems can be avoided if the terms and conditions are clearly set out, just as in a formal arrangement.

Banks

An alternative to asking friends and family is to borrow money from a bank. This has the advantage of being a formal arrangement, where everyone knows exactly where they stand. However, banks charge interest on money they lend. This means you have to pay them a fee in return for them lending you the money. Banks will usually leave you to run the business for yourself and make your own decisions, but they will insist on being paid, whereas you may be able to delay payment to friends. If you have a disappointing first few months or years, the bank may not be very understanding and you may even have to shut down and sell things off to pay off your debt. So be careful to discuss your requirements in full before borrowing from a bank, and to examine the worst-case scenario as well as the best.

There are two main options when borrowing from a bank:

• an overdraft. This is an arrangement that allows you to borrow money up to a certain limit if you need it. It is expensive and the bank can ask you to repay it at any time. You should never use an overdraft to invest in long-term projects because you would not be able to get the cash quickly if the bank asked for it back. However, if you end up needing only part of the overdraft then you only have to pay interest on the amount you borrow. An overdraft is useful for relatively small amounts, as a safety net, when you may or may not need to make use of the facility.

- a loan. This is an agreement to borrow a fixed sum of money over an agreed time. If you know how much you need and how long you need it for then a loan is better than an overdraft. It means you can plan your repayments and know exactly when it will be repaid.

Before borrowing from a bank you are advised to have a good business plan (see Chapter 4) explaining why you want the money, what you are going to use it for and how you will repay it. The bank may ask for some form of security in case there are problems.

This is known as collateral. For example, you may use your house as collateral: this acts as a guarantee and means that if you cannot repay the money you owe, the bank can take possession of your house.

Raising money from a bank may be particularly difficult for a new firm, especially if the person involved has little or no previous experience of running a business. Banks may be wary of lending to them because of the risk involved. Also, the business may only have a few assets to use as a guarantee for a loan. The interest charges on any loans may therefore be high because of the risks involved.

Web link

To find out more about what the banks offer in the form of overdrafts and loans and to compare their terms and conditions, visit their websites. For example: www.hsbc.co.uk

Business in Focus

Business in focus: UK Web Media

Jamie Harwood was still in his twenties when he set up his business, UK Web Media. Within five years the turnover of the business was around £10m.

Jamie's first idea for a website was www.marriagegiftlist.com. 'My uncle was getting married and the invitation listed three or four wedding gift lists,' he says. 'I thought it would be nice to have something online, consolidated in just one place.'

But starting an online business required money. When Harwood asked his family for financial backing, they refused, so he took out a £7,000 bank loan. His website, which still exists, flourished, although it didn't make him rich — but the experi-

ence led him to found UK Web Media in 2002. This business helps larger firms to advertise effectively on the internet.

Harwood says: 'The key is to have confidence in what you do and know what you do. My biggest tip is to find something you really, really enjoy. If you enjoy it, the fruits of the labour will follow.'

(Adapted from Fast Track)

Why do you think Jamie Harwood's family refused to lend him money, but the bank consented?

What do you think are the key factors that will determine the success of Jamie Harwood's businesses?

Do you think that enjoying being in business is enough to be successful?

Borrowing method	Advantages	Disadvantages
Overdraft	A flexible way of funding day-to-day financial requirements.	Have higher interest rates than loans.
	Interest is only payable on the amount you are overdrawn.	The bank can ask for repayment at any time.
Loan	You can match the term of a loan to your requirements.	No flexibility – you could be paying interest on funds you are not using.
	It is easier to budget for repayments.	You may have to offer some form of security (collateral).

Table 9.1 Overdrafts vs loans

Government assistance

The government is eager to help people to start up in business because it creates jobs and provides more choice for customers. To encourage entrepreneurs it offers advice – this can be found at local Business Link offices. Various financial incentives are also available. For example, the Small Firms Loan Guarantee scheme provides a form of insurance for banks to help small firms get loans. If you qualify for this, the government will guarantee the loan, so it is much more likely to be given.

Government grants are also available. A grant is a sum of money given to an individual or groups of individuals for a specific purpose. This will usually only cover a proportion of the total costs but as long as you fulfil the necessary conditions you will not have to repay anything. There are various grants available to start-ups from the European Union, Regional Development Agencies, Business Link, local authorities as well as private charitable organisations. However, there is a great deal of competition for such grants and you must meet each scheme's criteria (e.g. in terms of your location or size or how you intend to use the money). Also, a grant will only cover some of the costs – you need to meet the rest yourself.

Investors

Another way of raising finance is to bring in outside investors. In return for putting money into the business, they gain some control over it. You may not want to raise money this way if you want to remain totally in charge.

If the business has company status (see Chapter 8) it can sell ordinary shares. The buyer of an ordinary share:

- is an owner of the company
- has one vote per share. This means that the more shares an investor has the greater the control he or she has over the business.
- is entitled to receive dividends if they are paid out

For more information on shareholders, see Chapter 8.

By selling shares to raise money, the entrepreneur is involving other people in the decision-making, and will have to share the rewards. However, there will

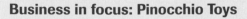

Business in Focus

Business in focus: Pinocchio Toys

Michael Sekulla's traditional toyshop, Pinocchio Toys, had been trading in Dunster, Somerset for less than a year when he began looking for ways to reach more customers. A website was the obvious route, but with no computer and limited funds the path seemed blocked. With help from his local Business Link, Michael successfully applied for a government grant to help buy the hardware he needed. The company now runs a thriving website, www.pinocchio-toys.co.uk, alongside the original shop.

According to Michael: 'We'd always planned to sell online, but we couldn't afford to invest a lot in computer equipment during the early months. Around that time, we had a visit from our local Business Link adviser who got us thinking about grants. We had to fill in a form setting out what we wanted and why. We also wrote our own plan outlining the business benefits we expected to gain from a grant. Putting our objectives on paper focused our thoughts and helped with filling in applications later on. We were very specific about our requirements. Knowing exactly what you want makes it easier to narrow down the grant options available. We looked at local authority websites, approached rural development agencies and, most helpful of all, used Business Link's Grants and Support Directory. We were prepared to put in what money we could afford, which was important because we found that few grants cover the full cost of a project.

Once we'd narrowed down the possibilities, we went through each grant's eligibility criteria in detail. Grant bodies want to see that you're committed and that you've thought everything through from a business point of view. Getting the grant was a big boost. It enabled us to start on the website six to nine months earlier than we'd planned and meant we had e-commerce capabilities in time for the key Christmas selling period.'

(Source: www.businesslink.gov.uk)

Question:

Why do you think the government provides grants for entrepreneurs and small businesses?

not be fixed annual interest repayments (unlike loans) and in a disappointing trading year the shareholders are likely to vote to reduce the dividends paid out (whereas banks would insist on the interest payments being met). If the business does struggle, all that can happen is that the investors lose the money they have invested, whereas with a loan the founders may become bankrupt trying to meet the interest payments. Another benefit that outside investors may bring with them is valuable experience that can help your business be more sucessful. They could even be suppliers or distributors, so having them invest could help develop a greater sense of partnership.

Key term
Bankruptcy occurs when an individual becomes insolvent (i.e. they cannot pay what they owe). You are declared bankrupt and then the court takes control of your earnings and allows you to repay the money over a given number of years.

Business in Focus

Business in focus: Body Shop
When Dame Anita Roddick needed money to open her second Body Shop, the bank refused to give her a loan. So she borrowed £4,000 from a friend, Ian McGlinn, in exchange for a half-share of the company. If Roddick had been able to get a bank loan for that £4,000 she would have been able to repay it over time. Instead, when she sold the Body Shop business in 2006 for £652m, McGlinn, who still held 22.4 per cent of the business, received £146m.

(Source: Adapted from *The Sunday Times*, June 17, 2007)

When selling shares in a new business, you may not feel like you are giving away anything valuable – and (unlike with a bank loan or other borrowing) if the business fails you don't have to pay back your investor. But as the Body Shop example shows, selling shares can prove to be expensive in the long run!

You may end up feeling annoyed that you are working 100 hours a week and taking a small salary, and you are sharing the money with people who have done nothing but put in some money!

With reference to the story above, do you think that selling shares is a bad way of raising finance?

Venture capital
Venture capital is a type of investment, typically provided by professional, outside investors to new, fast-growing businesses. It is generally in the form of cash, in return for shares in the business as well as interest payments. It is called venture capital because the investment is usually quite high risk. Most venture capital comes from investment banks or other financial institutions that look for what they hope will be successful businesses that they want to be involved with.

The downside for entrepreneurs of this form of finance is that venture capitalists usually get a say in company decisions. The television programme *Dragons' Den* highlighted the role of venture capitalists.

Business in Focus

Reggae Reggae sauce
Levi Roots, who was nominated for the best reggae singer award at the 1998 MOBO awards, persuaded TV investors on *Dragons' Den* to invest £50,000 in his sauce-making business. His Reggae Reggae sauce is now on sale in 600 Sainsbury's stores.

Dragons' Den judges Peter Jones and Richard Farleigh each paid Brixton-based Mr Roots £25,000 in return for a 20 per cent stake in his company.

The sauce was based on an old family recipe: it went on sale along with Mr Roots' record 'Proper Tings' (the Reggae Reggae Sauce song). The sauce was previously only available on Mr Roots' website or at the annual Notting Hill Carnival.

Sainsbury's buyer said the firm had been hugely impressed with the product. 'It fits perfectly with our ethos to encourage customers to try something new and our desire to help nurture smaller, niche suppliers, so we have pulled out all the stops to make it available in stores as quickly as possible,' he said.

(*Source*: Adapted from BBC News, http://news.bbc.co.uk/go/pr/fr/-/1/hi/uk/6424021.stm. Pub: 03/07/2007)

Questions:
Do you think £25,000 is a fair price for 20 per cent of the business?

What do you think are the advantages and disadvantages to Levi Roots of raising money from venture capitalists?

Business angels

'Business angels' are similar to venture capitalists. They are wealthy individuals who typically invest £10,000 upwards in new businesses. They are usually experienced business people and are able to offer advice to the entrepreneur.

Which source of start-up finance is the best?

The decision on how to raise business finance will depend on a combination of factors:

- Where can you get money from? If you already have a high level of loans you may find it difficult to get more. Do you have friends and family who will lend you money?
- What will it cost? What is the interest rate if you borrow money from a bank? Can you repay the money? Could you sell shares?
- When and how will you have to repay?
- Do you mind not having complete control of your business? If you do, then it may be better to borrow from a bank because although this involves paying interest the bank does not have a vote when it comes to decision-making.

In reality, the choices open to entrepreneurs may be quite limited. Also, it is likely that they will have to use a combination of sources to get their business up and running.

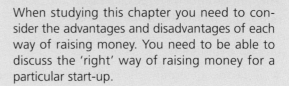

What do you think?

You have a great idea for a product that you think will make your fortune. However you need £50,000 to start up. A venture capitalist offers you the money in return for repayments of £5,000 a year for 15 years and 51 per cent of the business. Do you agree?

Examiner's advice

When studying this chapter you need to consider the advantages and disadvantages of each way of raising money. You need to be able to discuss the 'right' way of raising money for a particular start-up.

Summary

When you are starting up your business you will need money. This chapter has looked at the various sources of finance that might be open to a business such as friends and family, overdrafts, loans and shares. When choosing the right source of finance, entrepreneurs must consider a range of factors such as the cost, the availability and the impact on the control of the business.

Quick questions

1. What is meant by venture capital?
2. What is the difference between an overdraft and a loan?
3. What is a grant?
4. Outline one disadvantage of borrowing money from friends to finance your business.
5. Outline one disadvantage of taking out a loan to finance a business.
6. State one advantage and one disadvantage of using venture capital as a way of financing your business.
7. State one advantage and one disadvantage of selling shares as a way of financing your business.
8. State one reason why business start-ups sometimes have problems raising finance for their ideas.

Issues for analysis

- The differences between different sources of finance.
- The importance of costs, control and the time period for which the money is needed.

Issues for evaluation

- What factors determine the right source of finance for a start-up business?
- Is a loan the best way to finance a new business?

Analysis and evaluation questions

1 'My family could just about lend me the money' says Kylie Whinney, who wants to set up her own stables, 'but I don't really want to ask them. My market research shows the idea is a good one, I just need to raise the money to get it started.'

a Analyse the possible sources of finance Kylie might use to start her business, apart from her family.

b Discuss the advantages and disadvantages to Kylie of borrowing from friends and family.

2 According to Mandie Sufus, 'We have reached the point where we have borrowed what we can and I am worried about borrowing more. The question now is whether we want to raise more money in some other way or stay the size we are.' Mandie has grown her business Sporticus Ltd since she set it up five years ago and now owns five fitness clubs and health centres. She feels she could grow the business more, but is not sure how to finance such growth.

a Analyse the problems that higher levels of borrowing might cause Sporticus Ltd.

b Discuss the ways that Sporticus Ltd might raise finance, apart from borrowing more.

Assessment

Case study

When fashion journalist Natalie Massenet found she could not buy the latest designer fashions on the internet, she set up Net-a-porter.com. – an online luxury fashion boutique. Founded in London in 2000, the company raised finance from friends and private investors, and has convinced the world's most desirable fashion brands – including Fendi, Miu Miu and Jimmy Choo – to work with its website. Net-a-porter claims that customers spend an average of £475 per order, with 3,000 new customers buying from the website every month.

Questions

(30 marks, 40 minutes)
1 What is the company's average income per month from new customers? (3 marks)
2 Explain one advantage of selling via the internet rather than through physical stores. (3 marks)
3 Analyse the factors that might determine the future success of Net-a-porter.com. (9 marks)
4 Discuss the possible reasons why Natalie raised finance from friends and investors, rather than from loans. (15 marks)

10 Locating the business

When starting up and indeed when growing a business its location can be an important factor. It may affect many aspects of the business, such as costs and ease of access to resources. In this chapter, we consider the issues involved in choosing a particular location.

What you need to know by the end of this chapter:
• factors influencing start-up location decisions
• the impact of location on business success.

Choosing a location

The location of a business can have a significant impact on its success. It can affect demand: for example, setting up a tourist guide business is more likely to work in a city that attracts lots of visitors than in one that tourists tend to avoid. Location can also affect costs. Rental rates in a city centre are higher than for sites that are a long way out. Location can also affect your own enjoyment of being in business. For example, long commuting times can be tiring. Choosing the right location is therefore an important decision for an entrepreneur.

In some cases, there may be factors that have a major influence on where you need to be. For exam-ple, if you want to set up a shoe-repair business you probably want to be somewhere where there are lots of passers-by, such as in the city centre. Realistically, you cannot visit peoples' homes because the fee involved is low; equally, customers are unlikely to travel far to come and find you. Shoe-repair firms are therefore often located in small shops on main streets. The need to be close to demand drives the location decision in this case. However, many of the famous entrepreneurs who have made their fortune from computing (either websites or software) started out in their bedrooms. As they could do everything online, the physical location did not matter much. The type of business is therefore a key factor deter-mining the right location.

Real-life Business

Hewlett Packard

Bill Hewlett and Dave Packard were classmates at Stanford University in America. They founded HP in 1939 and built the company's first product in a garage. This was an audio oscillator – an electronic test instrument used by sound engineers. One of HP's first customers was Walt Disney Studios, which pur-chased eight oscillators to develop and test an innovative sound system for the movie 'Fantasia'. When Dave and Bill first set up they supposedly tossed a coin to see whether the business would be called Hewlett Packard or Packard Hewlett. Hewlett Packard grew to become a huge multi-billion dollar business. In 2004 the company bought back Bill and Dave's garage and restored it to the condition it was in 1939. You can see a video about the garage on the HP website.

Bill and Dave developed a highly successful and admired management approach known as 'The HP Way'. This included '...one of the first all-company profit-sharing plans—they gave shares to all employees. They were among the first to offer tuition assistance, flexi time, and job sharing... Today, the behaviour of the two founders remains a benchmark for business...'

According to Bill, the HP Way is 'a core ideology . . . [that] includes a deep respect for the individual, a dedication to affordable quality and reliability, a commitment to community responsibility, and a view that the company exists to make technical contribu-tions for the advancement and welfare of humanity.'

(Source: *Business Week*)

Figure 10.1 The original garage where Hewlett Packard started

Web link

If you want to know more, visit the Hewlett Packard website at www.hp.com

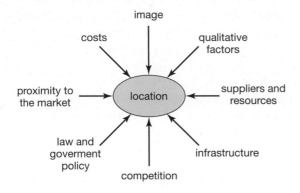

Figure 10.2 Factors affecting location

Other factors that need to be considered include:

- the costs of a given location. Basing a store in a busy shopping centre is expensive so you have to be sure that you can recover the costs through your sales. Do you need a shop at all, or can you simply sell online?
- the competition. In some industries it is felt to be desirable to be close to the competition. You may contribute to an area that becomes well known for its Chinese shops, art shops or jewellery shops, for example. On the other hand, you may feel there is an advantage in being the only accountant, DIY store, newsagent or café in your area.
- the law. There may be regulations on where you put your business, or planning permission (which

is needed from the local council) may restrict what you can to do to alter premises, forcing you to locate in one area rather than another to get the type of premises you want.

- the market – where are the customers and how far are they willing to travel? If you sell specialist goods such as sports cars, customers may be willing to travel to get to your showroom. If you sell what are called convenience goods such as milk and newspapers, customers will not be prepared to travel very far and so you need to be close to a suitable catchment area. However, if you send your products to your customers (e.g. if you are a mail-order business) or take your service to them (e.g. if you are a window cleaner or plumber) the need for your offices to be close to customers may not be so significant.
- suppliers and resources. If you need to be near a particular supplier or resource then this will obviously affect where you site your business. A sailing school, for example, needs to be near water!
- the infrastructure. This refers to the service and facilities that support business, such as roads, electricity, telephone services, and public transport. If your business involves the delivery of supplies or the finished product, if you want easy access to motorways or airports to speed up getting to see clients then the infrastructure will be an important consideration in location.
- qualitative factors. Sometimes the location decision will be made after careful financial calculations. However, the decision will also be affected by non-financial factors, such as the impact on your quality of life or the impact on a firm's image. For example, you might want to live and work in a particular area, or you might choose an area just because you know it well or you like the weather. These are known as qualitative factors.

Key terms
Infrastructure refers to the services and facilities that support day-to-day business activity.
Qualitative factors affecting location are factors that are not easily measurable, such as the quality of life.

Ben and Jerry

Back in 1966, in a school PE class, Ben Cohen and Jerry Greenfield found they hated running but loved food. Years later in 1978, Ben had been fired from a series of jobs while Jerry had failed for the second time to get into medical school. So, given that eating was their great passion and having completed a $5 correspondence course in ice-cream making, they opened an ice cream store in a renovated petrol station in Burlington, Vermont. The shop quickly became popular in the local community because of their innovative flavours, made from fresh Vermont milk and cream and 'large portions of whatever ingredients they felt tasted good on the day of making!' The inclusion of big chunks of chocolate, fruit and nuts distinguished them from any competitors.

In the early days Ben and Jerry were very bad at accounting. After two months they closed the store and put up a sign that said, 'We're closed to figure out whether we're making any money'. It turns out they weren't, but luckily they soon learnt how to do much better and went on to create a business that was eventually sold to Unilever for $326 million in 2000.

Ben and Jerry's has been very distinctive for its unusual flavours but also for its support of minority and disadvantaged groups and its political and environmental causes are promoted clearly on its ice cream tubs

Figure 10.3 Ben and Jerry's first shop

Business survival and location

The location of a business can be crucial to its survival. The location of a hotel, a restaurant or a new shop or factory can make all the difference between success and failure. In these cases, the location is important because:

- it can affect the costs of production. The rent of a site is a fixed cost. The higher the fixed costs, the higher the level of output needed to break even (see Chapter 13). The location can also affect the cost of labour (wages are typically much higher in some areas than others) and the cost of supplies (because it may cost more to transport materials to some areas than others).
- sales. If a store is in a good busy location this can boost sales and therefore increase profits
- image. The quality of some products is associated with particular regions (e.g. Scottish whisky, German beer, French wine): being based in these regions adds to the image of the product.
- the ease of getting the product to the market: the transport system and the location relative to the market can affect the speed of delivery which can help sales.

Key term
Fixed costs are costs that do not change with output.

What do you think?
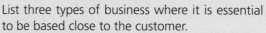

List three types of business where it is essential to be based close to the customer.
List three types of business where being near resources is more important.
Can you think of any businesses where the location is not an important consideration?

One of the problems facing businesses that are starting up is that they often lack the money to afford the best location. For example, someone setting up a new cafe may not be able to pay high-street rents and so may end up in a side street, away from most of the customers. Also, the best locations may already have been taken, meaning that the new business is immediately at a disadvantage compared with existing firms.

Examiner's advice

When studying this chapter you should examine the various factors that determine a firm's location. Think particularly about the factors that are relevant to start-up firms. You should be able to discuss the key factors that influence the location of a particular start-up.

Summary

The location of a business can have a significant impact on its performance. It can affect the costs, the accessibility to customers and the image of the business. Unfortunately, a start-up business may not be able to choose the location it would prefer because of issues such as a lack of finance.

Quick questions

1 State one way in which the location of a business might affect its costs.
2 State one way in which the location of a business might affect its demand.
3 Why might a business want to locate near its competitors?
4 Identify one qualitative factor that might affect a firm's location.
5 If a firm chooses a high-cost location, the output needed to break even will be higher. True or false?
6 State one particular problem that might face a start-up business when choosing a location.
7 State one type of business that would need to be located near specific resources.
8 State one type of business that would need to locate close to its customers.

Issues for analysis

- The impact of location on demand.
- The impact of location on costs.
- The impact of location on competitiveness.

Issues for evaluation

- Why is business location an important factor in determining a firm's success?
- What are the problems associated with start-up location decisions?

Analysis and evaluation questions

1 'Tea for Two' was Gemima's idea for a new business. Having seen the success of coffee shops, she felt sure that was a gap in the market for a chain of tea shops.

a Analyse the factors that might influence the location of a 'Tea for Two' tea shop.
b To what extent is the location of a 'Tea for Two' tea shop likely to determine the success of the business?

2 For several years Dave Wright had had a part-time job in a sandwich shop. At 18 he left school and set up his own sandwich shop.

a Analyse the possible consequences to Dave of choosing the wrong location.
b Discuss the way in which Dave might choose a location for his business.

Assessment

The home is the most popular location for a start-up. But what do you do when you want to expand – should you move or stay put? Many entrepreneurs are reluctant to move into an office and lose the benefits of working from home. However, staying at home may restrict their growth opportunities. One solution may be to outsource as much as you can (i.e. get others to do it for you).

Case study

Louise Leadbetter runs Honey PR, a national public relations business from her home in Shropshire. She uses a network of self-employed PR consultants who work from their own homes, rather than in an office provided by Louise. When she also became involved in importing scooters from America, Louise overcame the space problem by renting an unused cowshed from a local farmer at a low rent.

Caroline Putus runs Enjoy Riding, a horse riding school, from her home in Ipswich. She brought in specialist help from outside to fill her skills gap. She makes use of specialists to deal with the accounts and general administration. Caroline has focused on her core expertise of encouraging people to enjoy riding and has given the other elements of the business to others to do in their own offices.

(Source: Adapted from *The Sunday Times*)

Questions

(30 marks, 40 minutes)

1 Explain why many entrepreneurs start their businesses at home. (6 marks)
2 Analyse the possible problems of operating a business from home. (9 marks)
3 Discuss the key factors that might determine the best location for a horse-riding school. (15 marks)

Employing people

When you first set up your business, or as it grows, you are likely to need to employ other people. This brings with it advantages and disadvantages, which we examine in this chapter.

What you need to know by the end of this chapter:
- the types of employees used in small businesses
- the reasons, problems and difficulties of employing people
- the benefits and problems of using consultants and advisers.

Deciding to employ people

When you first set up in business you may well be operating on your own. Working on your own has advantages: you make decisions for yourself, do not have to consult others and can decide things quickly. However, there may come a point when you need others to help you out.

This may be because:

- you need a rest! Working on your own can be tiring and stressful. You may need help to make sure that your shop can be open every day, or that the phone is answered promptly. You may need cover for when you are on holiday, or time to focus on the administration of the business.
- you want to benefit from the expertise of others. You may be good at the fundamental service you provide (such as website design) but need help in other areas (such as accounting).
- you may need extra staff to meet the demand. With a growing number of customers you are likely to need more employees to serve them.

This means you need to employ other people.

The decision to employ other people is an investment decision and as such has an opportunity cost. Money invested into recruitment, training and salaries is not being used elsewhere in the business (e.g. in marketing). You have to be sure this investment is worthwhile and that the money is being spent wisely.

Legal issues

When deciding to employ people you must be aware of the numerous laws that relate to the employment and payment of staff (such as the minimum wage, which sets a limit to the lowest wage within the UK). These laws affect:

- the hiring process. You cannot discriminate against people because of their age, race, gender or sexual orientation. Employers must give employees a written contract of employment which sets out the terms and conditions of their employment.
- the payment system. Again, you cannot discriminate here (e.g. you cannot pay a woman less than you pay a man for the same job).
- redundancies and dismissals. For example, you may have to pay employees redundancy pay if their jobs no longer exist and you ask them to leave. If someone is not performing well, you should make sure that you warn them and give them the opportunity to improve before asking them to leave.
- health and safety. The workplace must be safe and employees must receive training in health and safety procedures.
- employee rights. For example, you must make sure you have appropriate insurance against injuries to employees. You must also be aware of employees' rights, such as the right to sick pay and maternity leave.

> **Key term**
> **Redundancies** occur when jobs no longer exist e.g. when a business has to close an outlet.

Forms of employment

One option entrepreneurs have if they need help with their businesses is to employ people full time. This may increase the resources of the business considerably but also increases fixed costs.

Other forms of employment include:

- part-time. Part-time employees might work mornings only or a couple of days a week. For example, as a new business, you might employ someone just for a few hours a week to help with the accounts or marketing or to do the cleaning. Clearly, this option is cheaper than employing someone full time. From the employee's perspective, part-time work can allow them to combine work with other aspects of their life, such as looking after their children.
- temporary. Temporary staff can be useful to help out when there is a rush in orders. Imagine you run a fireworks business – you are likely to be busy around October and early November leading up to Bonfire Night. Similarly, strawberry farms are busy in the summer and gyms are busier after New Year. During these periods it may make sense to employ extra staff. You would not want to hire people all year around because this would increase your costs during times when they are not needed.

The use of part-time and temporary employees can provide the business with an important degree of flexibility. It allows the business to respond to changes in demand and match supply to customer requirements. For example, part-timers can be used in shops to cover busy Saturdays: temporary staff can be used to cover the Christmas rush.

Business may also make use of consultants or advisers. This is because there may be times when you need specialist help. This may be on a one-off basis or for a particular project. Essentially, you are buying in their expertise. For example, you may want to employ a website designer or marketing adviser. Consultants and advisers have specialist skills and may only be used rarely, if at all. They have the advantage of seeing your business from the outside – they can take a dispassionate look at it and provide objective advice. They will have experience from other businesses they have worked with. On the other hand, they do not know your business as well as you do, so their advice may not always be entirely appropriate and, of course, their services may be expensive.

Business in Focus

Systems Associates

System Associates is an internet technologies company delivering software services to public and private sector clients. It is based in Maidenhead, has 25 employees and regularly uses skilled employees on short-term contracts.

Its managing director says: 'Short-term contractors give us both labour flexibility and the ability to bring in specialist skills as we need them.

For example, we recently won a major contract to build a portal for the new London-wide e-government agency, London Connects. Part of the project was to categorise and set up large chunks of online content. The skills required were highly specialised and our team was already at capacity, so we decided to employ a team of content editors on short-term contracts.

We sourced a selection of candidates using internet recruitment services that specialise in our sector. Interviews and reference checking were essential to make sure the employees' skills and experience matched their CVs. We also wanted to ensure a good fit with our existing project team.

We selected four employees who signed contracts with us before starting work. As with all our written agreements, they covered legal issues like terms and conditions but also included project schedules, deadlines and deliverables, fees payable and so on. We couldn't afford to keep on an employee who didn't meet expectations. We therefore specified a one-day notice period for the first four weeks, a safeguard that we often use in short-term contracts.'

(Source : www.businesslink.gov.uk)

Questions:

What problems might occur when using employees on short term contracts?
Why do you think System Associates doesn't simply hire more full-time staff?

Difficulties when working with others

Employing people also brings with it new challenges, such as working effectively with others and learning how to manage people. Managing people involves making sure they know what to do, motivating them to do the job properly and keeping control over the quality of their work and the deadlines for completion.

When you give someone else a task to do, this is known as delegation. Effective delegation is important if you employ others: there is no point hiring someone and then still doing all the work yourself. However, delegating is not always easy to do. Some people like to control things themselves and are not good at handing over tasks to others. Some people are not good at explaining what they want or at making sure the other person has the right resources and skills to do the job properly.

What do you think?

Would you be good at managing other people?

Key term
Delegation occurs when a superior entrusts a task to a subordinate.

Also, some people prefer working on their own without having to consult or inform anyone else about what they are doing. This type of person can find it difficult to make full use of their employees' talents.

Examiner's advice

When studying this chapter you need to be aware of the different ways of employing people and the advantages and disadvantages of each form of employment. You should be able to discuss whether a business should employ more people and what is the right method of doing so.

Summary

Although some businesses do operate with just one person, most entrepreneurs employ others to help them. This decision brings with it various challenges, including managing others, maintaining quality and making sure you are aware of the legal issues involved in hiring staff. However, the benefits include having more help to complete tasks, as well as gaining from the expertise and advice of others.

Quick questions

1. Why might a business employ part-time employees?
2. Why might a business employ temporary employees?
3. Why might a business employ a consultant?
4. State one problem of employing a consultant.
5. State one legal issue that a business must consider when employing staff.
6. State one problem you may have when managing someone else.
7. What is meant by delegation?
8. Is it better to hire a full-timer or a part-timer?

Issues for analysis

- Employing others and the impact on costs and the quality of service.

Issues for evaluation

- Should you run your business alone or employ others?
- Is using part time and temporary staff better than employing people full time?

Analysis and evaluation questions

1. Hannah had always worked on her own at the beauty salon but demand was becoming so high that she knew she needed extra help.
   a. Analyse the factors that might determine who Hannah hires.
   b. Discuss the advantages and disadvantages to Hannah of employing someone else.

2 Rory Beefheart has built up his antiques business on his own for the last five years. He has recently hired an employee to delegate much of the administration work to so that he can focus on dealing with customers, which he enjoys.

a Analyse the benefits to Rory of delegating work to his new employee.
b Discuss the possible problems of delegating work to his new employee.

Assessment

Case study

Norton Priory Museum and Gardens is an award-winning visitor attraction in Runcorn, Cheshire. It is one of the largest excavated monastic sites in Europe.

Its Managing Director says, 'Our business is open 362 days a year and demand fluctuates between seasons, so efficient staffing policies are essential. We're also a popular location for film and TV crews, plus we run frequent evening events, all of which require flexibility in working hours.

We make staff aware from the start that unusual working hours will be part of the job. However, we also make it clear that we're prepared to give as well as take. We offer a good working environment and excellent training opportunities. We've found people are willing to trade unusual or unsociable hours for the benefits we provide in other areas.'

Our financial structure as a charitable trust means we work to strict budgets, so traditional overtime doesn't always fit the bill. Overtime can be expensive, especially for the number of weekends and Bank Holidays that we need our employees to work. It's also part of our company culture to encourage a healthy work-life balance and paid overtime could undermine that.

We researched alternatives and now we use a combination of part-time employees and time off in lieu (TOIL) to meet variable demands on working hours. We also take on a number of graduate work placements and volunteers during our busiest season to take the pressure off regular staff.

We keep detailed records of hours worked, including weekly time sheets, and we review them regularly so that we can spot potential problems before the business or the individual suffers.'

(*Source*: www.businesslink.gov.uk)

Questions

(30 marks, 40 minutes)

1 Explain two factors that are likely to affect the number of visitors to Norton Priory Museum. (6 marks)

2 Analyse the possible reasons why Norton Priory Museum keeps a detailed record of hours worked. (9 marks)

3 Discuss the benefits to Norton Priory of using part-time and temporary employees. (15 marks)

Assessment of Section 1: Starting a business

Case study

Nick Wheeler's first venture in retail was little short of disastrous. 'I started selling hand-made shoes in the 1980s,' he says. 'I'd draw around people's feet and fax the drawings to a workshop in India. They'd make the shoes for £10 and I'd sell them for £50, which is very good value for shoes that are made to order.

'Unfortunately, because of the dodgy phone lines and early fax machines, the image got horribly distorted and the shoes that came back would fit only a pixie or a clown.'

After a short stint at management consultants Bain & Co, which confirmed his suspicion that he couldn't stand having a boss, Wheeler's second attempt at retail was launched in 1986. It proved to be much more successful, and today his shirt company, Charles Tyrwhitt, turns over £50 million a year. 'The difference was that I really understood the product and I had much better control of the production,' says Wheeler, 'If you want to succeed in retail, you need to have a real passion for whatever you're selling.'

His funding was unorthodox – an £8,000 legacy from a great-aunt and a remarkably successful investment in the form of a vintage sports car, which he bought for £17,000 and sold a year later for £100,000.

Wheeler also saw the potential of the internet very early as a way of developing his business. Online retailing has seen huge numbers of entrepreneurs enter the market over the past few years.

'It's very rare that you find somebody starting from nothing in conventional retail these days because the high price of high-street property means that they need huge capital investment,' says a retail analyst. 'In an increasingly competitive market, successful retailers are those who differentiate themselves.'

(Source: *The Sunday Times* May 13, 2007)

Questions

(30 marks, 40 minutes)

1   Nick Wheeler financed his business with his own money. Explain the advantages of funding a start-up in this way, as opposed to other sources of finance. (6 marks)

2   According to the article, the successful retailers are those who can successfully differentiate themselves. Analyse the ways in which a shirt retailer such as Charles Tyrwhitt might differentiate itself from competitors. (9 marks)

3   To what extent do you think the success of Nick Wheeler has been due to luck? (15 marks)

12 Calculating costs, revenues and profits

If you put yourself into the position of an entrepreneur planning a business, one of the first things that will come to mind is: 'Will my business make a profit? This is a sensible question for an entrepreneur to ask. To work out a business's profit (or loss) an entrepreneur will need to make estimates of the money that the business will earn and also its expected costs. If you were an entrepreneur you would need to think about what price to charge and also, quite possibly, about how you would keep your future business's costs as low as possible.

What you need to know by the end of this chapter:

- the distinction between total, fixed and variable costs
- why costs are important to a business
- how a business calculates its revenue
- how profit is calculated and its importance to a business
- the relationships between cost, price, revenue and profits.

The relationship between profit, cost and revenue

One of the most important relationships for a business is:

profit = total revenue − total costs

Profit is a very important objective for many businesses. This formula allows businesses to calculate whether they might make a profit and, if so, how much it might be.

Key term

Revenues are the earnings or income generated by a firm as a result of its trading activities.

Business costs

What is a cost? It is simply the expenditure a firm makes as part of its trading. Some of the expenses or costs firms face include payments for raw materials, fuel and components, as well as for labour (in the form of wages and salaries).

Firms face many costs or expenses. Some occur before the business starts trading (for example, the legal costs of setting up a business) while others have to be paid throughout the life of a business (wages and rent fall into this category). The costs faced by a business can be classified in a number of ways, though the most common is to divide them into fixed and variable costs.

Fixed costs

Fixed costs do not change when a business alters its level of output. As an example, a business's rent will not vary if there is an increase or decrease in the level of production. Other examples of fixed costs include management salaries and interest payments made by the business.

The graph below relates to XYZ Computers plc – a manufacturer of computers. You can see that whether the factory produces 10,000 or 70,000 computers each year, the fixed costs faced by the business will remain the same – £5m.

The reason that fixed costs do not alter is that XYZ Computers simply uses its existing facilities fully at times when it is receiving more orders. As a further example, in the run-up to Christmas a chocolate manufacturer might increase its output, thereby using its existing production facilities more fully. The firm's rent, rates and other fixed costs will be unchanged.

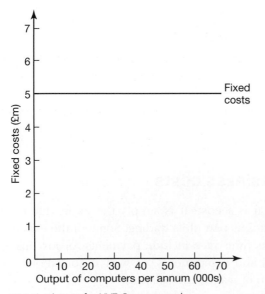

Figure 12.1 Fixed costs for XYZ Computers plc.

Looking at this graph, can you think of any benefits that XYZ Computers might gain from producing 60,000 computers rather than 30, 000 computers annually?

Variable costs

In contrast to fixed costs, variable costs alter directly with the level of a firm's output. This means that, a firm which is increasing its output is likely to have to pay higher variable costs, whereas a business reducing its output could expect variable costs to fall. Expenditure on fuel, raw materials and components are all examples of variable costs.

The XYZ Computer company faces variable costs of £500 for each computer it manufactures (see Figure 12.2); this is necessary to pay for the electronics, case and monitor. Thus, to produce 20,000 computers, the company faces variable costs of £10m (20,000 × £500); to manufacture 50,000 results in variable costs of £25m (50,000 × £500).

Variable costs are usually shown as a straight line.

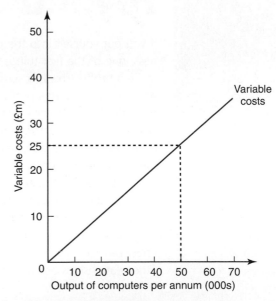

Figure 12.2 Variable costs for XYZ Computers plc

This suggests that expenditure on items such as fuel, labour, raw materials and components rises directly along with output. Variable costs are drawn this way for simplicity. In the real world, the line may gradually flatten out as businesses frequently negotiate lower prices when placing large orders. Thus, XYZ Computers may be able to purchase components more cheaply, so the variable costs associated with an output of 50,000 computers might, for example, be £22.5m. This means that the variable cost of one computer is actually £450, not £500.

Fixed costs and prices

As we have seen, the cost of making any product is made up of two parts:

- fixed costs
- variable costs.

A firm can help to keep costs of production for each individual unit to a minimum by producing on the largest possible scale. Consider the following two scenarios for the London Bicycle Company. This Company has fixed costs of £100,000 and each bicycle has variable costs of £50 for materials and labour.

Scenario A

The company produces 1000 bicycles during the year. Total production costs are £100,000 + (£50 × 1000) = £150,000

Average cost of producing one bicycle = £150

Scenario B

The company produces 5000 bicycles during the year. Total production costs are £100,000 + (£50 × 5000) = £350,000

Average cost of producing one bicycle = £70

Manufacturing in the circumstances of Scenario B would allow the company to set lower prices for its bicycles or to enjoy higher profits – or both.

Semi-variable costs

Some firms face costs which should be classified as semi-variable: they have fixed and variable elements.

Telephone costs are an example of a semi-variable cost. Most businesses pay a fixed, quarterly charge for line and equipment rental. In addition, they face charges for each call made. The line and equipment rentals are fixed as they do not change as the firm increases or lowers its production levels. However, call charges are variable – they are likely to increase along with output as more calls are made to suppliers and customers, for example. Thus, taken together these elements mean telephone charges are semi-variable.

Total costs

The calculation of total costs assumes that all the costs faced by a business are either fixed or variable. This means total costs can be calculated simply using the following formula:

total costs = fixed costs + variable costs

Total costs of production are an important piece of information for a business. Managers of a business can use this information when taking decisions on levels of output and prices to be charged. For example, firms that have very high levels of fixed costs, perhaps due to expensive equipment, will seek to produce large quantities of output. This reduces the effect of fixed costs on selling price by spreading them over a large quantity of sales.

Opportunity cost

In Section 1, we saw that there is another way of looking at costs, other than giving a monetary value

Level of production (thousand computers)	Fixed costs (£ million)	Variable costs (£ million)	Total costs (£ million)
0	5	0	5
10	5	05	10
20	5	10	15
30	5	15	20
40	5	20	25
50	5	25	30
60	5	30	35
70	5	35	40

Table 12.1 Cost information for XYZ Computers

to the resources used by a business. Economists use a concept called opportunity cost, which values a product in terms of what has been given up to obtain it. Thus, an accountant might value a factory extension at £250,000, based on the resources necessary to build it. An economist might say that the opportunity cost of the extension was a training programme for employees. This is because the management team of the business decided on an extension to the factory, rather than a training programme for employees.

Why do businesses calculate costs of production?

There are a number of reasons why it is important for a business to know the level of costs they are incurring as a result of their trading activities.

- Most businesses draw up financial forecasts or budgets which set out their production plans and the costs they expect to pay. It is an important part of management to ensure that costs are being kept within agreed limits.
- Businesses benefit from knowledge of their costs of production to allow them to set a price that ensures that they make a profit. This is known as 'cost-plus' pricing.
- Sometimes businesses are not able to control the price at which they sell their products – they might be a small firm in a very competitive market. In these circumstances it is important to know costs of production to decide whether it is possible to sell products at a profit. This will help the business's managers to make a dcision on whether to enter a market.

Business revenues

A business's revenue is its income or earnings over a period of time. You may also encounter the terms sales revenue or sales income, which have the same meaning. Businesses calculate the revenue from the sale of a single product as well as from their entire product range. In either case the calculation is the same:

revenue = quantity sold × average selling price

In most circumstances, a firm can exercise some control over the quantity it sells and hence over its revenue.

If a business reduces its selling price, it can normally expect to sell more. Whether this increases its revenue depends on the number of additional sales it makes as a result of reducing its price. If competitors also reduce their prices, then few extra sales will result and revenue will be reduced.

Similarly, a rise in price can be expected to reduce sales. The size of the fall in sales will depend on many factors, including the loyalty of customers and the quality of the products. The amount by which sales fall will determine whether the firm receives more or less revenue following its price rise. Some businesses sell products that are unique or regarded as highly desirable, perhaps because they are fashionable. Thus, some producers of fashion clothing, such as Gucci can charge high prices and still enjoy relatively high sales.

Web link

To find out more about Gucci (and its prices) visit www.gucci.com/uk/index2.html.

The relationship between price and sales revenue is explained by the concept of the price elasticity of demand (see Chapter 29).

What do you think?

If you were an entrepreneur planning a business, how might you estimate the costs of operating your business over the first year of trading? What people might you talk with? What other sources of information could you use?

Examiner's advice

Business studies is an integrated subject. It is important to explore the links that exist between the various modules of the subject when responding to questions. There are obvious links between the topic of business revenues and price elasticity of demand. It may be worth revising such linked topics together to allow you to explore the relationships in your examination.

Profits

A business makes a profit when, over a period of time, its revenue exceeds its total costs of production. The formula necessary to calculate profit is set out below.

profit = total revenue – total costs

A company's profits depend upon two main factors: profit margins and the quantity (or volume) of sales.

- A profit margin is the amount or percentage of the final selling price that is profit.
- The quantity a firm sells will also affect the amount of profits it earns. In general if a business sells a greater quantity of its products it will make more profit, so long as it does not have to reduce price to achieve higher sales.

How might a business use its profits?

One of the most important decisions taken by a business is how to use its profits – assuming that it makes any. The uses of profits can be divided into two categories:

- distributed profits – these profits are paid to the owners of the business, this will be in the form of dividends if the business is a company
- undistributed or retained profits – this portion of a business's profits are kept for investment in the business. Such profits may be used to purchase assets to help the business trade in the future. Examples include machinery, vehicles or properties.

The key issue in distributing profits is the balance between the short term and the long term. Distributing a high proportion of profits may keep the business's owners happy in the short term, but might not be in the interests of those wanting a long-term investment. Some owners want to see the company grow over a number of years and to benefit from owning a share of a more valuable business.

The importance of profit

For many businesses, profits are very important and are often used as a measure of success. Many people who invest in enterprises do so in the hope and expectation of making a handsome return on their money. For such investors it is not simply profits that are important, but rather the size of the profit. A larger profit means a greater return for the investor.

However, for many entrepreneurs profit is not the most vital factor. In the early stages of a business, survival may be the prime objective. Profits may become important later on – so long as the business survives. Even at a later stage in the life of a new business, the owners of the business may only aim to make a certain level of profit, this is termed 'satisficing'. Once the agreed level of profit has been achieved, the business's owners might pursue other goals such as leisure activities.

For some businesses, earning a profit may not be at all important. A number of businesses are not established with the aim of making profits. Charities, for example, do not seek to make profits. This type of business seeks to raise the maximum amount of income possible, or to provide a high-class product, while earning enough to cover costs. In 2007, Tenovus,

Business in Focus

Pieminister

Pieminister is a small business set up by Jon Simon and Tristan Hogg to produce a 'really good pie made from proper stuff'. The duo believed they had spotted a gap in the UK market in that they could not find suppliers of high quality pies. The business has acquired a reputation for producing high quality products and its sales have risen. The company's products are sold by some of the UK's finest shops and pubs and even the Queen has tasted Pieminister's products.

The business's pies are premium quality and offer the opportunity to sell at a high price and to enjoy a high profit margin. Its pies sell for between £2.50 and £2.95 each. However, by using the fresh, good quality ingredients, the business incurs significant variable costs in its manufacturing.

Web link

You can learn more about Pieminister at its website www.pieminister.co.uk.

What would be the effect on Pieminister's profits if the cost of ingredients for its pies increased significantly?

Should Pieminister try to increase its profits by reducing its prices?

one the UK's leading cancer charities, opened a innovative style of coffee house in Bristol. The aim of the coffee shop is primarily to raise awareness of issues relating to cancer and to encourage people to make donations directly to the charity. Obviously all the profits from 'Coffee Plus' will be used to finance research into cancer and care for cancer sufferers, but this is not the primary aim of the new business.

One step further: prices and profits

The relationship between prices and profits is complex and depends on a number of factors. A rise in price might be expected to increase a firm's revenues and, assuming costs only rise in proportion with sales, its profits. However, this assumes that most of the business's customers do not react to the price rise and continue to buy its products. It is realistic to assume that some sales will be lost following a price rise as customers switch to cheaper alternatives. However, it should increase the business's revenue, so long as consumers' purchasing decisions are not too sensitive to price changes. We consider the relationship between price changes and demand for products more fully on pages 214–217.

However, a price increase could be a response by a business to an increase in costs. In this case there may be little or no increase in the business's profits. The business may simply raise its prices to maintain its existing profit margin. A new, small business may be unable to increase its prices significantly in such circumstances for fear of setting its prices higher than competitors. This is likely to make it difficult for a new business to win customers.

So there are two key issues to consider when examining the relationship between prices and profits. First, does the price increase result in a higher profit margin for the business? Second, will the loss of sales resulting from the price increase more than offset the rise in price received from each sale?

Summary

Businesses face different types of costs – some increase along with the level of production while some do not. Costs are only one side of the coin – the other is revenue. An entrepreneur will deduct costs from revenue to arrive at a figure for profit. However, in the case of a start-up business it may be that the business may make a loss initially.

Quick questions

1 Complete the following formula: Profit = ? – total costs
2 Which one of the following is the best definition of variable costs:

a costs that do not change when output changes?
b costs that do change when revenue alters?
c costs that have no relationship with output?
d costs that change directly with output?

3 Is the following statement true or false? 'When drawn on a graph, variable costs always start at the origin (where the two axes intersect).'
4 Which two of the following would normally be considered to be fixed costs?

a fuel costs
b rent for an office
c raw material costs
d costs of insuring the business's premises.

5 State one reason why an entrepreneur might forecast costs for a start-up business.
6 Complete the following formula: Sales revenue = ... × average selling price.
7 Is the following statement true or false? 'An increase in variable costs will always lead to an increase in a business's prices.'
8 For which one of the following businesses is profit unlikely to be an important concept?

a Marks & Spencer
b Barclay's Bank
c Oxfam
d Norwich City Football Club.

9 Complete the following sentence: The profit margin is the ....
....
10 Why might an entrepreneur not be concerned about making profits in the first few months of trading?

Issues for analysis

- The relationship between a business's level of production and its total costs
- The importance for a business of calculating its costs before commencing trading.
- The relationship between selling price and a business's revenue.

Issues for evaluation

- Is profit the most important objective for a particular start up business?
- Will a business benefit from increasing its price?

Analysis and evaluation questions

1 Jo Dawson worked for many years in the City and, having recently retired, enjoys a generous pension. Being an active person she has recently opened a tanning shop in a rented high street property. Jo's major costs are the lease on the shop (£600 a month) and the rental payments for the tanning equipment. Business is steadily increasing after a slow start.

a Analyse why Jo's total costs might not increase proportionately with her sales. (8 marks)
b Discuss whether making a profit should be the most important objective for Jo in the management of her business. (15 marks)

2 Shaw Fu is a talented chef, but has no experience of running a business. He is in the final stage of planning his new restaurant. He intends to offer an authentic Chinese menu, based on the use of fresh, seasonal foods – it is important for him to have a selling point in what is a very competitive market. He knows these foods can vary in price and is concerned about what prices to charge for meals. However, he is confident that sales of beer, wine and spirits will generate large profit margins.

a Examine two reasons why it might be vital for Shaw to forecast his costs as part of his financial planning. (8 marks)
b To what extent might the prices Shaw charges for meals determine the future profitability of his restaurant? (15 marks)

Assessment

Case study

StarSparkles was established by Pauline Clifford in 2006. Her business idea was to decorate customers' shoes with individual designs in a range of colours, but all are sparkly as shown below.

Pauline offers a range of designs, including plac-

Figure 12.3 StarSparkle shoes

ing coloured sparkles on the toes or heels of shoes, or spelling out someone's name on the shoes. Her website (www.starsparkles.com) lists her prices for a range of customisations; for example, the price for colouring the toes of a pair of shoes with three or more colours is £40.

StarSparkles has relied heavily on publicity to promote its products and Pauline has been very successful in this aspect of managing her new business. Celebrity wearers of Pauline's customised shoes include Paris Hilton, Gwen Stefani and Britney Spears.

(Adapted from www.starsparkles.com)

Questions

(30 marks, 40 minutes)
1 Assume that Pauline raises the price for a 'three colour toe sparkle' to £50 per pair of shoes. As a result her sales fall from 200 pairs of shoes per month to 175. Calculate her old and new sales revenue per month for this service. (6 marks)
2 Analyse **two** possible factors that might influence whether or not Pauline would make a greater profit following the price increase outlined in Question 1. (9 marks)
3 Some people may argue that profits are the most important reason why Pauline established StarSparkles. To what extent do you agree with this view? (15 marks)

13 Using break-even analysis to make decisions

Before launching a new business, most entrepreneurs want to know how much of their good or service they will need to sell each week or month if they are to make a profit. This information can be an important part of decision-making for entrepreneurs. It can help them to answer questions such as 'Should I start this business?' or 'What might happen if my fixed or variable costs rise?'

What you need to know by the end of this chapter:
- the meaning of break-even and contribution
- how to calculate break-even output
- how to draw and complete break-even charts
- how to read a break-even chart and to illustrate profit or loss on them
- the impact of price and cost changes on break-even output and break-even charts
- the advantages and disadvantages of using break-even analysis.

What is break-even analysis and why is it used?

The break-even output is the level of output or production at which a business's sales generate just enough revenue to cover all its costs of production. At the break-even level of output, a business makes neither a loss nor a profit. Start-up businesses may use break-even analysis for a number of reasons:

- to help to decide whether the business idea will be profitable and whether it is viable.
- to help decide the level of output and sales necessary to generate a profit
- the results of break-even analysis can be used to support an application by a business for a loan from a bank or other financial institution
- to assess the impact of changes in the level of production on the profitability of the business
- to assess the effects of different prices and levels of costs on the potential profitability of the business.

Contribution

Contribution is an important part of break-even analysis. Contribution can be defined as the difference between sales revenue and variable costs of production. This is illustrated in Figure 13.1.

Contribution is calculated through the use of the following formula:

$$\text{contribution} = \text{revenue} - \text{variable costs}$$

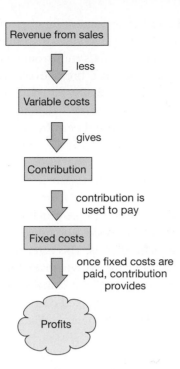

Figure 13.1

Contribution can be used to pay the fixed costs incurred by a firm. Once these have been met fully, contribution provides a business with its profits.

> **Key term**
> **Contribution** is the difference between sales revenue and variable costs; it is used to pay fixed costs and to provide profits.

Contribution can be calculated in two different ways:

1 If an entrepreneur decides to produce more than one product, he or she may calculate the contribution made by each product to paying fixed costs and providing profits. Using contribution avoids the need to divide up fixed costs between the firm's various products. This assists entrepreneurs in assessing the financial performance of each of their products.

2 Contribution can be calculated for the sale of a single product. This is known as contribution per unit. It is calculated by using the formula:

contribution per unit = selling price of one unit of output – variable cost of producing that unit

It is this second method of calculating contribution that is useful when calculating the break-even point.

Calculating the break-even point

An entrepreneur wishing to calculate break-even point will require the following information:

- the selling price of the product
- the variable cost of producing a single unit of the product
- the fixed costs associated with the product – remember, fixed costs do not change as the level of production alters.

This information is used within the formula set out below:

break-even output = fixed costs/selling price per unit – variable cost per unit

This formula can be rewritten, given that contribution is the result of taking away variable cost from the selling price of a product:

break-even output = fixed costs/contribution per unit

Using break-even: a case study

Sarah Patel is planning to open a new restaurant in Soho, West London. She has a lot of experience in the industry and plans to establish a restaurant with a reputation for serving high quality meals in a beautifully furnished building. Soho is a popular part of London and many people are looking to dine in the area. Sarah plans to call her restaurant 'The Holly'.

Sarah needs a loan to open The Holly. She has already looked at a building about a mile away which would seat up to 30 diners. She has produced the figures set out in Table 13.1.

Type of Cost or Revenue	Amount
Average selling price per meal at The Holly	£60
Variable costs per meal – ingredients, fuel, wages	£35
Monthly fixed costs of the new restaurant – lease for the property, rent & rates	£10,000

Table 13.1 **Sarah's analysis for The Holly**

Using this information, Sarah is able to calculate how many meals she would need to sell (or how many diners she has to attract) in her restaurant if the project is to break even.

break-even output = fixed costs/contribution per unit

Sarah knows her fixed costs will be £10,000 each month and this figure is entered into the top of the formula. To fill in the bottom, Sarah has to take away the variable cost of producing a meal from the price the customer pays for a meal. The contribution earned from each meal in Sarah's new restaurant is £25 (£60 – £35), so the calculation looks like this:

Monthly break-even output = £10,000/£35 = 400 diners

So, Sarah knows that, if her plan for The Holly is to break even, she will need to attract at least 400 customers each month. If she attracts more than 400 customers, the project will make a profit. Sarah plans to open The Holly on 25 evenings each month and would, therefore, break even if she had an average of 16 customers each night in the new restaurant.

While this calculation gives Sarah a quick guide to the number of customers her restaurant will need to break even, it tells her little more about the level of profit or loss The Holly might make. A break-even chart is one way to work out the level of profits the business will generate if her forcast is proved to be correct.

We can use a break-even chart to illustrate Sarah's plans to open The Holly.

Drawing a break-even chart

The first stage in constructing a break-even chart is to mark scales on the two axes. Sarah knows that The Holly can seat a maximum of 30 customers per night and that she normally opens for 25 evenings

each month. So her maximum number of customers each month is 750 (30 customers × 25 nights). So her scale on the horizontal axis runs from zero to 750.

The vertical scale on a break-even chart records costs and revenues. Normally, revenues are the highest figure. So Sarah has to calculate the highest possible revenue she could earn from her restaurant. At most she could attract 750 customers paying an average of £60 each. So the highest revenue she could possibly receive is (£60 × 750) = £45,000. If she marks her vertical scale from zero to £45,000, Sarah will have an appropriate range of values.

Having marked her scales, the first line to be drawn onto the chart is fixed costs. This is relatively simple as fixed costs do not change whatever the number of customers. So Sarah marks a horizontal line on the chart to show the monthly fixed costs she will have to pay – £10,000. This is illustrated in Figure 13.2.

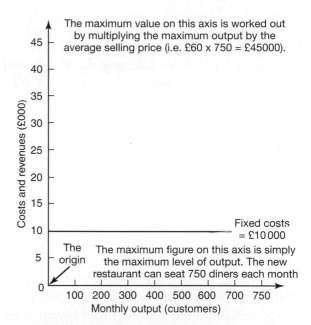

Figure 13.2 Fixed costs on Sarah's break-even chart

The next stage is to include variable costs. As variable costs are expenditure on items such as components and raw materials, these costs will rise along with output. If Sarah has an increasing number of people dining at The Holly she will need to buy more food and her wage bill will also rise.

Variable costs always start at zero. It is not necessary to plot variable costs at each level of production. Sarah can simply calculate variable costs for the highest possible level of output. This would occur if The Holly was full every night and the restaurant had 750 customers each month. So, the highest variable costs

Sarah could encounter are to provide 750 meals each having a variable cost of £35. The highest variable cost would therefore be £26,250 (£35 × 750). Sarah marks this point onto her break-even chart as shown in Figure 13.3 and draws a straight line from this point to the origin.

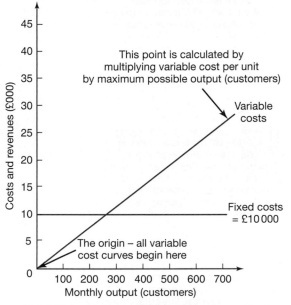

Figure 13.3 Adding variable costs to Sarah's break-even chart

The next task for Sarah in drawing her break-even chart is to add together fixed and variable costs. The results can be entered onto the chart as total costs. Sarah will calculate total costs at zero output and maximum output (750 customers per month). She can mark these two points onto her chart and join them with a straight line.

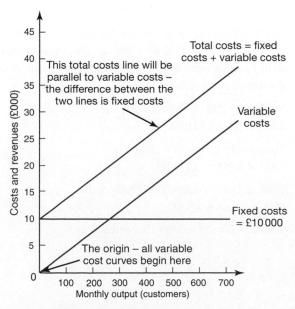

Figure 13.4 Adding the total costs line to Sarah's chart

1   If The Holly has no customers in a month, it will not incur any variable costs. At zero output, total costs are the same as fixed costs. In Sarah's case, this will mean a total costs figure of £10,000 per month.
2   At the other extreme, The Holly might be full, with 750 customers each month. Sarah will add together fixed costs (still £10,000, of course) and variable costs at full capacity (750 customers' meals each having variable costs of £35) equal to £26,250. So, total costs for the restaurant in these circumstances will be £36,250 (£10,000 + £26,250).

The line connecting these two points is equal to total costs. If it is drawn correctly, it should be parallel to the variable costs curve.

The last stage in constructing Sarah's break-even chart is to add on a line showing the revenue The Holly will earn. Sarah has already calculated that an average customer spends £60 on a meal in her restaurant. Following the approach we used for costs, Sarah works out her revenue if the restaurant has no customers and if it is full every evening during a month.

1   The first situation is easy. If The Holly does not have any customers, it will not have any revenue. So the revenue line begins at the origin.
2   If the restaurant is full, Sarah expects each of the 750 customers to pay £60 on average. If The Holly attracts this level of custom, it will earn £45,000 (£60 × 750).

Figure 13.5 shows the break-even chart with the revenue line included. To make the chart easier to read, the variable costs line has been left out.

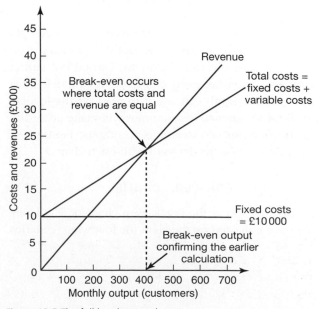

Figure 13.5 The full break-even chart

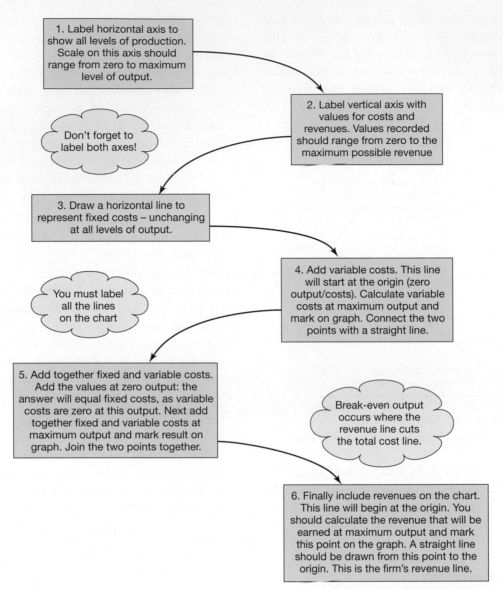

1. Label horizontal axis to show all levels of production. Scale on this axis should range from zero to maximum level of output.

2. Label vertical axis with values for costs and revenues. Values recorded should range from zero to the maximum possible revenue

Don't forget to label both axes!

3. Draw a horizontal line to represent fixed costs – unchanging at all levels of output.

4. Add variable costs. This line will start at the origin (zero output/costs). Calculate variable costs at maximum output and mark on graph. Connect the two points with a straight line.

You must label all the lines on the chart

5. Add together fixed and variable costs. Add the values at zero output: the answer will equal fixed costs, as variable costs are zero at this output. Next add together fixed and variable costs at maximum output and mark result on graph. Join the two points together.

Break-even output occurs where the revenue line cuts the total cost line.

6. Finally include revenues on the chart. This line will begin at the origin. You should calculate the revenue that will be earned at maximum output and mark this point on the graph. A straight line should be drawn from this point to the origin. This is the firm's revenue line.

Figure 13.6 In summary: drawing break-even charts

The break-even chart tells Sarah that she needs 400 customers each month if The Holly is to break even. This confirms the calculation we carried out earlier. However, a break-even chart provides much more information. Sarah can use it to read off the level of profit or loss her new restaurant will make according to the number of customers it attracts. Figure 13.6 summarises how to draw a break-even chart.

Reading break-even charts

Figure 13.7 shows the break-even chart for The Holly. We have indicated on the chart the following scenarios.

- If The Holly attracts 200 customers each month, the restaurant will make a loss as this figure is less than break-even output. The financial position of the business will be:

Revenue (200 customers paying £60 each) = £12 000

Total costs [costs of £10 000 + (200 × £35)] = £17 000

With 200 customers The Holly will make a loss = £5000

This loss is illustrated on the vertical axis.

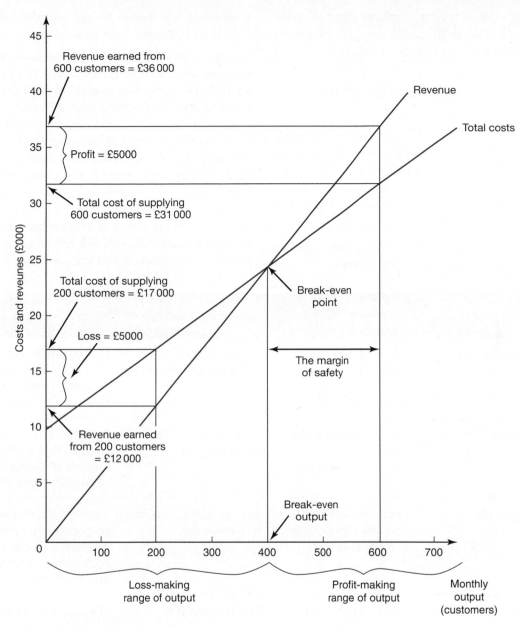

Figure 13.7 Reading break-even charts

- If The Holly attracts 600 customers each month, the restaurant will make a profit as this figure is greater than break-even output. The financial position of the business will be:

Revenue (600 customers paying £60 each) = £36,000

Total costs [costs of £10 000 + (600 × £35)] = £31,000

With 600 customers The Holly will make a profit = £ 5,000

The amount of profits at this level of output is shown on the vertical axis.

It is, of course, possible to read off the level of profit that Sarah's restaurant will make, whatever the number of customers it attracts each month.

This is one way in which a break-even chart is of value to an entrepreneur. It can be used to read off the expected profit or loss at various levels of output. If the entrepreneur believes that he or she can achieve a certain level of sales, this technique will provide guidance on whether this is likely to be profitable or not.

The margin of safety

A break-even chart can be used to show the margin of safety. The margin of safety is the amount by which a firm's current level of output exceeds the level of output necessary to break even.

If Sarah's new restaurant is successful and attracts 600 customers each month, the margin of safety will be 200 customers. This means that, in these circumstances, The Holly could lose 200 customers monthly before it began to make a loss.

Changing variables and break-even analysis

Break-even analysis can assist entrepreneurs in planning and operating their businesses. Break-even analysis can identify the number of sales a business needs to make to generate a profit at certain levels of costs and prices. However, break-even can deal with more complex circumstances including:

• analysing the impact of changing costs and/or prices on the profitability of the business

• deciding whether to accept an order for products at prices different from those normally charged.

In spite of its relative simplicity, break-even provides entrepreneurs with an effective and clear method of analysis and can assist in making decisions, such as setting prices or accepting one-off orders.

Break-even analysis can show the consequences for a business in terms of changing profits (or losses) that may result from changes in fixed and variable costs or alterations in the firm's selling price. This is important for the planning of new businesses and also for businesses that operate in environments which alter frequently. It is too simplistic for entrepreneurs to assume that costs will remain constant or that prices in their markets will not alter over a period of

Change in business environment	Effect on break-even chart	Impact on break-even output	Other effects
Rise in variable costs	Total cost line **pivots** upwards	Greater output necessary to break-even	Due to rise in costs greater revenue (and so more customers and sales) are necessary to break-even.
Fall in variable costs	Total cost line **pivots** downwards	Smaller output required to break-even	Each sale incurs lower costs so that a smaller number of customers is needed to cover costs
Rise in fixed costs	Fixed cost line and total cost line move upwards in a **parallel shift**	Greater output required to break-even.	Business incurs greater costs before earning any revenue, so more sales will be required to cover costs and break-even
Fall in fixed costs	Fixed cost and total cost lines make **parallel shift** downwards	Smaller output is necessary to break-even	The business's overall costs are lower and hence fewer sales will be required to break-even
Rise in selling price	Revenue line **pivots** upwards	Break-even is achieved at a lower level of output	Each sale will provide the business with greater revenue while costs are unaltered. Hence fewer sales will be necessary to break-even
Fall in selling price	Revenue line **pivots** downwards	Break-even is reached at a higher level of output.	Every sale will earn the business less revenue so, as costs are unchanged, more sales will be required to earn sufficient revenue to break-even.

Table 13.2 The effects of changing costs and prices on the break-even point

time. Using break-even analysis for a number of 'what if?' scenarios can increase the value of the technique in financial planning and decision-making.

Table 13.2 illustrates the general effects of changing costs and prices on the break-even point of a business. To calculate the precise effect of changes at a particular level of production, it is necessary to conduct calculations or to construct a break-even chart.

Sarah is conscious that rental values of properties in the Soho area of London are rising rapidly. She realises that the rent of the Georgian building in which The Holly is located is likely to rise and that this will increase her overall costs. If this happens this will reduce the profitability of the new enterprise. Sarah is concerned that a substantial rise in fixed costs (to say £12,500 each month) might make the business unattractive in financial terms.

with fixed costs at £10,000 a month a revenue of £24,000 was sufficient to break even. With the increased level of fixed costs, Sarah needs to attract sufficient diners to give the restaurant a monthly income of £30,000 and a contribution of £12,500 to ensure that break-even is achieved.

Sarah's other fear is that she may be forced to reduce her prices because of increasing competition from other restaurants in west London. She believes that it may be necessary to cut the average price of a meal in The Holly from £60 to £55. Sarah recognises that if she lowers her prices the restaurant will need to attract more customers to break even. Alternatively, the level of profit earned from a given number of customers will fall. The effects of reducing prices by £5 per meal are shown in Figure 13.9. This assumes that all costs are unchanged.

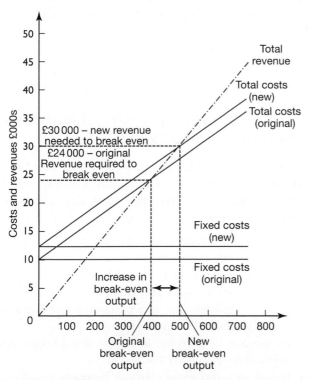

Figure 13.8 Break-even output and rising fixed costs

Figure 13.8 illustrates the effect of a rise in fixed costs on The Holly. The chart highlights that a rise in fixed costs results in Sarah's restaurant requiring a greater number of diners (500 rather then 400) to break-even. This occurs because given the increase in costs faced by The Holly, the restaurant will need to earn higher revenue to cover its costs. Originally,

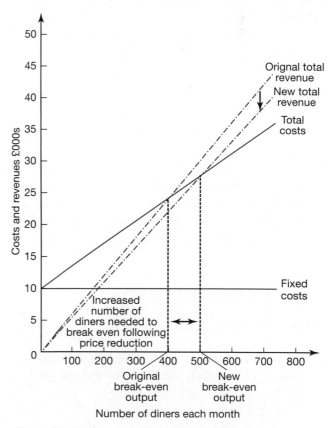

Figure 13.9 Break-even output and reduced prices

Had Sarah been in a position to increase her prices, a smaller number of diners would have been needed to break even. The analysis above would have been reversed.

Business in Focus

Classical Prom Company

The wet weather during the summer of 2007 caused great problems for the Classical Prom Company. The company had planned a series of classical music concerts at locations throughout England including Dorset. Gloucestershire, Warwickshire and Sussex. However, the bad weather meant that sales at the concerts failed to reach break-even output.

A spokesperson for the company said that only two of the nine concerts planned reached 75 per cent of the sales necessary to break even. Sales went well during the early spring when the weather was sunny, but stalled once the rains began in June.

What actions could the company take with regard to a) its prices and b) its costs to reduce the level of ticket sales required to break even?

In what way does this case illustrate a fundamental weakness of break-even analysis as a technique of financial planning?

Entrepreneurs can take actions to reduce the level of production or output necessary to break even. So if a business is able to increase its price, fewer units of output will need to be sold to break even. A reduction in fixed or variable costs will have a similar effect.

What do you think?

Would an increase in price always increase the chance of a start-up business breaking even in its first year of trading?

Break-even and non-standard prices

A similar analysis would have resulted if Sarah had been approached by a customer and offered the chance to provide a large number of meals at a price below her normal average of £60. Suppose a local theatre offered her a contract to fill her restaurant one night each week as part of its 'View & Dine' package. The theatre may only offer Sarah a fixed price of £50 per diner, but guarantee a minimum of 25 diners on that evening. Sarah could take this into account in her business planning and decide whether it is an attractive offer using break-even analysis. In this case she may be tempted. Assuming her fixed costs for one night are £334 (£10,000/30) and that her contribution per unit is now £15 (£50–£35), The Holly would break even on this offer with (just over!) 22 diners and the contract is for 25 as a minimum. Sarah might also think that this is a good way of publicising The Holly. If they enjoy the experience, diners might return and pay full price, or tell friends about it.

Break-even analysis and market research

To be most effective, break-even analysis should be supported by market research. Sarah knows that she needs 400 diners each month is she is to break even. If her market research reveals that this is likely, this will be a major reason for her to go ahead and open the restaurant. However, if the projected figure is lower, the enterprise is unlikely to be profitable.

The advantages and disadvantages of break-even analysis

Most financial techniques have advantages and disadvantages, and break-even analysis is no exception. The advantages offered by break-even analysis include the following:

1 It is a simple technique allowing most entrepreneurs to use it without the need for expensive training. Because of this it is particularly suitable for newly established and small businesses.
2 It is a technique that can be completed quickly, providing immediate results.
3 Its use can be of value in supporting a business's application to a bank for a loan.
4 By using break-even charts a business can forecast the effect of varying numbers of customers on its costs, revenues and profits.
5 Break-even analysis can be used to analyse the implications of changing prices and costs on the enterprise's likely profitability.

Web link

Computers are highly effective for calculating break-even output using different prices and costs. This website offers an example of software that can be used for this purpose: http://downloads.zdnet.co.uk/ 0,1000000375,39148679s,00.htm

However, break-even analysis has a number of shortcomings:

1 It assumes that all products are sold. So Sarah might assume that she will attract 600 customers each month. She will order the necessary food and hire sufficient staff. However, if only 500 turn up, she will not make the profit indicated for 600 customers on the break-even chart.

2 It is a simplification of the real world. Businesses do not sell all their products at a single price and calculating an average is unlikely to provide accurate data. The technique is also difficult to use when a business sells a number of different products.

3 Costs do not rise as steadily as the technique suggests. As we have seen, variable costs can rise less quickly than output because of the benefits of buying in bulk.

4 A break-even analysis will only be as accurate as the data on which it is based. If costs or selling prices are incorrect, then the forecasts will be wrong.

So break-even analysis offers some support to an entrepreneur looking to start a business. However, it is only a gudeline and its value should not be overstated. Perhaps most important, entrepreneurs should bear in mind that the value of the technique depends on the use of reliable data for costs, prices and expected sales.

One step further

In reality, most break-even charts are more complicated than the ones we have drawn in this unit. An entrepreneur considering whether or not to start a business may find that the level of fixed costs is not constant throughout the range of output that he or she is planning to produce.

So a small manufacturing business might find that once its orders reach a certain level it requires a second factory and that, as a consequence, its rent and business rates suddenly increase. This results in a sudden step in the enterprise's fixed costs once that level of output in reached. This is illustrated in Figure 13.10 below.

This sudden rise or discontinuity has an effect on the business's total costs and also on its forecast profitability at higher levels of output. In general, costs rise, reducing profitability and increasing the level of output required to break-even.

This has several implications for entrepreneurs. First, they must consider whether at some point their fixed costs are likely to increase and to be aware of

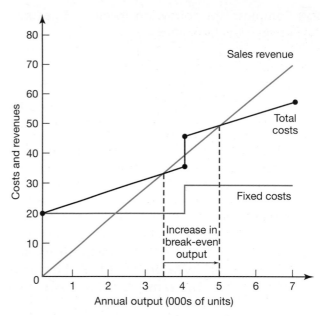

Figure 13.10 Increase in break-even output

the impact of this on their profitability. It may be that there are distinct benefits to working on a smaller scale. They may also consider whether costs are really fixed. In the longer term is it probably true to say that all costs are variable. Arguably, this means that break-even anlysis is of less value in the longer term.

Summary

Break-even is a useful technique for entrepreneurs who are starting a business. It allows them to consider the effects of different prices and costs on potential profitability, as well as helping to make a judgement on the viability of the business. However, it has significant weaknesses, such as assuming all production is sold. It is valuable to entrepreneurs as long as these weaknesses are recognised.

Quick questions

1 Which one of the following statements relating to break-even output is true?

1 It is the level of output at which sales revenue equals total costs.

2 It is the level of output at which variable costs equal sales revenue.

3 It is the level of output at which variable costs and total costs are equal.

4 It is the level of output at which profits are greatest.

2 Complete the following formula: Sales revenue – variable costs = ...

3 'Contribution always equals profits.' True or false?

4 Complete the following formula:

Break-even output = fixed costs divided by ....per unit

5 The selling price of Sally's hand-knitted sweaters is £90. The variable cost of each one is £40. Her monthly fixed costs are £1000. Market research suggests that she will sell 16 sweaters per month. Should she start producing sweaters on the basis of this information?

6 Sally discovers that her competitors sell hand-knitted sweaters for £120. she thinks she could do the same. Does this alter the decision on whether or not to go ahead with the business?

7 Is the following statement true or false? 'At levels of output below break-even, the total revenue line will be below the total costs line, while at output greater than break-even, the total revenue line will always be above the total cost line.'

8 Is the following true or false? 'A fall in variable costs per unit will always reduce break-even output.'

9 Does the total revenue line pivot or shift when there is a fall in prices?

10 Is the following statement true or false? 'The level of profit or loss on a break-even chart can be shown by the vertical distance between sales revenue and variable costs.'

Issues for analysis

These mainly relate to the use of break-even charts and calculations.

- The possible effects of a 5 per cent rise in variable costs on break-even output.
- The market price for the business's products increases by, say, £5.
- Methods of reducing the volume of output and sales necessary to break even.

Issues for evaluation

- How valuable is break-even to a decision about whether or not to start up a particular business?
- Do the shortcomings of break-even analysis mean that it is not worth entrepreneurs using it as part of their business planning?

- To what extent does the effective use of break-even analysis depend upon high quality primary market research?

Analysis and evaluation questions

1 Michael Bertolotti has the following data for his home cleaning business 'Helping Hands':
- Fixed costs per month of operation: £2,700
- Average contribution per house cleaned: £36.

He plans to offer his service in a nearby town for the first time. Two larger cleaning firms already operate there. He conducts a limited amount of primary market research and is confident that if he reduces his price (resulting in a contribution per unit of £30), he will be able to enter this new market successfully.

a Michael plans to reduce his price and therefore his contribution per house cleaned to £30. Analyse **two** possible implications of this decision. (8 marks)

b To what extent might break-even analysis help Michael to take this decision on whether to sell his service in the nearby town? (15 marks)

2 Jamie Lee is an artist and has just launched a business painting portraits of people and animals. Her bank manager has suggested that Jamie should try to reduce the level of output and sales she needs to break even. Because of Jamie's effective use of her website and a very competitive pricing policy, she already has sufficient commissions to keep her busy for at least the next nine months. Jamie's fixed and variable costs are low and she thinks they are easy to forecast.

a Examine **two** actions that Jamie might take to reduce the level of output needed for her new business to break even. (8 marks)

b To what extent do you agree with the bank manager's view in **these circumstances**? (15 marks)

Assessment

Case study

Nick Hess's attempt to operate a sustainable food retailing business in Devon failed. He marketed Foodeaze as a 'carbon-neutral' business. Its USP was that it was a sustainable business in that it did not damage the environment and could trade without threatening the welfare of future generations.

The business sells a range of local foodstuffs as well as operating a bar and restaurant. All the food sold in the restaurant was prepared from the ingredients sold at Foodeaze. Supplies were delivered from local farms using vehicles running on bio-diesel. The financial planning for the business was thorough and at first all went well. Within five weeks of opening the business was close to its break-even level of sales.

However, the opening of a new store nearby selling similar products led to sales falling and break-even becoming a distant possibility. After three months of trading, Foodeaze ceased operations due to mounting losses. Nick Hess said he had factored in the opening of the new store into his business plan, but had underestimated its impact.

(Adapted from: BBC News 16th May 2007
http://news.bbc.co.uk/1/hi/england/devon/6660947.stm)

Questions

(30 marks, 40 minutes)

1 Assume the following financial information applies to Foodeaze in its fifth week of trading:
   - Average revenue received from each sale was £20.
   - The variable cost of this sale was £12.
   - Break-even required 1400 customers weekly.
   - The number of customers achieved was 1200.

2 Calculate the loss made by Foodeaze in its fifth week of trading. (6 marks)

3 Analyse the possible sources of information that Nick Hess used to construct his break-even analysis. (9 marks)

4 To what extent does the experience of Nick Hess and Foodeaze show that break-even analysis is of little value to an entrepreneur starting a new business? (15 marks)

14 Using cash-flow forecasting

Making sure the business has sufficient cash to pay its bills as they become due is one of the trickiest tasks for a new entrepreneur. It can be made easier by forecasting the flows of cash in and out of the enterprise, to identify periods when the busienss might be short of cash. It is, however, vital that entrepreneurs appreciate the importance of managing cash carefully. What you need to know by the end of the chapter:
• the meaning of the term 'cash flow'
• the reasons why entrepreneurs draw up cash-flow forecasts
• the structure of a typical cash-flow forecast
• the techniques entrepreneurs use to forecast cash flow.

What is cash flow?

A potentially profitable enterprise can fail because of poor management of cash flow. Equally, an unprofitable new business can enjoy a period in which it has plenty of cash – before the bills arrive!

Cash flow and profits are two very different concepts:

• As we saw in Chapter 12, a business makes a profit if, over a given period of time, its revenue is greater than its expenditure. A business can survive without making a profit for a short period of time, but it is essential that it earns profits in the long run.
• Cash flow relates to the timing of payments and receipts. Cash flow is important in the short term, as a business must pay people and organisations to whom it owes money.

Unless a business manages the timing of its payments and receipts carefully, it may find itself in a position where it is operating profitably but is running out of cash regularly. This could be because it is forced to wait for several months before receiving payment from customers. In the meantime, it has to settle its own debts.

Businesses are especially vulnerable to cash-flow difficulties in their first months and years of trading. It is for this reason that many financial institutions demand evidence that entrepreneurs have planned the management of cash for a new enterprise before granting a loan.

Key terms
Cash flow is the movement of cash into and out of a business over a period of time.
Cash flow forecasts state the inflows and outflows of cash that the managers of a business expect over some future period.

What do you think?

Why might an entrepreneur starting an online business find it easier to manage his or her cash during the first months of trading?

Why do newly established businesses forecast cash flows?

There are two main reasons why an entrepreneur might forecast the cash flow of a proposed business.

- To support applications for loans. Almost all new enterprises require loans to enable them to become established (and also during periods of expansion). Banks and other financial institutions are far more likely to lend money to a business that has evidence of financial planning. It is reassuring for the bank that the entrepreneur understands the importance of cash and has planned carefully to avoid cash-flow crises. Cash-flow planning gives the bank more confidence that the entrepreneur will be able to make the repayments of the loan as and when they are due.
- To help avoid unexpected cash-flow crises. Twenty percent of newly established businesses fail within two years of starting trading. A high proportion of these fail because of cash-flow difficulties. Planning can help avoid such difficulties. Cash-flow planning helps to ensure that newly established businesses do not suffer from periods when they are short of cash and are unable to pay their debts. By forecasting cash flows, a business can identify times at which it may not have enough cash available. This allows them to make the necessary arrangements to overcome this problem.

Newly established businesses are particularly vulnerable to cash-flow problems for a number of reasons:

- They often have to offer customers time to pay to win them away from established firms – this delays the receipt of cash.
- Suppliers may demand immediate payment from newly established businesses who have not had time to develop a good record for paying suppliers – thus cash flows out immediately.
- New businesses usually have to spend heavily on marketing to bring their enterprises to the attention of potential customers. This can lead to a heavy outflow of vital cash.
- New businesses often do not have reserves of cash that have been built up from previous trading periods.

It is during the early months of trading that many new businesses face the most severe cash-flow difficulties. Costs can be high, leading to a large outflow of funds. Simultaneously, the business may receive little revenue as sales may be low and customers may want time to pay. It is easy to see that without careful planning many new businesses may run out of cash during this period. This is the cause of a large number of business failures.

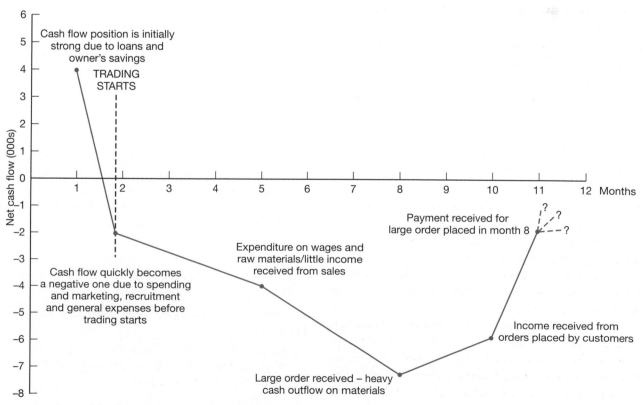

Figure 14.1 Pressures on the cash flow of a new enterprise

Real-life Business

'Spark of Inspiration' was set up by Sonia Wilkinson in 2005. It sells educational toys and actively encourages parents to provide them for children in place of computer games. Spark of Inspiration's toys include creative toys such as kits for making models or mosaics, board games for the family, puzzles and thinking games.

When Spark of Inspiration was first established Sonia wanted to import some cotton bags from India to help her to promote her business. This decision placed pressure on Sonia's early cash-flow forecasts. As a start-up business, tax rules meant that Spark of Inspiration had to pay Value Added Tax (VAT) on its imports and then claim the money back at a later date.

1   Why did this tax rule place extra pressure on Spark of Inspiration's cash flow?

Web link

You can read more about Sonia's business at www.sparkofinspiration.co.uk.

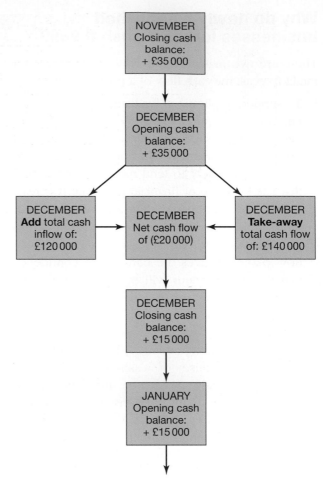

Figure 14.2 Opening and closing balances

Constructing cash flow forecasts

A simplified cash-flow forecast is illustrated in Figure 14.2.

Suppose, in this example, that the cash outflow forecast for December is £160,000. What would be the closing balance for December in these circumstances? Although cash-flow forecasts differ from one another, they usually have three sections and are normally calculated monthly. An essential part of cash-flow forecasting is that inflows and outflows of cash should be included in the plan at the time they take place.

1   Cash in – the first section forecasts the cash inflows into the business, usually on a monthly basis. This section includes receipts from cash sales and credit sales. Credit sales occur when the customer is given time to pay: normally 30, 60 or 90 days.

2   Cash out – the cash out (or expenditure) section will state the expected expenditure on the goods and services. Thus, a typical section might include forecasts of expenditure on rent, rates, insurance, wages and salaries, fuel, and so on. At the end of this section the total expected outflow of cash over the time period in question would be stated.

3   The net monthly cash flow is calculated by subtracting the total outflow of cash from the total inflow. The final section of the forecast also has the opening balance and the closing balance. The opening balance is the business's cash position at the start of each month. This will, of course, be the same figure as at the end of the previous month. The net monthly cash flow is added to the opening balance figure. The resulting figure is the closing cash balance for the month. It is also the opening balance for the following month.

A typical format for a cash flow forecast is shown in Figure 14.3.

		January	February	March	April	May	June
1 Cash in	Cash sales						
	Credit sales						
	Total Inflow						
2 Cash out	Raw materials						
	Wages						
	Other costs						
	Total outflow						
3 Net monthly cash flow	Net monthly cash flow						
	Opening balance						
	Closing balance						

Figure 14.3 A typical format for a cash-flow forecast

Examiner's advice

Although you should understand how to construct a cash flow forecast, it is unlikely that you will be asked to do this in an examination because of time constraints. You may be asked to:

- fill in missing figures to show that you understand the structure and calculations
- identify problems that might occur – to demonstrate that you understand what the forecast tells you!
- propose solutions to the cash flow problems you have identified.

Constructing cash flows – a case study

Steve Marshall is planning to buy a bookshop. Steve knows that he needs to forecast his cash flow to help him to identify times when he might experience problems. Knowing when he is likely to be short of cash gives him the chance to arrange an overdraft or short-term loan. His bank is unlikely to advance him a loan unless he constructs a cash-flow forecast.

- Steve has made the following forecasts about his business for the first four months of trading from June until September.
- Steve has raised £75,000 from a bank loan and his savings to buy the lease on a property and to purchase a stock of books. He also intends that this money will be used to pay his start-up marketing costs.

- He expects his business to have an opening cash balance of £2,000 at the start of June.
- He anticipates his cash sales to rise steadily for each of the four months (from £5,750 to £9,215) as his business becomes better known. However, he has already received an order to supply books to a local college. The order is for £10,000. He expects payment in September, but will buy the books in June at the same time as he purchases his initial stock.
- Each month Steve orders books from his suppliers to replace stock he has sold.
- He has to pay his own wages and those of a part-time assistant. These normally amount to £1,500 each month.
- Other costs, including his rent, rates, heating and lighting amount to £1,500 each month in June and July, but are higher in August and September.
- Steve's cash-flow forecast is shown in Table 14.1.

Steve's cash-flow forecast illustrates many of the key principles. An important figure for each month is shown in the row entitled 'Net monthly cash flow'. This simply records the balance between the inflow and outflow for the month: June is a good example of how this operates. In June, Steve expected to receive £5,750 from book sales. At the same time he planned to spend £94,500 on his initial stock of books as well as supplying the college's order, but also on marketing, wages and rent. So, in June he expected his net cash flow (cash inflows less cash outflows) to be minus £13,750 (£80,750 – £94,500). In cash-flow forecasts, negative figures can be shown in brackets or with a minus figure in front. Hence, the figure entered for net monthly cash flow in June could be (£13,750).

	June	July	August	September
Cash in				
Savings & borrowings	75000	0	0	
Cash sales	5750	7500	8475	9215
Credit sales	0	0	0	10000
Total cash inflow	**80750**	**7500**	**8475**	**19215**
Cash out				
Purchase of lease on shop	30000	0	0	0
Purchase of books	59000	4500	5000	6100
Wages	1500	1500	1500	1500
Marketing costs	2500	1500	975	400
Other costs, e.g. rent	1500	1500	1605	1630
Total cash outflow	**94500**	**9000**	**9080**	**9630**
Net monthly cash flow	**−13750**	**−1500**	**−605**	**9585**
Opening balance	2000	−11750	−13250	−13855
Closing balance	−11750	−13250	−13855	−4270

Table 14.1 **Steve Marshall's cash-flow forecast**

This case study also highlights one of the key advantages of cash-flow forecasting. Steve's business will be short of cash during June, July, August and, to a lesser extent, September. The closing balances for these months indicate that he will require a maximum of £13,855 of additional cash to enable him to pay his rent, wages, and so on. Knowing this in advance means that Steve can take steps to avoid a cash crisis, possibly by agreeing an overdraft with his bank.

Christina Domecq

In 2003, Christina Domecq had a business idea. Driving to a meeting she checked her voicemail and discovered that she had 14 messages. She had to spend time writing them out for later reference. She wondered whether it would be possible to receive voicemail as text messages. It was a simple, but a unique idea and a business was born.

Figure 14.4 Christina Domecq

By 2007, SpinVox, the company she set up to convert voicemail messages into text, has 300 employees and a million users of the service. SpinVox currently converts voicemail messages in English, Spanish, French and German, but is planning to add Italian to the list. SpinVox has been valued at £100 million.

Christina is 30 years old and was born in Spain and is a member of the Domecq sherry family and, as such, she has entrepreneurial spirit running in her veins. She was educated in America and was probably always going to be a successful businesswoman. By the age of 20 she had set up an IT consultancy with a £7 million turnover. Christina was voted Ernst & Young's Young Entrepreneur of the year in 2007.

Christina and her cofounder Daniel Doulton are always innovating to grow SpinVox further by, for example, launching Social Networks through SpinVox, a service that allows people to post to their blogs and social networking sites just by speaking into the phone. Their messages get conveyed to text and immediately posted to sites such as Facebook.

> **Web link**
>
> To find out more about SpinVox, visit www.spinvox.com

Sources of information for cash-flow forecasts

Using market research can reduce the risk of inaccurate cash-flow forecasting. Market research can establish the prices customers are prepared to pay and the probable level of demand for a firm's products. It is important for entrepreneurs to use the results of primary market research to help them to anticipate sales revenue and hence cash inflow. Secondary research will probably be of limited value in these circumstances, as any new business is likely to have some unique characteristics and the market is likely to have changed since previous secondary research was completed.

> **Key term**
>
> **Trade credit** is a period of time given by suppliers before customers have to pay for goods or services

Other possible sources of information for constructing cash-flow forecasts include the following.

Suppliers

A new business's suppliers can provide information in two ways. First, they will provide information on the costs that the entrepreneur will have to pay to purchase raw materials (books in the case of Steve Marshall's bookshop), fuel or marketing services such as advertising. Second, and most important, suppliers will advise of trade credit terms they are willing to offer. If suppliers give customers time to pay for goods or services this means that the cash outflow will not occur for a period of time – usually 30 or 60 days. This is a vital piece of information because it helps the entrepreneur to enter the cash outflow in the correct month of the forecast and obviously has implications for net cash flow figures as well as opening and closing balances.

Business Link

This is a government-funded organisation offering advice and support for new and small businesses. It has an informative website and operates on a regional basis meaning that its support is based on knowledge of local markets. Business Link offers a range of online courses as well as contacts with local advisors who can use their experience to assist new entrepreneurs in constructing effective and realistic cash-flow forecasts.

Web link

Look at www.businesslink.gov.uk for details of the support offered to new and small businesses by this organisation.

Banks

Most high street banks offer a range of support services for new businesses. Often, these are linked to opening a business bank account and/or taking out a business loan. Banks also supply software to help entrepreneurs with the practical aspects of constructing a cash-flow forecast.

It is important that an entrepreneur researches the likely costs of operating a new business. There will not be any past trading records to use as guidance for drawing up the first forecast and it is easy to underestimate likely costs or to be optimistic about timings of inflows. Late payment contributes to the failure of an estimated 10,000 – 15,000 firms each year in the UK, with small firms owed, in total, an estimated £50,000 million each month in 2007, according to the Small Business website.

Businesses can use cash-flow forecasts in the same way as they use break-even analysis to forecast a number of 'what if' scenarios. It can be particularly important for a new business to consider the impact on its cash flow if sales are lower than forecast, if costs are higher or – and this is highly likely for a new business – if customers do not pay on time. Equally, by using spreadsheets, entrepreneurs can assess the implications for cash flow of accepting a new, large order.

Web link

Visit www.smallbusiness.co.uk for further information on all aspects of running a small business, including the management of cash flow.

Most modern businesses use spreadsheets to construct their cash-flow forecasts. This technology makes analysing cash flows simpler and quicker and automatically adjusts all the figures when a single change is made to the data.

Trade credit and cash flow

There are many reasons why a new business might want to offer its customers time to pay – a process known as giving trade credit. A new business can only establish itself by winning customers from competitors or by 'creating' new customers. In each case, allowing customers time to pay is likely to be considered an attractive aspect of the supply of goods or services. In effect, this reduces the pressure on the customer's cash flow as the outflow of cash is delayed. One way to look at trade credit is to think of it as a free, but very short-term loan. The provision of trade credit will help a new business to win customers.

Granting trade credit may also help the business to charge slightly higher prices, which can aid profitability in the long term. Customers may be willing to pay a slightly higher price in return for being allowed 30 or 60 days' grace before having to pay their bills.

However, the downside of granting trade credit to customers is clear. It delays inflows of cash and imposes additional pressures on the enterprise's own cash flow. This can make it more difficult to manage and it may mean that the business has to borrow from its bank, incurring costly bank and interest charges. However, granting trade credit is a possible strategy for a new business so long as it has planned its cash flow carefully and is certain it has made arrangements for those difficult times when cash outflows exceed cash inflows.

One step further: late payment

Late payment occurs when customers settle bills after the agreed date. In a 2005 survey approximately 8,000 small businesses were surveyed as to the extent of this problem. Table 14.2 below summarises the results.

The problem of late payment appears to be greater in the manufacturing sector, though the most pronounced statistic here is that a high proportion of newly established businesses are unwilling (or perhaps unable to afford) to offer trade credit. By demanding

Percentage who said...	All firms	Primary sector	Manufacturing	Services
Major problem	10%	5%	18%	10%
Minor problem	18%	13%	28%	22%
No problem	43%	54%	39%	42%
Don't offer customers trade credit	28%	28%	15%	25%
Don't know/No response	1%	0%	1%	1%

Table 14.2 The extent to which late payment is a problem

(Source: Annual Survey of Small Businesses 2005, Institute of Employment Studies)

payment on, or before, delivery entrepreneurs can ensure cash flows into the business promptly.

A further reason why late payment may have become less of a problem for small firms in recent years is the Late Payment Act, 1998. This law became fully operational in 2002 and gives small businesses the right to claim interest on outstanding debts at 8 per cent above the Bank of England's current base rate. (For example, at the time of writing this would allow a small business to charge 13.75 per cent interest on an outstanding invoice.)

However, the problem of late payment has not gone away. Research by the Institute for Employment Studies has shown that as businesses grow late payment becomes a more pressing issue. For businesses that employ between 50 and 250 people, 43 per cent of managers reported late payment as a problem.

Summary

This unit has shown how important it is for entrepreneurs to manage cash carefully and avoid cash crises. This is a particularly important issue for new businesses and success is more likely if cash flow is forecasted as accurately as possible. It is likely that most new entrepreneurs will benefit from advice in planning cash flow.

Quick questions

1 Complete the following sentence by filling in the missing word:

Cash flow relates to the .... of a business's receipts and payments.

2 Businesses are particularly vulnerable to cash flow difficulties in the first few years of trading. True or false?

3 For which two of the following reasons might businesses construct cash flow forecasts:

- to increase the profit made per unit of production?
- as a means of forecasting the next year's profit?
- to support applications for loans?
- to avoid financial problems during periods when they may be short of cash and unable to pay suppliers.

4 Complete the following formula by filling in the missing word. 'Cash inflow per month minus Cash outflow per month equals ....,'

5 If Balmer Ltd has an opening cash balance in May of £24,750 and a net cash flow for May equal to (£14,250), which one of the following will be its opening balance for June:

- £39,000?
- £24,750?
- £38,500?
- £10,500?

6 If a business has a net cashflow for June of £35,000, and an opening balance of (£12,500), what is its opening balance for July?

7 Is the following a description of cash sales or credit sales? 'These occur when a business allows customers time to pay, normally 30 or 60 days.'

8 Complete the following formula: Opening balance – net monthly cash flow = ...\ ....

9 Is the following statement true or false? 'Negative figures in cash flow forecasts are normally shown in brackets.'

10 Is the following statement true or false? "Suppliers can be very helpful to an entrepreneur when drawing up a cash flow forecast as they can provide information on costs as well as the timing of payments".

Issues for analysis

- The trend or 'story' within a specific cash flow forecast – is the position improving or worsening?
- The sources of information for a forecast and considering their reliability.
- The methods available to a particular business to improve its cash flow position and the advantages and disadvantages of their use.

Issues for evaluation

- Is this business viable given its forecast cash position?
- How useful is this forecast to the business? Is it reliable?
- Does this business face cash-flow problems above and beyond what might be expected for a new business of its type?
- What would be the optimal action for a business to take to improve its cash-flow position?

Analysis and evaluation questions

1 Laura Deeman's new business is about to commence trading. Laura is offering an online dating service for customers aged over 50. She markets her business as being for wealthy clients who are short of time. She intends to provide a premium service including online video clips of clients. Online dating is a volatile market and one in which consumer spending varies unexpectedly.

This is a new enterprise and very different from existing dating websites. Laura has considerable experience of running small businesses. She has planned her cash flow carefully and, although she anticipates a negative closing balance for the first eight months, this does not exceed £7,500 in any month. By the end of the year Laura forecasts a small positive closing balance of £950.

a. Analyse **two** possible sources of information that Laura might have used to forecast the cash flow position of her business. (8 marks)

b. To what extent do you think that Laura can rely upon her cash-flow forecast? (15 marks)

2 The cash-flow forecast below was drawn up as part of the financial planning carried out by Tom Martell. Tom plans to establish a business providing a professional chef service throughout London. Professional chefs plan and cook high-quality meals in the homes of their clients. Tom's business is targeted at wealthy people who don't have time to prepare meals for dinner parties at home.

Tom has conducted primary research throughout higher income groups in London. He has very limited financial resources, but has received much support from his bank.

	January	February	March
Cash in			
Cash sales	1900	2050	2245
Credit sales	0	0	1370
Total cash inflow	1900	2050	3615
Cash out			
Wages	750	795	850
Raw materials	1400	1535	1625
Marketing costs	950	450	150
Other costs	1550	300	300
Total cash outflow	4650	3080	2925
Net monthly cash flow	–2750	–1030	690
Opening balance	1000	–1750	–2780
Closing balance	–1750	–2780	–2090

Table 14.3 Tom Martell's cash-flow forecast

a Examine two actions that Tom might take to improve his forecast cash flow position. (8 marks)

b Tom has decided **not** to go ahead with his business idea. To what extent does the cash-flow forecast support his decision? (15 marks)

Assessment

Case study

Kate Chant is in the process of starting a new business. Bungay Herbs will supply fresh herbs ready wrapped to delicatessens throughout East Anglia.

	April	May	June
Cash in			
Savings & borrowings	40000	0	0
Cash sales	2500	3000	4475
Credit sales	0	0	6750
Total cash inflow	**42500**	**3000**	**11225**
Cash out			
Purchase of greenhouses	36000	0	0
Purchase of equipment	4500	0	0
Wages	1450	1600	1700
Marketing costs	3000	1800	1720
Other costs, fuel, seeds	4255	3000	2345
Total cash outflow	**49205**	**6400**	**5765**
Net monthly cash flow	−6705	−3400	5460
Opening balance	2500	−4205	−7605
Closing balance	−4205	−7605	−2145

Table 14.4 Kate Chant's cash-flow forecast

Kate intends to supply a range of the most commonly used herbs including parsley, mint, dill, oregano, sage and chives. The herbs will be supplied still growing in small pots of compost to ensure freshness.

Kate owns a smallholding and has substantial experience of growing plants and of running a business. However, the new enterprise has meant that she has had to invest in new greenhouses and other essential equipment as well as taking on two part-time employees. In addition, she has to spend heavily on marketing her new business to suitable retailers in East Anglia. She has also agreed to offer 60 days' trade credit to her customers to help build up a customer base.

Drawing up the cash-flow forecast above for the first three months of trading was essential in order to persuade the bank to grant her a loan to cover the start-up costs. The loan will also help her to manage her start up costs.

Questions

(30 marks, 40 minutes)

1 Assume that Kate decides to change her forecasts for June. She reduces income from cash sales to £4,150 and increases marketing costs to £1,900. In the light of these changes calculate
  • total cash inflow
  • total cash outflow
  • net monthly cash flow
  • opening balance and
  • closing balance
  for **June** only.(5 marks)

2 Examine **two** possible benefits to Kate resulting from drawing up her cash-flow forecast. (9 marks)

3 To what extent has the construction of the cash-flow forecast shown above made it more likely that Bungay Herbs will survive its first year of trading? (16 marks)

15 Setting budgets

At the stage when an entrepreneur is planning the finances of a business, it is not certain that the entrepreneur will go ahead with the enterprise. Forecasting revenues, costs and profits, collectively known as setting budgets, is an important element in planning the business. If an entrepreneur can have confidence in the likely accuracy of budgets, they can play an important part in decision-making, including whether the business is likely to be viable in the future.

What you need to know by the end of this chapter:
- the differences between income, expenditure and profits budgets
- why businesses set budgets
- the ways in which businesses set budgets
- the problems businesses encounter when setting budgets.

What are budgets?

Budgets are financial plans for a future period of time. Firms plan their earnings and revenues using budgets. Budgets are usually drawn up on a monthly basis, over the period of a financial year.

In the last chapter we considered cash-flow forecasts which are also financial plans and a different type of budget. Sometimes they are called 'cash budgets'. However, in this chapter we concentrate on budgets relating to earnings, expenditure and profits.

> **Key terms**
> **Budgets** are financial plans for the future looking at revenue from sales and expected costs over some time period.

Types of budgets

- **Sales revenue or earnings budgets**. These set out the business's expected sales revenue from selling its products. Important information here includes the expected level of sales and the likely selling price of the product. A start-up business may have forecast relatively low revenue budgets during its first few months of trading. It is likely that the sales revenue budgets will be increased as the business becomes better known.

- **Expenditure budgets**. These are also called cost or production budgets. Businesses need to plan their expenditure on labour, raw materials, fuel and other items which are essential for the process of production. These set out the expected expenditure on a monthly basis on these items.

- **Profit budgets**. By combining sales revenue and expenditure budgets it is possible to calculate expected profits or losses. For many new businesses it may be that a profit is not made during the first months or even years of trading. For many start-up businesses survivial is more important than making a profit in the early stages of trading.

Setting budgets can help the business achieve its objectives. If, for example, a business has growth in sales as a major objective, the budgets will reflect this with higher revenues being forecast, but also higher costs of production planned for.

What do you think?

Would you start a business that was not expected to make a profit during its first year? What reasons might you have for your decision?

The process of creating budgets

Before firms can start to write their budgets for the coming year, they need to carry out some research. This may involve:

- analysing the market to predict likely trends in sales and prices to help plan sales revenue
- researching costs for labour, fuel and raw materials by contacting suppliers and seeing if they can negotiate price reductions for prompt payment or ordering in bulk
- considering government estimates for wage rises and inflation and incorporating them into future sales revenue and expenditure budgets.

Once a business has collected the necessary data, it is normal to start by drawing up expected revenues from selling products – the sales revenue budget. This is the first budget because, once a firm knows its expected sales, it can plan production. This enables the business to forecast the costs associated with producing enough to match planned sales. For a new business it is likely that sales will rise from a fairly low level during the first year of trading. It is vital in the setting of budgets that expendtiure matches this. It is impossible for a business to increase its sales without producing more of its goods or services to supply to customers.

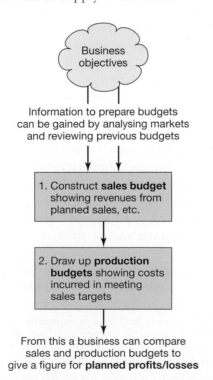

Figure 15.1 Drawing up budgets

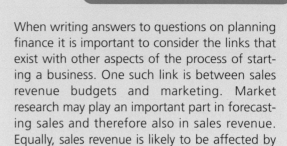

Examiner's advice

When writing answers to questions on planning finance it is important to consider the links that exist with other aspects of the process of starting a business. One such link is between sales revenue budgets and marketing. Market research may play an important part in forecasting sales and therefore also in sales revenue. Equally, sales revenue is likely to be affected by the actions of competitors and the success of the new business's promotion.

Once production budgets and sales budgets are completed, it is possible to compare revenues and expenditure. This allows entrepreneurs to forecast profits (or losses) for the future trading period.

Setting budgets – a case study

Vixen Soap Ltd is due to start trading in two month's time. The company's owners, Paul and Hayley Hills, are planning to manufacture a range of hand-made soaps. The company intends to produce a range of soaps including those made from olive oil, lavender, camomile and champagne, as well as organic soaps. The intention is to sell these products using the internet and an effective website has been developed to promote the new company and its products as well as to provide a method of selling the soaps.

Paul and Hayley have prepared a detailed business plan including sales, expenditure and profit budgets for the first year of trading. They conducted extensive primary and secondary market research, which suggested that the company's unique range of high-quality products will prove popular and sales are expected to rise steadily. However, initial costs are expected to be high as the company builds up a stock of products ready for sale.

Paul and Hayley began the process of setting budgets by estimating the company's sales using the market research data. By combining the likely volume of sales with the expected prices, the sales revenue budget was developed. For example, Hayley has forecast that in January the company would sell 5,000 bars of scented and flavoured soap at £1.49 each, giving a sales revenue of £7,450.

	January £	February £	March £
Sales of scented/flavoured soaps	7450	12560	17500
Sales of organic soaps	2765	3400	4125
Total sales	10215	15960	21625
Purchases of raw materials	19500	14010	15550
Packaging	1215	1105	1350
Wages & salaries	3000	2850	2995
Marketing & administration	2450	2400	2450
Other costs	975	1100	1075
Total costs	27140	21465	23420
Profit/Loss	−16925	−5505	−1795

Table 15.1 Vixen Soap's budgets

Once the level of forecast sales was decided, it was possible for the company to calculate its expected costs of production. As with many start-up businesses, production costs are initially high. The company has to build up a stock of its full range of soaps to enable it to supply custsomers promptly. At the same time, production costs have to reflect likely sales. So, variable costs of production are forecast to rise in February and March as sales increase.

The company's sales revenue, expenditure and profit budgets for its first three months of trading are shown above.

Why do businesses draw up budgets?

There are a number of reasons for planning future costs and revenues by setting budgets:

- Budgets assist a business to control its finances by planning expenditure over a future period, usually a year. Budgets help to ensure that a business does not spend more than it should. If the entrepreneur makes sure that expenditure does not rise above the budget, costs should not get out of control. This is very important for a start-up business, as it is unlikely to be profitable initially and control of costs will be vital.
- Budgets act as targets for entrepreneurs. For example, a sales revenue budget can encourage and stimulate employees to increase sales so that the budgeted revenue is achieved, or even exceeded.

Budgets help to coordinate decisions within a business. For example, a growing business will set increasing budgets for sales revenue and expenditure. This will encourage employees to aim for higher sales and facilitate this by allowing them access to increased resources.

- As a new business grows it is impossible for a single person to manage all a business's budgets effectively to ensure that costs are controlled and planned revenues earned. Responsibility for budgets can be given to other employees within the budgets – a process known as delegated budgets. A system of delegated budgets allows a number of people within the enterprise to share responsibility for making sure that financial plans are met.
- The process of budgeting encourages entrepreneurs to think carefully about the future prospects of the business and its ability to meet its objectives. Setting budgets makes entrepreneurs think about the factors at work in the market (such as trends in consumers' tastes) and how the business may respond to them. It also focuses attention on expected costs and how to minimise them.

Key terms

A **budget-holder** is responsible for the use and management of a particular budget.

Delegated budgets exist when firms give control over budgets to relatively junior employees.

Difficulties in setting budgets

Setting a budget is not always an easy exercise, especially for a newly established business. Here are some of the reasons:

- **It may be difficult to forecast sales accurately**. Entrepreneurs may find it difficult to estimate their sales when setting the sales revenue budget. For a new business this is a particular problem, as there are no trading records on which to base forecasts. It is always easier to set a budget if a previous year's figures can be amended – for example increasing sales by 5 per cent if the market is growing. A new business is highly dependent on its market research to forecast sales. If this research is inaccurate, sales forecasts will probably prove incorrect. Changes in tastes and fashions can occur rapidly, especially in the music and clothing industries, making accurate forecasts more difficult to achieve. Similarly, the pace of change in high technology industries, such as personal computers, makes the process of planning sales very tricky.
- **The danger of unexpected changes**. Forecasting events for the next year is fraught with difficulty. An entrepreneur may face an unforeseen rise in costs – for example, the 30 per cent rise in fuel costs during 2006. This can increase expenditure above budgets reducing their accuracy and effectiveness as a control mechanism.
- **Decisions by governments and other public bodies**. These can make it difficult to set accurate budgets. During the year to August 2007, the Bank of England raised interest rates from 4.50 per cent to 5.75 per cent. This is likely to have increased the costs of any business that had borrowed money. An unexpected increase in the rate of inflation can increase costs However, unexpected changes can also affect sales. a health scare, for example, such as that affecting the alleged safety of wireless internet connections, can have a substantial impact on sales revenue.
- **Using entrepreneurs' time effectively**. Setting budgets can be a time-consuming task, especially for a new business. There is a risk that the entrepreneur or manager may spend too long setting budgets and not devote sufficient time to other tasks. On the other hand, rushing the setting process may result in inaccurate budgets. This could prove counter-productive if sales revenue targets are unachievable and demotivate employees. Another risk is that expenditure budgets may fail to control costs effectively, damaging the financial performance of the enterprise.

Sources of information for budgets

The would-be entrepreneur faces a particular problem in compiling budgets – he or she has no previous trading records on which to base sales and expenditure figures. Clearly, if a business has traded for several years, much of the budgeting process can be based on the outcomes of previous financial years. Among other things, this enables entrepreneurs to predict trends in sales and seasonal effects with a greater chance of accuracy.

So, what sources of information are available to draw up the first budgets for a new business?

Similar businesses

It is possible that owners of similar small businesses will be prepared to offer advice and guidance so long as the new business does not pose a direct threat to them. A small business from a different geographical area might be prepared to discuss likely sales figures and associated costs, safe in the knowledge that the new business will not be a competitor. For example, someone considering opening a bed-and-breakfast business in one area of the country may find owners in other regions willing to offer support.

Professional organisations

Many types of businesses operate in markets where there are professional organisations who are able to offer advice on setting up in this line of business. This advice may extend to helping to forecast sales and associated costs. The website given below is an example of the type of advice that is available from professional organisations.

Web link

To see the help that is available on starting a bed-and-breakfast business, go to www.bandbowner.com

---

Banks and government organisations

As we saw in Chapter 14 on cash-flow forecasts, banks and government organisations such as Business Link can provide help with many aspects of drawing up budgets. Besides offering technical support on the process to be used, these organisations may have knowledge of local market conditions that

Business in Focus

Basic foodstuffs

In 2007, the price of many foodstuffs is expected to rise substantially. There are three main causes of the expected increases in the price of staple foods such as bread, milk and sugar.

The price of oil is rising (which affects the cost of nearly everything else: farmers face high costs to operate machinery and delivery costs rise as well).

Developing countries such as China and India are enjoying rapid rises in incomes. More affluent consumers in these countries are spending some of their extra income on food (including foods that they haven't traditionally eaten much of such as meat), meaning that demand for grain to feed livestock is increasing forcing up prices.

The increasing use of biofuels is another reason why the price of basic foods is rising. Land that was previously used to grow crops for food is now used to grow crops to make biofuels.

Give examples of small businesses that may experience problems as a result of the rise in price of basic foodstuffs.

These rises in prices are expected, so they do not represent a problem for small businesses when setting budgets'. Do you agree with this view? Justify your decison.

Zero budgeting

An alternative approach used by a number of firms when setting expenditure budgets is zero budgeting. Using this technique, each budget is set at zero at the start of the budget-setting process. Employees responsible for the areas covered by the budget have to bid for a budget and to justify any money they request.

Should start-up businesses draw up budgets?

It is difficult for start-up businesses to compile accurate budgets, partly because they do not have any financial records on which to base their forecasts. The danger is that they may make decisions based on budgets that are not accurate and which will ultimately be unhelpful to the business. For example, a pessimistic forecast of sales revenue may encourage an entrepreneur to sell at a lower price than necessary.

It is possible to argue that placing great reliance on budgets for a start-up business may be inappropriate if the business is not seeking to maximise profits. An entrepreneur who is, for example, seeking to supply a high-quality product may be better advised to focus on the results of primary market research.

Summary

The process of budgeting starts with an assessment of likely sales (and perhaps the use of market research) before forecasting expenditure. Drawing up financial plans can help entrepreneurs to assess the potential of their business ideas in terms of profits. It is a tricky process for a new business, but can help a business to obtain finance from banks and other investors.

Quick questions

1 Is the following statement true or false? 'Sales volume and average selling price are the key pieces of information needed to construct an expenditure budget'.
2 Drawing up budgets involves a series of activities. Place the four statements below in the correct order.
   - Draw up production budgets.
   - Construct sales budgets.
   - Establish the business's objectives.
   - Analyse markets and previous budgets to gather information.
3 Complete the following sentence by filling in the missing words. 'A .... budget is constructed first because it gives an indication of likely .... on raw materials, wages and other costs.'
4 Of what is the following a definition: 'a person responsible for the use and management of a particular budget'?

5 State **two** reasons why a newly created business should draw up sales and expenditure budgets.
6 Complete the following sentence by filling in the missing spaces. 'Entrepreneurs find it difficult to ...... sales revenue budgets because there are no .... on which to base forecasts.
7 List **three** reasons why a new bakery may be unable to forecast its sales accurately during its first year of trading.
8 Is the following statement true or false? 'An unexpected rise in the rate of interest may increase the costs of a small business and make its expenditure budget inaccurate.'
9 Of what is the following a definition? '.......... exist when budgets are automatically set at nil and budget-holders have to argue their case to receive any funds.'
10 Is the following statement true or false? 'Setting budgets can be more difficult for new businesses than for established businesses.'

Issues for analysis

- The reasons why an entrepreneur involved in a business start-up would draw up budgets and the benefits that might be derived from this process.
- The problems that an entrepreneur might encounter when preparing a first set of budgets for a start-up business.
- The sources of information that might be used for compiling budgets and whether or not they are likely to prove to be accurate.

Issues for evaluation

- Are other measures more useful to predict the performance of a new business, for example the results of primary market research?
- Are budgets so likely to be inaccurate for a new business that their use offers few benefits to entrepreneurs?

Analysis and evaluation questions

1 A & L Treasures Ltd is the brainchild of Alison Heaps and Louise Yates. The company supplies gifts for birthdays, Christmas and special occasions. The business has the objective of beautiful, high-quality gifts at a fair price while exceeding its customer's expectations. They also intend offering employees excellent working conditions. The two partners worked in insurance before starting their business. A & L Treasures operates a website as well as a shop in London. Alison and Louise expect to sell most gifts online at certain times of the year.

a Examine **two** problems that Alison and Louise may face when drawing up the first set of budgets for their new company. (8 marks)

b To what extent might Alison and Louise's profit budget provide the best evidence in judging the likely future performance of A & L Treasures? (15 marks)

2 Jonathan Parks founded his computer consultancy two months ago. He supplies his service to other small businesses and to people who use computers at home for leisure purposes. He specialises in troubleshooting and installing new computer systems and software. After providing computing services to friends the demand for his services was such that he realised he could start a business. Market research confirmed this. Jonathan has reached agreement with suppliers and already has sufficient stock on hand to meet his customers' needs.

a Analyse the possible sources of information that Jonathan might use to draw up his expenditure budget. (8 marks)

b Jonathan expects to face some difficulties in drawing up his budgets for his first year of trading. Discuss whether this means that the budgetary process will be of no benefit to him. (15 marks)

Assessment

Case study

Debbie Marsh plans to transform her roadside stall selling soft fruit and vegetables in the summer months into a year-round farm shop and café. Debbie and her husband own and run a farm near Malpas in Cheshire. Debbie's plan is to create a shop from an existing farm building, with the help of a bank loan and some financial support from the farm. The shop will sell home-made cakes and puddings, ready-made meals, chutneys and jams, as well as the home-grown soft fruits and fresh vegetables. Customers will also be able to buy eggs from the Marsh's free-range hens and rare-breed meat from Gloucester Old Spot pigs. Debbie hopes to benefit from the current trend towards healthy eating and buying local food. Debbie expects to sell her products at premium prices, even though she faces tough competition from other farm shops in the locality.

Debbie plans that her 30-seat café will offer freshly prepared hot and cold meals, soups, cakes and scones. It will be located in a landscaped garden with a children's playground. A nearby paddock with piglets and hens will help to keep children entertained while parents shop.

	June £	July £
Sales of fruit & vegetables	1976	2324
Sales of meat	2215	2456
Café sales	670	756
Total sales	4861	5536
Purchases of raw materials	2440	2750
Fuel costs	175	156
Wages	975	1095
Marketing & administration	2080	1250
Interest charges	375	435
Total costs	6045	5686
Profit/Loss	−1184	−150

Table 15.2 Debbie's first budget

Questions

(30 marks, 40 minutes)

1 Use the following information to construct Debbie's sales, expenditure and profit budget for August. Sales of fruit and vegetables: £2,500, sales of meat and also café sales are 10 per cent higher than in July. Raw materials and wages are £3,000 and £1,200 respectively, while fuel costs are unchanged. Interest charges are the same as July and marketing and administration charges are £1,100. (7 marks)

2 Analyse two difficulties that Debbie may have encountered in drawing up her first budget. (8 marks)

3 Debbie's husband does not believe that Debbie needs to draw up budgets for her new business. To what extent do you agree with this view? (15 marks)

16 Assessing business start-ups

This is perhaps the most important stage of planning a business. All the work is complete – you have your idea, the market research has been conducted and analysed and the financial plans drawn up. Will it work? Well, it depends on what you are trying to achieve as an entrepreneur and how you regard risk. No business venture is bound to succeed. At this stage you are trying to assess whether the risk is such that you can go ahead with it.

What you need to know by the end of this chapter:
- the objectives that entrepreneurs may pursue when establishing businesses
- how to assess the strengths and weaknesses of a business plan
- the reasons why business start-ups can be risky
- the major reasons why start-up businesses fail.

Business objectives

There is a wide range of reasons why people start their own businesses. Table 16.1 below illustrates some of the key reasons identified in a 2005 survey of over 8,000 owners of newly established small businesses.

> **Key term**
> **Business objectives** are goals or targets pursued by businesses that shape the decision-making of entrepreneurs.

What do you think?

If you were to start your own business once you have completed your education, what would be your reasons? Do the statistics in Table 16.1 surprise you in any way?

Reason	All businesses	Businesses without employees	Businesses with employees
Independence, being own boss	28%	27%	32%
To make money	11%	10%	14%
To develop an idea	13%	13%	11%
To develop a hobby or skill	10%	11%	5%
To benefit the community	3%	4%	2%

Table 16.1 Major reasons for starting a business
(Source: Annual Survey of Small Businesses 2005, Institute of Employment Studies)

Having considered the reasons why people start their own business, it is possible to develop them into possible objectives when running a business.

- **To have greater control over your life**. The immediate appeal of starting a business for many people is not to be answerable to a boss. The idea of independence at work is very appealing. Entrepreneurs like to be able to take time off when it suits them and to be able to make their own decisions, rather than having to act on the instructions of a line manager.

  Entrepreneurs who start a business with this objective may engage in 'satisficing'. This means that the entrepreneur does not aim to gain the highest possible sales or profits but to generate sufficient income for a reasonable standard of living. Satisficing allows an entrepreneur to enjoy leisure time and activities.

- **To develop an idea**. Many entrepreneurs have an idea for a product which they are convinced will be a winner and set out to develop this idea into a commercial product. Developing an idea is the basis for a viable business if there is sufficient demand for the product and if it is produced at a price that customers will be willing to pay.

Figure 16.1 Levi Roots with his sauce

The BBC television series Dragons' Den has featured many such people. One of the most memorable contestants was the charismatic Rastafarian singer Levi Roots who developed 'Reggae Reggae Sauce'. This sauce is designed to complement chicken dishes and is premium priced at £4.50 per bottle. Despite the pricing policy (or maybe because of it) Levi's business has proved successful. Having gained financial backing from venture capitalists following his appearance on Dragons' Den, his business had sold over 500,000 bottles of his sauce by mid-2007, and won a contract to supply Sainsbury's.

Web link

You can discover more about Levi's business at www.reggaereggaesauce.com

- **Maximising profits**. It is perhaps surprising that making money does not appear to be the most popular reason for starting a business and therefore that this is not the major objective of most entrepreneurs. However, some entrepreneurs do see themselves as becoming very wealthy and following in the footsteps of businessmen such as James Dyson and Richard Branson. To maximise the long-term profits of the enterprise, business growth is essential. In the short term, profits may not be as high as possible. For example, prices may need to be lowered to achieve higher sales or costly advertising campaigns may be used to enter new markets. The long-term intention, however, is to generate maximum profits.

- **To benefit the community**. Some enterprises are established to help others in the community rather than to make money. Usually, such businesses aim to support disadvantaged people (people who are poor or ill), for example – or to improve or protect the environment in some way. These are sometimes referred to as social enterprises. Social enterprises are businesses with a social purpose working in the UK or internationally to deliver lasting social and environmental change. Well-known social enterprises include Cafédirect, The Big Issue, the Eden Project in Cornwall and Jamie Oliver's Fifteen. However, there are many other social enterprises operating in a wide range of industries, from farmers' markets and recycling companies to transport providers and childcare.

HICEC

The Highlands and Islands Community Energy Company (HICEC) is a 'non-profit' business. It provides free advice and funds for renewable energy projects developed by community groups to benefit their community. The company is based in the Highlands and Islands of Scotland. It offers support from the earliest stage of a renewable energy project idea through to helping to ensure it is running properly once completed.

It has a voluntary board of directors appointed for their specialist knowledge and involvement in renewable energy and community development. The company was established in 2004 and currently has 11 employees.

One of HICEC's recent projects was at Alness. It supported the Alness Golf Club in installing a 6 kilowatt wind generator to reduce the Club's energy bills. The HICEC provided a grant of £12,000 to finance the project. As a result of this project the Club will become carbon neutral. Alan Black, Captain of Alness Golf Club, said: 'Our turbine has attracted considerable interest from golf clubs, both local and as far afield as Ireland. This system enables us to assist with heating the clubhouse in the winter and powers the club's electric caddy carts in the summer.'

(Source: Adapted from Community Energy News www.hie.co.uk/HICEC/CE_news_JAN07%20.pdf)

Assessing the strengths and weaknesses of a business plan

Making a judgement on the strengths and weaknesses of a business plan or idea obviously depends upon the precise nature of the business. Research has shown that one of the most important elements in the success (or failure) of a retail business is its location. In contrast, this is unimportant for an online business. However, a number of vital and common elements of a plan can be identified. These can be presented as a series of questions that any potential investor would ask.

- **Is there a demand for this product?** This is probably the most fundamental issue in assessing a business plan. Many entrepreneurs have an idea for a product that they expect to sell, only to find

that what they thought was a unique and imaginative idea is not as popular as expected. Market research can provide evidence of whether demand may exist. Primary research is likely to provide more accurate and reliable evidence as it should be up to date and focus on the precise product in question. If research is insufficient in scope, not up to date or lacking in any other way this might be a reason to doubt the viability of the enterprise. Anyone assessing a business plan should look behind sales forecasts to discover and make judgements about the reliability of the data.

- **What is the competition?** There are several questions that entrepreneurs and potential investors need to ask about the competition. First, is there competition? It is unusual for an entrepreneur to come up with an idea for which no competition exists and, even if it doesn't at the outset, it will if the product is successful. For example, other firms may produce rival products if Levi Roots' 'Reggae, Reggae Sauce' continues to sell in large quantities. In these circumstances the strength of the business plan may depend upon the existence of a watertight patent or other protection for a business idea. In the 2005 survey of small and medium sized businesses, over 20 per cent of respondents said that competition was the major hurdle to success.

> **Key term**
> **Insolvency** – a business is insolvent if it doesn't have enough assets to pay its debts as they fall due. An individual is insolvent if he or she is unable to discharge his or her debts as they fall due.

- **Has the business planned its cash flow management?** For most new businesses, cash flow is a critical issue. Shortages of cash in the early stages of managing a business may mean that the business is unable to pay its debts on time and this may result in insolvency. The first line of evidence of cash flow as a strength of a business plan is the existence of a cash-flow forecast. Further investigation should reveal whether this has been carefully researched and whether inflows reflect expected sales and credit terms.

- **What is the experience of the entrepreneur?** If you read the biographies of the entrepreneurs that appear throughout this book, you will realise that few of them enjoyed instant success. Usually, successful entrepreneurs have learned a lot from previous and unsuccessful attempts at starting a business. So an entrepreneur's CV can be highly revealing when assessing the strengths and weaknesses of a business plan. In the case of less experienced entrepreneurs, it may be important to discover what advice, if any, they have sought in the planning of their business.

- **Will it make a profit?** Although not all businesses set out with the objective of making a profit, this is an important objective for most enterprises. Many businesses take time to break even and to move into profitability. A business plan that suggests immediate and large profits may be inaccurate but, one that fails to forecast a profit for the foreseeable future will also be unattractive to investors, suppliers and potential employees. Profits budgets will provide evidence of the entrepreneur's expectations but, as with all financial plans, it is crucial to make some assessment of the sources used to compile the forecasts.

Overall, a business plan has to 'fit together'. The elements should relate to one another and tell a consistent story – and this is particularly true of the financial planning element of the plan. So, for example, the market research data should be reflected in the sales figures and the cash inflows and the expenditure budget should reflect the level of sales. Experienced professionals looking at an entrepreneur's business plan will scrutinise such details carefully.

Why business start-ups can be risky

From an entrepreneur's point of view, risk is the possibility of encountering misfortune that may threaten the survival of the business. The risks for a business start-up come from two main sources:

- financial risks
- operating risks.

Real-life Business

Jamie Oliver is credited by some writers with making cooking cool. However, his talents extend beyond the kitchen. Jamie was born in 1975 into an entrepreneurial and catering family. His family run a successful pub and restaurant in Essex.

Jamie is well known for his campaign against the use of processed and unhealthy ingredients in school dinners. By the age of 16, Jamie knew he wanted to be a chef, so he attended Westminster Catering College, followed by a period of study in France, before returning to London to work. He spent valuable time at the River Café where he learnt to create the fresh and simple food which has become his signature.

This led him into filming 'The Naked Chef': by 2007 he had filmed eight series of this programme. This popular series resulted in publishers showing great interest and by 2007 Jamie had eight books to his name.

In 2002 Jamie combined his entrepreneurial flair and willingness to take a financial risk with his culinary talents. He created the Fifteen Foundation – a restaurant which was also a social enterprise. The restaurant (with branches in London, Cornwall, Melbourne and Amsterdam) offers top-class food while providing professional training for youngsters from disadvantaged backgrounds. The launching of

Figure 16.2 Jamie Oliver

this enterprise required considerable finance by Jamie. It has since become a commercial and social success.

Web link

To find out more about Jamie Oliver's social enterprise business 'Fifteen' visit www.fifteen.net

Financial risks

We have seen earlier in this chapter and also in the chapter on cash flow that shortages of cash can pose a serious threat to a business's continued operations. Cash flow poses a particular risk for a business start-up because they are frequently unable to negotiate credit terms with suppliers meaning they have to pay for materials and services on ordering or delivery. At the same time a new enterprise may have to offer trade credit as a marketing tool to attract customers away from rivals. The result is that cash outflows may occur before inflows giving the potential for liquidity problems.

A start-up business may not have significant financial resources in the form of savings or access to external sources of finance such as overdrafts. This reduces the ability of a new business to survive a poor trading period. An established business, with a successful trading history, may be able to persuade a bank to lend it money, or suppliers to delay payment. This is less likely to be an option for a start-up business. In the 2005 Annual Survey of Small Businesses, over 28 per cent of entrepreneurs said that obtaining finance was a problem.

Business start-ups face other financial risks too. Some new businesses may borrow large sums of money to finance the purchase of important assets such as property or vehicles, or to pay for marketing campaigns to raise awareness of their products. Over time they may experience problems in repaying high levels of debt – especially if sales are below expectations. This can become a particular problem when interest rates are rising.

Operating risks

A start-up business does not have an established list of clients from whom it can be reasonably certain that it will receive orders, so future sales are more difficult to predict with any degree of accuracy. If the business fails to reach the level of sales that it has forecast, it may encounter cash problems that could threaten its future.

A start-up business is at risk because of the potential reactions of competitors. They may respond to the emergence of a start-up business by reducing prices and/or engaging in advertising campaigns. These actions will be designed to drive up the new enterprise's costs and to reduce its revenues by making it more difficult to acquire customers. Price reductions by competitors can be a particularly

effective weapon if consumer's demand is particularly sensitive to prices.

> **Key term**
> **Capacity** is the maximum output a business can produce when using all its resources to their maximum extent.

A further operational source of risk to a start-up business is the extreme under-utilisation of its capacity. A new business may incur the costs of providing a large amount of capacity in the expectation of rising sales over time. However, in the short term, the business has to bear the costs of such capacity levels while its sales revenues are low. If sales do not increase in line with expectations, it may find that its costs are excessive. For example, an entrepreneur opening a new restaurant has to pay rent and rates on the property, wages to cooking and waiting staff and other costs such as marketing. If only a few of the restaurant's tables are occupied each evening, cash-flow problems might mean that the business's future is in jeopardy.

Why start-up businesses fail

There is a close relationship between the factors that make new businesses risky propositions and the reasons why they fail. The failure of a small enterprise is a common event in the UK. The government has stressed official figures which show that there were 4.3 million businesses employing 250 or fewer people in the UK in 2005, compared with only 3.7 million in 1997.

However, almost half of all businesses that started during the 12-month period between 2001 and 2002 did not survive until 2005, according to a survey of its business banking customers by Barclays Bank. The Bank has tracked the closure rates of its business accounts over the past 13 years and found that about 12 per cent of year-old businesses have disappeared six months later. The annual rate of closure levels out after a business has survived for five years, dropping to 6 per cent during the seventh year of trading.

What do you think?

Why might the rate of survival for start-up businesses have improved in recent years?

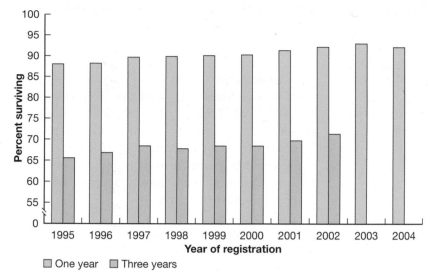

Figure 16.3 The percentage of enterprises surviving one year and three years after registration, UK, 1995–2004
(Source: DTI Small Business Service, taken from 'Survival rates of VAT-registered enterprises, 1995–2004: Key results', URN 09/963, published Feb 2007, Chart 4)

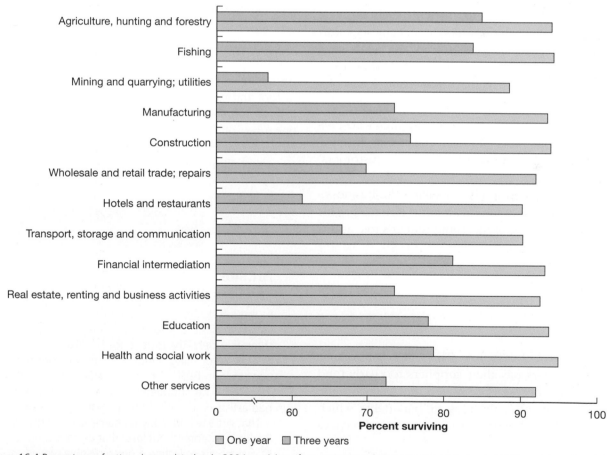

Figure 16.4 Percentage of enterprises registering in 2004 surviving after one year and percentage registering in 2002 surviving after three years, UK industry sectors
(Source: DTI Small Business Service, taken from 'Survival rates of VAT-registered enterprises, 1995–2004: Key results', URN 07/963, published Feb 2007, Chart 1)

Reasons for business failure vary according to the type of business and the market in which it is operating.

It can be seen from Figure 16.4 that survival rates vary according to the sector of the economy in which the business operates. Hotels and restaurants appear to have a high rate of failure after three years, with about 38 per cent not surviving this period. In contrast, businesses established in the fields of agriculture, forestry and fishing appear more secure. In part, this may be because more people establish small hotels and restaurants and that they are more vulnerable to changes in tastes and fashions; and it also likely to be affected by trends such as cheaper air travel.

However, a number of key reasons exist that can contribute to the failure of business start-ups, irrespective of the sector of the economy in which they operate. These include the following.

Poor management

The UK Insolvency Helpline cites 'poor management' as the prime reason for the failure of a business. This is more likely in the case of a start-up business, where it is likely that the entrepreneur will have limited experience of management. One issue for new managers is that they do not always appreciate the need to bring in experts to help when necessary. Bringing in people who are experts in fields such as sales, finance and technical innovation at an early stage can make the difference between success and failure for a start-up business. There are a number of other manifestations of poor management in the early stages of a new business, including:

- relying too much on a single supplier who fails to deliver on time. This can mean that the new business is unable to meet its own customers' needs promptly.
- not focusing sufficiently on selling the business's good or service in the first months of trading. This is a vital element of the entrepreneur's role at this stage of the enterprise's life.

Financial problems

This is another crucial reason for the failure of start-up businesses. Terminal financial problems take a number of forms:

- Poor control of cash flow. This can occur because entrepreneurs pay their suppliers too early (and before it is necessary), buy too much stock in the expectation of high sales or bad debts which occur when customers receive goods and services but do not pay for them.
- Failure to pay taxes such as VAT. The fines for not paying business taxes promptly can rapidly wipe out the profits of a small business.
- Overspending. Spending on unnecessary luxuries such as expensive office furniture or luxury cars can contribute to suffering heavy outflows of cash and failure to generate profits.

- Loss of financial support. If an investor pulls out of a start-up business, it may face insurmountable financial difficulties.

Lack of demand

A start-up business might find that its sales are substantially lower than it forecast, for a number of reasons. One possibility is that its market research was insufficient or incomplete and suggested that sales would be higher than expected. Other reasons for low sales include changing tastes and fashions or competitors reducing prices.

External shocks

Small and newly established businesses are particularly vulnerable to unexpected external events. External shocks can take a number of forms. They include unexpected rises in costs (for example, energy costs rose substantially in 2006 and again in 2007) or the emergence of new competitors or products which can result in a slump in sales. Other types of external shocks can also affect demand for a start-up business's products. Many small hotels and restaurants suffered badly as a result of the outbreak of foot and mouth disease in 2001. As a consequence a large number of new businesses failed, primarily because of unexpectedly low sales revenues. Government figures put the cost to the tourist industry at £6 billion.

Business in Focus

Art Site

Art Site, an online business selling paintings and sculptures, lasted only nine months before it collapsed in debt. But for Peter Rankin, one of the three founders, the experience felt like years.

'The awful thing about it is that lots of other people get hurt,' he says. 'The family gets involved. The suppliers are owed money. We had artists who took it very personally with us.'

That Art Site had many fundamental failings, Mr Rankin now admits, not least that its basic premise of making art collecting more accessible proved as flawed as so many other dotcom failures.

The final nail in the coffin came when the company spent thousands of pounds on a show based on the promise of money from an investor. The cheque was cashed but promptly bounced, leaving the Art Site seriously in the red.

'He led us up the garden path. I vowed I would never do this again without a financial person who I trusted 100 per cent,' says Mr Rankin.

Peter Rankin had to sell his house to clear the debts and it was six months before he felt capable of doing anything new, let alone take another job.

(Source: FT.com at: www.ft.com/cms/s/c787057c-5602-11da-b04f-00000e25118c,dwp_uuid=4f86d546-8cf5-11da-9daf-0000779e2340.html 15th November, 2005)

Summary

Entrepreneurs start businesses with a range of objectives, and a surprising proportion are not financial. In contrast, it is financial problems that pose the major risk to a business and lead to the failure of many new enterprises. However, poor management also contributes to the closure of many new businesses.

Quick questions

1 Is the following statement true or false? 'The major objective for entrepreneurs in the UK when starting a business is to make money.'
2 Complete the following sentence by filling in the missing spaces. 'For many people, the immediate appeal of starting a business is not to be .... to a boss.'
3 What is meant by the term 'satisficing'?
4 Is the following statement true or false? 'Developing an idea is the basis for a viable business if there is sufficient demand for the product and if it is produced at a price that customers will be willing to pay.'
5 What are the similarities between the following enterprises: Cafédirect, The Big Issue and Fifteen?
6 Which of the following is not likely to be an important issue in assessing a business plan?
a Has the business planned its cash flow management?
b What is the competition for the business?
c What experience does the entrepreneur have?
d Will the entrepreneur engage in satisficing?

7 Distinguish, with examples, between financial risks and operating risks.
8 Is the following statement true or false? 'Approximately 50 per cent of business start-ups do not survive for three years.'
9 State two ways in which poor management might lead to the failure of a start-up business.
10 Give two examples of external shocks which may result in the failure of newly established businesses.

Issues for analysis

- Identifying key strengths and weaknesses of a specific business plan, taking into account its objectives and market.
- The objectives of establishing a business can affect the reasons for failure.
- Examining the consequences of entrepreneur's actions for the survival of the business.

Issues for evaluation

- What are the key factors that determine the degree of risk in a specific business venture?
- What is (or are) the most important reason(s) for the success or failure of a start-up business?

Analysis and evaluation questions

1 Sam's business idea is to set up as a visiting massage therapist. She plans to visit people in their own homes and to offer massages and aromatherapy. Sam has conducted market research among friends and family and forecasts consistent sales figures. She has low fixed costs and forecasts positive cash flows from the outset of trading. Sam expects the business to offer sufficient profits in the first year to give a 30 per cent return on capital. She has no experience of running a business but considerable knowledge of massage and aromatherapy.

a Examine the potential strengths of Sam's business idea. (8 marks)
b Discuss the factors that may determine whether or not Sam's business will survive the first three years of trading. (15 marks)

2 Earlier in this chapter we encountered Jamie Oliver's social business 'Fifteen'. Before answering the questions below find out more about this business by visiting www.fifteen.net.

a Analyse why Jamie Oliver might have established this business. (8 marks)

b To what extent do you consider 'Fifteen' to be a risky business start up? (15 marks)

Assessment

Case study

Perfect Pizza is one of the UK's leading pizza delivery and takeaway businesses, with well over 110 stores throughout the country. Since 1982, the company has grown nationally and plans to add a further 20 franchised stores to its network by the end of fiscal 2007/08. The expansion will not stop there as over 100 new stores are in the pipeline for the next five years.

Owner Manji Bagri says: 'I have a background in finance and operating independent fast-food outlets. However, I felt it was time to do something new. I wanted to work for myself, but with the help of a franchisor. I have operated a franchise previously and appreciate its benefits and, having looked at the product and brand of Perfect Pizza, I decided to take this route.

The best thing about franchising is that it provides the opportunity to duplicate a tried and tested business model. With the right amount of enthusiasm and drive it can succeed. You pay to be part of a strong brand – one that is well known throughout the UK and is synonymous with quality. Independent pizza delivery operators couldn't afford the high level of marketing expenditure.

Perfect Pizza offers an excellent back up service in terms of training, financial advice, marketing and product development. Lots of people open up pizza businesses but only a small number succeed. There is a high turnover of staff in the pizza delivery business, so it can be tough to find good people, but we have a very friendly approach to our employees and look after them well – as a result we tend to hold onto our staff.'

(Source: Adapted from www.perfectpizza.co.uk)

Web link

You can find out more about Perfect Pizza at www.perfectpizza.co.uk

Questions

(30 marks, 40 minutes)

1 Explain Manji's likely objectives in taking up a Perfect Pizza franchise. (6 marks)

2 Analyse the strengths that a bank may look for in Manji Bagri's business plan before agreeing to a loan to support the start-up business. (9 marks)

3 To what extent do you agree with the view that by opting to run a Perfect Pizza franchise Manji Bagri's business was certain to succeed? (15 marks)

17 Unit One Assessment

Case study

Babies with attitude

Figure 17.1 A baby with attitude

Eddy Choi was delighted when he heard he was about to become a father. When the baby was born, Eddy rushed to the shops to buy clothes for his little boy. However, when he got there Eddy was disappointed with the choices available – everything looked pretty boring (and very blue). He wanted to buy his boy clothes with a 'bit more attitude and style'.

Eddy felt there was a gap in the market for more exciting baby clothes. After looking around online, and doing some other secondary market research, Eddy was sure he had found a good business opportunity. His findings showed the market size was big and market growth looked appealing. After much debate and discussion with his wife (who said she thought he was mad) Eddy eventually decided he was going to start up his own baby clothing business. Before making the final decision he asked 20

friends what they thought of his idea and they were very positive indeed.

So last month Eddy decided that he would give up his job as a clothes shop manager and start his own baby clothes line called 'Ready to Rumble'. His best friend Jazz is going to help him design the clothes in his free time. (Jazz is very creative and has lots of great ideas. His main job is guitarist with a band that is often touring.)

They will use other firms to produce the clothes for them. Eddy has already spoken to others in the industry and made useful contacts. He has approached Mothercare, a major retailer of baby clothes, with some initial drawings but Mothercare felt the clothes would not fit in with their other lines. He was told to return in a year or so when his products had got some track record in terms of sales. However, Eddy has found two independent shops that are willing to take some of his clothes for a trial period. Jazz, meanwhile, is setting up a website so they can sell direct.

Eddy and Jazz have decided to form a partnership because they think a company sounds too complicated and unnecessary. As they have known each other for years, they do not feel that any formal agreement is necessary. They grew up together and rarely argued.

Eddy and Jazz have decided to trademark their clothes and the firm's logo. To get the business going, they will put in £20,000 each (all of their savings) and they have approached the bank with a business plan for a loan for another £40,000. This should give them all they need to get the logo designed professionally, to start advertising the business on the internet and get some clothes produced.

The plan is to buy clothes on average for £3; other variable costs are estimated to be £2 per item. They will sell the clothes on average for £9 each. They are going to operate out of a small room in Jazz's flat which they will turn into an office if they can clear out all the guitar equipment. (They haven't asked Jazz's wife about this yet.) Eddy has no space at all at his house.

They will pay themselves relatively little to begin with and they estimate their annual overheads will be around £40,000 a year. From his chats with others in the business and his own experience, Eddy estimates they will sell 8,000 items in the first year but that this will grow by 20 per cent in Year 2 and a further 25 per cent in Year 3 as the brand becomes known. With good negotiating skills, Eddy think he can keep the variable costs the same for the first three years but overheads will probably grow by 10 per cent a year. Although the amounts of money involved are quite small, Eddy has already budgeted carefully for spending on different items. Eddy knows that businesses take time to establish themselves but both he and Jazz think this venture will only be worthwhile if they can make a profit by the end of the third year.

Case study questions

Section A : 20 marks. You are advised to spend no more than 20 minutes on this section.

a What is meant by the term 'profit'? (2 marks)

b What is meant by 'secondary market research'? (2 marks)

c State two items that should be in Eddy and Jazz's business plan. (2 marks)

d Calculate the profit Eddy and Jazz will make in the second year if their estimates are correct. (6 marks)

e Explain one possible benefit to Eddy and Jazz of budgeting. (4 marks)

f Explain one possible benefit to Eddy and Jazz of getting a trademark for the name of their new clothes label and their designs. (4 marks)

Section B: (40 marks)

a Analyse the factors that might determine the demand for Eddy and Jazz's baby clothes. (10 marks)

b To what extent do you think that Eddy and Jazz setting up as a partnership is a wise decision? (15 marks)

c If you were the bank manager, would you lend Eddy and Jazz the £40,000 they want? Justify your answer. (15 marks)

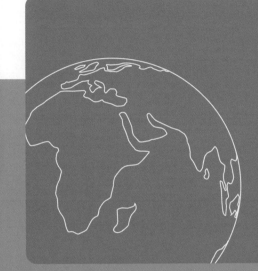

unit two

THE AQA STORY CONTINUED...

Unit 1 focuses on new businesses and the issues they face when starting up. Unit 2 focuses more on medium-sized organisations and the issues faced by managers when trying to make the business more successful. It examines businesses that are already established, analyses the issues that managers have to deal with when running an organisation and looks at how they can improve business performance.

Managers face decisions in all of the functional areas: marketing, operations, people and human resource management. In Unit 2 we consider how decisions in these areas can help a business to be more successful. For example:

- By recruiting and training more effectively, and motivating employees more successfully, the performance of staff may result in better customer service and more sales.
- By adapting the way that products are marketed, the sales of the product may be boosted and a decline in sales may be avoided.
- By improving the quality of products, there will be less waste and fewer mistakes; this again is likely to increase customer satisfaction and boost sales.
- By controlling the way money is used within the business, managers can help to ensure that resources are used appropriately and not wasted. Good management of finances can help to ensure that a business has sufficient cash, is generating satisfactory levels of profits and has the finance it needs to pursue new projects

At AS level, the businesses considered tend to be medium-sized enterprises operating within the UK, rather than more complex multinational organisations. At A2, we study bigger businesses and consider the international environment.

The Unit 2 examination

The examination is made up of two data response questions worth 40 marks each. It lasts 1 and a half hours. Unit 2 accounts for 60 per cent of the total marks at AS level.

The data items may be based on real businesses or may be fictional. Each item will have a number of questions, covering the different functional areas of marketing, finance, operations and human resources. An overview of the unit is shown below.

The relative weighting of the skills being assessed on the two units are shown below:

	Unit 1	Unit 2
	%	%
Content	35	27
Application	28	23
Analysis	20	28
Evaluation	18	22

As you can see, there are more marks on this paper for the higher level skills of analysis and evaluation, making Unit 2 more demanding than Unit 1. However, once you have studied Unit 1, your skills should continue to develop, putting you in a good position to get the most out of Unit 2.

18 Using budgets

In Chapter 15 we followed the process of preparing financial forecasts for revenue, expenditure and profits. This chapter picks up the story once trading has commenced and focuses on comparing actual figures with the forecasts – a monitoring process known as variance analysis. We shall see this is an important part of financial management.

What you need to know by the end of this chapter:

- how variances are calculated
- the ways in which variances are used to analyse budgets
- how variances can be used by businesses in the process of decision-making
- the benefits and drawbacks of using budgets.

Monitoring budgets

Setting budgets is only the first stage in the budgetary process. Once a business has planned its sales revenue and expenditure, it is essential to monitor the accuracy of these financial plans by comparing the budget figures with the actual figures resulting from the business's trading.

What do you think?

The owners and managers of many small businesses do not use budgets. Why don't they?

Budgets can also provide a wealth of information to help managers take decisions on how to improve the performance of the business:

- **Analysing budgeted and actual expenditure**. This provides information on how successful the business is at controlling its costs. As a business grows it is possible to judge the ability of different parts of a business to manage its expenditure against given targets. If one area of a business is regularly overspending its budgets, managers may take action to reduce expenditure and, by so doing, increase profitability. Relevant actions might include addressing issues such as poor motivation of employees, problems with quality or not using capacity fully. Of course, if a business, or part of a business, fails to meet expenditure budgets regularly it may be because the budgets are too low to be achievable.
- **Analysing sales revenue**. A business that fails to meet its sales revenue budgets for one or more of its products may need to consider why this is occurring. Prices may be too high when compared with those of competitors, the business may not be advertising sufficiently or not targeting the correct market segments or the quality

and/or design of the product may be inadequate. Good managers will use the information from analysing budgets to make decisions to improve the business's sales performance.

- **Analysing profits budgets**. Profits below budget are likely to be a cause of concern for most businesses. These can be caused by excess expenditure, by revenue falling short of expectations, or by a combination of these factors. This scenario may prompt managers to examine means of cutting expenditure as well as boosting sales revenue.

Variance analysis

Key terms

Variance analysis is the process of investigating any differences between forecast data and actual figures.

The process for monitoring budgets is known as variance analysis. A variance occurs when an actual figure for sales or expenditure differs from the budgeted figure. Actual sales and cost figures can be higher or lower than planned; similarly actual sales revenue figures may be higher or lower than budgets. The two categories of variance are shown in Table 18.1.

The process of calculating a variance is simple as shown in Table 18.2. It simply involves a comparison between the budgeted figure and the actual figure.

What do you think?

What might you do as the owner of a small business if your budgets suggest that the enterprise will make a small loss over the next financial year?

The business had forecast that its sales revenue would be £840,000. However, the actual figure was £790,000. In this case the variance (or difference) is £50,000. It is an adverse variance because it will result in the business's profits being lower than forecast, or its loss larger than forecast. In contrast the business's fuel costs are only £70,000 – £5,000 less than the budgeted figure. In this case this is a favourable variance because this will result in the business's profits being larger than forecast (or a smaller loss than budgeted).

Carrying out regular variance analysis can give a business advance notice that its financial plans are inaccurate. Variance analysis can be carried out each month and will show before the end of the financial year that the firm's finances are not as planned. This allows the business to take action to reduce expenditure or increase revenue at an early stage. Figure 18.1 summarises the range of actions that businesses may take in response to adverse and favourable variances.

Favourable variances	Adverse variances
A favourable variance exists when the difference between the actual and budgeted figures will result in the business enjoying higher profits than shown in the budget.	An adverse variance occurs when the difference between the figures in the budget and the actual figures will lead to the firm's profits being lower than planned.
Examples of favourable variances include: • actual wages less than budgeted wages • budgeted sales revenue lower than actual sales revenue • expenditure on fuel is less than the budgeted figure	Examples of adverse variances include: • sales revenue below the budgeted figure • actual raw material costs exceeding the figure planned in the budget • overheads turn out to be higher than in the budget
Possible causes of favourable variances: • wage rises lower than expected • economic boom leads to higher than expected sales • rising value of pound makes imported raw materials cheaper	Possible causes of adverse variances: • competitors introduce new products winning extra sales • government increases business rates by unexpected amount • fuel prices increase as price of oil rises

Table 18.1 **The two categories of variance**

Revenue/cost	Budget figure (£)	Actual figure (£)	Variance
Sales revenue	840,000	790,000	£50,000 – adverse
Fuel costs	75,000	70,000	£5,000 – favourable
Raw material costs	245,000	265,000	£20,000 – adverse
Labour costs	115,000	112,000	£3,000 – favourable

Table 18.2 Calculating variances

Firms may also need to respond to favourable variances. Production costs which are lower than planned may be regarded as beneficial. But sales revenue which is greater than anticipated might be caused by the firm selling more products than planned. In these circumstances, the business might not have sufficient supplies to meet future customer requirements. This could result in the loss of long-established customers and should be avoided.

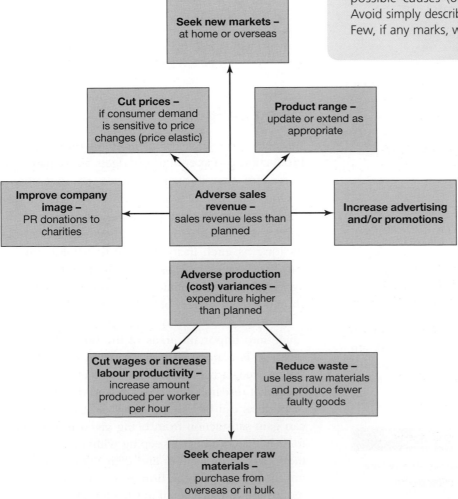

Figure 18.1 Responding to adverse variances

Real-life Business

The White Company

Founded in 1994 by Christian Rucker, The White Company specialises in supplying a wide range of stylish home accessories and clothing, principally in the colour white. Initially, the company sold its products by mail-order and became one of the UK's fastest growing retailers selling 2,500 different products. In 2003, The White Company opened its first retail store in Sloane Square in London. By 2007 the company was operating 17 retail outlets from Guildford in the south, to Edinburgh in the north.

Figure 18.2 Christian Rucker

Drawing up budgets for the new retail outlets has proved to be challenging for the managers at The White Company. The budget for sales revenue for the company's shops has been increased 20 per cent for the next financial year. In 2005 the company's retail sales exceeded the budget by 30 per cent.

Question:

Is it possible that the managers at The White Company gain little benefit from using budgets because the company's sales are growing so quickly?

Web link

You can find out more about The White Company at www.thewhitecompany.com

Delegated budgets

In recent years, firms have given control of budgets to individuals and teams at all levels within the business. This has been accompanied by a reduction in the number of managers and an attempt to give workers more control over their working lives. Allowing them to take some decisions relating to finance through delegated budgets is an important part of this. The intentions behind these changes are to:

- reduce the number of managers, cutting wage costs
- motivate employees by giving them more diverse and responsible jobs
- help encourage employees at all levels to play a part in decision-making and problem-solving.

Many companies have made use of delegated budgets in an attempt to improve their performance. Their use has also been extended to organisations in the public sector, for example hospitals, schools and colleges.

Web link

Many of the UK's banks offer advice on setting and using budgets. Lloyds TSB is no exception. Visit the link below to refresh your memory of setting budgets as well as about monitoring them. www.lloydstsbbusiness.com/support/businessguides/budget.asp

Using budgets

Budgets are used to control finances effectively. Production or expenditure budgets allow managers to ensure that a business does not overspend. Senior managers receive their own budgets and can allocate them between the various parts of the department or area for which they are responsible. As long as each individual budget-holder makes sure that she or he does not spend more than the agreed figure, the businesses overall expenditure should remain under control.

Budgets allow senior managers to direct extra funds into important areas of the business. So, if a business is concerned that its product range is not selling well, it may increase its budgets in the areas of market research, and research and development.

Budgets can be used to motivate staff. Employees can gain satisfaction from being given responsibility for a budget, and from keeping within it. As a result, their level of motivation and their performance may improve, benefiting the firm as a whole. (We look at motivation in more detail in Chapter 23.).

Sales revenue budgets can also be used as targets for employees. Employees may be motivated to improve their performance by the existence of targets in the forms of sales revenue budgets. If successful this can increase the business's revenue and possibly its profitability.

The disadvantages of budgets

If a business intends that some of its employees should manage budgets (known as delegating budgets), then training will be required. The cost of the training could be substantial, depending on the skills of the workforce. Furthermore, there could be teething problems in the forms of errors or delays as employees adjust to the new roles and responsibilities.

Allocating budgets fairly and in the best interests of the business is difficult. Some managers may be skilled at negotiating large budgets for the areas for which they are responsible. This might be at the expense of more worthy areas. So, for example, a manager responsible for the sales force may receive a large budget allocation, while insufficient funds are given to the manager responsible for production.

Budgets normally relate to the current financial year only. So, managers might take a decision to keep within the current budget which is not actually in the longer-term interest of the business. For example, a decision to reduce the size of a workforce for budgetary reasons might result in competitors gaining more of the market over the next few years because those businesses are able to supply sufficient quantities of the good or service.

Summary

After reading this chapter you should know how managers calculate variances and the meaning of the results. Variances can be positive or adverse and managers should take appropriate actions in response to these variances. The process of setting budgets offers a number of advantages to businesses, especially if the process is delegated to junior employees within the organisation. However, there are a number of drawbacks to using budgets, such as the cost of training employees to set and monitor budgets.

Quick questions

1 Distinguish between a sales revenue budget and an expenditure budget.

2 State *two* reasons why a manager might analyse an expenditure budget.

3 State *two* reasons why a sales revenue budget might be higher than forecast.

4 Of what is the following a definition: 'The process of investigating any differences between forecast data and actual figures'?

5 Complete the following sentence by filling in the missing word. 'An .... variance exists when the difference between the actual and budget figures will lead to a firm's profits being lower than expected.'

6 Polly Ltd's budgets for the next financial year are as follows. Total expenditure – £945,000, sales revenue – £1,200,000. Its actual figures were Total expenditure – £956,000, sales revenue – £1,250 000. Calculate the variances for total expenditure, sales revenue and profits. In each case state whether the variance is adverse or favourable.

7 Pip & Sons Ltd sales revenue for the last financial year was £3,500,000. The company's sales revenue was 10 per cent less than expected. Calculate the variance and state whether it was adverse or favourable.

8 Which one of the following is an adverse variance?

a sales revenue higher than forecast

b expenditure on wages lower than forecast

c raw material costs higher than stated in the budget

d fuel costs lower than stated in the forecast.

9 Is the following statement true or false? 'Managers do not need to take any action if variances are favourable.'

10 State one reason why using budgets throughout a business might improve its financial performance.

Issues for analysis

- Identifying adverse and favourable variances and explaining the possible causes of these variances.
- Suggesting actions managers might take in response to adverse or favourable variances.
- The advantages and disadvantages of using budgets in specific circumstances.

Issues for evaluation

- How valuable is variance analysis to a start-up business?
- To what extent do the results of variance analysis represent a problem for a business?
- Do the benefits of delegating budgets outweigh the disadvantages of doing so?

Analysis and evaluation questions

1 Hannah Marshall is one of Britain's emerging talents in the field of dress design. Hannah launched her debut collection of twelve 'darkly minimalist' dresses, entitled 'Quiet Noise', to an international audience in February 2007.

Figure 18.3 Hannah Marshall designs

Hannah has said in interviews that she needs to develop a sound knowledge of business finance to complement her creativity. She has had to draw up business plans in order to gain financial support from creative funding bodies such as NESTA. Hannah is seeking further investment in her business.

a Examine the benefits that Hannah might receive from drawing up budgets for her business. (8 marks)

b Discuss whether or not Hannah Marshall would have benefit from conducting variance analysis on her costs and sales in the months following the launch of her debut collection. (15 marks)

Web link

You can find out more about the progress of Hannah's business at www.hannahmarshall.com

2 John Arlott has just conducted variance analysis after the first month of trading for his hotel. John opened his south Devon hotel in July and has been very impressed by its success. Selected elements from his variance analysis for the hotel's first month are shown below.

Item	Budget	Actual	Variance
Sales revenue	7 275	11 005	3 730 F
Marketing	1 250	2 000	750 A
Wages	2 400	2 754	354 A
Supplies of food & drink	1 046	1 340	294 A
Profit	(1 550)	950	2 500 F

Table 18.3 John Arlott's variance analysis

Although John has some experience in managing businesses, this is his first attempt at managing a hotel. He trusted to instinct rather than market research when planning the finances of his new enterprise, although he has marketed the business heavily. He is, however, a little concerned that most of his expenditure budgets have recorded adverse variances.

a Analyse possible reasons why John's sales revenue variance was favourable for the first month of trading. (8 marks)

b One of John's relatives has decided to invest in the hotel. Discuss whether or not John's variance analysis supports this decision. (15 marks)

Assessment

Case study

In Chapter 15 we met Debbie Marsh, who was in the process of opening a farm shop and café on the family farm near Malpas in Cheshire. The shop sells fruit and vegetables as well as eggs and meat from the farm. Debbie expected to benefit from the current trend towards healthy eating and buying local food. After the first two months' trading, Debbie was able to compare her actual trading figures with the budgets she had drawn up.

Questions

(30 marks, 40 minutes)

1 Complete Debbie's variance analysis by filling in the blank spaces in the table below. (7 marks)
2 Examine *two* possible reasons why Debbie's Sales revenue budget might have shown an adverse variance in June. (8 marks)
3 Debbie said she was 'very, very disappointed' with the financial performance of her new business during its first two months of trading. To what extent do you agree with her? (15 marks)

	JUNE			JULY		
	Budget £	Actual £	Variance £	Budget £	Actual £	Variance £
Sales of fruit & vegetables	1976	1780	196 A	2324	2320	
Sales of meat	2215	2155	60 A	2456	2500	44 F
Sales of cakes and pies	670	790	120 F	756	780	24 F
Total sales	4861	4725	136 A	5536	5600	
Purchases of raw materials	2440	2220	220 F	2750	2790	
Fuel costs	175	175	0	156	169	13 A
Wages	975	950	25 F	1095	1050	
Marketing & administration	2080	2160	80 A	1250	1300	
Interest charges	375	375	0	435	430	5F
Total costs	6045	5880	165 F	5686	5739	
Profit/Loss	−1184	−1155	29 F	−150	−139	

Table 18.4 **Debbie's variance analysis**

19 Improving cash flow

We saw in Chapter 14 that planning cash flow is an essential element of a successful business start-up. This chapter looks further at cash-flow management and considers issues that can occur in relation to cash flow once a business starts trading. Essential elements of cash-flow management at this stage of a business's life are identifying causes of cash-flow difficulties and proposing solutions appropriate to the circumstances.

What you need to know by the end of this chapter:
- the factors that can lead to businesses having cash-flow problems
- the actions that small and medium-sized businesses can take to improve their cash-flow position
- the ways in which the careful management of cash-flow can improve a business's performance.

Causes of cash-flow problems

Arguably the major cause of cash-flow problems is lack of planning. Many businesses, once established, do not forecast in this way and are thus at risk of unforeseen problems.

A number of other factors can contribute to cash flow difficulties:

- overtrading – this occurs when a business expands quickly without organising funds to finance the expansion. Rapid growth normally involves paying for labour and raw materials several months before receiving payment for the final product. If this occurs over a prolonged period, a business can face severe cash-flow problems.
- allowing too much trade credit – most businesses offer trade credit – allowing customers between 30 and 90 days to pay. This helps to win and keep customers. However, if a firm's trade credit policy is too generous, it may lead to cash-flow difficulties as cash inflows are delayed. In such a situation a business may find itself unable to pay its bills when they are due as it has not received payment from its customers.
- poor credit control – a firm's credit control department ensures that customers keep to agreed borrowing limits and pay on time. If this aspect of a business's operation becomes inefficient, cash inflows into the firm may be delayed. In some cases, a customer may not pay at all (this

is known as a 'bad debt'). In these circumstances it is highly likely that a firm will encounter problems with its cash flow.

Key terms
Trade credit is offered when purchasers are allowed a period of time (normally 60 or 90 days) to pay for products they have bought.

What do you think?

Is it inevitable that a new business will have cash-flow problems?

Monitoring cash flow

It would be foolish for businesses to imagine that their cash-flow forecasts will always prove to be accurate. A number of factors can lead to incorrect cash flow forecasts:

- inaccurate assumptions – people may make mistakes regarding the future levels of sales for the business, the prices they will receive for their products and especially the timescale within which customers will pay them. A firm's forecasts

Steve Marshall's cash-flow forecast – June	Budget	Actual
Cash in		
Savings & borrowings	75000	75000
Cash sales	5750	5230
Credit sales	0	0
Total cash inflow	**80750**	**80230**
Cash out		
Purchase of lease on shop	30000	29500
Purchase of books	59000	60000
Wages	1500	1450
Marketing costs	2500	2400
Other costs, e.g. rent	1500	1500
Total cash outflow	**94500**	**94850**
Net monthly cash flow	**–13750**	**–14620**
Opening balance	2000	2000
Closing balance	–11750	–12620

Table 19.1 Monitoring Steve Marshall's cash flow.

of the cash it will earn can, of course, be too low or too high. If a competitor suddenly increases prices, for example, this may lead to higher cash sales than expected.

- unexpected costs – prices of raw materials may increase without warning. The cost of labour may rise (for example, the introduction of the minimum wage). Similarly, machinery breakdowns can impose unanticipated pressures on a business's cash flow.
- inexperience – this is often the cause of poor quality cash-flow forecasting. Many people set up firms with relatively little experience of managing a business. Forecasting the amounts and timings of cash inflows and outflows accurately in this situation is very difficult.

In Chapter 14, we saw that Steve Marshall had drawn up a cash-flow forecast as part of his financial planning for the opening of his bookshop. The table above shows the actual cash movements that took place during his first month of trading in comparison with Steve's forecast. It is apparent that Steve's cash position is slightly worse than he forecast. He expected to have a closing balance of (£11,750) whereas it is (£12,620). This may mean that he needs to increase his overdraft above the amount he originally thought that he would need.

Entrepreneurs need to assess the significance of any unexpected figures when analysing forecast and actual cash figures. There are a number of possible causes when considering cash variances:

- it might be a one-off occurrence that will not happen again – such as a cancelled order (or an unexpectedly large one)
- it could be due to seasonal variations such as Christmas or the summer period – this can be important for certain types of businesses such as toy shops or garden centres
- more critically, it may be part of a continuing trend – whether sales are rising or falling steadily, there will be cash implications
- it could be self-correcting – a surge in demand followed by a slump, and in this case no action will be required.

Methods of improving cash flow

Identifying potential cash flow problems is only part of the solution. Businesses have to decide how they are going to improve their cash position. A number of techniques can be used to improve cash flow.

Improved control of working capital

Working capital is the finance available to the business for its day-to-day trading activities. Working capital is available to a business when its customers pay for the goods or services they have received. Working capital is used to pay wages, and for fuel and raw materials. There are a number of techniques set out below that a business may use to improve its working capital.

Negotiate improved terms for trade credit

Most firms receive some trade credit from their suppliers. This means they are given 30 or 60 days to pay for supplies. If a business can persuade suppliers who have previously been reluctant to offer trade credit to do so, it will improve its cash position. Remember, cash flow management is a matter of timing – delaying payments always helps. Another important move might be to extend existing trade credit agreements from, say, 30 to 60 days, or 60 to 90 days.

Offer less trade credit

Similarly, a business can help its cash-flow position by offering its customers less favourable terms for trade credit. This may require all customers to pay for products within 30 days, whereas in the past trade credit was for 60 days. However, this decision may result in a loss of customers as they move to competitors who offer more favourable credit terms.

Debt factoring

Debt factoring is a service offered by banks and other financial institutions. If businesses have sent out bills (also termed invoices) which have not yet been paid they can 'sell' these bills to gain cash immediately. Factoring debts in this way provides up to 80 per cent of the value of an invoice as an immediate cash advance. The financial institution then organises the payment of the invoice and makes a further payment to the business concerned. It is usual for the financial institution to retain about 5 per cent of the value of the invoice to cover their costs.

Many small firms believe that to lose up to 5 per cent of their earnings means that factoring is uneconomic – it can eliminate much of their profit margin. However, factoring does offer benefits:

- The immediate cash provided by the factor means that the firm is likely to have lower overdraft requirements and will pay less interest.
- Factoring means businesses receive the cash from their sales more quickly.

Debt factoring is generally used by small businesses. Businesses with a turnover above £1 million normally use an alternative technique (called invoice discounting) where the company retains the administration of the deal within the business. This way, its customers need not know that the company is using a debt factoring service. This can help a business to retain the confidence of its customers. The figure below illustrates the stages involved in debt factoring.

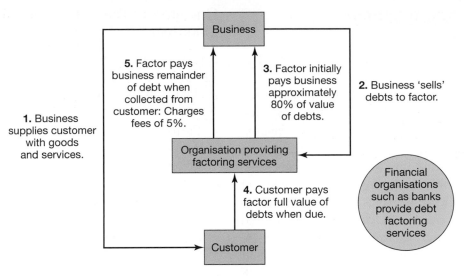

Figure 19.1 Debt factoring

Arrange short-term borrowing

The majority of businesses have an agreed overdraft with their bankers. An overdraft allows a business to borrow flexibly according to its needs up to an agreed limit. Overdrafts can be expensive, but are reasonably economical and flexible when a business only borrows a set amount for a short period. As an alternative, a business may decide on a short-term loan to provide an injection of cash into the business. A short-term loan is likely to have a lower rate of interest and the option to pay the loan back over two years or so may be attractive to a business that is short of cash.

> **Key terms**
> An **overdraft** is a flexible loan on which a business can draw as necessary up to some agreed limit.

> **Web link**
> We have already seen that Business Link is an important source of advice for entrepreneurs. It offers support to entrepreneurs in managing cash flow. One aspect of this support is case studies of businesses that have managed their cash effectively. One of these case studies can be seen at http://tinyurl.com/38xmr2

Sale and leaseback

This method of improving cash flow has been widely used by businesses over recent years. It entails a business selling a major asset – for example, a building – and then leasing it from the new owner. This provides a significant inflow of cash into the business, improving the cash position, but commits the firm to regular payments to lease the asset. In 2006, Austin Reed, the clothing retailer, sold a large building in Thirsk for £1.78 million. The company subsequently leased the property back from its buyer, while enjoying a boost to its cash position.

> ### Real-life Business
>
> **Laurence, Scott and Electromotors**
>
> The future of a Norfolk company was under threat in 2007 after it experienced cash flow problems. Laurence, Scott and Electromotors owns a large factory in Norwich and makes large electrical motors for ships, power stations, oil and gas industries and employs approximately 200 people. Administrators kept the company running while a solution to the company's problems was sought. A union spokesperson said that the company has a 'healthy' order book with an estimated £17 million of orders.
>
> *How might the management team at Laurence, Scott and Electromotors solve this company's cash flow problems? Justify your decision.*

Cash flow and business performance

Effective planning and monitoring of cash flow reduces the risk of a business facing a cash crisis. However, it cannot remove the risk completely. Even experienced and highly-trained managers can make errors. In particular, changes in the external environment, especially sudden and unexpected change, can result in inaccurate cash flow forecasts and firms experiencing cash shortages. In July 2007, a number of garden centres faced problems as sales fell due to unseasonally wet weather. Having already purchased supplies of plants and other garden equipment, these businesses were relying on selling them within a short period of time. The fall in sales meant that cash inflows were below expectations and some garden centres faced problems in paying bills as they fell due.

A business can benefit in a number of ways from effective and careful management of cash flow:

- **Reduced borrowing costs.** If managers can predict periods of cash flow difficulty and take appropriate actions, then it is less likely that the business will need to use its overdraft facility as fully as might have been the case. This can reduce interest charges significantly. If a business exceeds its overdraft limit then its bank is likely to impose penalty charges. Reducing interest charges means that a business will face lower costs and higher profits.
- **Good relations with suppliers.** Careful management of cash makes it more likely that a business will be able to pay suppliers promptly and in full. Many suppliers offer discounts for prompt payment and this can help a business to reduce its costs.
- **Public relations.** Businesses experiencing cash problems may lose the confidence of their customers who doubt their ability to continue to supply goods and services. In such circumstances customers may no longer place orders; this is almost certain to exacerbate the problem and may result in the company being unable to continue trading.

One step further: other ways of identifying cash-flow problems

It is essential that managers of small and medium-sized businesses recognise the signs of cash-flow problems at the earliest possible stage. There are several sources of evidence that they may consider.

- **Customers' finances and behaviour.** Many small businesses only sell to one or two customers and, if they face problems, the consequences for the business's cash position can be critical. One step that managers and entrepreneurs may take is to employ a credit agency. Credit agencies have access to databases which hold up-to-date financial information about businesses. Credit agencies often know if a business is experiencing credit difficulties before anyone else. Other, softer forms of evidence of customers having cash problems include delays in payments, and difficulties in contacting relevant employees.
- **Changes in market conditions.** A number of indicators exist to show that the market for the business's products could be altering. Rises in interest rates, the emergence of new competitors or new technology being used in products or the method of production could suggest that the business may encounter lower sales and potentially, cash problems. Successful managers are always alert to market developments and take action immediately.
- **Using financial forecasts.** Keeping financial forecasts up to date and analysing variances regularly can provide an early warning system that all is not well. This may seem an obvious action but many entrepreneurs face a heavy workload and do not always continue to forecast cash flow once the business has traded for some time.

Summary

This chapter has emphasised that managing cash flow is an ongoing task for entrepreneurs. It is important that they are alert to causes of cash problems and respond promptly and appropriately to any difficulties. There are significant benefits to all businesses, but especially to small and medium-sized ones, from managing cash effectively.

Quick questions

1. Is the following statement true or false? 'Drawing up detailed cash flow forecasts eliminates all risks of cash flow problems'.
2. Of what is the following a definition? 'This occurs when a business expands quickly without organising funds to finance the expansion.'
3. Is the following statement true or false? 'Businesses are particularly vulnerable to cash flow difficulties in the first few years of trading or when starting a major new project.'
4. Complete the following sentence by inserting the missing word. 'An .... is a flexible loan on which a business can draw, whenever necessary, up to some agreed limit.'
5. Which one of the following might not help a business to improve its working capital position:

a. offering customers shorter periods of trade credit?
b. using the services of a debt factor?
c. persuading suppliers to provide extended trade credit?
d. stockpiling raw materials in preparation for future production?

6. State **two** reasons why a manager might draw up an inaccurate cash-flow forecast.
7. Complete the following sentence by filling in the blank spaces. 'sale and leaseback entails a business selling a major .... – for example, a building – and then leasing it back from the new ....'
8. Is the following statement true or false? 'A business will not face cash-flow problems if it offers customers the same trade credit terms as it receives from its suppliers.'
9. Complete the following sentence by filling in the blank spaces. 'Businesses experiencing cash-flow problems may lose the .... of customers who doubt their ability to continue to .... goods and services.'
10. Is the following statement true or false? 'Paying bills promptly can result in an increased level of profit.'

Issues for analysis

- Considering a business's cash flow forecast including the relationships between cash inflow and outflow variances
- Establishing the causes of a particular business's cash-flow difficulties.
- Explaining actions that business may take to improve their cash position.

Issues for evaluation

- To what extent should a manager be concerned about a particular cash-flow position?
- What is the major cause of a business's cash-flow weaknesses – or strengths?
- What are the implications for a business resulting from effective management of its cash flow?

Examiner's advice

Do use numerical and written evidence when considering a business's cash-flow position. The numbers will show a trend – which ultimately might be improving or getting worse. However, there may also be important snippets of information in the accompanying text in an examination question. This may help you to judge the major cause of the cash problems or the most effective action that managers may take in response.

Analysis and evaluation questions

1. Alex Griffin identified a gap in the market for individualised, innovative, designer-made products rather than the mass-produced goods available from most high street retailers. After a year of research he developed a website on which customers could buy and sell highly individualised products. Alex described his site as a 'superboutique'. Bouf.com is the site on which to buy and sell limited edition, custom-made and unique goods. Its products include fashion, food and furniture, all sorts of gadgets, footwear and gifts. Many products are only available in small quantities and the range is always changing.

a Analyse why Alex's business might have encountered cash-flow problems in its first months of trading. (8 marks)
b To what extent might the success of Alex's business depend upon the effective planning and monitoring of cash flows? (15 marks)

2 Smith & Son Ltd is a small business supplying equipment to the printing industry. The company has a long cash cycle – many months from starting to manufacture the equipment to the point where the customer pays. Some of its customers are very slow to pay.

The company's cash position for the last two months is shown below.

a Examine *two* possible reasons why Smith & Son Ltd's closing balances for January and February have adverse variances. (8 marks)
b Discuss the actions that Smith & Son Ltd might take to improve its cash flow position. (15 marks)

	January Forecast	January Actual	February Forecast	February Actual
Cash in				
Cash sales	24500	25769	26500	26440
Credit sales	176300	156500	180150	168750
Total cash inflow	200800	182269	206650	195190
Cash out				
Purchase of materials	101500	103200	104500	105112
Wages	24500	25050	25230	25976
Overheads	67240	67200	68000	68543
Fuel, seeds, other costs	6555	6410	7150	7020
Total cash outflow	199795	201860	204880	206651
Net monthly cash flow	1005	−19591	1770	−11461
Opening balance	−12500	−12500	−11495	−32091
Closing balance	−11495	−32091	−9725	−43552

Table 19.2 Smith & Son Ltd's Cash-flow forecast

Assessment

Case study

Here we continue the story of Kate Chant's business, Bungay Herbs, which sells fresh herbs to supermarkets in East Anglia. At the end of May, after two months' trading, Kate is able to compare her cash-flow forecast with the actual inflows and outflows of cash.

Kate owns a small-holding, has a lot of relevant business experience and is confident her business will succeed. Her cash sales have been better than expected and her credit sales look positive, though she has had to offer 60 days' trade credit to build up a customer base. She is awaiting payment from two supermarkets for large orders that she supplied.

In addition, she has to spend heavily on marketing her new business to suitable retailers in East Anglia.

Questions

(30 marks, 40 minutes)

1 Outline *two* reasons why Kate's cash-flow position might be less strong than she forecast. (6 marks)

2 Analyse *two* actions Kate might take to improve her business's cash-flow position. (9 marks)

3 To what extent should Kate be concerned about the cash-flow position of her new business after two months' trading? (15 marks)

	April Forecast	April Actual	May Forecast	May Actual
Cash in				
Savings & borrowings	40000	40000	0	0
Cash sales	2500	2850	3000	3098
Credit sales	0	0	0	0
Total cash inflow	**42500**	**42850**	**3000**	**3098**
Cash out				
Purchase of greenhouses	36000	38050	0	0
Purchase of equipment	4500	4410	0	120
Wages	1450	1460	1600	1510
Marketing costs	3000	3200	1800	1790
Other costs, fuel, seeds	4255	4078	3000	3150
Total cash outflow	**49205**	**51198**	**6400**	**6570**
Net monthly cash flow	−6705	−8348	−3400	−3472
Opening balance	2500	2500	−4205	−5848
Closing balance	−4205	−5848	−7605	−9320

Table 19.3 **Kate Chant's cash-flow forecast**

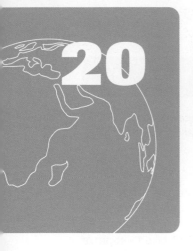

20

Measuring and increasing profit

Profit is the main goal of many, but not all, businesses. However, it is important to think further about profits. What is a good level of profit for a particular business? It is too simple to say that a bigger profit is better than a smaller one; it needs to be compared with something. It is also naïve to think that a business can always increase its profits by increasing prices or cutting costs – whether this succeeds depends upon a number of factors. Finally, profits and cash flow are very different things – a profitable business can be short of cash.

What you need to know by the end of this chapter:
• how to calculate net profit margins and what the results mean
• how to calculate the return on capital and what the results mean
• how businesses can improve their profitability and the strengths and weaknesses of these approaches
• the distinction between cash and profit and the implications of this for businesses.

Profit as an objective

We saw in Chapter 12 that profit is calculated by deducting total costs from the total revenue received by a business over a given time period. Profit is a very important objective for many businesses and it is one way of measuring the success of a business. However, a simple profit figure is not as revealing as it might appear. It is simple to assume that if one firm makes a larger profit than another, it must be more successful. This might not be the case. It is important to consider two factors when making a judgement on a business's profits:

1 What level of sales was necessary to generate the profits? If a firm achieves a high level of profits from a relatively small number of sales, it may be considered very successful.

2 How much money was invested into the project to produce the profits? Obviously, a larger investment would be expected to result in a higher level of profits.

We can make a more meaningful judgement about a business's performance if we compare its profits with something else in a simple calculation. Calculating ratios that compare profits to sales or capital invested into the business allows us to make more informed assessments of a business's performance.

Net profit margins

A business calculates its net profits by deducting all its costs of production from its sales revenue. This figure is normally referred to simply as profit (and hence profit margin), and this is what we will do. The profit figure is useful to managers and others interested in the performance of a business, but more so when compared to the sales revenue the firm received in the sale trading period.

The formula for calculating the profit margin is shown below.

$$\text{net profit margin} = \frac{\text{net profit} \times 100}{\text{sales revenue}}$$

	Units sold	Sales revenue £	Total costs £	Profit £	Net profit margin %
Business A	25,000	2,400,000	2,050,000	350,000	14.58
Business B	9,750	975,000	799,500	175,500	18.00

Table 20.1 Calculating net profit margins.

If the firm makes a loss, then its profit margin will be negative.

It is possible to calculate a profit margin for a single product, or for the business's entire output. For a business that sells a single product at a standard price, these two figures should be the same. However, in reality the majority of small and medium-sized businesses sell a range of products at a variety of prices. (So, for example, in the 'Real-life business' example given later in this chapter, the farmer might have a different profit margin for peas, cabbages and cauliflowers.)

The table below illustrates the calculation of net profit margins for two firms during the same financial year.

We can see from Table 20.1 that even though Business A makes a higher level of profits than Business B (£360,000 as compared with £175,500), its profit margin is actually lower. Thus, in some senses Business B could be considered more successful. If it achieved the same level of sales as Business A, and maintained its profit margin, its profits would be £432,000 – 18 per cent of £2,400,000.

In general, higher profit margins are preferable to lower ones, as a higher profit margin is likely to lead to greater overall profits. This should meet with the approval of the business's owners, assuming that their objective is to make the largest profits possible.

However, it may be that a business would have to reduce its price to achieve higher sales and this would reduce its profit margin and, in turn its level of profits. In Table 20.1 Business B achieved its sales revenue by selling 9,750 units of output at £100, with an average cost of £82 per unit of output.

It may be that to sell enough units to generate sales revenue of £2,400,000, Business B will have to reduce its price to £90. If its cost of production remains at £82 per unit, the overall position will be as shown in Table 20.2.

It might be, however, that the managers at Business B would be able to reduce costs of production per unit as it increases its scale of production. It may reduce the costs per unit by buying raw materials in bulk, or by using its capacity more intensively and thereby lowering fixed costs per unit of production. If its managers achieve this, it may help to maintain the business's profit margin.

What do you think?

Imagine you are about to launch your new business and are deciding what profit margin you want. What factors would you take into account in making this decision?

	Units sold	Sales revenue £	Total costs £	Profit £	Net profit margin %
Business B	26,667	2,400,000	2,186,694	213,036	8.88%

Table 20.2 Business B's profit margin as it reduces price to increase sales.

Real-life Business

Farmers

Farmers have complained that competition from overseas and demands from UK supermarkets have made the growing of cauliflowers during the winter months unprofitable. Most UK-produced winter cauliflowers are grown in Kent and Cornwall, which are relatively frost-free.

One grower, Geoff Philpott, who is from Broadstairs in Kent, said that many farmers were considering not growing cauliflowers in the future. 'I had to forego supplying one supermarket about eight weeks ago when we got down to a price of 15 pence (per cauliflower) for me, which was 23 pence below the cost of production.'

What is Geoff Philpott's current profit margin on the sale of cauliflowers?

What would be his profit margin if he received 47.5 pence per cauliflower?

(Source: BBC News, at http://news.bbc.co.uk/1/hi/england/6679557.stm, 22 May 2007)

Return on capital invested

An alternative means of making a judgement about a business's profits is to consider the amount that was invested initially. The calculation is fairly simple, using the formula set out below:

$$\text{Return on capital} = \frac{\text{net profit} \times 100}{\text{capital}}$$

Suppose an entrepreneur purchases a corner shop for £100,000 and in the first year of trading earns a profit of £6,000. The return on capital for this first year of trading would be 6 per cent.

As with the profit margin, a higher figure is preferable. However, it might be that the corner shop will earn higher profits (and a higher return on capital) in future years. Many investments are long-term projects and it may be too simplistic to make a judgement on the results of a single year's trading. Some investments (for example in property) are designed to produce returns over many years and hence making judgements on a single year might be considered premature.

Equally important in such a decision is the alternative use to which the capital invested could be put. In effect, entrepreneurs need to consider the opportunity cost. In this instance, the entrepreneur may consider that her money would produce a similar return if it had been held in an interest-paying bank account, with much less risk.

Risk is an important issue to consider when reading a return on capital figure. Risk is the threat that an investment may fail and that the investor may lose all or part of the capital invested. When judging an investment figure it is vital to take risk into account. A high return on a capital figure may be needed if an investment is considered risky. An investor putting capital into purchasing property may want a high return on his investment. This would act as compensation for the risk of a fall in the property prices and a reduction in the value of his investment. An investor putting money into a lower risk project may be satisfied with a lower return on capital.

Examiner's advice

When calculating return on capital – or profit margins, always show your workings, in case of error. Also, do think about what is a reasonable figure. If the return on capital is very high – say 125 per cent – look again at your figures to check that they are correct.

Improving profits

In 2007, a survey by The Royal Bank of Scotland revealed that over 25 per cent of small businesses said that increasing profits was their 'main objective'. There are a number of methods that a business can use to achieve this aim.

Reduce costs of production

This is perhaps the first consideration of many managers when considering how to increase profits. If a business can maintain its prices while reducing its costs of production, then profit margins will increase. So long as sales do not decline, its profits will rise. However, there are a number of risks in taking this action. First, the reduction in costs may result in lower quality goods or services being supplied. This could result in a loss of customers which could prove counter-productive and ultimately reduce profits.

In 2007, IBP Conex Ltd, a Glasgow company that manufactures plumbing components such as taps and pipes, transferred some of its manufacturing to Poland to take advantage of substantially lower wage rates. However, this move led to the loss of 66 jobs in Glasgow and some adverse publicity for the company.

Increase prices

The other obvious option is to increase the price at which the business sells its products. An increase in revenue per unit with costs stable will boost profit margins. However, this is a risky option as an increase in price may lead to existing customers seeking alternative suppliers and potential new customers looking elsewhere. The success of this decision depends on the importance of price in the decision to purchase. The manager of a luxury hotel may be able to increase prices for accommodation and food with little effect on sales. In contrast, a small town-centre café may find a high proportion of its customers move elsewhere if prices are raised.

In 2007, cheese-makers in Leicestershire increased prices for Stilton cheese from £7.80 a kilo to £8.30. In part this was due to rising milk prices. Stilton producers were hopeful that customers would be loyal to the brand and that the impact on sales would be limited allowing profits to be maintained, if not increased.

Improve the business's efficiency

An efficient business uses a minimal amount of resources to produce its goods or services. Managers can take a number of decisions to increase the efficiency of their businesses and thereby reduce costs with positive implications for profits.

Use capacity more fully

A business's capacity is the maximum amount that it can produce. If this capacity is used fully then the business's fixed costs are spread across more units of output helping to reduce average cost. At the same time, more units of output are produced, and hopefully sold, thereby increasing revenue.

Many small UK airlines operate Jetstream 41 aircraft which can hold a maximum of 29 passengers. Profits from operating these aircraft can be increased

Figure 20.1 A Jetstream 41 aircraft

if the aircraft is full, or nearly full, on flights. In this context a full aircraft means that the airline is using its capacity as fully as possible. The costs of operating a full aircraft are only a little higher and more passenger fares will increase revenue.

Reduce the number of substandard products

If a business produces products that are not of the right quality, then it incurs additional costs. This is because it has paid to produce goods that it cannot sell. These must either be scrapped or reworked to make them saleable. In either case costs rise. Any management decisions (for example, training employees to monitor quality) that help to reduce the number of poor quality products will help to reduce costs of production and enhance profitability.

Improve methods of production

Decisions to improve the efficiency of the production process can help to reduce costs and to improve profitability. On the island of Jersey, a number of businesses have been encouraged by the Island's government to recycle cooking oil for use to fuel vehicles. This helps to reduce disposal costs of the oil, as well as reducing expenditure on petrol or diesel.

Eliminate unprofitable aspects of production

A business can take decisions to close down certain aspects of its operations that are making a loss. This can lead to increased profits for the remaining parts of the enterprise as the business uses it resources in the most efficient manner. In 2007, the UK airline First Choice reduced the routes it flies by ending all flights to and from Cardiff in South Wales. The company said that this decision was 'in line with customer demand'. This decision would allow First Choice to concentrate its resources on more popular and profitable routes.

Hornby

Hornby is one of the UK's best known manufacturers of toys. The company sells a range of well-known brands, including Scalextrix and Airfix. The company's profits in 2007 were £8.1 million and were considered disappointing. However, the company is confident that this will improve in the future. The company expects to see a major contribution to future sales and profits from the Airfix model brand, which it purchased recently. At the same time the company is transferring much of its production from Margate in Kent to China to take advantage of lower costs.

Question:

To what extent might the move to China and the purchase of the Airfix brand ensure that Hornby's profits are higher in the future?

The distinction between cash flow and profits

Profit is the surplus of sales revenue over total costs, if any exists. Just because a business is profitable, it does not mean that it will hold large sums of cash, or even have enough cash. There several reasons why this situation might arise.

- First, the business might sell large amounts of goods or services at profitable prices by offering customers 60 or 90 days' trade credit. This will mean that the business has to find cash to buy supplies and pay employees several months before the cash from the sale of the product flows into the business. This problem can be exacerbated if the business pays its suppliers promptly.
- Alternatively, a business such as a jeweller might hold large amounts of (expensive) stock for customers to view before making a choice. This will entail large amounts of cash being tied up in the form of stocks and not available to the business for other purposes.
- A business may have paid for fixed assets and used large sums of cash to do so. These assets may support the business over many years, and will lead to future inflows of cash. However, the outflow of cash would be at the start and may place pressure on a firm's finances.

So, a profitable business may find itself short of cash and possibly unable to settle its bills as they fall due. This could lead to the firm becoming insolvent and having to cease trading. A cash crisis is a major reason why many small and medium-sized businesses fail.

In the long-term, however, a business has to make a profit to satisfy its owners. They have invested funds into the business, quite possibly by purchasing shares, and expect to see a return on their investment. This is only possible if the business makes a profit in the longer term. A business may survive for some time without making profits if its owners are prepared to be patient, but cash has to be managed carefully in the short-term to ensure that bills can be paid on time.

One step further: thinking more about profits

Current profits are a useful measure of the success of a business. As we have already seen, by comparing profits to sales revenue or the amount of capital invested into a project we can make them more meaningful still. However, current profits do not provide a complete measure of a business's success, however we present them.

It may be, for instance, that a business is currently making relatively low profits in comparison to other similar businesses. This might occur because the owners of the business are investing in researching new products or are offering low prices to achieve consistent growth in sales. Both of these actions are intended to boost future profits, so it may be important to take a longer-term view of a business's profitability.

Not all business owners are motivated solely by profits. Research by the Royal Bank of Scotland in 2007 revealed that only 6 per cent of small business owners surveyed set up their businesses to make money. Other reasons were the desire to be their own boss or to turn a hobby into a business. In such cases the business's owners may pursue a policy known as 'satisficing' whereby a certain level of profits is deemed acceptable and after that other goals such as maximising leisure time or the prestige of the business are pursued.

Summary

Profit figures are more meaningful when compared with sales revenue or the amount invested in a project. Simple calculations produce relevant figures. Businesses have a range of methods of improving profits, but all have some potential drawbacks and none are guaranteed to succeed. Finally, there are other ways of assessing a business's performance apart from the size of its profits – whatever they are compared with.

Quick questions

1. Complete the following sentence by filling in the missing spaces. 'A profit margin is calculated by dividing the business's profit by .... and multiplying the answer by 100.

2. Chorlton Cakes Ltd's sales revenue for last year was £800,000. Its profits were £120,000. What was the company's profit margin?

3. A business has a profit margin of 12 per cent and its profits were £60,000. What was the business's sales revenue for the period?

4. If Prentiss Ltd makes a loss of £850,000 on sales of £4.25 million, what is its profit margin?

5. Is the following statement true or false? 'An increase in price will always increase a business's profits.'

6. If Chorlton Cakes Ltd invested £150,000 in a new factory and it made a return on capital of 15 per cent in its first year of trading, what were its profits?

7. Is the following statement true or false? 'A reduction in costs of production may have undesirable side effects.'

8. Is the following statement true or false? 'A reduction in prices can, in some circumstances increase a business's sales revenue.'

9. Complete the following sentence by filling in the missing spaces. 'A profitable business may find itself short of .... and possibly unable to settle its .... as they fall due.'

10. Is the following statement true or false? 'A cash-rich business is certain to make a profit.'

Issues for analysis

- Understanding how to make profit figures more meaningful through comparison with other factors, such as sales revenue or the sum invested.
- Recognising the strengths and weaknesses of the various actions a business might take in an attempt to improve profitability
- Appreciating the difference between cash flow and profits and the importance of this for businesses.

Issues for evaluation

- Does a particular level of profits represent a good performance by a business?
- What is the best way for a given business to improve its profitability?

Analysis and evaluation questions

1. Bowles Farm Ltd sells a range of fruit juices from crops grown on the farm. The company's major sales are in the autumn when its fruit harvest is complete. The company originally just sold a range of apple and pear juices, but has expanded in recent years to sell organic juices at higher prices. The company sells mainly through major retailers, on a 60-day credit basis. However, the company's IT manager is developing a website with the aim of selling directly to customers.

   The company is investing in increasing its production by planting new orchards and expects to increase sales by 100 per cent over the next five years. The company is profitable but its managers would like to receive higher profit margins.

   a. Analyse two reasons why Bowles Farm Ltd is a profitable company but experiences cash flow problems. (8 marks)

   b. Discuss the actions that Bowles Farm Ltd's managers might take to increase the company's profits. (15 marks)

2. Jack Marshall in one of Suffolk's few remaining offshore fishermen. He operates from Lowestoft harbour and sells his catch locally in season. Despite the heavy investment in his boat, his business is profitable. However, he is unhappy at the profit margin he receives on selling fish to local shops and hotels. Jack is considering buying a van and paying a driver to transport his fish to London to sell at higher prices. Prices in London are about 35 per cent higher than in London.

   a. Examine two ways that Jack might increase his profit margin. (8 marks)

   b. To what extent might actions to improve Jack's profits lead to cash flow problems in the short-term? (15 marks)

Assessment

Case study

Perfect Weddings & Honeymoons specialises in providing a complete service in arranging overseas and UK weddings. The company: 'strives to be creative and offer individuality to every wedding couple, constantly researching new and unusual wedding locations, new destinations and improving on the venues that are available in each location.' They aim to : 'ensure that you have the wedding of your dreams without the stress and worries that usually accompany such a joyous occasion.'

The company assists customers in: 'choosing the ideal wedding destination and venue, arranging all of the legal documentation and liaising with the venue to ensure that the wedding is a complete success.'

The business competes in this market with other much larger businesses, some of which provide a wide range of holidays. However, the market is growing as more couples choose to marry overseas.

(Source: Adapted from www.perfect-weddings.net/AboutPerfectWeddings.htm)

Web link

To learn more about this business visit www.perfect- weddings.net

Questions

(30 marks, 40 minutes)

1 Assume that the company enjoys a 12 per cent profit margin on a wedding for a particular couple. If it costs the company £3,500 to arrange it, what price will it charge? (5 marks)
2 Analyse the likely implications for the business's profits of a price increase. (10 marks)
3 To what extent is this business able to decide upon its chosen profit margin? (15 marks)

Section 4: People in business

21 Organisational structures

Deciding how to organise the people in the business becomes increasingly important as a business grows. When first established, a business may only have one or two employees (or even none at all) and working with people is likely to be straightforward. However, as the business becomes established and more people are hired, then it is important (and more difficult) to work with people as efficiently as possible. This chapter considers how small and medium-sized businesses can structure their businesses to do this.

What you need to know by the end of this chapter:

• how issues such as levels of hierarchy, spans of control, work loads, delegation and communication flows affect the structure of the organisation

• the roles that are carried out in the organisation by directors, managers, team leaders and supervisors

• how the structure of an organisation can affect the performance of the business.

What is an organisational structure?

An organisational structure is the way in which a business is arranged to carry out its activities. The organisational structure, which may be shown in an organisation chart, sets out:

• the routes by which communication passes through the business

• who has authority (and power) and responsibility within the organisation

• the roles and titles of individuals within the organisation

• the people to whom individual employees are accountable and those for whom they are responsible.

Some businesses change the structure of their organisation rapidly and regularly: some entrepreneurs believe that they should be continually reorganising their firms to meet the demands of a dynamic marketplace. By improving the organisational structure

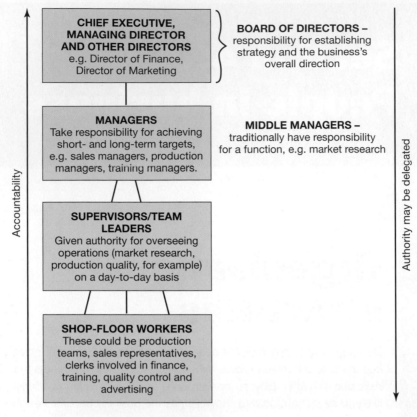

Figure 21.1 A simplified organisational chart

on a regular basis a business is better able to meet the needs of its customers.

A principal reason for the regular change in organisational structures is the pace of external change. All businesses have to ensure that they are able to compete with rival firms. Keeping costs to a minimum is an important part of competing successfully, and is a common factor in a business's decision to change its organisational structures.

Key elements in organisational structures

There are several important elements that entrepreneurs need to consider when designing or adapting organisational structures.

Workloads and job allocation

The most fundamental decisions that managers have to take about the structure of their business are about who is going to do which jobs, and how much work a person can reasonably be expected to complete within a working day or week. Good decisions in these areas can help to make a business more effective and cost-efficient.

As a small business develops, the entrepreneur will not be able to carry out all the tasks necessary for its operation. It is likely that the entrepreneur will focus more on managing the enterprise, while newly appointed employees can carry out more basic duties.

For example, an entrepreneur opening a hairdressing business may spend most of the working day cutting and styling hair. Entrepreneurs running very small or micro businesses will complete administrative tasks in the evenings. But as the business grows the hairdresser will employ other people to cut and style hair and will spend more time on managerial issues. If the entrepreneur opens other hairdressing salons, there may come a poiint where he or she is exclusively a manager.

A medium-sized business will also be able to employ some specialists to, for example, manage finances or to carry out marketing or research activities. Appointing specialists and allocating them appropriate tasks is one way in which a manager can improve the performance of a business. A marketing manager may, for example, enable the business to achieve a higher level of sales. In contrast an IT specialist may help the organisation to reduce costs and increase profit margins. Business with efficient organisation structures will draw on the strengths and abilities of people in the way they allocate tasks.

Managing workloads effectively can help businesses to control costs. A workload is the duties and tasks that an employee is expected to complete in a given time period, such as a day or week. For example, your teachers may be expected to teach 22 hours in each week during term. Workloads involve a question of balance. Using staff time fully is important to avoid times at which people are idle while the business continues to incur wage costs. However, over-burdening employees with duties can mean that people are forced to work under pressure, resulting in mistakes being made, and dissatisifed customers.

Some managers make use of part-time and temporary employees to cope with fluctuations in the level of activity within the business. This can, by maintaining the workload of full-time employees at an acceptable level, help the business to continue to operate efficiently during periods when demand fluctuates.

What do you think?

Can you think of occupations where it is not always easy to measure or forecast the workloads of employees?

Levels of hierarchy

Key terms

Levels of hierarchy refer to the number of layers of authority within an organisation. That is, how many levels exist between the Chief Executive and a shop-floor employee.

A **span of control** is the number of subordinates directly responsible to a manager.

The **chain of command** is the line of communication and authority existing within a business. Thus, a shop-floor worker reports to a supervisor, who is responsible to a departmental manager, and so on.

A fundamental element of any organisational structure is the number of levels or layers of hierarchy. Organisations with a large number of layers (or levels) of hierarchy are referred to as 'tall'. That is, there are a substantial number of people between

the person at the top of the organisation and those at the bottom. Figures 21.2 and 21.3 illustrate both tall and flat types of structure.

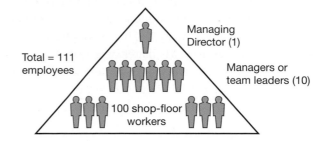

(a) A 'flat' organisational structure has few levels of hierarchy (three) and a wide span of control. Many UK businesses have implemented this form of organisational structure.

Figures 21.2 'Flat' organisational structures

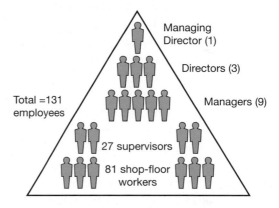

(b) A traditional 'tall' organisational structure has five layers of hierarchy and a narrow span of control. In spite of the firm employing more people, it has fewer shop-floor employees than the 'flat' stucture above.

Figures 21.3 'Tall' organisational structures

What do you think?

Surveys of employees have shown that the majority of people prefer to work within a 'flat' organisation. Why might this type of structure be particularly popular with junior employees?

Traditionally, UK businesses have tended to use 'tall' organisational structures as they have grown. Once businesses have adopted a tall organisational structure they have long chains of command from those at the top of the organisation to those at the bottom. Businesses with many layers of hierarchy frequently experience communication problems as messages moving up and down the organisation pass through many people and may be distorted or not passed on.

Attracted by the prospect of faster and more effective communication, and influenced by Japanese and American companies, many UK businesses have either adopted or moved towards flatter organisational structures. However, the process of flattening structures (commonly termed delayering) has led to businesses operating with significantly wider spans of control.

Spans of control

A span of control is the number of people who report directly to a manager. Spans of control and levels of hierarchy have a relationship. An organisation with a wide span of control will have relatively few levels of hierarchy – the 'flat' organisation in Figure 21.2. Conversely, 'tall' organisations have many layers of hierarchy, but narrow spans of control. Figure 21.4 illustrates a broad and a narrow span of control. Manager A has a span of control of two. This is because the two supervisors B and C are the only employees who are directly responsible to him. Supervisor B has the widest span of control – five workers are responbile to her.

A narrow span of control allows team leaders, supervisors and managers to keep close control over the activities of the employees for whom they are responsible. As the span of control widens, the subordinate is likely to be able to operate with a greater degree of independence. This is because it is impossible for an individual to monitor closely the work of a large number of subordinates. A traditional view is that the span of control should not exceed six, if close supervision is to be maintained. However, where subordinates are carrying out similar duties, a span of control of ten or even twelve is not unusual. It is normal for a span of control to be less at the top of an organisation. This is because senior employees have more complex and diverse duties and are, therefore, more difficult to supervise.

Key terms
Delegation is the passing of authority (but not responsibility) down the organisation structure. Thus, a junior manager might be given the authority to conduct a market research campaign, but responsibility for the overall success of the campaign remains with the senior employee.

Delegation

Delegation is the passing down of authority through the organisation. In a very small organisation, an entrepreneur or manager may be able to make all the necessary decisions and carry out many managerial tasks. He or she may not necessarily have the experience or knowledge to do this as effectively as possible, but lack of finance may preclude the employment of specialists.

However, as an organisation grows, this may become more difficult – it becomes impossible for the entrepreneur to take all decisions. Because of this, the structure adopted by the organisation might need to be adjusted as it develops. One key strategy entrepreneurs might adopt is to delegate authority as the organisation increases in scale. Giving people more authority is likely to lead to wider span of control. Wider spans of control can operate effectively if junior employees have been delegated authority to take decions. This reduces the workload on their manager or team leader, as he or she does not have to monitor all subordinates so closely, freeing time for other duties.

The extent to which an organisation adopts delegation as a key element in its organisational structure depends upon the the entrepreneur's view of control. Some entrepreneurs like to retain as much control of decision-making as possible, and only delegate when the pressure of their workload makes this essential.

Web link

Business Link provides practical information about delegation. You can read this by following the link below: http://tinyurl.com/2mdg54

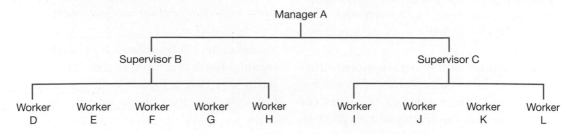

Figure 21.4 Spans of control

Communication flows

Communication is the exchange of information between two or more parties. A well-structured organisation will be designed to facilitate the effective flow of communication throughout the organisation. Communication flows in several directions within an organisation:

- up and down the organisation. This entails the passing of information down from senior to junior employees and from junior to senior employees.
- across the organisation. A well-designed organisational structure will also offer employees at the same level in the business sufficient chance to communicate effectively.

In part, communication will flow smoothly through the enterprise if unnecessary levels of hierarchy are not established. As we saw earlier, communication is more likely to be disrupted if it has to pass through several people. Spans of control are also important in this regard. Communication is more likely to flow efficiently if the spans of control are designed to fit in with the abilities of employees. So if junior employees are well trained and motivated it may be possible to operate with a wider span of control.

However, effective communication does not simply depend upon the structure of the organisation. Other factors, such as efficient use of information and communications technology and the holding of meetings and briefings can have a great impact as well.

Centralisation and decentralisation

Centralisation and decentralisation are opposites. A centralised organisation is one where the majority of decisions are taken by senior managers at the top (or centre) of the business. Centralisation can provide rapid decision-making, as few people are likely to be consulted. It should also ensure that the business pursues the objectives set by senior managers. Decentralisation gives greater authority to employees lower down the organisational structure.

Workforce roles

An entrepreneur who is designing a structure for a new organisation, or amending an existing one, is likely to consider a number of roles for employees as part of the process.

Directors

Directors are found as part of the workforce of a company – either private or public. Directors are proposed by the Chief Executive of a company and take up the role if they are subsequently elected by shareholders.

The role of directors is largely strategic – they set and oversee the achievement of long-term goals for the business. Directors can be executive or non-executive. Executive directors are employed by the company in a senior capacity, possibly with responsibility for a part or function of the business such as marketing. Non-executive directors are not employed by the company and are usually appointed because they have a particular knowledge or skill. Their main role is to offer advice at board meetings.

What do you think?

The government and other stakeholders have often called for non-executive directors to be critical of companies when their actions are not in the interests of the stakeholders and particularly of the shareholders. Why do you think that some non-executive directors do not act in this way?

Directors exist within relatively small, private, limited companies but are likely to fulfil broader roles than in larger companies because smaller companies employ fewer people.

Managers

Managers carry out a range of duties. These are often categorised as planning, organising, motivating and controlling. Managers normally have authority over a number of junior employees and plan and monitor short- and medium-term strategies for the business.

In a small business, the owner may carry out the duties of manager and director looking after all the planning for the business as well as organising and controlling day-to-day activities. This is one reason why many entrepreneurs are very busy people!

Web link

You can find out more about what managers do by visiting the Management Resources website at: http://tinyurl.com/2uwrkf

Supervisors

Supervisors represent a link between managers and the business's shop-floor workers. They are the first rung of management and in regular contact with shop-floor workers. Supervisors are delegated some authority by managers to take decisions on day-today issues such as staffing or tactics to meet deadlines. Supervisors also act as a line of communication between managers and shop-floor workers.

> **Key term**
> **Operatives** or **shop-floor workers** are those who work at the lowest level in an organisational structure. For example, in a retail setting they would be the shop assistants.

Team leaders

Team leaders carry out many of the same functions in organisations as supervisors. However, the use of the term 'team leader' implies that the business operates in a different way. Team leaders make less use of authority than supervisors and are used in a role which supports shop-floor employees. Their role is to facilitate the work of more junior employees and to help them to attain the business's objectives. Organisations that take this approach rely heavily on delegation of authority and there tends to be trust between employees at all levels.

How organisational structure affects business performance

The aims of an entrepreneur when first designing an organisational structure will be to:

- keep a tight control on costs and
- meet customers' needs as fully as possible.

This is a tricky balance to achieve, particularly at times when an organisation is growing. In such circumstances it is necessary to alter the structure frequently, and it can be difficult to achieve both of the above aims at all times.

Keeping control of costs

Controlling costs allows a business to improve its profit margin or to increase sales as a result of price increase, while maintaining an existing profit margin. A competitive business will have costs under control. A number of aspects of the design of an organisation's structure can help to control costs.

Allocating workloads so as to make the best use of employees' time is an integral part of controlling labour costs. The ideal organisational structure will have employees busy, but not overburdened so that they are unable to carry out their jobs effectively. Managers have to use experience and observation to try to have the right number of people allocated to various aspects of the organisation's operations.

Good upward flows of communication can be helpful in this regard. Junior employees who report back on the effectiveness of their own work and that of their colleagues will help managers to make good decisions on work allocation and to use expensive resources effectively.

Using flatter organisational structures can help a business to keep its costs under control. By creating an organisational structure with fewer employees (often the number of managers is reduced) wage costs are likely to be reduced, offering the business more freedom in pricing or the opportunity to improve profit margins. One way to achieve this is through having minimal layers within the organisation. In particular, businesses may create structures that have relatively few middle managers, preferring to delegate authority to relatively junior employees. Managers often receive substantial salaries, so employing only as many as necessary can help to minimise wage costs.

However, the success of this approach does depend upon having relatively junior employees who are able to cope successfully with additional tasks and greater authority. This will require planning and investment in training.

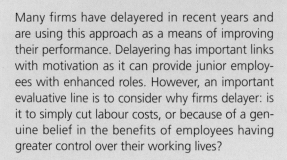

> ### Examiner's advice
>
> Many firms have delayered in recent years and are using this approach as a means of improving their performance. Delayering has important links with motivation as it can provide junior employees with enhanced roles. However, an important evaluative line is to consider why firms delayer: is it to simply cut labour costs, or because of a genuine belief in the benefits of employees having greater control over their working lives?

Business in Focus

TIO

A Scottish organic vegetable grower and processor is creating up to 20 new jobs as it expands its business. TIO (This Is Organics) is investing £2.5 million in expanding the company's cold storage facilities which will enable the business to deal with much larger orders from customers. One of TIO's major customers is Tesco, which it supplies with root vegetables such as carrots and parsnips.

The new facilities will see TIO's workforce expand from 47 to 67 within a few months and will have an impact on the company's organisational structure.

What roles might TIO's new employees fulfil within the company?

In what ways might these changes affect TIO's ability to meet the needs of its customers?

Web link

To find out more about TIO, visit www.tio.co.uk

Meeting customers' needs as fully as possible

Satisfying customers is a vital part of being a successful business. Satisfied customers are likely to provide further orders and may be a source of good publicity for a business. In turn, this may attract new customers. Offering a better service to customers is an important way in which business can improve its performace. (We look in more detail at customer service in Chapter 35.)

Reducing the number of levels of hierarchy in an organisation through delayering provides junior employees with greater opportunities for decision making within, and control over, their working lives. For example, a receptionist in an hotel who is authorised to make room switches without reference to a manager might be able to meet the needs of a disabled customer quickly and efficiently by effecting a transfer to a ground-floor room. This may also help to motivate employees and to improve their performance at work. Being given authority to make changes may encourage relatively junior employees to, for example, investigate causes of customer dissatisfaction and to take appropriate action.

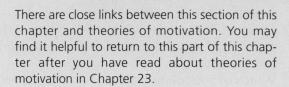

Examiner's advice

There are close links between this section of this chapter and theories of motivation. You may find it helpful to return to this part of this chapter after you have read about theories of motivation in Chapter 23.

Both delegation and decentralisation can be doubly beneficial to managers in a business. They can reduce the workload of senior managers, allowing them to focus on important long-term issues such as developing new products or entering new markets. At the same time, it offers junior managers an opportunity to develop their skills in preparation for a more senior position.

Effective communication flows through an organisation is a crucial part of meeting customers' needs as fully as possible. If an organisation is unsuccessful in communicating customer complaints or requests to those who may be able to to take the necessary actions, it is very unlikely that customers will be satisfied in the future. In the same way, successful businesses draw on the creative ideas of employees at any level in the organisation. If these are communicated successfully, a business may be in a better position to meet the needs of customers.

Summary

There are a number of key decisions that a manager has to take in relation to the organisational structure. These include levels of hierarchy, spans of control, work loads, job allocation and delegation. A business can improve its performance in terms of costs and meeting customers' needs by adopting an appropriate organisational structure.

Quick questions

1 Which of the following will be shown on an organisational chart:
a the roles and titles of people within the organisation?
b the names and addresses of customers?
c details of suppliers?
d the business's stakeholders?

2 Complete the following sentence by filling in the missing words. "............... is the passing of .... from a manager to a subordinate."

3 Of what is the following a definition: 'The number of layers within an organisation'?

4 Of what is the following a definition: 'The number of subordinates directly responsible to a manager'?

5 Which of the following is not associated with a 'tall' hierarchical structure:

a many levels of hierarchy within the organisation?

b wide spans of control?

c a long chain of command?

d a large number of people between the person at the top and those at the bottom of the organisation?

6 Complete the following sentence by filling in the missing terms. 'A ...... organisational structure contains few levels of hierarchy, but a ...... span of control.'

7 What is the difference between a supervisor and a team leader?

8 Complete the following sentence by filling in the missing terms. 'A manager carries out four functions: ...., ..., ... and ....'

9 Complete the following sentence by filling in the missing terms. '.................... are proposed by the Chief Executive of a company and take up the role if they are subsequently elected by ....'

10 State two ways in which restructuring an organisation might help to improve its performance.

Issues for analysis

- Explaining ways in which changes in organisational structure can affect the performance of a business.
- Appreciating the effect of changes in some elements in an organisation's structure on others.
- Understanding the effects on changing the organisation's structure of the job role's of the business's employees.

Issues for evaluation

- Do changes in the organisation's structure result in an improvement in the performance of the business?
- What are the key elements of an organisation's structure that contribute towards its performance?

Analysis and evaluation questions

1 Beech Ltd manufactures windows and doors and sells its products throughout the South West of England. The company is enjoying rising sales and is expanding. The company's HR manager wants to delegate greater authority to shop-floor employees and to widen the span of control of the company's supervisors. The company's production line currently has 48 employees and four supervisors. The intention is to increase production line employees to 60 without any increase in supervisors.

a Analyse the possible effects of these changes on the job roles carried out by Beech Ltd's supervisors. (8 marks)

b Discuss whether this decision will inevitably reduce the company's costs of production. (15 marks)

2 Val's Bakery is found in three towns. The shops sell bread and cakes produced at a bakery behind one of the shops. Val has decided to delegate authority for managing the shops to a senior shop assistant in each branch. This will allow her to concentrate on the production side of the business. She intends to supply more bread and cakes to other businesses as well as to her own shops.

a Examine the effect that delegation might have on the jobs of the senior shop assistants. (8 marks)

b To what extent might delegation improve the performance of Val's Bakery? (15 marks)

Assessment

Case study

Tom Smith opened his construction firm five years ago. Since then it has grown steadily. Much of the business's work is building extensions and carrying out repairs, although he does occasionally build a new house. He employs six people and enjoys working with them on the building sites – Tom is a carpenter. He does his paperwork in the evenings.

However, the growth of his business has led to the need for changes. He has an increasing number of managerial duties to carry out, such as planning, and his customers are asking if he can help with issues such as drawing up building plans and helping them to get planning permission for changes to their properties. Tom feels his business can earn additional revenues from these changes. However, he will need more staff and will not be able to be on building sites to monitor the work.

Questions

(30 marks, 40 minutes)

1 Explain the likely effects of these changes on communication flows in Tom's business. (6 marks)

2 Analyse how Tom's role might change as his business grows. (9 marks)

3 Discuss whether Tom's plans to improve the service he gives to customers can only be achieved by increasing his costs. (15 marks)

22 Staff performance, recruitment, selection and training

For many businesses, and particularly those supplying services, having a workforce that performs well is a central part of success. So it is important that managers can measure how well their workforce is performing and then take actions to improve its performance. Improving the performance of the workforce might entail recruiting new employees, retraining existing ones, or possibly both.

What you need to know by the end of this chapter:
- the ways in which managers can measure the performance of the workforce
- how businesses recruit and select employees
- the ways in which recruitment and selection can improve the performance of the workforce
- the methods of training used by business and the benefits and drawbacks of training.

Measuring workforce performance

Before managers decide on changes to the workforce as a result of recruitment or training it is important to assess the performance of the existing workforce. A number of measures are available to businesses to assess the performance of their employees. Armed with this knowledge, managers are then in a better position to implement appropriate changes to improve the performance of the workforce and the business overall.

Labour productivity

$$\text{Labour productivity} = \frac{\text{output per period}}{\text{number of employees at work}}$$

This is perhaps the most fundamental indicator of the performance of a group of employees and has implications for a business's costs and hence the prices that it can charge. Productive workers produce larger quantities of output per worker per time period, and this is a measure that is relatively easy to calculate.

Labour productivity depends upon factors such as the extent and quality of capital equipment available to the workforce as well as its skills and degree of motivation. Thus it is possible for managers to take a range of actions with the intention of improving labour productivity figures. Research indicates that overall labour productivity in the UK increases by about 2 per cent per annum. This improvement in efficiency reduces the labour costs involved in producing a typical unit of output. Improvements in labour productivity allow businesses to enjoy increased profit margins or to reduce prices (while maintaining profit margins), hopefully leading to increased sales.

What do you think?

What actions might the manager of a fast food restaurant take to improve the productivity of his workforce?

We look at the topic of productivity in more detail on pages 248–250.

on pages 248–250.

Labour turnover

$$\text{Turnover} = \frac{\text{number of staff leaving during the year} \times 100}{\text{average number of staff}}$$

This ratio measures the proportion of a workforce leaving their employment at a business over some period of time, usually one year. Low wages and inadequate training, leading to poor morale among employees, may cause high levels of labour turnover. Another cause is ineffective recruitment procedures, resulting in the appointment of inappropriate staff. Other reasons include redundancy and retirement.

Some level of labour turnover is inevitable. Managers seek some level of labour turnover to bring new ideas into a business, but not so high as to impose excessive recruitment costs. The 2007 Annual Survey by the Chartered Institute of Personnel and Development (CIPD) revealed that labour turnover in the UK was 18.1 per cent in 2007, compared with 18.3 per cent in 2006 and 15.7 per cent in 2005.

Managers attempt to manage labour turnover to achieve a balance between bringing new employees with enthusiasm and ideas into the business against the costs of recruitment and the loss of experienced and skilled employees. Figure 22.1 below shows that the impact of labour turnover of most businesses (56 per cent) surveyed has a minor negative impact on performance. This suggests that most businesses face a higher labour turnover than desired or that they face unexpected recruitment costs.

Key terms

Labour productivity measures the relationship between the amount of labour used in production and the quantity of outputs of goods or services.
Labour turnover is the percentage of a business's employees who leave the business over some period of time (normally a year).
Absenteeism occurs when an employee is not present at his or her place of work.

Real-life Business

	0%	1–10%	11–20%	21%+
Senior managers & directors	53	10	13	24
Managers & professionals	31	19	25	25
Administrative, secretarial & technical	19	16	24	41
Services (customer, personal & sales)	19	14	20	47
Manual & craft workers	16	17	33	35

Table 22.1 Labour Turnover, by occupational group – categories of labour turnover rates (Source: Chartered Institute of Personnel Development Annual Survey, 2007)

Why do you think that Services occupations (e.g. customer services) has a higher rate of labour turnover than senior managers and directors?

Does this matter?

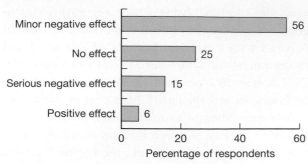

Figure 22.1 The effect of labour turnover on organisational performance
(Source: Chartered Institute of Personnel Development Annual Survey, 2007)

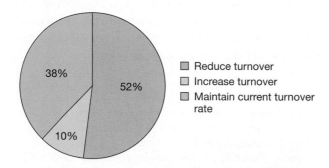

Figure 22.2 Organisations' stated aims when surveryed on labour turnover
(Source: Chartered Institute of Personnel Development Annual Survey, 2007)

Absenteeism

$$Absenteeism = \frac{number\ of\ staff\ absent\ (on\ one\ day) \times 100}{total\ number\ of\ staff}$$

Absenteeism occurs for a variety of reasons, including industrial accidents and illness. The term is frequently used to describe a situation where an employee is absent from work frequently and without good reason. So, it may be used as a measure of the morale and motivation of a workforce. High levels of absenteeism can dramatically increase a business's costs.

Health & safety

$$Health\ \&\ safety = \frac{number\ of\ working\ days\ lost\ per\ annum\ for\ H\ \&\ S\ reasons \times 100}{total\ number\ of\ possible\ working\ days}$$

This measures the safety of the working environment. A dangerous working environment not only lowers employee morale but may also damage the performance of the workforce. Absence due to accidents and injuries in the workplace increases the labour costs incurred by a firm and can lead to adverse publicity.

Managers need to measure employee performance to assess the efficiency (and competitiveness) of the workforce. In service firms (where labour costs are a

high proportion of total costs) this can be a particularly important factor. Measures of employee performance also help to assess whether a workforce is fully motivated.

Planning for an effective workforce

Before a business recruits, selects or trains employees, it must establish future labour needs. This is not simply a matter of recruiting sufficient employees. Those recruited must have the right skills and experience to help the organisation achieve its corporate objectives. Managers will draw up a human resource or workforce plan to detail the number and type of workers the business needs to recruit.

Businesses require a range of information when developing human resource plans:

- They need to research to provide sales forecasts for the next year or two. This will help identify the quantity and type of labour required.
- Data will be needed to show the number of employees likely to be leaving the labour force in general (labour turnover). Information will also be required on potential entrants to the labour force.
- If wages are expected to rise, then businesses may reduce their demand for labour and seek to make greater use of technology.
- The plan will reflect any anticipated changes in the output of the workforce due to changes in productivity or the length of the working week.
- Technological developments will impact on planning the workforce.
- Developments in this field may reduce the need for unskilled employees while creating employment for those with technical skills.

Developing the workforce

One way to improve the performance of employees and the business is to recruit employees with the appropriate skills from outside the organisation. An alternative is to train existing staff to develop their skills and knowledge. Both options can be expensive and take time.

Recruiting and selecting employees

Firms can alter the composition of their workforce through recruitment. The process of recruitment is summarised in Figure 22.3 below.

The human resource department normally plays a key role in the recruitment and selection process. However, the increasing influence of Japanese business practices on British businesses has meant that

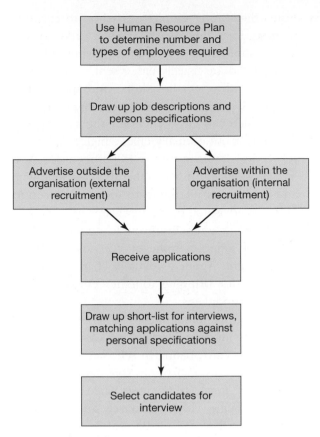

Figure 22.3 The recruitment process

These documents form an important part of recruitment and selection. Candidates' applications should be compared against the person specification and those applicants having the 'best fit' should be invited to interview. At interview, the job description might form the basis for the interviewer's questions.

Examiner's advice

It is easy to get bogged down in the detail of recruitment and selection procedures. While such knowledge is fundamental, it is vital to think about how successful different approaches to recruitment and selection might be in helping to improve the performance of a business.

Key terms

Recruitment and selection is the process of filling an organisation's job vacancies by appointing new staff.

Job descriptions list the duties and responsibilities associated with a particular job.

Person specifications outline the skills, knowledge and experience necessary to fill a given position successfully. These are also termed job specifications.

Internal recruitment takes place when a business looks to fill a vacancy from within the existing workforce.

External recruitment occurs when a business invites applications for vacant posts from any suitably qualified candidates.

Training is the process whereby an individual acquires job related skills and knowledge.

some firms no longer have a separate human resource department. In these circumstances, managers or teams responsible for the relevant area of the business may oversee the process of recruitment.

The recruitment process

The start of recruitment is to draw up job descriptions and person specifications.

Job descriptions relate to the position rather than the person. Typically, job descriptions might contain the following information:

- the title of the post
- employment conditions
- some idea of tasks and duties.

Person or job specifications set out the qualifications and qualities required in an employee. They refer to the person rather than the post and include:

- educational and professional qualifications required
- character and personality needed
- skills and experience wanted.

In 2007, over 80 per cent of businesses surveyed by the CIPD said that they were experiencing recruitment difficulties. The key reasons for recruitment difficulties cited were a lack of necessary specialist skills (65 per cent), followed by higher pay expectations (46 per cent) and insufficient experience (37 per cent). Appointing people who have the potential to grow but who currently don't have all that's required is the most frequently used initiative to overcome recruitment difficulties.

Internal and external recruitment

Firms may recruit internally through promotion or redeployment from within existing employees. This offers a number of benefits:

- candidates will have experience of the business and its culture and will be familiar with the firm's procedures
- internal candidates may not require induction training
- internal recruitment provides employees with opportunities for promotion
- it avoids the need for expensive external advertising
- selection may be easier as more is known about the candidates.

However, internal candidates are drawn from a limited pool of employees and the skills and experience of this group of people may be insufficient to meet the needs of the business. This is more likely in the case of smaller businesses and with senior appointments.

Managers may be keen to have a wider choice of candidates and may seek to recruit externally. This can result in applications from higher quality candidates, especially if recruitment is through national media or nationally-based recruitment agencies. External recruits may bring fresh ideas and enthusiasm into the business. This can be a vital factor in an organisation with a low level of labour turnover.

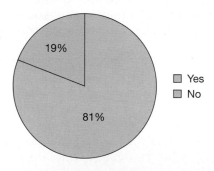

Figure 22.4 Percentage of businesses that advertise all vacancies internally
(Source: Chartered Institute of Personnel Development Annual Survey, 2007)

External recruitment is likely to be very expensive. It also carries a greater risk as candidates are not known to the business. Firms can recruit externally by using a range of methods:

- Firms 'headhunt' employees who are currently working for other organisations in order to offer them employment. Those employees who are headhunted are usually either senior managers or people with specialist skills, perhaps in short supply. Specialist executive recruitment agencies exist which can target precisely the right type of candidates, but normally charge high fees.
- Job centres are run by the Department for Work and Pensions to bring together those seeking work and businesses intending to recruit. Job centres may also advise on training available to workers.
- Employment agencies provide employers with details of suitable applicants for posts they may have vacant. Agencies usually charge considerable fees for bringing together employers and potential candidates.
- The government operates a number of training schemes to improve the skills and knowledge of the workforce. Participating in schemes such as New Deal offers firms a chance to consider the skills and aptitude of possible employees while they are on a training scheme. This is a relatively low-risk strategy and a cheap means of recruitment.

Recruitment can be an expensive exercise. Research in 2007 showed that the average cost of external recruitment for a new employee is over £4,300. For senior managers and directors this figure rises to £10,000.

However, many managers would argue that these figures are less costly than appointing the wrong employee and perhaps having to repeat the process.

What do you think?

Why is it more expensive to appoint a senior employee?

Selection

A number of selection techniques exist. Because of the high costs resulting from recruiting the wrong people, firms are investing more resources and time in the recruitment and selection process.

Interviews remain the most common form of selection technique. Interviews can involve one or two interviewers, or even a panel. They are relatively cheap and allow the two-way exchange of information, but are unreliable as a method of selection. Some people perform well at interview, but that does not necessarily mean they will perform well at work.

Psychometric tests reveal the personality of a candidate. Questions are used to assess candidates' honesty, commitment or ability to fulfil a particular role.

As managers become more aware of the high costs of poor selection decisions, they have made increasing use of assessment centres. In such centres, a number of candidates are subjected to a variety of selection techniques over a period of between two and four days. These might include some or all of the following:

- simulations of circumstances that might occur within the job
- a variety of interviews
- role-plays involving a number of the candidates and assessment centre staff
- psychometric tests.

Evidence suggests that assessment centres are efficient at selecting employees for managerial positions. They are substantially more expensive than operating interviews, but their better performance compared with more traditional selection techniques might make them more cost effective in the long run.

How recruitment and selection can improve a workforce

Recruiting and selecting the right employees can improve the quality of a business's workforce. For example, appointing employees with the following types of skills can allow the business to meet the needs of its customers more effectively:

- **Innovative employees**. Such employees can introduce new ideas into the business, either in relation to the way that production is carried out or new ideas for products. They may bring knowledge and experience from other businesses.
- **Information technology skills**. Most businesses use information technology in some way within the business – perhaps to monitor stocks or to collect information on customer preferences.

Method of selection	Not used	Rarely used	Occasionally used	Frequently used
Formal Interviews	8	5	10	77
Telephone interviews	39	23	23	1
Assessment centres	53	12	19	16
Online tests	71	10	11	9
Group exercises (eg role playing)	54	18	18	10
Personality & aptitude tests	44	12	26	18

Table 22.2 **Methods of selection used by a sample of 843 UK businesses in 2007**
(**Source**: Adapted from CIPD Annual Survey on Recruitment, Retention & Turnover, 2007)

What evidence is there in this table that businesses attempt to minimise costs of selection?

- **Customer service skills**. Dealing effectively with customers and responding to their needs (and complaints) is an important element of successful business performance. Customers who are dissatisfied may move to other businesses and also act as a source of adverse publicity for the business.

Obviously, there are many other skills that new employees can bring into a business. For many businesses, and especially those in the services sector, the quality of the workforce is a crucial element in competitiveness. Some businesses base their advertising on the job-related skills that their employees possess For example, IKEA, the home products retailer, makes the most of the quality of its workforce in its advertising.

However, recuitment can also weaken the performance of a workforce in the short-term. Bringing in new employees who may be unfamiliar with the business's procedures and customers can result in errors and work being completed more slowly than usual.

Of course, recruitment and selection is not the only way to improve the quality of a workforce. Many businesses opt to give employees job-related skills through a programme of training.

Training

Training is a process whereby an individual acquires skills and knowledge. This can help him or her to develop, as well as assisting the organisation in achieving its objectives.

Almost all employees receive training at some point during their working lives. For example, they may receive training when commencing a new job. This is known as induction training and is intended to introduce an employee to the business. Induction training may provide employees with information on the following:

- important policies such as health and safety, and disciplinary procedures
- the layout of the factory or office
- their new colleagues
- the basic duties of the job.

Induction training enables a new recruit to become more productive quickly. It can prevent costly errors resulting from employee ignorance and also make a new employee feel welcome, thereby reducing labour turnover.

Center Parcs

Center Parcs opened its first holiday village at Sherwood Forest in July 1987, offering short-break holidays on a year round basis. Since then it has expanded its operations opening three further holiday villages.

Figure 22.6 Center Parc pool

Each holiday village is set in a forest environment, typically 400 acres in size, and provides high-quality accommodation in fully equipped villas, apartments and lodges, which are set among trees and streams. Each village offers an extensive range of sports and leisure activities plus numerous restaurants, bars and retail outlets and an 'Aqua Sana' spa facility. Woodland, water and a natural healthy environment are the essential elements of a Center Parcs break.

The company has the following statement on its website: 'We value high quality staff and the contribution they make in achieving guest satisfaction and value, recognising employee commitment drives business success.'

Why might Center Parcs have such a clear and highly prominent statement on its website?

Web link

You can find out about Center Parcs at www.centerparcs.co.uk

Employee attitudes to training

A CIPD survey in 2005 entitled *Who learns at work?* found that:

- 78 per cent of the respondents had received some form of training in the previous 12 months
- 94 per cent of the respondents who had undertaken training believed that it helped them to do their job better
- 20 per cent of respondents had undertaken training, whether personal or work-related, in their leisure time
- of those people who had undertaken training outside work, 38 per cent completed training for purely work-related reasons.

The CIPD survey suggests a generally favourable attitude towards learning at work on the part of employees and that many employees display commitment to their own learning. Many employers are seeking to take advantage of this level of commitment.

Types of training

Off-the-job training involves training outside the workplace, either at a college, university, or some other training agency. External courses may take the form of lectures and seminars, self-study or open learning.

On-the-job training does not require the employee to leave the workplace. He or she learns from experienced employees through observation and work shadowing. The trainee may work through instruction manuals or receive guidance from senior employees.

The costs and benefits of training

In spite of the fact that it incurs costs, and can sometimes be disruptive, training offers organisations a number of benefits, as shown in Table 22.3.

Government support for training

The government encourages training in various ways. Through the Department for Innovation, Universities and Skills it funds a range of training schemes such as modern apprenticeships and the 'New Deal'. It also promotes the cause of training through its 'Investors in People' scheme.

Firms that meet the requirement for training of employees (in particular for training employees to assist in meeting corporate objectives) are entitled to use a logo identifying them as meeting this particular standard. This may assist the business in its dealings with customers and other businesses.

Examiner's advice

It is important to appreciate the benefits and drawbacks of techniques such as training. Questions with high mark allocations will often require students to assess the strengths and weaknesses of particular techniques in given circumstances. It will, therefore, be necessary to apply information such as that set out above when responding to this type of question.

What do you think?

Why might employees be attracted to businesses that provide good quality training programmes?

Costs	Benefits
Training uses up valuable resources that could be utilised elsewhere in the organisation.	Training can improve employee performance and hence the competitive position of the business.
Training means that employees are unavailable to the organisation for a period of time.	Training should improve employee motivation and productivity.
Employees, once trained, may leave for better jobs.	Training is a core component of HRM and assists organisations in achieving strategic objectives.
Some managers believe training their staff can lessen the degree of control they have over their subordinates.	A reputation for training will assist organisations in attracting and retaining high quality employees.

Table 22.3 The costs and benefits of training

One step further: employer branding

Employer branding can be defined as creating a perception of the business as a really good place in which to work in the minds of current employees and key stakeholders such as customers and shareholders. A survey of 895 businesses in the UK by the Chartered Institute of Personnel and Development (CIPD) in 2007 revealed that 69 per cent of businesses consider that they have an employer brand. Employer brands are important to smaller businesses: 64 per cent of businesses with less than 250 employees and 66 per cent of employers with 251-201 employees claim to have an employer brand.

Employers offered three main reasons for developing a distinctive employer brand:

- Over three-quarters of businesses surveyed said that it was a vital part of the recruitment process. They used a strong employer brand to help them to attract high-quality employees.
- Other managers believed that a clear employer brand helps to improve the external perceptions of the business. This could help sales in the long term.
- Some businesses use employer branding as a USP and as a means of differentiation from other businesses in the same sector.

Most businesses use employer branding in all materials relating to recruitment and selection.

Summary

A high-quality workforce can be a valuable competitive weapon for businesses. There are a number of ways of measuring the performance of the workforce: labour productivity and turnover are probably the most important of these. Businesses attempt to improve the quality of their workforces through recruitment and training, in the expectation of enhancing competitiveness.

Quick questions

1. State three ways of measuring the performance of a business's workforce.
2. A business has a workforce of 800 employees and last year had a labour turnover figure of 13 per cent. How many people left the business during the year?
3. A sports car manufacturer produces 840 cars each year with a workforce of 42 employees. Calculate its labour productivity in terms of cars produced per employee per year.
4. The following list contains four activities undertaken by businesses during the recruitment process. Place them in the correct sequence:

   - Draw up short list.
   - Draw up job description and person specification.
   - Place job adverts in the media.
   - Use assessment centre to select candidates.

5. Which business term does the following sentence define? 'These outline the skills, knowledge and experience necessary to fill a given position successfully.'
6. Which of the following is an advantage of internal recruitment:

   - The business has access to a larger pool of candidates?
   - It helps businesses to bring in new ideas?
   - There is less likely to be a need for induction training?
   - It is particularly suitable for a firm that is expanding quickly?

7. Complete the following sentences by filling in the missing words. 'On-the-job-training does not require the employee to .... the workplace. He or she learns from .... employees through observation and .... shadowing.'
8. Which of the following is not a means by which the government encourages training:

   - psychometric testing?
   - New Deal?
   - Modern Apprenticeships?
   - Investors in People?

9. Of what business term is the following a definition? 'The process whereby an individual acquires job-related skills and knowledge.'
10. Which of the following is a type of off-the-job-training:

    - observing other employees?
    - lectures at a local college?
    - work shadowing?
    - receiving guidance from senior employees?

Issues for analysis

- The arguments for and against using internal or external recruitment in given situations.
- The short- and long-term effects of recruitment on the performance of a business.
- The case for and against a specific business investing in training.

Issues for evaluation

- Do the benefits of a programme of recruitment outweigh the costs of the programme?
- To what extent might a programme of recruitment and selection improve the performance of a particular business?
- Should a specific firm invest in training its employees?

Analysis and evaluation questions

1 Sandlers Ltd owns and operates 12 department stores in the north of England. It employs 500 people and has attempted to recruit from within. The company's sales staff has not received much training and large numbers of customers have complained about the level of service they receive. Sandlers' Managing Director has decided that the company should invest in a major programme of training for its 390 sales assistants.

a Analyse the ways in which Sandlers Ltd might measure the performance of its workforce. (8 marks)

b To what extent can the company rely upon its 'major programme of training' to improve the performance of its workforce? (15 marks)

2 Parsley & Sons Ltd is a medium-sized business manufacturing components for the electronics industry. The company is experiencing growth after a long period of stability and low labour turnover. The company employs large numbers of skilled employees and has found recently that it is losing its best employees to competitors. It has spent heavily on training in recent years.

a Analyse the case for and against Parsley & Sons Ltd recruiting its new employees externally. (8 marks)

b Discuss the extent to which Parsley & Sons Ltd can determine the performance of its workforce. (15 marks)

Assessment

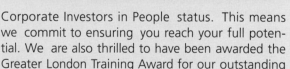

Case study

Red Carnation Hotels (RCH) has eleven outstanding luxury hotels – in the UK, Switzerland, South Africa and the USA:

> 'Presented with elegance, style, and grace, because our business is to make your visit so enjoyable you want to come back.
>
> The Red Carnation Hotel Collection is distinguished by an absolute commitment to attentive service and the comfort of each and every guest. Are you that someone who has a passion for surpassing guest expectations and thrives on offering unrivalled service?'

On their website, they introduce some of their team members. They also show how the dedication of their employees is recognised, through the benefits and rewards that they offer.

> 'Our training and development is second to none, so much so that we have been accredited with Corporate Investors in People status. This means we commit to ensuring you reach your full potential. We are also thrilled to have been awarded the Greater London Training Award for our outstanding achievements in workplace training.'

(Source: Adapted from Red Carnation Hotels' website at www.redcarnationhotels.com)

Questions

(30 marks, 40 minutes)

1 Explain the possible benefits to RCH of using external recruitment. (6 marks)

2 At one point, RCH's labour turnover was reported to be 29 per cent. Examine the possible implications for the business of this figure. (9 marks)

3 To what extent can RCH's recruitment and training policies guarantee an improvement in the performance of the hotels? (15 marks)

23 Theories of motivation

Motivating people is very important for businesses. If the people in a business work hard and to good effect, the performance of the business is likely to be good. A lot of theories have been written about the factors that motivate people. This chapter considers a few of them and encourages you to research others.

What you need to know by the end of this chapter:
• the different views of the sources of motivation
• theories of motivation that reflect the different sources of motivation
• the strengths and weaknesses of the selected theories of motivation.

Key terms
Motivation describes the factors within individuals that arouse, maintain and channel behaviour towards a goal. More simply, it is the will to work.

Productivity measures the relationship between the resources put into an activity and the resulting output.

What is motivation?

Motivation describes the factors that arouse, maintain and channel behaviour towards a goal. There are two ways we can think about motivation at work and what causes it:

• Motivation can be the will to work due to enjoyment of the work itself. This implies that motivation comes from within an individual employee.
• An alternative view of motivation is that it is the will or desire to achieve a given target or goal that is the result of external factors, such as the promise of a reward, or to avoid the threat of punishment.

The first of these views assumes that motivation lies within the individual employee, and the second that it is the result of some external stimuli. People in the workplace have differing views on the sources of motivation. A survey revealed that nearly 90 per cent of employers believe that money is the main motivator, while employees rank pay fourth, behind an interesting job, security and achievement.

What do you think?

What motivates you – internal desire or external stimuli? Does it vary according to the circumstances?

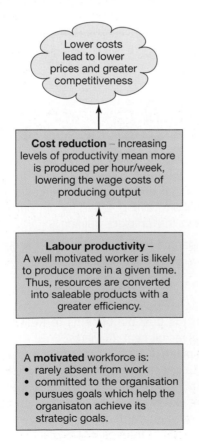

Figure 23.1 How motivation can aid productivity

This distinction is an important one and you should bear it in mind when considering theories of motivation and how, in practice, entrepreneurs and managers can motivate other people.

Why is motivation important?

Whatever its nature, motivation is an important factor for all businesses. Organisations whose workforces possess high levels of motivation tend to show the following characteristics:

- a low level of absenteeism by employees at all levels within the business
- relatively few employees deciding to leave the organisation, giving a low level of labour turnover
- good relations between managers and other employees
- high levels of productivity from the labour force.

A business that enjoys the benefit of a highly motivated workforce is also likely to have a productive workforce. Low production costs offer firms two opportunities:

- to sell their products more cheaply
- to maintain price levels and enjoy greater profits.

A high level of motivation within a workforce offers a business other benefits, too:

- Motivated employees are usually contented, making it easier for businesses to attract other employees – the firm will have a reputation as a 'good' employer. This helps to build the employer brand.

- Modern businesses protect their public image and spend vast sums of money to enhance it. The motivation (and thus the performance) of the workforce can be an important element of creating a positive corporate image.
- Over recent years, firms have become increasingly aware of the need to compete in terms of quality and customer service. If businesses are to compete in these ways, motivated employees are essential.

So, any entrepreneur or manager seeking to improve the performance of his or her workforce may be able to do so by taking steps to improve employee motivation. Understanding the various potential sources of motivation is an important part of taking such a step.

How can businesses motivate employees?

Many different views exist on motivation, and they differ because it is not clear why people work. Is it to gain money, to enjoy social interaction with other humans, or to fulfil personal needs such as achievement and recognition? Or a combination of some or all of these? If managers can identify the main reasons why their staff work, they can determine how best to motivate them at work. It is possible to classify theories of motivation into a number of groups or schools of thought. Three such schools are set out in Table 23.1. (We consider another school of thought in 'One step further' on page 172.)

School of thought	Key writers	Essential ideas
Scientific School	Frederick Winslow TAYLOR (1856–1917)	Motivation is an external factor achieved through money. Employees should be closely supervised and paid piece-rate. Time and motion studies determine efficient means of production and workers are trained and told how to operate.
Human Relations School	Elton MAYO (1880–1949)	This brought sociological theory into management and accepted that employees could be motivated by meeting their social needs. More attention was given to the social dimension of work (e.g. communication, working as groups and consultation between managers and employees).
The Neo-Human Relations School of Management	Abraham MASLOW (1908–1970) and Frederick HERZBERG (1923–2000)	This school highlighted the importance of fulfilling psychological needs to improve employee performance. Motivation, according to Maslow and Herzberg, depended upon designing jobs to fulfil psychological needs.

Table 23.1 Schools of thought on motivation

Examiner's advice

You do not have to know the theories of any particular writer on motivation. You can choose to study the ones on the pages that follow, or any others in which you are interested. However, you should know about at least one theory that relates to financial motivation, and another that considers other factors as a source of motivation.

The School of Scientific Management

Motivating workers became an important issue as the size of businesses increased in the late nineteenth century. Managers developed the division of labour to its fullest extent in an attempt to increase efficiency and improve competitiveness. The introduction of mass production methods, along with the use of division of labour, increased the numbers of people working in factories. At the same time, their tasks became monotonous.

Against this background, managers began to investigate ways of increasing employee motivation to improve competitiveness and employee satisfaction. Frederick Winslow Taylor was the most notable of these early writers on motivation and became known as 'the father of scientific management'.

Taylor began to advise and lecture on management practices and became a consultant to car manufacturer Henry Ford. Taylor's theories were based on a simple interpretation of human behaviour, that people were motivated solely by money – his term was 'rational man'. He combined this principle with a simple interpretation of the role of the manager: to operate the business with maximum efficiency.

The key elements of Taylorism

1 The starting point of Taylor's approach was work-study. He measured and analysed the tasks necessary to complete the production process. He used a stopwatch to measure how long various activities took and sought the most efficient methods of completing tasks. He encouraged the use of the division of labour, breaking down production into small tasks.

2 From this he identified the most efficient employees and the approaches they adopted. Using these as a basis, he then detailed 'normal' times in which duties should be completed and assessed individual performance against these norms.

3 Employees were provided with the equipment necessary to carry out their tasks. This principle extended to giving stokers (men shovelling coal) a shovel of a size appropriate to their physique to maximise their efficiency. They were also given elementary training and clear instructions on their duties.

4 Because, according to Taylor, employees were only motivated by money, the final stage of the system was to design and implement a piece-rate pay system. Under a piece-rate system, employees are paid according to the amount they produce. Taylor, however, developed differential piece-rate systems to encourage efficiency among employees.

Taylor also believed in close supervision of the workforce to ensure that they continued to make the maximum effort possible, motivated by pay.

What do you think?

Is pay the only thing that would motivate you at work? Can you think of circumstances in which this might not be the case?

Taylor's views were unpopular with shop-floor employees. His systems forced them to work hard and, by raising productivity levels, placed the jobs of the less efficient workers under threat. Taylor's approach raised efficiency and productivity, so businesses did not need as many employees. His ideas resulted in strikes and other forms of industrial action by dissatisfied workers.

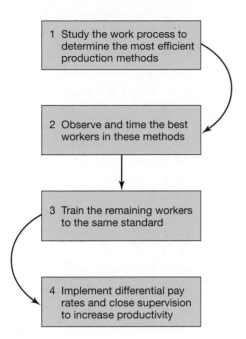

Figure 23.2 The essential features of Taylorism

Taylor's legacy

It is easy to dismiss Taylor and his ideas. His entire philosophy was based on the belief that employees were motivated only by money. He ignored any social dimension of employment and made employees work very hard for what was a meagre wage. His ideas resulted in workers endlessly completing monotonous tasks. There was considerable hostility towards his ideas and opposition from politicians and the business community.

However, Taylor made a significant and enduring contribution to the management of business organisations. He established management as a scientific subject worthy of research and study. His approach was adopted by many premier figures in the business community in the early decades of the century, including Henry Ford. His techniques encouraged the use of mass production and the conveyor belt system. Furthermore, his work provided a starting point for a later and more people-centred approach to management.

Real-life Business

Frederick Winslow Taylor

Taylor was born in Philadelphia in March 1856, the son of a lawyer. He was a brilliant scholar and, after attending Harvard University, trained as an engineer. He spent many years working for Midvale Steel Company in Philadelphia, eventually becoming chief engineer.

While at Midvale, Taylor introduced work-study. Under this technique he observed employees at work and suggested ways of eliminating wasted time and effort by workers. This became the basic principle of his scientific approach to management.

Taylor was a talented inventor, but he decided to become a consultant to spread his ideas on scientific management. His most notable work was at the Bethlehem Steel Company, where his ideas achieved enormous increases in productivity.

Taylor retired at the age of 45. He spent much of his remaining life as a writer and lecturer. His most notable book was The Principles of Scientific Management, published in 1911. He died in 1915, having had a profound impact upon the management of business.

Examiner's advice

Avoid considering Taylor simply in negative terms. Certainly, many of his ideas would not be acceptable in modern businesses, but others (for example, simple piece-rate pay and work-study) have endured. A balanced assessment of Taylor should take into account the lasting elements of his approach, as well as the shortcomings.

The Human Relations School

A fundamental weakness of the Scientific School was that its work ignored the social needs of employees. This, and the obvious unpopularity of the ideas of Taylor, led to the development of the Human Relations School. This school of thought concentrated on the sociological aspects of work. Its foremost member was an Australian-born psychologist, Elton Mayo (1880–1949). Initially, Mayo was one of Taylor's disciples, believing in the importance of scientific management to business efficiency.

Examiner's advice

Many students just think of Mayo in terms of communicating with bosses, and his emphasis on social and sporting facilities. However, this is only part of his work. He advocated the benefits to employers and employees of working in teams – this aspect of his work is an important issue within many businesses today.

The Hawthorne effect

Mayo's views altered as a result of research he conducted at the Western Electric Company in Chicago. The research was to examine the effects of changes in lighting on the productivity of workers at the company's Hawthorne plant. Previous experiments on lighting and productivity had produced unexpected results. Researchers had anticipated that improving lighting would increase productivity because giving workers better working conditions would allow them to work harder and earn more money. They were astonished when productivity increased not only in the group who were given improved lighting, but also among a group whose lighting had not changed.

It became apparent that the employees were responding to the level of attention they were receiving as part of the investigations and because they were working together as a group. This became known as the 'Hawthorne effect'. As a result of this and similar experiments, Mayo stressed the importance of 'social man' within the workplace. From these experiments, Mayo concluded that motivation was dependent upon:

- the type of job being carried out and the type of supervision given to the employee
- group relationships, group morale and the sense of worth experienced by individuals.

The implications of the 'Hawthorne effect'

Following the publication of Mayo's findings, managers gradually became more aware of the importance of meeting the social needs of individuals at work. Social environments at work and informal working groups were recognised as having positive influences upon productivity.

The acceptance of Mayo's views led to a number of developments in businesses during the 1940s and 1950s, many of which remain today:

- Personnel departments were established to ensure that employees' social needs were met at work wherever possible.
- Employees were provided with a range of sporting and social facilities to foster the development of informal groups among employees.
- Works outings and trips became a familiar part of an employee's year (for example, Marks & Spencer organises short-break weekends for its employees).
- Managers gave more attention to teams and teamworking.

Mayo's recognition of the importance of teamworking is perhaps his most enduring testimony. Many firms have organised their workforce into teams, for example, John Lewis and Toshiba.

Web link

For more information about John Lewis, visit www.john-lewis-partnership.co.uk

Mayo's work took forward management in general, and motivation in particular. He moved the focus onto the needs of employees, rather than just on the needs of the organisation.

The Neo-Human Relations School

This could also be called the new Human Relations School. Abraham Maslow and Frederick Herzberg are recognised as key members of this particular school. They began to put forward their views in the 1950s. While the Human Relations School, associated with Elton Mayo, highlighted the sociological aspects of work, the Neo-Human Relations School considered the psychological aspects of employment. This school argued that motivation lies within each individual employee: managers merely need the key to unlock the motivational force.

By focusing on the psychological needs of employees, Maslow and Herzberg encouraged managers to treat their employees as individuals, with different needs and aspirations. Their work emphasised that, because people are different, the techniques required to motivate individuals will also differ.

Business in Focus

Graduates

A 2007 survey by accountants Ernst and Young has shown that graduates rate training and development more highly than the salary they will receive. About 44 per cent of those responding to the internet survey rated training opportunities most highly among potential first employers. Only 18 per cent of the 1,051 graduates (mainly in accountancy) who responded to the poll voted for salary and benefits as their top concern.

Ernst and Young said the kind of people voting in the poll on its graduate web page were likely to be those who had studied for accountancy degrees and who had some vocational experience. Salary and benefits, and work/life balance, came in second and third places respectively. Placed fourth in the importance stakes in the poll was the reputation of a business at 12 per cent; people and culture came fifth on 8 cent.

(Source: Adapted from BBC News, http://news.bbc.co.uk/1/hi/education/6957082.stm)

Do the results of this survey show that pay as a motivator is outdated and irrelevant for today's managers?

Maslow's hierarchy of needs

In 1954, Maslow published his 'hierarchy of needs', setting out the various needs that, he argued, every one attempted to meet through working. Maslow presented his hierarchy of needs as a triangle with basic needs shown at the bottom and his so-called higher needs towards the top.

Maslow's argument was a relatively simple one. Employees, he argued, have a series of needs they seek to fulfil at work. These are in a hierarchy – once a lower level need is satisfied, individuals strive to satisfy needs further up the hierarchy. Abraham Maslow established five levels of human needs that can be satisfied through employment.

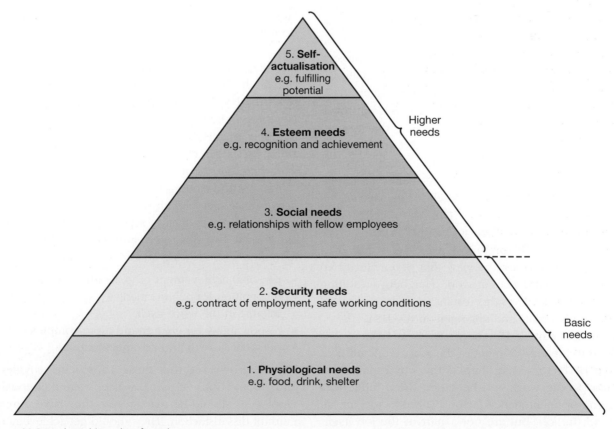

Figure 23.3 Maslow's hierarchy of needs

Maslow's level of need	Examples	Means of satisfying needs
1 Physiological needs	Food, water, shelter, clothing	Through pay and a warm and dry working environment
2 Security needs	A safe and secure working environment for employees	Implementing a proper health and safety policy, providing employees with contracts of employment
3 Social needs	Contact and friendships with other employees	Social and sporting facilities, opportunities to work in groups
4 Esteem needs	Achievement, recognition and self-respect	Delegating authority to junior employees, offering promotion opportunities
5 Self-actualisation	To fulfil one's potential completely	Providing opportunities to take new responsibilities and to develop new skills

Table 23.2 An explanation of Maslow's hierarchy of needs

The key point of Maslow's argument was that a business could motivate its employees by offering them the chance to fulfil a higher level of need once a lower one was satisfied. So once an employee's basic needs had been met, perhaps through a system of fair pay, he or she could be motivated further by the offer of secure and continuing employment. Similarly, a worker whose social needs were met through employment could next be motivated by the opportunity to satisfy self-esteem needs. This could be achieved by taking responsibility for a major project, offering the chance of achievement and recognition.

Maslow's theory was attractive to managers from the outset. It offered a more individualistic approach to motivating employees, recognising that not all people are the same. Managers had long realised that what motivated one person would not necessarily motivate another. Maslow's theory offered an explanation and an alternative approach for managers.

Frederick Herzberg's two-factor theory

Herzberg's two-factor theory was the result of a study designed to test the view that people face two major sets of influences at work. Herzberg's resulting theory was based on the results to questions asked of 200 accountants and engineers in the USA.

The first part of Herzberg's motivation theory is related to the environment of the job. He identified a range of factors that shaped the environment in which people work and he called these influences hygiene or maintenance factors. These factors are all around the job, but are not a part of the job itself.

Herzberg's research identified a number of hygiene factors, including the following:

- company policies and administration
- supervision of employees
- working conditions
- salary
- relationship with fellow workers (at the same level).

Herzberg's crucial finding was that hygiene factors do not lead to motivation, but without them employees may become dissatisfied. So, according to Herzberg, an employee cannot be motivated by pay, but might be dissatisfied by inadequate financial rewards. Hygiene factors were so named because Herzberg believed attention to them would prevent hygiene problems. It is important to note that Herzberg's research classified pay as a hygiene factor and, therefore, as unable to motivate.

The second finding of Herzberg's research established those factors with the ability to motivate – the motivators. These factors relate to the job itself and can be used to positively motivate employees. He identified the following factors as motivators:

- personal achievement of goals and targets
- recognition for achievement
- interest in the work itself
- responsibility for greater and more complex duties
- personal growth and advancement.

Herzberg believed that these approaches (hygiene and motivation) must be used simultaneously. Employees should be managed so they have a minimum of dissatisfaction. They should get achievement,

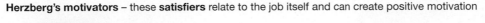

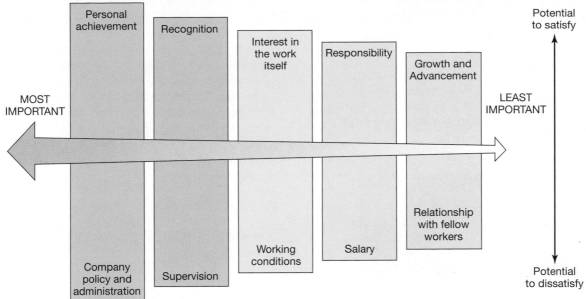

Figure 23.4 Herzberg's hygiene and motivational factors

recognition for achievement, take interest in their work and be given responsibility to allow them to grow and develop within their work.

Assessing the work of the Neo-Human Relations School

The research and writing of Maslow and Herzberg has had a major impact on the way in which businesses have managed their employees. Although there are differences in their approaches, many similarities also exist. As illustrated in Table 23.3, Herzberg's motivators broadly correspond with Maslow's higher needs.

Both have the major advantage in that they were not simply theoretical writings – practical implications for management were within the theories. Both authors encouraged managers to utilise their employees' abilities by giving them challenging tasks.

Weaknesses do exist within these theories, of course. Herzberg's assertion that pay cannot be used to motivate might be true of many employees in wealthy, developed economies. However, this may not be the case with workers in poorer, developing countries. Equally, Maslow's theory is based upon a hierarchy and the assumption that individuals move from one level to the next. His work has been criticised on the grounds that people do not move through these needs in the same order. It also assumes that, once a need is fulfilled, it loses its power to motivate. This may not be the case, especially with the higher needs.

	Maslow	Herzberg
Motivation factors (higher needs)	• Self-actualisation needs • Esteem needs • (Higher needs)	• Achievement • Recognition • Responsibility • Interest in work • Personal growth
Maintenance factors (lower needs)	• Social needs • Security needs • Physiological needs • (Mainly lower needs)	• Company policy and administration • Supervision • Working conditions • Relationship with fellow workers

Table 23.3 Herzberg and Maslow compared

Business in Focus

Frederick Herzberg

Frederick Herzberg was born in Massachussetts in the USA in 1923. He attended City College, New York before enlisting in the army. During his military service he witnessed the survivors at Dachau concentration camp.

Figure 23.5 Frederick Herzberg

Herzberg gained a PhD in Psychology at the University of Pittsburg and began to turn his attention to business management. He became Professor of Management at Case Western Reserve University, where he established the Department of Mental Health. In 1972 he joined the University of Utah's College of Business.

Herzberg developed a reputation as one of the most influential thinkers on people at work and employee motivation. He combined his deep knowledge of employee psychology with a series of practial experiments in the workplace. His book 'Work and the Nature of Man' (1966) was voted one of the ten most important books on management theory and practice in the twentieth century. He died in January 2000.

Examiner's advice

Motivation is a popular topic in examination questions and a popular subject with students. However, many answers receive low marks because students do not apply their knowledge to the scenario in the question. Many questions on motivation ask you to consider whether the events in the scenario can be explained in terms of relevant theory. The skill is, therefore, to analyse whether the theory 'fits' the scenario.

One step further: Process theories of motivation

Process theories of motivation look at what people are thinking about when they decide whether or not to put effort into a particular activity. Examples of such theories include expectancy and equity theories. They try to capture the process that employees go through when making choices with goals in mind. Unlike the other theories of motivation we have considered, they see the individual as an active decision-maker, rather than trying (in the case of the Neo-Human Relations School) to meet certain needs. Process theories emphasise the actual process (or method) of motivation.

Victor Vroom's expectancy theory

This theory argues that motivation depends on employees' expectations of the results of their efforts. If employees know what they want from an outcome and believe they can achieve it, they will be motivated.

If an employee was promised and therefore expects particular childcare facilities to be available, but due to over-demand they turn out not to be, the employee's expectations might be damaged so much that they might withhold effort, withdraw their commitment, or even resign. This employee is not looking for a particular need (such as promotion) to be satisfied, and therefore theories such as those put forward by Maslow or Herzberg might not be appropriate to explain the behaviour in this situation.

Adams' equity theory

This theory related motivation to the potential rewards that are promised to an individual. John Stacey Adams gave the name 'equity theory' to the simple assertion that members of any workforce wish to be treated fairly or equitably in relation to others. Adams argued that employees are in a constant process of 'comparing' themselves (in terms of pay or working conditions) to colleagues or employees in other businesses. If employees consider themselves to be treated unfairly, their motivation and effort may be reduced.

Web link

You can find out more about the equity theory of motivation at www.businessbells.com/adamsequitytheory

Quick questions

1 Read the following two options and then decide which of the four statements set out below is correct.

Option A: the will to work due to the enjoyment of work itself.

Option B: the will or desire to achieve a given target or goal.

- Only statement A is a correct definition of motivation.
- Only statement B is a correct definition of motivation.
- Both statements are correct definitions of motivation.
- Neither statement is a correct definition of motivation.

2 Is the following statement true or false? 'A highly motivated workforce can help a business to improve its image.'

3 Which writers on motivation were responsible for the following two concepts:
- rational man
- social man.

a Taylor and Maslow?
b Taylor and Mayo?
c Mayo and Herzberg?
d Maslow and Herzberg?

4 State two ways in which improving motivation might improve a business's performance.

5 Place these essential elements of Taylorism in the correct order:

a Implement differential pay rates and close supervision.
b Study the work processes to determine the most efficient production methods.
c Train all the workers to master the most efficient methods.
d Observe and time the most efficient workers.

6 Mayo would have supported the use of the following techniques to motivate employees with one exception. Which one is the exception:

a works outings and trips?
b the provision of sports facilities?
c the use of teams within businesses?
d the use of piece-rate pay systems?

7 Complete the following sentence by filling in the missing spaces. Mayo's research at the .... Plant in Chicago was to examine the effects of changes in lighting on the .... of workers.

8 Place the following four needs from Maslow's hierarchy in the correct order (from lowest to highest):

a esteem needs
b security needs
c physiological needs
d social needs.

9 'Salary, working conditions, company policies and administration and recognition are all hygiene factors.' True or false?

10 Is the following statement true or false? 'Maslow's higher needs roughly correspond with Herzberg's motivators.'

Issues for analysis

- Explain the factors that may motivate employees in given circumstances.
- Offer an explanation supported by relevant theory on how a business might improve the motivation of its workforce in particular circumstances.

Issues for evaluation

- What might be the most effective means of motivating an employee or group of employees?
- To what extent is it possible to motivate an entire workforce?
- Discuss whether it is possible to motivate a workforce in particular circumstances?

Analysis and evaluation questions

1 Dennis Muir owns and manages a garden centre selling plants and a range of gardening equipment. He is a wealthy man who started the business when he retired as an accountant. He employs five full-time and some part-time staff – the precise number depends upon the time of the year. Dennis is concerned that his labour turnover is high and that his workers are not as productive as he would like or expect. Dennis is not sure whether to increase pay or to use other methods of motivation.

a Analyse the factors that might motivate Dennis at work. (8 marks)

b To what extent might Dennis be able to improve the motivation of his workforce by increasing pay? (15 marks)

2 Michelle Twigg is an ex-model and the founder of 'Twiggie's' an upmarket hairdressing chain based in London. She is in the process of opening three new hairdressing branches – this will bring the total to eleven. Michelle is concerned that, as her business has grown, she has not been able to supervise it as closely as she would like. Her employees seem to have become less productive and there has been an increase in customer complaints. Michelle is wondering whether to increase the pay of her employees, especially that of her branch managers.

a Examine why improving pay might improve the motivation and performance of Michelle's workforce. (8 marks)

b Discuss whether or not motivational theories might be of any assistance to Michelle in these circumstances. (15 marks)

Assessment

Case study

A majority of employees who work in small and medium-sized business say that they prefer this scale of organisation because they 'feel more at home'. This supports the view that small and medium-sized businesses offer working environments that are comfortable yet stimulating.

This working environment within a small or medium-sized business is in contrast to that operating within large businesses. In the latter employees are unlikely to know people who work in other departments or areas of the business and may feel that they have little in common. This can make it more difficult for employers to ensure that the entire workforce is working towards shared goals.

In large businesses employees are also more likely to feel that their contribution at work has little effect on the overall performance of the business. They can view themselves as a very small cog in a very large wheel. This is likely to decrease levels of motivation. Smaller businesses appear less likely to de-motivate employees in this way and their scale allows flexible working practices offering employees more variety and a greater say in determining their working lives.

(Source: Adapted from BBC News at: http://news.bbc.co.uk/1/hi/business/2943734.stm, 15th May 2007)

Questions

(30 marks, 40 minutes)

1 Using examples from the text, explain two possible sources of motivation for an employee in any business. (6 marks)
2 Examine the problems that the manager of a small business might face in motivating his or her workforce. (9 marks)
3 To what extent does motivational theory suggest that it is more difficult to motivate employees in a large business? (15 marks)

24 Motivation in practice

Workforce performance is often a key indicator of the overall performance of a business. A highly motivated workforce can help to give a business a competitive edge over its rivals. This need to enhance competitiveness has been the driving force behind many practical attempts to improve employee motivation. Chapter 23 considered the theoretical bases for employee motivation. This chapter takes this a step further and examines the practical methods that businesses can adopt for this purpose.

What you need to know by the end of this chapter:
- the financial methods that may be used to motivate employees
- how job design can be used as a technique of employee motivation
- the techniques and benefits of empowering employees
- how working in teams can improve employee motivation and performance.

Financial methods of motivation

Managers and organisations use a variety of pay systems in an attempt to improve the performance of their workforce. Despite attention given to the views of Herzberg, which suggest that monetary methods of motivation are of limited value, pay remains a major incentive.

Salaries and wages

Most employees in the UK receive their payment in the form of salaries or wages. Salaries are expressed in annual terms (e.g. a production manager might be paid a salary of £30,000 per year) and are normally paid monthly. Salaried employees are not normally required to work a set number of hours per week though their contract of employment may state a minimum number of hours.

On the other hand, wages are usually paid weekly and employees are required to be at work for a specified number of hours. Employees are normally paid a higher rate (known as overtime) for any additional hours worked.

Piecework

Under this pay system, employees are paid according to the quantity they produce. Thus, an employee on a production line might receive an agreed amount for each unit of production they complete. Piecework is common in a number of industries in the UK including textiles, electronics and agriculture.

Piecework offers businesses a number of advantages and disadvantages. Since the implementation of the minimum wage, employers have faced additional problems in using piecework. Employers using piecework have to ensure that their employees earn at least

Writer	Opinions on the motivational powers of pay
Frederick Taylor	Taylor saw pay as the primary motivating factor for all workers. He referred to workers as 'economic animals' and supported the use of piece-rate.
Abraham Maslow	He saw pay as a reward permitting employees to meet the lower needs on their hierarchy.
Frederick Herzberg	Pay is a hygiene factor and a possible cause of dissatisfaction. In a few circumstances pay might be a motivator if, for example, it is used as a recognition for merit.

Table 24.1 Opinions on pay

the minimum wage rate per hour. The UK government introduced the minimum wage on 1 April 1999. This legislation covered full- and part-time employees as well as temporary workers and those on piecework. Since then the wage has increased steadily and at rates above inflation and the average increase in wages. This has benefited low-paid employees, but has imposed an additional cost burden on businesses.

When the minimum wage was initially introduced, businesses argued that it would result in around 80,000 job losses. These fears have proved to be unfounded and the government has raised the minimum wage rates every year since its introduction. In October 2007 the rate for employees aged over 21 was increased to £5.52 (compared with £3.60 when it was introduced in 1999). Workers aged between 18 and 21 received £4.60 an hour from October 2007.

Key terms

Fringe benefits are rewards received by employees in addition to their wages or salary. Common examples include company cars and private health care.

Performance-related pay exists where some part of an employee's pay is linked to the achievement of targets at work. These targets might include sales figures or achieving certain grades in his or her annual appraisal.

Piecework (also called piece-rate) is a system whereby employees are paid according to the quantity of a product they produce.

Fringe benefits

These are sometimes referred to as 'perks'. Fringe benefits are those extras an employee receives as part of their reward package. Examples include the following.

- a company car (or a mileage allowance for an employee's own car)
- luncheon vouchers
- private health insurance
- employers' contributions to pension schemes
- discounts for company products.

Firms tend to use fringe benefits to encourage employee loyalty and to reduce the number of employees leaving the firm. A danger of the widespread use of fringe benefits is that costs can increase quickly, reducing profitability.

Performance-related pay (PRP)

Performance-related pay (or PRP) has become more widely used over recent years and has developed along with employee appraisal systems. PRP is only paid to those employees who meet or exceed some agreed targets. Under PRP, employees are paid for their contribution to the organisation, rather than their status within it.

Businesses of all sizes have introduced PRP. Examples include Cadbury's and Nissan, as well as schools and colleges from the public sector. PRP remains popular, and many employees support linking some element of pay to performance.

Business in Focus

Rascals Day Nursery

A nursery proprietor in London became the first person to be prosecuted for breaking the UK minimum wage laws in August 2007. Teresa Aguda, owner of Rascals Day Nursery in Walthamstow, was fined £2,500 after being prosecuted by HM Revenue & Customs (HMRC). She also pleaded guilty to obstruction, and had to pay £500 in costs.

Aguda was prosecuted after refusing to let HMRC staff enter the nursery to check if she was paying her staff the right amount of money. The judge at Waltham Forest Magistrates' Court called Aguda's refusal to co-operate 'a scandalous breach of the National Minimum Wage legislation'.

The National Minimum Wage Act 1998 implies a right to the minimum wage into contracts of employment, so a worker who has been underpaid can commence legal proceedings to recover the difference between the wages paid and the National Minimum Wage. It is presumed that the worker has been underpaid unless the employer can prove otherwise.

HMRC has been specifically looking at the nursery sector, where staff are traditionally low paid. The hairdressing industry has already been scrutinised, and the hospitality and hotel industries are said to be next.

(Source: Adapted from The Workplace Law website, at www.workplacelaw.net/display.php?resource_id=9022)

What impact do you think that Mrs Aguda's actions will have had on the motivation and performance of her staff?

What advice might you offer to Mrs Aguda regarding the future motivation of her staff?

However, there have been criticisms of the huge bonuses paid to some senior managers and directors of moderately successful companies.

Criticisms of PRP

A number of criticisms of performance-related pay have been put forward:

- Many employees perceive PRP as fundamentally unfair. This is particularly true of those working in the services sector where employee performance is difficult to measure. Employees fear that they might be discriminated against because they do not get on with the manager who conducts their appraisal interview. This can result in their performance worsening, not improving.
- A majority of businesses operating PRP systems do not put sufficient funds into the scheme. Typically, the operation of a PRP scheme adds 3–4 per cent to a business's wage bill. This only allows employees to enjoy relatively small performance awards, which may be inadequate to change employee performance.

Developments in PRP

Increasing numbers of businesses are implementing a system known as variable pay. Some managers argue that a business's performance often depends upon the achievements of the few.

Variable pay is really a development of PRP. It is similar in that it rewards employee performance, but there are differences. PRP operates according to a formula used throughout the company. Variable pay is far more flexible and the potential rewards for star employees are greater. If the business performs well employees benefit under variable pay, but can suffer financial penalties in a less successful period.

However, management consultant Peter Newhouse & Co. believe that variable pay has a limited impact on motivation, and that a recent survey shows poorly designed variable pay systems can demotivate.

Web link

Read the views of Peter Newhouse at www.peternew house.com/services/index.html

Some managers remain unconvinced of the value of PRP, no matter how sophisticated the scheme. The widespread use of PRP may, in part, be an attempt by managers to keep pay rates down for the majority of employees. PRP, or variable pay, treats employees as individuals limiting the ability of trade unions to bargain collectively.

Key term

Employee appraisal schemes assess and evaluate the performance of workers over a period of time with the intention of improving their performance.

Examiner's advice

PRP remains a highly topical issue. While there are a number of arguments in favour of it, a central weakness remains. This can be explained in terms of the theory we covered in Chapter 23. Writers such as Maslow and Herzberg argued that money has limited power to motivate employees. PRP, no matter how it is implemented, has more in common with Frederick Taylor's views of motivating employees.

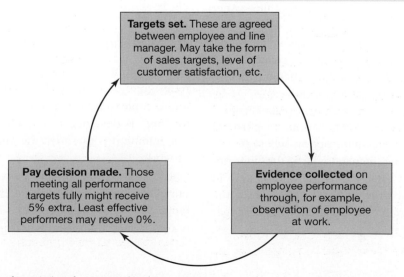

Figure 24.1 The operation of a typical performance-related pay system

Profit sharing

Profit sharing is a system whereby employees receive some of the business's profits. This is a type of performance-related pay, but one that may not discriminate between the performances of individual members of staff. Such payments, which may vary according to salary or wage, are distinct from and additional to regular earnings.

Profits are paid out to employees immediately in the form of cash or company shares. Profit sharing in the form of ownership of shares in the firm has, in a few cases, also involved participation by employees in the firm's management.

Profit-sharing schemes may improve employees' loyalty to the company. These schemes can help to break down the 'them and us' attitude. Under profit-sharing schemes, a greater level of profit is regarded as being of benefit to all employees, and not just senior managers and shareholders. Employees may be more willing to accept changes designed to improve the business's profitability.

The danger with profit-sharing schemes is that they can be too small and fail to provide employees with a worthwhile payment. On the other hand, if schemes are too generous, the company may have insufficient funds for capital investment.

Share ownership

This can be a development of profit-sharing schemes. Some businesses pay their employees' share of the profits in the form of company shares. Share ownership schemes vary enormously in their operation. Here, we consider two of the main schemes operated by UK companies.

Some businesses offer employees the opportunity to purchase shares after saving for a period of time. After say, five years, employees can purchase shares at the price they were at the start of the savings scheme. This is a popular type of scheme, though tax changes have made it more difficult to operate. Other businesses offer employees free shares as an incentive.

Share options are a form of share ownership normally aimed at senior managers. About 14 per cent of UK companies operate share option schemes.

Under share options, managers have the opportunity to buy company shares at some agreed date in the future, but at the current share price. Thus, the current share price might be £2.50 and the manager is given the option to purchase 1,000 shares in three years' time at this price. In three years the market price of shares may have risen to £3.50. This offers the manager the chance to purchase the 1000 shares for £2,500 (£2.50 × 1,000) and to sell them immediately for £3,500, giving a profit of £1,000. If the share price falls over the three-year period, the manager will choose not to buy the shares.

> **Key terms**
>
> **Variable pay** is a flexible form of performance-related pay which offers employees a highly individual pay system related to their performance at work.

Non-monetary forms of motivation

Non-monetary methods of motivation tend to focus upon the design of employees' jobs. Employees can be motivated by asking them to do a job that is challenging and interesting. A good job should have at least a number of the features listed below.

- Employees carry out duties that result in a definite end product.
- Clear and challenging goals give employees something to aim at. Goals should be demanding, but not unattainable.
- Employees should be able to identify easily their contributions to the organisation.
- Jobs should be designed so that jobholders are involved in planning their own schedules of work, choosing their work methods, and coping with problems as they arise.

The main methods of non-monetary motivation attempt to incorporate some of these features into the working lives of employees.

Job enrichment

Job enrichment occurs when employees' jobs are redesigned to provide them with more challenging and complex tasks. This process, also called 'vertical loading', is designed to use all employees' abilities. The intention is to enrich the employee's experience of work.

Frederick Herzberg was a strong supporter of job enrichment. He believed that enrichment provided employees with motivators that increase the satisfaction they might get from working.

Job enrichment normally involves a number of elements:

- redesigning jobs so as to increase, not just the range of tasks, but the complexity of them
- giving employees greater responsibility for managing themselves
- offering employees the authority to identify and solve problems relating to their work
- providing employees with the training and skills essential to allow them to carry out their enriched jobs effectively.

Job enrichment involves a high degree of skill on the part of the managers overseeing it. They must ensure that they do not ask employees to carry out duties of which they are not capable.

Key terms

Job design is the process of grouping together individual tasks to form complete jobs.
Job enrichment occurs when employees' jobs are redesigned to provide them with more challenging and complex tasks.

Real-life Business

Tyrells

Founded in 2002, Tyrells Potato Chips produces gourmet hand-cooked potato and vegetable crisps which are sold at high-end retail outlets including Harrods, Harvey Nichols and Waitrose. Tyrells is the only UK crisp manufacturer to grow its own potatoes and hand-fry them on its Herefordshire farm. Tyrells employs 45 people and supplies around 300,000 packets of crisps to 4,000 customers every week.

The Founder of Tyrells Potato Chips, William Chase, values the role his employees play and have played in the company's success. 'We now have a small team here at Tyrells, all fully trained in all aspects of the chip-making process. Everyone enjoys being part of a growing company and we all contribute individually to the success of the company, and are passionate about producing real food, with pedigree.'

(Source: Adapted from Tyrells website at www.tyrellspotatochips.co.uk)

In what way do you think William Chase motivates his employees?

Is it easier to put motivation theory into practice in a growing company?

Web link

Find out more about Tyrells at www.tyrellspotato chips.co.uk

Job enlargement

Job enlargement does not increase the complexity of tasks carried out by an employee. Instead it increases the number of similar duties. It is also termed 'horizontal loading'.

A number of firms operating a policy of job enlargement simply require employees to carry out a number of similar tasks. Thus, a receptionist might be asked to carry out a number of duties in addition to dealing with telephone and personal enquiries from customers. The receptionist may also be asked to maintain records of petty cash and update customer records for example.

Job enlargement offers benefits to the employee in that carrying out a range of duties, rather than a single one repeatedly, may stimulate their interest. The business gains an advantage from having an employee able to carry out a wider range of duties, possibly reducing its labour costs.

Job rotation is a particular type of job enlargement. Under this system employees switch regularly from one duty to another. Thus, a supermarket may require employees to spend a week on the checkout, a week stacking shelves and a week dealing with customer enquiries. Rotation may reduce the level of monotony, but does not increase the challenge of the job.

Business in Focus

Today was fun

Sharyn Wortman is the CEO of Today Was Fun. It is an organic tea company that she runs from a barge in Putney, London. The company supplies a range of organic and eco-friendly teas. The extract below is from the company's website.

'Make every day fun

If we can't, at the end of each working day, say Today was Fun, we're in the wrong business. To ensure we can say it, we pour our hearts into everything we do and we:

- play well with others
- respect everyone
- eat well

Figure 24.2 Sharyn Wortman

- listen and learn
- dream
- wear comfortable shoes
- laugh whenever possible.

And we keep in mind that there is more to life than work. So don't call us on Fridays because we won't be in. Monday to Thursday we'll be hard at work sending as much fun + wisdom around the world as we can. But on Fridays we work on ourselves.

Some of us paint on Fridays, some write, some sing and others take time to be with their families. As a result we're happier humans. See if you can tell next time you deal with us.

(Source: Today Was Fun website at www.today-wasfun.com)

To what extent do you think that Sharyn's approach to motivation will result in a high level of performance from her workforce?

Web link

See what they get up to on Fridays by visiting the company's website at www.todaywasfun.com/makingitfun.htm

What do you think?

Why do you think that Sharyn Wortman treats her employees in this way?

Key term
Job enlargement entails giving employees more duties of a similar level of complexity.

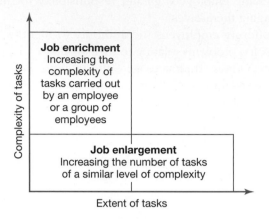

Figure 24.3 Job enrichment and job enlargement

Employee empowerment

Empowerment involves redesigning employees' jobs to allow them greater control over their working lives. Empowerment gives employees the opportunity to decide how to carry out their duties and how to organise their work.

Empowerment can make work more interesting as it offers opportunities to meet a number of individual needs. Empowered workers can propose and implement new methods of working as they bring a new perspective to decision-making. They may spend a part of their working lives considering the problems they face and proposing solutions.

Key term
Empowerment is a series of actions designed to give employees greater control over their working lives

Empowerment would receive the approval of Maslow and Herzberg. It provides motivators, as well as offering employees the opportunity to fulfil higher needs.

Employees require training if they are to be empowered. They are unlikely to have the skills necessary to schedule tasks, solve problems, recruit new employees and introduce new working practices. It takes time to implement empowerment and teething problems are common.

Business in Focus

The Co-operative Bank

The Co-operative Bank estimates that it has saved £10 million since implementing an employee suggestion scheme in 1992. The employee proposing the idea is awarded 5 per cent of the first year's savings, up to a maximum of £25,000. However, only 12 per cent of the Bank's employees say that financial rewards are the main reason for offering ideas. Most want to see their ideas put into practice and the performance of the Bank improve.

Teamworking

Teamworking exists when an organisation breaks down its production processes into large units instead of relying upon the use of the division of labour. Teams are then given responsibility for completing the large units of work. Team members carry out a variety of duties including planning, problem-solving and target-setting.

A number of different team types operate within businesses:

- Production teams – many production lines have been organised into distinct elements called 'cells'. Each of these cells is staffed by teams whose members are multi-skilled. They monitor product quality and ensure that production targets are met.
- Quality circle teams – these are small teams designed to propose solutions to existing problems and to suggest improvements in production methods. The teams contain members drawn from all levels within the organisation.
- Management teams – increasingly, managers see themselves as complementary teams establishing the organisation's objectives and overseeing their achievement.

There has been a major trend in businesses towards teamworking over recent years. Teamworking is a major part of the so-called Japanese approach to production and its benefits have been extolled by major companies such as Honda and John Lewis.

Web link

John Lewis operates own 26 John Lewis department stores, 185 Waitrose supermarkets, an online and catalogue business and makes extenive use of teamworking. Visit the company's website at www.johnlewispartnership.co.uk

In particular, look at the company's video about its relations with its employees – or 'partners', as they are called. This can be found on the page entitled 'The Partnership Spirit'.

Teamworking offers employees the opportunity to meet their social needs, as identified by Maslow; Herzberg identified relationships with fellow workers as a hygiene factor. However, much of the motivational force arising from teamworking comes with the change in job design that usually accompanies it. Teamworking requires jobs to be redesigned, offering employees the chance to fulfil some of the higher needs identified by Maslow, such as esteem needs. Similarly, teamworking offers some of the motivators, for example achievement.

Organisational structure and motivational techniques

In many ways, the structure of the organisation determines the non-financial motivational techniques that can be used. A flatter organisational structure with wider spans of control is likely to provide more opportunities, and arguably a great need for, delegation. If this is the case, then the design of jobs is more likely to incorporate factors such as job enrichment, employee empowerment and teamworking. In an organisation with a flatter structure, managers are likely to be overwhelmed by their workloads unless they delegate some activities to more junior employees.

In contrast, a business utilising a taller organisational structure with narrower spans of control, but more levels of hierarchy is likely to have to take a different approach to motivating its employees. The opportunities for motivating through job design may be more limited, though use may be made of techniqies such as job rotation. However, the use of techniques that rely on signififcant amounts of delegation may be inappropriate. This type of organisation may make greater use of financial methods of motivation.

One step further: team pay

Team pay is a method of linking the pay of employees to the level of performance that they have achieved in a team. Team pay means that all members of a team receive some sort of financial incentive when a goal or target is reached. The goals might be financial, sales related or expressed in terms of quality. Team pay might be a supplement to basic pay or it might represent the entirety of an employee's pay.

Team pay is a very attractive technique, as more businesses adopt flatter organisational structures and make more use of delegation. Modern businesses using these approaches to organising their employees require a workforce that can be flexible in its ability to deliver improvements in quality, profitability and customer service.

Team pay aims to reinforce behaviour that leads to effective teamwork. It encourages group endeavour rather than just individual performance. It can be argued that pay systems that encourage the individual do not foster teamwork. In addition, it is argued that managers treat team members as individuals only, rather than relating to them in terms of what the team can achieve. An appropriate balance has to be struck between individual performance and the individual's performance in a team.

Summary

Employers can use financial and non-financial techniques to motivate employees. A range of financial techniques is used. Some of them are linked closely to the amount a worker produces, others to the profitability of the business. Non-financial techniques of motivation centre on the design of the employee's job, the degree of authority that the employee is given and the opportunities to work as a member of a team.

Quick questions

1 'Under this pay system, employees are paid according to the quantity they produce.' Of what is this a definition?

2 Which of the following best describes the term 'overtime':

a The amount paid for each unit of production?

b The hourly wage rate paid to supervisors who oversee other workers?

c The hourly wage rate paid for any hours worked over the normal amount?

d Any hourly wage rate in excess of the minimum wage?

3 Which of the following is not a fringe benefit:

a overtime payments paid to employees?

b private health insurance?

c discounts on company products?

d a company car?

Team Pay	Individual Merit Pay
Rewards teamwork and co-operation	Creates internal competition
Encourages group to improve work systems	Encourages withholding of information
Increases flexibility and ability to respond to changing needs	Individuals try to improve system — results in failure
Not incorporated in base pay	Decreases flexibility
Encourages information sharing and communication	Incorporated into base salary
Focus on wider organisation	No focus on wider organisation

Table 24.2 Contrasting approaches: team pay vs individual pay
(Source: 'Institute of Employment Studies Report 281: Team working and pay' by M Thompson, May 1995
http://www.employment-studies.co.uk/summary/summary.php? id=281)

4 Complete the following sentence by filling in the blanks. 'Performance-related pay (PRP) rewards employees for their .... to an organisation rather than their .... within it.'

5 '................. / ...... is a development of PRP. It rewards performance, but it is more flexible and offers far greater rewards for 'star' performers.' Which of the following terms could be inserted in the space:

a piecework pay?
b hourly pay?
c bonus pay?
d variable pay?

6 State two possible benefits of profit sharing.

7 Which of the following should not be a feature of a well-designed job:

a Employees carry out a variety of duties?
b Employees earn an hourly pay rate in excess of the minimum wage?
c Employees are given clear and challenging goals?
d Employees are able to identify their contribution to the organisation?

8 Complete the following sentences by filling in the missing words. '...... / .... occurs when employees' jobs are redesigned to provide them with more .... and .... tasks.'

9 What is the alternative name for job enlargement?

10 Of what is the following a definition? 'This involves redesigning employees' jobs to allow them a greater degree of control over their working lives.'

Issues for analysis

- The ways in which different financial rewards may affect the motivation of employees.
- The possible implications of job design for employees' motivation.
- How the structure of the organisation might influence motivation.

Issues for evaluation

- To what extent might a particular approach to motivation improve the motivation and performance of the workforce?
- Do the benefits of a particular method of motivation outweigh its costs?
- What is the main influence on the motivational techniques used by a business?

Analysis and evaluation questions

1 Gibble and Co. Ltd is a long-established manufacturer of fountain pens. It is a traditional business with a tall organisational structure. Its products are recognised as being of the highest quality and it charges premium prices for its products. Its most expensive pen sells for £1,250. Despite the company's profits reaching record levels, its managers are seeking ways to improve the performance of its workforce. Some managers believe that pay is not the best way to improve motivation and employee performance.

a Examine how the company might use monetary methods of motivation to improve the performance of its workforce. (8 marks)
b To what extent is it inevitable that the company will use non-financial methods to motivate its workforce? (15 marks)

2 Philly Ltd is a cheese manufacturer, based in Dorset. The company has grown steadily over recent years and the size of its workforce has doubled. Employee performance has not been at the levels the managers would like and they are not convinced their use of job rotation on the shop floor has been entirely successful. The company has not made large profits in recent years. At the latest Board meeting the Director of HR has suggested the wide-scale implementation of employee empowerment. There is a lot of opposition to this suggestion from long-serving managers.

a Examine the advantages and disadvantages of the company's use of job rotation. (8 marks)
b Discuss the case for and against the company empowering its employees. (15 marks)

Assessment

Case study

Keith Abel, 43, runs the UK's most successful organic delivery company from Abel & Cole's London HQ. In 2006, The Financial Times rated Abel & Cole the UK's 14th best company to work for. The company delivers to 25,000 households in southern England. In 2007 it expanded and a delivery service began in the Midlands, and in Manchester.
(Source: Adapted from Abel & Cole's website at www.abel-cole.co.uk)

At Abel & Cole's HQ in South London there are photos of rosy cheeked employees in the reception area. Keith Abel believes that no-one should be stuck at a reception desk all day. Abel is a cheerful man and dressed very casually despite being at work. Below his office is the company's games room. There are also guitars and keyboards lying around for jamming sessions after work, and in a well-equipped kitchen the company's lunch club is flourishing. Each day two people cook for everybody else.

The company treats its staff well. They receive free fruit and vegetables, pensions, a bike scheme and the best summer picnics in the world. More importantly, their rights are respected, they get fair pay, good management, and first pick of all new vacancies. The company has promoted many people into new, challenging roles and employs a full-time trainer to support them.

(Source: Adapted from The Antipreneurs, Times Online at http://business.timesonline.co.uk/tol/business/related_reports/entrepreneurs/article1893344.ece?token=null&offset=12)

Web link

To find out more about Abel & Cole, visit www.abel-cole. co.uk

Questions

(30 marks, 40 minutes)

1 Explain two ways in which Abel & Cole put motivation theory into practice. (6 marks)

2 Analyse the possible problems that the company may face in motivating its employees as the business expands. (9 marks)

3 To what extent do you think that the advantages of Keith Abel's approach to motivation outweigh the disadvantages? (15 marks)

Section 5: Marketing and the competitive environment

25 Effective marketing

In this chapter we consider the importance of marketing and the way in which it contributes to the effectiveness of a business and its success. We examine the different elements of marketing and examine how the effective management of marketing decisions can improve the competitiveness of a business.

What you need to know by the end of this chapter:
• the meaning of marketing
• the difference between niche and mass marketing.

All organisations need customers. The purpose of all businesses is to understand and provide the goods and services that customers want. Indeed, according to Peter Drucker, a very influential management writer, there is only one valid purpose for a business, which is 'to create a customer.'

Marketing is the function of the business that is responsible for understanding customer needs and developing the right products, setting the right price and promoting and distributing products in the right way. Marketing provides the link between the customer and the production function of the business. Marketing ensures that what is being provided is actually wanted and needed (i.e it is something of value), communicates this to customers and makes the product available to them at a price that provides value for money.

For the business success the activities of the different business functions must be integrated effectively.

Figure 25.1 Interpreted business functions

The importance of marketing

Effective marketing occurs when a firm fully understands the requirements of its customers and is able to meet these needs successfully. The marketing function helps the organisation to provide a product that the customer wants, is affordable, is perceived as good value and that leaves the customer and the organisation itself satisfied with the transaction.

Marketing is an ongoing process because:

- customers' needs change over time (e.g. the increasing interest in health issues has increased demand for health clubs and reduced demand for high-fat foods)
- competitors enter the market with their own offerings and so businesses must respond to this
- firms' own strengths change and develop.

Effective marketing will, therefore, change over time to ensure there remains a good match between customers' needs and the business's own strengths. Effective marketing will lead to high levels of customer satisfaction, which means that customers:

- are more likely to come back and buy more
- are more likely to tell their friends to come and try the products
- may be more willing to try new products launched by the business
- may become loyal to the product and less likely to switch to competitors

What do you think?

Customers have become more interested in environmental issues and health issues. This has affected the demand for some products. What other changes in customer demand do you think there have been in recent years?

Real-life Business

Hugh Davidson

Hugh Davidson is a marketing writer who has advised many large companies around the world. One of his books is called *Offensive Marketing*. According to Davidson, 'Offensive marketing involves every employee in building superior customer value very efficiently for above average profits.' This is an interesting definition of marketing in that it highlights that:

- everyone is involved in marketing because everyone affects the quality of the service and the customer's impression of the product
- it is important to develop value for money that is better than your competitors' not just the same
- it is important to use resources efficiently (i.e. you must think about how much you spend on marketing and measure the returns from different types of spending)
- the aim is not just to do well but to achieve profits that are above average – the mark of a truly successful business.

Defining marketing

A formal definition of marketing should include the following features:

- It is an exchange process – that is, it is two way. The business offers the customer a good or service and in return receives something, usually payment.
- It is mutually beneficial because both sides should gain from the exchange. Customers should be satisfied with the product and firms should make a profit (assuming that the firm is a profit-making organisation). Firms are unlikely to give away products for nothing.

- It aims to identify and anticipate customer needs. Entrepreneurs need to understand their customers to know what to offer them. However, it is not always enough to just identify customers' needs: in fact, sometimes the customers may not know themselves what their needs and wants are. In some markets, such as fashion and film, firms have to anticipate what customers will want in the future. They have to predict trends even before most customers know what these trends will be.
- It aims to delight customers. Nowadays satisfying customers may not be enough, as many other firms are doing this. It's much better to delight the customer, so that they are more than satisfied and more likely to buy from you.

The purpose of marketing is to match the abilities and strengths of the business to the needs of the market. A business aims to supply goods and services that customers want and that will generate suitable rewards for the organisation.

What do you think?

What was the last item you bought that cost over £20? Are you happy with your purchase? Would you say it was good value for money? Why?

Marketing involves a whole range of activities, including finding out what customers want, developing new products, packaging and promoting the products, and setting the price. All these activities are aimed at developing and providing goods and services which will satisfy the customer (so he or she will buy it), and make a profit for the firm (assuming that is the business objective).

The more effective the marketing, the better the value provided for customers and the greater the rewards the business should be able to make.

The purpose of marketing

The purpose of marketing is to ensure that the organisation meets the customers' needs in the present and in the future. Marketing is therefore a dynamic process. To be effective it must work with the other functions of the business to influence:

- what is produced i.e. the precise nature of the firm's offerings; for example in terms of design, features and quality

- how many are produced? Marketing must estimate likely sales, which in turn influences the quantity of goods and services the business must be able to provide
- the range of products offered (e.g. how extensive the menu or wine list should be in a restaurant; how many different models should be displayed in a store)
- the price at which products are sold; this therefore determines how much can be spent on materials and the transformation process if a profit is to be made.

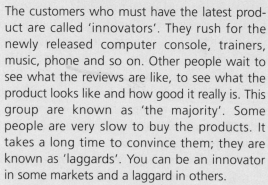

What do you think?

The customers who must have the latest product are called 'innovators'. They rush for the newly released computer console, trainers, music, phone and so on. Other people wait to see what the reviews are like, to see what the product looks like and how good it really is. This group are known as 'the majority'. Some people are very slow to buy the products. It takes a long time to convince them; they are known as 'laggards'. You can be an innovator in some markets and a laggard in others.

What type of buyer are you when it comes to products such as films, mobile phones, trainers, perfumes, or albums.

Market segmentation

Within any market, different segments may exist. A market segment is a group of people with similar needs and wants. For example, within the market for newspapers there are some readers who are most interested in sport, others who want financial news, and others who want celebrity gossip. Different newspapers have been developed to target these different groups.

Within the chocolate market the demand can be segmented into groups such as:

- snacking. This is chocolate that you buy and eat there and then (e.g. a Mars bar)
- sharing. This is chocolate that you buy and take home to share with others (e.g. Cadbury's Heroes)
- gift. This is chocolate that you buy to give to others (e.g. Thornton's chocolates)

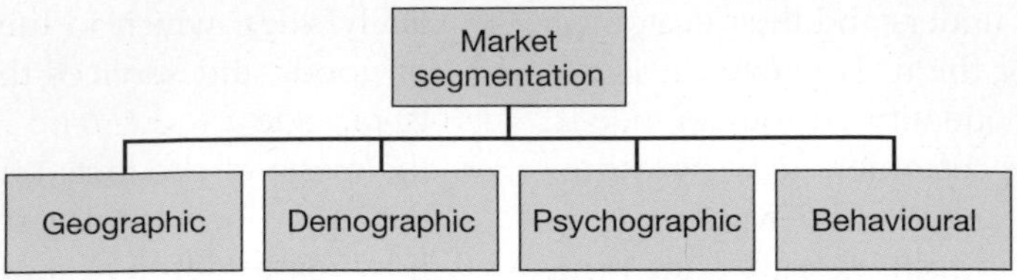

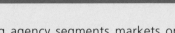

Figure 25.2. Types of market segmentation

Key terms

A **market segment** exists when there is a group of clearly identifiable needs and wants.

There are various ways in which a market may be segmented, including:

- **Geographic segmentation**: this focuses on the impact on demand of factors such as the location of customers or the climate in different regions. Cars sold to Africa, for example, will have to withstand high levels of heat; cars sold to Scandinavia will need to cope with the cold. In Japan flats are usually quite small as land is in demand and is expensive. As a result, washing machines and fridges have a smaller capacity than in America.
- **Demographic segmentation**: this focuses on the impact of factors such as age, gender, income, occupation, marital status and stage in the family life-cycle. In the toys market, for example, the type of toys three-year-olds will play with is very different from those wanted by 13-year-olds. When you are single, you may be looking for a city centre, one-bedroom flat; when you are married with children you may want a three-bedroomed house with a garden, near a good school and out of the city.
- **Psychographic segmentation**: this focuses on the impact of factors such as your personality, lifestyle, values, social class and attitudes. Are you someone who likes belonging to a group? Are you someone who is very ambitious? Do you want material things? Do you care how products have been made and their impact on the environment? These factors might all influence the way a product is promoted and the actual design of the product. Some holidays may be designed for adventurous, outgoing types. Others might target customers wanting a package hotel holiday in Spain.
- **Behavioural segmentation**: this focuses on why you buy a product (what benefit you seek), when you buy (the occasion) and your usage rate. Do you buy chewing gum to help you stop smoking? To have fresh breath? To help protect your teeth? Because you think it helps keep you calm? Do you tend to buy flowers to celebrate, or to apologise? Do you buy turkeys at Christmas or at other times during the year? When do you buy thank you cards or chocolates? Are you a light, medium or heavy user?

Business in Focus

The advertising agency segments markets or lifestyles into the following customer groups:

- Resigned: Rigid strict individuals oriented to the post. Brand choice based on familiarity, safety and economy.
- Mainstreamer: Domestic, conformist, conventional and sentimental. Favours big well-known, value for money, 'family' brands.
- Aspirer: Materialistic, acquisitive, focused on image. Attractive packaging is important.
- Explorer: Energetic and independent. Brand choice highlights difference, sensation and adventure. The first to try new brands.

What do you think?

What products do you think are segmented in terms of:

- Gender?
- Age?
- Income?
- Life-style?

Next time you watch the television, look at the adverts and try to see the motivations that are being targeted.

How do you think the hotel market is segmented? What about the magazine market? The music market?

For a market segment to appeal to a business it must be:

- measurable, so you can identify it exists and measure its size to decide on the likely earnings
- accessible, so you have the resources to offer what would be required and be able to get your products to the customers
- profitable, so you can meet customer needs and your own needs at the same time.

By segmenting a market effectively, managers can identify which segments it wants to target. By understanding the requirements of a particular segment it can develop the marketing mix to meet these needs more closely. Hopefully, this should increase sales and boost brand loyalty. Effective segmentation should lead to effective marketing, with businesses providing exactly the right product in the right place at the right time and price. However, the more a market is segmented the more variations there are to the product, and its marketing has to be adjusted for each item: imagine producing a different type of cleaner for the sink, oven, shower, toilet, floor, door handles, carpets, work surfaces, windows, walls and so on. Each one may meet a very specific need, but coordinating and providing such a range of products may be expensive. If possible, it would be easier and cheaper to produce an all-in-one cleaner to cover many, if not all, of these functions. The firm may well get cheaper inputs if it buys in bulk and can spread one set of marketing costs over more units.

Businesses may therefore have to trade off the appeal of segmenting and meeting specific groups of needs more precisely with the benefits and cost advantages of producing a limited range of products on a larger scale.

Niche marketing

Niche marketing occurs when a firm targets a specific segment of the market. For example, Aston Martin targets the luxury sports car market, Umbro targets only the football market and Brompton produces fold-up bicycles so that commuters can take them on the train.

By focusing on a niche, a firm can understand the specific requirements of the group and ensure its offering meets the group's needs precisely. It can tailor-make its marketing approach and avoid wasting time and money on activities that are not relevant.

Niche marketing is quite common for entrepreneurs. This is because:

- it focuses on just one segment of the market and therefore the resources required may be relatively small and this makes it affordable and feasible for a start-up business
- by focusing on a segment of the market this may not be perceived as a threat by larger, established firms. If a start-up is perceived as a real threat, the established firms may cut prices or try to influence stores to get them to stop distributing the product.

Business in Focus

Fentimans drinks

Figure 25.3 Fentimans drinks

Fentimans is a niche producer of a range of 'botanically brewed drinks'. The range at the moment includes: Dandelion and Burdock, Curiosity Cola, Victorian Lemonade, Shandy, Seville Orange and ginger beer. Its website states:

'The company was founded in 1900 and since then has focused on botanic brewing. This is a simple process involving herbs and plant roots. The products ferment for several days and all of the bottles have a sediment at the bottom.

As the original and traditional adult soft drink, Fentimans has always claimed to have no 'style' whatsoever (well, not for the sake of it – we're all substance)...'

Web link

To find out more about Fentimans, visit www.fentimans.com

However, there are dangers associated with niche marketing:

- The total number of customers is likely to be quite low and therefore if anyone changes his or her mind and switches to something else, this can have a significant effect on the total demand.
- If the product does prove to be successful then larger firms may be attracted by this success and enter the market. Small firms may struggle to match the power and resources of larger firms and so may lose their share of the market.

Business in Focus

Cobra Beer

The founder of Cobra Beer is Karan Bilimoria. The beer, which is actually brewed in the UK, despite its Indian image, is smoother and less gassy than many of its rivals. This made it an ideal product for Indian restaurants, where customers could drink several pints with their meal to take out some of the heat of the curries. When it was launched in 1989, Cobra Beer therefore targeted the restaurant niche. After the success in this niche, Cobra was moved into the mass market. It is now distributed through supermarkets and off-licences and promoted on television. It is also sold around the world, including India.

What marketing changes do you think have had to be made as Cobra beer has moved from niche to mass marketing?

Key terms
Niche marketing occurs when a business focuses on a particular segment of the market.

Mass marketing

A mass market approach targets the majority of the market. This usually involves high volumes of production and much higher capacity levels than niche marketing. This may make it unrealistic for most start-up businesses, especially given the high levels of promotion needed to generate the necessary demand to make mass production viable. However, over time a niche product may become more mainstream and therefore niche products may be moved into the mass market.

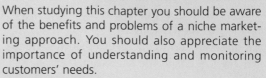

One step further: Market orientation vs product orientation

A market-oriented (or market-led) business is one that bases its decisions on customers' needs. It continually monitors its environment to find out what customers want, what competitors are offering and what changes are occurring in the market. By being market-oriented, a firm should be able to ensure that the product or service it provides matches its customers' needs. If there is a high level of competition, firms need to be market orientated to survive; if they are not, rivals will meet customer needs more effectively and reduce their sales. Any entrepreneur wanting to succeed should make sure there is demand for his or her product. This will usually be done via market research to try and identify the likely level of sales. This needs to be an ongoing process if the business is to remain market orientated.

By comparison, a product-oriented (or product-led) business focuses more on what it can produce and hopes that this will fit with customer requirements. This is a very risky approach because the firm may end up producing something the customer does not want. If an entrepreneur assumes that because he or she likes the idea, everyone else will also like it, this is being product oriented.

Although being product oriented is less likely to succeed than being market oriented, it can work if the customer has limited choice (for example, in some countries of Eastern Europe, governments only allowed a few firms to produce particular products and so customers had to buy what was available). In other countries local firms may be protected against foreign competitors, which also reduces customer choice. If it is lucky, the business may happen to produce a product that people want, or in some cases inventors come up with products that customers did not know they wanted until they arrived. However, over time, as customers find alternatives (for example, as markets are opened up to more competition) product-oriented firms are likely to suffer.

Summary

Marketing is an important function of a business and links the firm to its customers. It tries to understand customer needs, develop a marketing approach that meets these needs and then communicates this to the customers. At the heart of marketing is the importance of providing excellent value to customers and at the same time meeting the organisation's own objectives. The effectiveness of the way the marketing activities of a business are managed will have a major impact on its success. Better marketing means more satisfied customers and a greater chance of success.

Quick questions

1. What is meant by marketing?
2. Why is marketing a dynamic process?
3. 'Marketing should be a mutually beneficial process.' What does this mean?
4. What is meant by niche marketing?
5. State two reasons why a start-up business might undertake niche marketing.
6. State one problem of niche marketing.
7. Identify one way in which marketing actions can affect other business functions.
8. Identify one way in which other business functions can affect marketing actions.

Issues for analysis

- The benefits of market segmentation.
- The benefits of niche marketing.

Assessment

Issues for evaluation

- Consider the importance of marketing in determining a firm's success.
- Consider the benefits of segmentation.

Analysis and evaluation questions

1. Takako Yamuda works as the marketing manager for a chain of hotels. The owners are keen to grow the business and want to know what sort of hotels they should be providing to meet market needs.

   a. Analyse the ways in which the market for hotels may be segmented.
   b. Discuss the possible benefits of segmentation for Takako's business

2. Susie Shoots is the new managing director of GoodRead, a small chain of bookshops that has been established for over 50 years. Susie feels the business has lost touch with the market and this, in part, explains the loss of sales in recent years. 'We must become more market oriented' said Susie at a recent management meeting. 'We must also recognise that our best way forward is to adopt a niche marketing strategy.'

   a. Analyse the possible benefits to GoodRead of becoming more market oriented
   b. Discuss the advantages and disadvantages of adopting a niche marketing strategy for GoodRead.

Case study

Just Lamps supplies nothing but lamps, specialising in bulbs for audio-visual projectors. It therefore adopts a niche marketing approach. It originally started out selling replacement bulbs to schools and universities, but the business grew much faster when the Berkshire company targeted audio-visual equipment retailers, which now account for 90 per cent of its sales.

Founded by David Bethell and Marc Murray in 2002, the firm claims to source lamps for 6,000 models of projectors from manufacturers such as Sony, Panasonic and Epson.

Questions

(30 marks; 40 minutes)
1. What are the key features of a niche market? (6 marks)
2. Effective marketing involves understanding your customer needs. Analyse how Just Lamps might ensure it meets its customer requirements. (9 marks)
3. Discuss the possible advantages and disadvantages to Just Lamps of pursuing a niche-marketing approach. (15 marks)

26 Designing an effective marketing mix

A customer is influenced by many factors when deciding whether or not to purchase a product. The combination of these factors is known as the marketing mix. By developing an effective marketing mix, a business can meet the needs of its customers successfully. In this chapter we examine the different elements of the marketing mix.

What you need to know by the end of this chapter:
• the meaning of the marketing mix
• the influences on the marketing mix
• the importance of an integrated marketing mix.

Introduction to the marketing mix

The marketing mix comprises all the elements associated with a product that affect whether or not the customer decides to buy it. A broad range of factors may affect customers' purchasing decisions.

Consider why a customer might choose to shop in one supermarket rather than another. The list below contains a number of factors affecting this decision.

• How far away is it?
• How easy is it to park?
• What is the range of products like?
• Are the prices competitive?
• What facilities are there (for example, a coffee shop)?
• Are the staff friendly and helpful?
• What services are provided (such as carrying shopping to customers' cars)?
• Does the supermarket offer a loyalty card?

There are clearly many factors that influence a consumer's decision to choose one business rather than another and these are all part of the marketing mix. An effective marketing mix offers the customer the right mix of benefits at the right price. Improving the mix will involve changing or enhancing the combination of elements affecting the customers' buying decision.

The marketing mix is often simplified and is commonly described as 'the 4 Ps'. This approach identifies four elements in the mix (all beginning with the letter P):

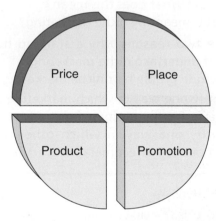

Figure 26.1 The marketing mix

1 Price – how much are customers charged for the product and what are the terms of payment (e.g. can you put a deposit down and pay in instalments)? How does this price compare with that of rivals?

2 Product – this includes the many different aspects of a product, such as its design, its quality, its reliability, its features and its functions. For example, you may buy something principally because of its style (e.g. Bang & Olufsen, and Apple), its reliability and durability (e.g JCB or Caterpillar) or the brand values (e.g. DKNY and Gucci).

3 Place – this is the way the product is distributed. Is the product sold direct to the customer or through retail outlets? Can you buy online, or do you have to travel some distance to get to a shop where it is sold?

4 Promotion – this is the way the firm communicates information about the product to the customer. For example, it may use advertising or a salesforce to highlight its strengths. The promotion of a product will affect the image that customers have of the product and their awareness and understanding of the benefits of the product.

> **Key term**
> The **marketing mix** is the combination of elements that influence a customer's decision whether or not to buy a product.

What is an effective marketing mix?

The key thing to remember when discussing the marketing mix is that it must be part of an integrated approach for it to be effective. This means that all the different elements of the mix must work together and complement each other. There is little point trying to develop a high-priced, exclusive brand to target high-income earners if it is then distributed through bargain outlets.

In a well-managed mix, the elements fit well together and enhance the overall value provided to the customer. Think about when you last bought a mobile phone; you probably thought about the brand name, the features and design of a particular model, the various pricing plans that existed on networks, the length of the contract, the terms of insurance and any special offers available. Many different factors would have combined to influence you.

Having said this, the nature of the product and market conditions will mean that some elements of the mix are more important than others for particular products. For example:

- If you have a car insurance business you may invest heavily in advertising to generate the enquiries and a sales team to take enquiries: if you own a local bakery, you may not spend much on advertising at all and rely more on word of mouth and having the right location.
- If you are a setting up a luxury hotel you may search for a long time to find the right place for your outlet: if you are a web based business you may operate from home.

Business in Focus

Simon Woodroffe

Figure 26.2 Yo! Sushi

Simon Woodroffe revolutionised the fast food industry when he launched Yo! Sushi in the UK. A former roadie, lighting technician and TV executive, Woodroffe opened his first Yo! Sushi restaurant in 1997 using his life savings of £150,000. He has sold the franchise around the world and has extended the brand into clothing.

Woodroffe has also launched Yotel! This is an unusual hotel chain that combines elements of Japanese capsule hotels with first-class service. It offers a cheap but stylish option for business travellers. The rooms have the feel of space-age pods; they are 7ft by 8ft and 7ft high. Rooms consist of a bed and an en suite, featuring integrated gadgets such as the 'techno wall' with clothes storage, a pull-down desk, charging points and Wi-Fi internet access, as well as mood lighting and flat-screen televisions. In 2007 he opened an Yotel! at Gatwick airport.

According to Woodroffe, 'Successful entrepreneurs come in all shapes and sizes – but I think having an overactive brain is probably common to them all. I sometimes think it could be a chemical imbalance. I know for myself that sometimes I have so much energy it's slightly... uncomfortable.'

(Adapted from: *The Observer*, Sunday December 29, 2002)

- If you are selling gift-type products then packaging may be very important to attract the customer and impress the consumer. If you sell computer equipment to businesses, packaging may be important only in terms of protecting the items during transportation.
- If you are selling exclusive hand-made shirts, a high price may be used to reflect quality. If you are selling caravan holidays a low price may be important in order to compete.

What really matters for the mix to be effective is that the various elements combine and complement each other in such a way that the customer believes that the product provides better value for money than the competition. Improving the marketing mix may therefore involve:

- offering more benefits in relation to the price, perhaps by adding additional features
- promoting the benefits of the product more effectively so the customer identifies more closely with it or understands more clearly what it does
- making the product more accessible so that it is easier for customers to buy.

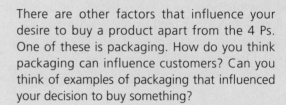

What do you think?

You are responsible for the marketing of:

a luxury cruise holidays in the caribbean
b family hotel holidays to Spain

How would your marketing mix differ for these two products?

It is important to see the four Ps model as a rather basic model of what influences a decision to buy, or not buy, a product: the buying process is a very complicated one and involves many different factors. For example, we are influenced by factors such as the people who serve us, the way in which we can buy the product (e.g. can we order online or not?) and the ease with which the features of one product can be compared with others. The mix should be thought of as anything connected with a product or service that influences the buyer's decision.

Examiner's advice

You need to remember that the right marketing mix depends on many factors, such as the type of the product and the competitive situation. You need to be able to analyse the marketing mix in the given context.

To make a business more effective, the entrepreneur needs to develop an outstanding marketing mix, with each element complementing each other.

What do you think?

There are other factors that influence your desire to buy a product apart from the 4 Ps. One of these is packaging. How do you think packaging can influence customers? Can you think of examples of packaging that influenced your decision to buy something?

One step further: the seven Ps

Some business writers now talk of the 7 Ps, rather than the 4 Ps. In addition to the original 4 Ps, these include:

- people – a well-trained, well informed, polite staff can influence people to buy from one shop rather than another. Customer service is an important marketing weapon. (This is examined in more detail in Chapter 35)
- physical environment – factors such as the layout, decor and parking can be an important influence on which restaurant, pub or store a person chooses.
- process – the ease of ordering and paying can influence a purchase. Many supermarkets have introduced self-scanning to reduce queues and attract customers.

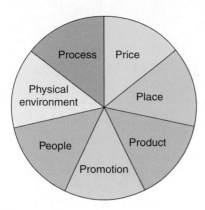

Figure 26.3 The seven P's

Summary

Your decision whether or not to buy a product depends on many different factors, which are collectively known as the marketing mix. One model of the marketing mix is known as the '4 Ps', which refers to the Price, Product, Promotion and Place; these are important elements that will combine to determine the appeal of a product. Effective marketing involves identifying and anticipating customer needs correctly and combining the elements of the marketing mix in a way that provides excellent value for money.

Quick questions

1 What is meant by the marketing mix?
2 What is meant by promotional activities in marketing?
3 What factors might affect the selection of the right marketing mix?
4 What is meant by an integrated marketing mix?
5 State one product that is distributed very widely and one that is only available in a few select places.
6 State one high-price brand of a product and one low-price brand in the same market

7 State one type of product that is advertised on television a great deal and another that is not advertised on television very much if at all.
8 State one product where you might think for several weeks and do lots of research before buying. State one product that you tend to buy quickly and without much thought.

Issues for analysis

- What influences the impact of the marketing mix on sales.
- The relationship between the marketing mix and the type of product.

Issues for evaluation

- What influences the relative importance of elements of the marketing mix.
- Is one element of the marketing mix more important than the others?
- What factors would make you change the marketing mix?

Analysis and evaluation questions

1 The Whole Tooth is a private dental practice in an exclusive part of London.
   Fresh is a business that produces bottled water.

a Analyse the key elements of a successful marketing mix for The Whole Tooth.
b To what extent is the marketing mix of the two businesses likely to be similar?

2 You may have started or be about to start looking for a university for a degree course.

a Analyse the factors that might influence your choice of university.
b Discuss the marketing actions a university might take to attract more students.

Assessment

Case study

Bouf Superboutique

'When other's zig, you zag....right? Problem is, when it comes to shopping, bland high street chains have made it mission impossible to stand out from the crowd. Think white iPod earphones, flat-pack Ikea furniture and Topshop t-shirts on every street corner, in every city in the world.

We weren't very happy about this lack of creativity so we decided to sort it out once and for all. As designers, we knew there was a heap of original products out there...the problem was finding them! So we quit our jobs and created Bouf.com, the ultimate boutique, specialising in unique and limited edition products from the world's best artists, designers and niche brands, for individuals who think for themselves. From Fashion, Food and Furniture, to Gadgets, Footwear and Gifts!

Everything we sell is unique, rare or limited edition, and hand-picked by us so you know you're getting something special. And if that wasn't enough, we're about to introduce our revolutionary bespoke service, so that you can tweak our products or design your own, and get something even more unique to you! We're still young, but we're adding more unique products to our collection and growing each day.'

(Source: www.**bouf.com**)

Case study questions

(30 marks, 40 minutes)

a What do you think of Bouf as a brand name? Do you think that it helps the business? (6 marks)

b If you were a marketing consultant to Bouf, analyse the factors that might influence the prices you set. (9 marks)

c To what extent is the choice of products offered by Bouf sufficient to guarantee the success of the business? (15 marks)

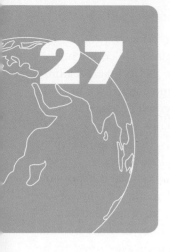

27

Using the marketing mix – product

The marketing mix is made up of several elements. The product itself is a crucial element of the mix. Many marketing specialists argue that the product is the most important element of the marketing mix because it is the product that directly meets customer needs. In this chapter we examine the different aspects of the product in marketing.

What you need to know by the end of this chapter:
• the influences on the development of new goods and services
• Unique Selling Points/Propositions (USP)
• Product Portfolio Analysis
• the product life cycle.

Introduction: The product

The products of a business refer to the goods and services it provides: what the customer is actually buying. The nature of a product can have a significant influence on the way it is marketed.

The nature of a product can be analysed on three levels:

1 The **core benefit** it provides. i.e. what does it actually do? For example, it may clean clothes, make you look smarter, help you to communicate or help you to move from A to B.

2 The **tangible product**. For example, what are the physical dimensions of the product, what features has it got, what does it look like, how reliable is it?

3 The **additional benefits** it provides (this is called the 'augmented product'). For example, what guarantees are given to the customer? What are the brand values and what do they convey to the buyer? What services are provided (for example is installation free)? Is there any after-sales service?

Businesses may compete in different ways: either via their tangible products or via their intangible features. Two washing machines may have different physical features: for example, either one may have a bigger washing capacity, be more environmentally friendly, be more user friendly or provide a quicker,

better wash. A laptop may be lighter, more stylish, have a bigger memory or a faster processor than another. These are tangible features. Look at the shaving market to see how products are developed to compete: three blades, four blades, strips on the razor to soften the skin, razors shaped and designed for women and even razors that pulsate to give a closer shave. The tangible product is being enhanced to provide more benefits.

Alternatively, a business might focus on the augmented benefits of a product, such as additional insurance cover, its brand values or a free delivery service. Free installation, an extended guarantee or a 24-hour helpline are all ways of competing via the augmented product.

The effective development of a product therefore involves the right combination of benefits (whether they are tangible or intangible). Improving the product will involve changing and enhancing these benefits to ensure they match customer needs. Many food items are now organic, or salt free, for example, because increasing numbers of customers are interested in these type of products.

Remember that any changes to a product have cost implications, and may also have other resource implications, for example in terms of the people and equipment needed to provide it. Promising to be at the scene of a car breakdown within an hour, or to deliver a pizza within 45 minutes is only good marketing provided you have the resources to fulfil the promise.

Unique Selling Point/Proposition (USP)

A USP is something distinctive about a product that sets it apart from its competitors. It could be the speed of delivery, the designer, the technical features, the materials used or the guarantee given (i.e. it could either be the tangible or augmented product).

Developing a USP potentially enables a firm to charge more, as demand may be less sensitive to price. It also helps to develop a brand loyalty. However, any USP needs to be protected if possible (e.g. through a patent or trademark) as competitors are always looking to imitate anything that is successful. What may be 'unique' one year may become 'standard' in the future, so businesses need to be looking to innovate continually.

> **Key term**
> A **USP** is a feature of a product that makes it distinctive.

> **Business in Focus**
>
> ### Heli-Beds
>
> Heli-Beds is an independent bed retailer. They describe themselves as 'the same day delivery people'. The company's USP is that if you order a bed by lunchtime they will deliver it on the same day.
>
> > **Web link**
> >
> > www.helibeds.co.uk
> > What are the implications for the business of making this promise, in terms of their resources?

> **What do you think?**
>
> Can you think of any products or businesses that you use that you think have a USP?

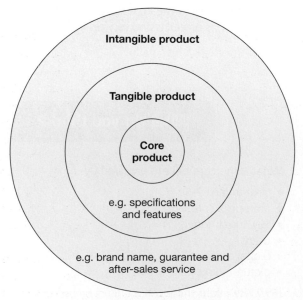

Figure 27.1 The three levels of a product

Making a successful product

A successful product is designed to meet customer requirements. These requirements may have been identified through market research. The design of the product should also take account of the production process. A well-designed product can save on costs, can be made easily to a consistent quality and meets the needs of customers very precisely.

Firms may succeed in the market by launching products that meet new needs or existing needs more effectively, by offering a more reliable product or by producing it more cheaply than the competition, enabling the firm to lower the price. Having the right product at the right price increases a firm's competitiveness.

The development process for a new product has a series of stages. First, the idea must be generated from somewhere. Then it must be developed and tested. Finally, it must be launched.

Some firms try to rush the design and development stage because they are so eager to get the product out on to the market to earn money. However, it is often the case that more time spent developing the product results in a much greater chance of long-term success. Approximately four out of five new products fail, which shows how risky developing new products can be and the importance of getting it right before launching it.

Business in Focus

Ben & Jerry's

Like all organisations, Ben & Jerry's, the ice cream business, has had its fair share of product failures as well as its many successes. Unlike most other businesses, they celebrate these failures on their website where you can visit the 'flavour graveyard'. Failures include 'Fudge central', the 'Vermonster' and 'Oatmeal cookie chunks'.

Web link

To find out more about the flavours that didn't work, visit: www.benjerry.co.uk/flavourgraveyard/

Do you think Ben and Jerry's undertake a great deal of market research before launching a product. If so, why do some fail? If not, why not?

Analysing the existing position

When deciding on what marketing actions to take, such as whether to invest in developing a new product, a firm will want to examine its existing position. Only by assessing how its products are doing will it be able to decide what to do next.

This process of analysing the position of the firm makes use of techniques such as the product life cycle model and product portfolio analysis (PPA).

The product life cycle

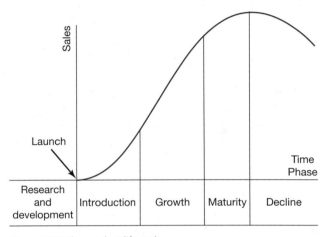

Figure 27.2 The product life cycle

The product life cycle traces the sales of a product over its life. The typical path for a product can be divided into five stages.

1. The research and development stage

During this stage, the basic idea for the product is developed and tested. Mock-ups of a design may be made, models of a product may be produced or a new recipe may be taste tested. This stage can be expensive for a firm and no revenue is being generated during this period. This is a time of high risk because the product may never be developed successfully and the investment at this stage may not be recovered. For example, it took James Dyson 15 years and over 5,000 prototypes of the Dyson vacuum cleaner before he got it right, highlighting the time and money that can be used up in the development phase.

The length of the research and development process will vary from product to product. In the case of new pharmaceuticals, it may take several years to develop and test products before they can be launched, whereas developing a new design for a greetings card is likely to take months rather than years. Some products, such as newspapers, are modified on a daily basis (although significant changes, such as the size of the paper or whether to switch to colour are far less frequent).

2. The introduction (launch) stage

This is the stage at which the product or service is launched and put on sale. Many product ideas will never actually reach this stage. They are abandoned after prototypes have been produced and tested. In the launch phase, promotion costs will be relatively high to make potential customers aware of the product; therefore a loss is still likely to be made. Producers may also struggle to get firms to stock their products or customers to try their service at this stage if the business is new, with no proven track record. Buyers may be reluctant to risk switching to or trialling a new product, particularly if there are heavy costs involved in doing so. For example, if there is a penalty payment for switching from one credit card, mortage company, electricity company or gas company to another, customers are more likely to stick with their existing providers.

3. The growth stage

If the product becomes known and accepted by customers, sales should grow. At this stage, it should be slightly easier to get distributors to stock the products, as they will be more confident of sales and therefore willing to stock them. The firm should begin to make profits at this stage, as revenues begin to outweigh costs. (For example, sales of wine, teeth-whitening formulas, smoothies, men's cosmetics and laser eye-surgery are all in their growth stage in the UK.) At this stage, you need to make sure you can meet the demand and manage the growth process. You may be taking on more staff, buying more equipment and expanding your premises: if this is happening rapidly it can be difficult to keep control. Making sure you can meet deadlines and maintaining quality can be major problems at this time.

Of course, some products never reach the growth stage: they are launched but are never successful and sales fail to take off.

4. The maturity and saturation stage

At this point in a product's life, the growth of sales slow down. The product may have been in the market for some time and competitors may well have launched similar products. (Products such as washing machines and televisions are currently in their maturity stage.) The maturity stage can last for years in some cases. There is no rapid expansion and managers must consider what to do next with the product: for example , should funds be invested to try and boost sales or should the product be scrapped?

5. Decline

Eventually, the sales of any product are likely to fall. The business may find it more difficult to get the product distributed at this stage and may be forced to cut the price to maintain sales. For example, you will have seen reduced-price CDs or books in the bargain areas of shops: the price has been reduced to try to increase sales. Products such as board games and bow ties are in their decline stages in the UK.

> **Key term**
> The **product life cycle** shows the sales of a product over its life time.

Business in Focus

Segway

The Segway was expected to revolutionise the way we travelled. It is a self-balancing scooter that was launched in 2001 by Dean Kamen, its American inventor. He imagined that this environmentally friendly form of transport would immediately catch on. The Segway can travel up to 12 miles an hour. However, when the Segway was launched in the UK the government declared it could not be driven in any public place. It was too fast to be driven on the pavement but not safe enough to be driven on the road. This decision by the government had significantly reduced demand for the Segway in the UK.

A recent study found that it took a few minutes to grasp the basic skills of Segway riding and three hours to become proficient. A rider simply leans forward to move forward and back to stop. On the original model, steering is controlled by twisting a handlebar grip. On a newer version, riders push the column left or right.

What do you think could be done to increase the sales of the Segway?

Using the product life cycle

Managers may use the product life cycle model to identify which stage a product is in at any given moment and then adjust the marketing mix accordingly. For example, promotion may be used to announce the launch of a product in the introduction phase but to stress the differences with competitors in the maturity phase. The price may be high initially if the product has some unique features, but have to be reduced in later stages as competitors enter the market. Distribution may be difficult to get at first when a product is new, but easier over time when it has begun to prove itself. The business should be able to improve the firm's performance by recognising or anticipating where the product is in its life cycle and adapting the marketing mix accordingly.

What do you think?

How else might the marketing mix change at different stages of the product life cycle?

Extending sales in the product life cycle

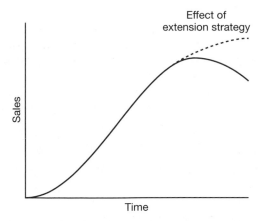

Figure 27.3 Extension strategies

A firm may try to prevent the sales of a product going into decline by using extension strategies. Methods to do this might include the following:

- increasing the usage of the product on any given occasion – for example, shampoo products always advise you to wash once then rinse your hair and wash again, thereby doubling the usage rate.
- encouraging the use of the product on more occasions – for example, Head & Shoulders was seen by consumers as a product to use when dandruff was already present. The company tried to change this perception to get people to use it all year round to prevent dandruff, as well as cure it.

- reducing the price – as products approach the maturity stage, firms often cut the price to maintain sales. The success of this depends on the sensitivity of demand to price changes.
- adapting the product – look around a supermarket and you will see endless examples of 'new, improved' products or products with added X, extra Y or less Z!. These are all ways of trying to keep the consumer interested in the product.
- introducing promotional offers – another technique often used by firms to try and prevent sales from falling is to have competitions or offers to boost their sales.
- changing the image of the product – this has been done with a number of drinks, such as vodka and cider, which have had their image changed to appeal to a younger audience. New versions have been launched, such as vodka and mixers and cider with ice, and the branding and packaging have been changed to revitalise the image.

Key term
An **extension strategy** occurs when marketing activities are changed to prevent sales falling

Business in Focus

The iPhone

The Apple iPhone downloads music and videos and has been described by Steve Jobs, the founder of the company, as a 'magical device' that has revolutionised the industry. The iPhone has no conventional buttons but instead uses a large touch-screen. The firm has patented keyboard technology on the 11.6mm thick phone, calling it 'multi-touch'. It is essentially a computer with a blank screen that users configure so they can operate the monitor with their fingers.

'We are all born with the ultimate pointing device – our fingers – and iPhone uses them to create the most revolutionary user interface since the mouse,' said Mr Jobs. A full touch keyboard is available for text messaging and there is a built-in two megapixel camera.'

Some people queued for days in America when the iPhone was first released in 2007. Apple said buyers visiting its stores would not be able to walk out with more than two iPhones each.

Apple's target was to sell 10 million iPhones in its first year and grab itself a 1 per cent share of the mobile phone market. The iPhone took two years to develop.

(Source: Adapted from:

http://news.bbc.co.uk/go/pr/fr/-/1/hi/
technology/6246063.stm, 1/9/2007
http://news.bbc.co.uk/go/pr/fr/-/1/hi/
technology/6250192.stm, 29/6/2007)

How long do you think the product life cycle will be for the iPhone?

How might Apple try to extend its product life cycle?

What do you think?

Can you remember any products that are not on sale any more? Why do you think they were taken off the market?

What new products have been launched recently? Do you think they will be successful?

How long do you think they will be on sale for? Why?

Product launch and capacity utilisation

The capacity of a firm refers to the maximum amount it can produce at a particular moment in time. This will depend on its resources, such as the number and skills of its employees and the level and quality of its capital equipment and technology. Capacity utilisation refers to the amount that a firm is producing at any moment, compared with the amount it could produce. For example, a 50 per cent capacity utilisation means that a firm is producing half as much as it could be making; 25 per cent utilisation means it is producing a quarter of what it could produce. Having low capacity utilization is bad practice because resources are being wasted, and the firm is being inefficient because it could produce and sell more.

Key terms
Capacity measures the maximum possible output a business can produce with its given resources.
Capacity utilisation measures the existing output as a percentage of the maximum possible output.

When a firm first considers launching a product, it must predict the likely level of sales because this will determine the capacity it will need. In the early stages of the product life cycle, sales will usually be less than in the maturity phase, so if it enters the market with enough capacity for peak sales, the capacity utilisation will be low early on. This can be expensive because, although the firm has the resources to produce, say, 100,000 units, it may only be producing 20,000. This means that the cost per unit will be high – the cost of the equipment and staff have to be covered by relatively few sales. As the sales grow over time, these fixed costs can be spread over more units, thereby reducing the cost per item. On the other hand, if the firm sets up with a low capacity, it means that if demand does grow it may not be able to exploit this in the short run. In the long term a firm can, of course, increase capacity if sales are high enough. However, the decision to increase capacity may involve high levels of investment, so the firm must be confident that sales will continue to stay high to make sure that the new higher level of capacity is utilised.

Product life cycle and cash flow

The cash flow of a business at the start of a product's life cycle is likely to be negative. This is because cash has to be spent researching and developing the product before any sales have occurred. Even when the product is launched, the firm is likely to be spending more money at first to promote it than is coming in as income. This means the business will need to monitor its cash flow effectively in the early stages to make sure it does not run out!

As sales enter the growth phase, the cash flow should become positive. This is because by this stage, there should be less need for extensive promotion as customers should be more aware of the product and also income should be higher.

In the maturity phase, there may be a need to spend money on re-promoting the product if sales are to be maintained. As a result, cash flow may begin to fall, but nevertheless it will usually remain positive due to the relatively high inflows. With falling sales in the decline phase, cash flow will drop.

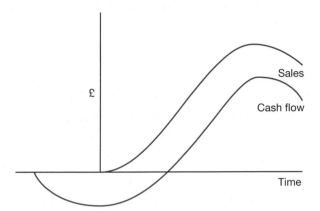

Figure 27.4 Sales and cashflow during the product lifecycle

The value of the product life cycle model

The product life cycle model is valuable because it highlights the fact that marketing policies have to be adjusted at different stages in the development of a product.

However, it is important to remember the product life cycle is just a model and its shape will vary considerably between products. In the case of a new single release by a band, for example, the life span may be just a matter of weeks, whereas Marmite was launched in the early twentieth century and is still in its maturity phase. Toys often have short life cycles but some of them, such as Barbie dolls, have been around for many years. So marketing decisions in relation to the product life cycle are not clear cut; some products in decline have had to be taken off the market because they cannot be made viable; others, such as the drink Tango, have been rebranded and brought back to great success.

Often, it will only be clear in retrospect what stage a product was in; what appeared to be a slight dip may turn out to be the decline of a product, or what appears to be a decline may only be a temporary drop in sales and this only becomes clear later on. Unfortunately, businesses have to make decisions as they go. They do not have the luxury of waiting to see what would have happened if they had not acted.

Another limitation of the product life cycle model is that it traces the sales of one product over time. Most businesses have several products and therefore it is important to look at its overall position.

Product portfolio analysis

Most firms have more than one product – some have hundreds. (For example, at the time of writing, Unilever owns a huge number of brands, including Bertolli, Birdseye, Findus, Hellman's, Knorr, Lipton, Slim-Fast, Comfort, Domestos, Dove, Lux, Pond's and Sunsilk, to name but a few.) The range of products and services a firm has is known as its 'product portfolio'. As part of its planning process, a business will examine the position of these products in their markets. This is known as 'product portfolio analysis'. One of the most famous models of portfolio analysis was developed by the management consultancy Boston Consulting Group and is known as the 'Boston matrix'. This model analyses the position of a firm's products in terms of their market share and the growth of the markets they operate in.

Types of product in the Boston matrix

Each circle in the Boston matrix represents one particular product or service. The size of the circle illustrates the turnover of the product; the bigger the circle the higher the turnover. The firm's products can be classified according to their market share and the growth of the market in which they operate.

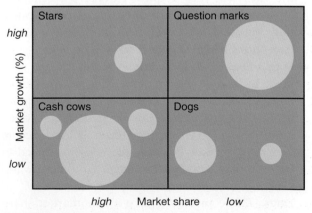

Figure 27.5 The Boston matrix

Key terms:
Product portfolio analysis examines the market position of a firm's products.
The Boston matrix is a method of product portfolio analysis that examines the products of a business in terms of their market share and the market growth.

- **Cash cows** are products that have a high market share but are selling in a slow-growing market. In some cases, this type of product will be the market leader in a mature market. Although the market may not be growing very fast, this may be because it has grown in the past leaving little room for further expansion. For example, the market for washing machines is quite big but is not actually growing very fast now; given the size of the market a brand with a high market share will have sales worth millions of pounds. By comparison, the market for hybrid cars and organic food is still relatively small but has potential for very fast growth.

  A cash cow already has a large market share, so much of the promotional work will have been done already. The product is likely to have a good distribution system and people will be aware that the product exists. The firm is used to producing the product in relatively large volumes and so the cost per unit should be fairly low. As a result, this type of product is likely to bring in high levels of cash for the firm. This can be used to finance other products.

- **Question marks** (or 'problem children'). These are products that have a small market share of a fast-growing market. These products may go on to be very successful, but equally they may fail. They are quite vulnerable and their future is uncertain (hence the name). There is a high degree of risk associated with these products because you cannot be sure they will succeed. They need protecting by the firm and they require extensive marketing. Most new products are question marks because their future is so uncertain (although there are exceptions when a product takes off quickly).

- **Stars**. These products enjoy a large share of a market that is growing rapidly. They are highly successful products for the business: however, they are usually expensive in terms of marketing. Money must be spent to ensure they retain their position in a growing market. For example, they may need to be promoted heavily to maintain customer awareness and to increase distribution in the market.

- **Dogs**. These products have a low market share and are selling in a slow-growing market. A firm may want to get rid of these products unless they think they can improve their sales. However, dogs can sometimes be revived. Lucozade used to be seen as a drink to help sick people get better, until it was very successfully repositioned as a sports and energy drink.

The value of the Boston matrix

The Boston matrix provides a snapshot of the position of all of a firm's products at a particular moment in time (whereas the product life cycle focuses on just one product). This enables managers to see whether they have a balanced portfolio (i.e an appropriate mix of products) or not. It can help a business to be more effective by providing an overview so the manager can take appropriate actions. For example:

- If a business has too many 'dogs', it may have insufficient new products to keep it going in the future. As a result, it may want to invest in new products.
- If, however, a business has lots of cash cows, it is generating relatively high levels of cash but, again, needs to think about the future: cash cows tend to be dominant products in markets that have already grown. A firm may want and need to be involved in newer markets as well and should therefore look to develop some star products.
- If a firm has too many question marks it may be quite vulnerable – question marks need protective marketing to maintain and grow their position in the market: this may drain a firm's resources.

With an appropriate mix of products, the cash cows can be used to finance the development of question marks and turn them into stars: this way the firm uses money from established markets to enter new markets and so protect its future.

Product portfolio analysis, therefore, provides a good basis for effective marketing planning:

- Dog products may be sold off or production and sales halted.
- Star products may be invested in to maintain their position.
- Cash cows may be 'milked' to provide funds.
- Question marks may be protected.

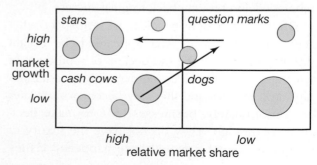

Figure 27.6 The Boston matrix (2)

One step further: the new product development process

There are several stages in the new product development process:

1 **Idea generation**

    Ideas for new products can be gained from a whole range of different sources such as customers, the firm's own research department, competitors, focus groups, employees, salespeople or trade shows.

2 **Idea screening**

    The aim of this stage is to identify unworkable ideas before investing significant resources to them.

    The screening process involves deciding whether:
    - there is a suitable target market for the product
    - it is technically feasible for the business to provide the product at an appropriate cost.

3 **Concept development and testing**

    This stage involves developing the marketing idea further and examining the engineering details. This includes decisions regarding:
    - the essential product features
    - the benefits the product provides

- the way in which the product can be produced
- the ways in which cost targets can be achieved.

    The concept then needs testing; perhaps via a focus group or other forms of market research.

4 **Business analysis**

    This stage looks at the financial data in detail to make sure the product can make a suitable level of profit. For example, business analysis considers:
    - the likely selling price based upon competitor analysis and customer feedback:
    - the estimated sales volume
    - the estimated break-even output and level of profits.

5 **Testing**

    This stage develops the product further and tests whether it actually works. For example, it may include:
    - producing a physical prototype or mock-up
    - testing the product in typical usage situations
    - undertaking market research
    - making adjustments where necessary
    - producing an initial run of the product and selling it in a test market area to determine customers' reaction.

6 **Technical implementation**

    This develops a plan to get the product produced and launched. It includes:
    - an estimate of the resources required
    - an engineering plan for production
    - details of the suppliers to work with.

7 **Launching the product**

    This stage sees the launch of the product. This includes promoting it to let potential customers know it is arriving and organising the distribution.

As you can see, developing a new product requires many different skills, including marketing and operations. Often, new product development teams will be cross functional, meaning that they include employees from different departments so that the idea is examined from different perspectives.

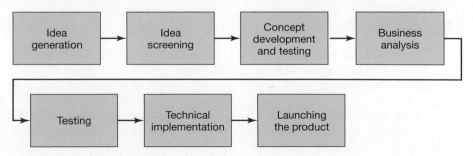

Figure 27.7 The new product development process

Summary

The product is one of the most important elements of the marketing mix: after all, customers buy a product for the benefits it provides. These benefits may be core, tangible or augmented. Managers will want to consider the position of their goods and services in terms of the product life cycle and may want to adjust their marketing accordingly. Managers will also consider the overall position of the portfolio of their products: this may be done via the Boston matrix. The effective management of a firm's products will play an important role in its overall success.

Quick questions

1 What are the stages of the product life cycle?
2 What is meant by an extension strategy?
3 What is meant by product portfolio analysis?
4 What is meant by a 'cash cow'?
5 What is a 'dog' product?
6 What is meant by a Unique Selling Point?
7 Give an example of how a firm might change its marketing actions at different stages of the product life cycle.
8 What is meant by a balanced product portfolio?

Issues for analysis

- The importance of a balanced portfolio.
- The relationship between the product life cycle and marketing activities.
- The relationship between cash and the product life cycle.

Assessment

Issues for evaluation

- What is the relative importance of the product in the marketing mix.
- What is the value of the product life cycle model and the Boston matrix.
- What are the most appropriate actions to take at different stages of the product life cycle or with different products in the portfolio?

Analysis and evaluation questions

1 According to Zak Zefferelli, a highly successful record producer: 'The key to being a successful act is to have a good USP. The key to a successful music label is to have a balanced portfolio of groups and individual performers.'

a Analyse the benefits to an act of having a good USP.
b Discuss the possible advantages to a record label of having a balanced portfolio.

2 'When we launch a new product there is always a worry that it will not take off.' says the marketing manager of a well-known perfume business.

a Analyse the relationship between cash flow and the stages of the product life cycle for a perfume product.
b Discuss the actions a perfume business might take if sales of one of its brands are falling.

Case study

Barbie, the best-selling fashion doll, was launched in 1959. The doll is produced by Mattel, Inc., and is a major source of revenue for the company. Ruth Handler, the creator of Barbie, watched her daughter Barbara at play with paper dolls, and noticed that she often enjoyed giving them adult roles. At the time, most children's toy dolls were representations of infants. Realizing that there could be a gap in the market, Handler developed the idea of an adult-looking doll.

The first Barbie doll wore a black and white zebra striped swimsuit and ponytail, and was available as either a blonde or brunette. Around 350,000 Barbie dolls were sold during the first year of production. Since then Barbie's appearance has been changed many times.

Barbie was one of the first toys the promotion of which was based extensively on television advertising: this approach has now been copied widely by rivals. It is estimated that over a billion Barbie dolls have been sold worldwide in over 150 countries and Mattel claims that three Barbie dolls are sold every second.

Barbie products include not only the range of dolls with their clothes and accessories, but also a huge range of Barbie branded goods such as books, fashion items and video games. Barbie has also appeared in a series of animated films including *Toy Story 2*.

Mattel estimates that there are well over 100,000 Barbie collectors. Ninety percent are women, at an average age of 40, purchasing more than twenty Barbie dolls each year. Forty-five percent of them spend upwards of $1,000 a year.

Vintage Barbie dolls from the early years are the most valuable at auction, and while the original Barbie was sold for $3.00 in 1959, a mint-boxed Barbie from 1959 sold for $3552.50 on eBay in October 2004. In recent years, Mattel has sold a wide range of Barbie dolls aimed specifically at collectors, including porcelain versions and depictions of Barbie as a range of characters from television series such as *The Munsters* and *Star Trek*.

In June 2001, MGA Entertainment launched the Bratz range of dolls, a move that gave Barbie her first serious competition in the fashion doll market. In 2005 figures showed that sales of Barbie dolls had fallen by 30 per cent in the United States, and by 18 per cent worldwide, with much of the drop being attributed to the popularity of Bratz dolls.

In April 2005, MGA Entertainment filed a lawsuit against Mattel, claiming that the 'My Scene' range of Barbie dolls had copied the look of Bratz dolls.

(Source: Adapted from: http://en.wikipedia.org/wiki/ Barbie_dolls)

Case study questions

1 Explain two possible reasons for the success of Barbie (6 marks)
2 Analyse the extension strategies used to maintain the sales of Barbie (9 marks)
3 Discuss whether the recent loss of market share to Bratz means that sales of Barbie are doomed. (15 marks)

28

Using the marketing mix – pricing

The price of a product can have a major influence on its appeal and whether or not customers think it is good value for money. In this chapter we examine the factors influencing the price of a product and different pricing strategies. Getting the price right is an important element of effective marketing because it will determine whether customers believe they are receiving value for money.

What you need to know by the end of this chapter:
- the different pricing strategies that are used
- the different pricing tactics that are used
- the influences on pricing decisions.

How price affects purchasing decisions

The price of a product plays an important part in our decision about whether or not to buy it. If the price is too high, we simply cannot afford the product even if we want to! Even if we can afford it we may decide it is not value for money if the price seems too high compared to the benefits the product offers. The success of the low-costs airlines such as Ryanair in gaining market share at the expense of firms such as British Airways shows how much the price can influence demand.

The price will, therefore, often play a significant role in the purchasing decision. However, the relative importance of price is likely to vary according to the product and the particular circumstances. For example, if two garages opposite each other are charging different prices for petrol, we are likely to choose the cheaper one. We are unlikely to be loyal to a particular brand of petrol. When buying a wedding ring, however, we do not always go for the cheapest! Similarly, when buying clothes and shoes we may be willing to pay more for an item if we think the brand justifies this.

Even if you wanted to choose the cheapest price it can be difficult to compare prices directly – look at how complicated the price structure is for mobile phones or electricity. The structure of special rates, different tariffs, different options is designed to make it difficult to know which is actually the best deal.

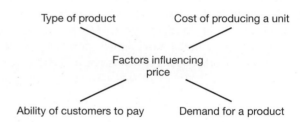

Figure 28.1 Factors influencing price

Factors determining the price of a product

The price of a product will depend on the following range of factors.

The type of product

Demand for some products is more sensitive to price than others. When you are looking to buy a new microwave, for example you are likely to look online or go to a shop that stocks several models. You may even go to a couple of different outlets to compare what they offer. This type of product is called a 'shopping good' because you shop around to find a good deal. These products are very sensitive to price differences. So managers will make the price comparable to that of their competitiors.

Other products are known as specialty items. These include high performance cars and luxury watches. Customers are likely to be willing to travel some distance to find these items and are heavily influenced by their design and branding factors. These products are less sensitive to price changes because they are so unique, so firms are likely to increase price. The sensitivity of demand to changes in price is measured by the price elasticity of demand. We examine this in more detail in Chapter 29.

The cost of producing a unit

Although in the short run a firm may sell an item at a loss to get it established in a market, in the long run a product will nearly always have to generate a profit. This means the price has to be greater than the cost per unit. Some organisations (such as museums and hospitals) are non-profit making and so do not necessarily have to cover their costs. However, most firms in the private sector have to make a long-term profit to survive. The price therefore cannot fall below the unit cost for too long.

The ability of customers to pay

If the economy is doing well and customers have high income levels a firm may be able to increase price because customers can afford to pay more. If, however, incomes are falling customers may be more sensitive to the price and look for a better deal (or delay purchasing at all); this may delay any price increases by firms.

The demand for a product

The level of interest in and demand for a product will also affect the price that firms can charge. In the UK in 2007 a smoking ban was introduced in public places such as pubs. This led many pubs to create outdoor areas where people could smoke. This in turn led to a big increase in demand for outdoor heaters and this pulled up their price. Similarly, when there are many investors wanting to buy the shares of a company, the share price usually increases because of the additional demand.

Competitors

The price that a business sets for its product must take account of competitors' prices. If competitors are offering a similar product or service and it is easy to switch from one to the other, firms are likely to set similar prices to each other.

This is why businesses will often stress the particular benefits of what they are offering, so they can justify a higher price. If customers believe a product provides better value for money, they may still buy it even if it is more expensive. Stella Artois beer, for example, ran a very successful 'reassuringly expensive' campaign in the UK, stressing that you pay more for high-quality lager.

There are now many websites offering price comparisons; this makes demand more sensitive to price as customers are looking around more and comparing is easier to do.

Pricing points

Some businesses aim to have a given range of products at particular pricing points in the market (e.g. the top or bottom end of the market) depending on the brand image and other elements of the marketing mix. Some businesses produce several different brands, priced at different levels. For example, a business may produce several different watches (often under different brand names): some in an exclusive range, some for the mass market and some discounted items.

The firm's objectives

The price charged by a firm will be influenced by its objectives. If a firm has a particular profit target, this will influence the price that is set per unit. If it wants to achieve £10,000 profit and expects to sell 20,000 units, it must make £0.50 profit per unit, if this is possible. If, however, it is aiming for a high market share (at least in the short run) it may be willing to sell at a lower price if this will help boost sales.

> **Key term**
> The **objective** of a business is the target it sets out to achieve.

The stage in the product life cycle

The price of a product is likely to be changed at different stages in the product life cycle. For example, when the product is in the maturity stage, the price may need to be reduced to avoid losing sales to competitors.

The rest of the marketing mix

The price a firm charges depends on the other elements of the marketing mix.

A heavily branded consumer product (such as Nike trainers or Coca Cola) will be expensive compared to own-brand products, for example. An exclusive four-star restaurant will charge more than a fast-food store. A designer boutique will charge more than Primark.

Typically the price will be higher if the product:

- has a unique selling point
- is perceived as being exclusive
- is in high demand
- is sold through exclusive outlets

There are therefore many factors that can influence the price of a product, and setting the price is a complex decision. If managers understand these influences, they can market their products more effectively by setting the right price for the market conditions. Managers can judge, for example, whether a price cut makes sense, given the market conditions.

Of course, a price is not fixed forever and there are a number of times when a firm might reconsider the price it is charging for a product. In the following sections we consider different pricing strategies and approaches.

Pricing strategies for new products

When a product is first launched into a market, a firm has to decide what price to charge.
They have a number of options:

- **Penetration pricing.** This strategy uses a low price to enter the market and gain market share. This makes sense if there are cost advantages from producing on a large scale. In some markets a high level of investment is required to set up, for example to invest in premises and equipment. Once this investment has been carried out a firm may want to generate high levels of demand to spread the costs over many units. A low entry price might help do this.

  Penetration pricing is also beneficial if the market is price sensitive (price elastic) in that a lower price will generate significantly higher sales and increase revenue (see Chapter 29).
- **Price skimming.** This strategy uses a high price to enter a market. Even though the price is high, some people may still be eager to try a new product. Once sales from this group of people have been exhausted, the price can be dropped to attract a new group of customers. When this group is exhausted, the price can be cut again. A price skimming strategy is appropriate if the firm can protect its idea or invention so that competitors cannot enter with a cheaper version in the early stages. (As we saw in Chapter 2, it may be protected using a trademark, which protects the firm's logo, or a patent, which protects a new invention.)

Price skimming makes sense if the market is not particularly price sensitive (i.e. this is known as price inelastic), so that a price cut would generate a relatively smaller increase in sales. This strategy is often used with new technology: the latest computer or computer accessory enters the market with a high price, which then falls quite rapidly a year or so later.

- **Competitive pricing** – some firms set their price at the same level as their competitors or deliberately undercut their rivals. The John Lewis Partnership claims it is 'never knowingly undersold'. Esso operates a 'Pricewatch' to monitor competitors' prices. Many retailers (such as Wyevale Garden Centres) offer to refund the difference if you can find a similar product cheaper in another local store. Competitive pricing is common when consumers can easily make a direct comparison between different products.
- **Price taking** – price takers are firms that accept the price which dominates in the market. A small independent electrical retailer, for example, may have to accept the price set by the major sellers, such as Currys. Independent bookshops may have to follow the prices of major bookstores, such as Waterstones.

Figure 28.2 Pricing strategies

Ratner's

Gerald Ratner was a highly successful businessman in the 1980s who brought jewellery to the high street. At the time, most jewellery was expensive and was sold through traditional outlets that were not in the city centre. Ratner built up an empire of shops selling basic, cheap jewellery and other items that appealed to the mass market. His success was built on providing basic products at a low price. This had not been done before in the UK in the jewellery market.

However, in 1991 Ratner made a speech in which he appeared to criticise his own products. He said that some of his company's earrings were cheaper than a Marks and Spencer sandwich but probably wouldn't last as long; he also said some of his own products were 'crap'. The media picked up on the speech and eventually Ratner was forced to resign. He later launched an internet-based jewellery business.

> **Key terms**
> **Penetration pricing** is a pricing strategy aimed at gaining market share via a low entry price
> **Price skimming** occurs when a high initial price is set for a product when it enters the market and the price is reduced over time.

By understanding these pricing strategies managers can decide on the best price to set when launching a new product.

Pricing tactics

Pricing tactics are short-term policies aimed at achieving a particular objective. These include:

- **Loss leaders** – a loss leader is a product sold at a loss to generate business for other (profitable) products sold by the firm. For example, supermarkets often sell a few well-known products at a loss and publicise the prices of these few products heavily. This increases the number of people using their shop and boosts the sales of other products. Similarly, photocopier and printer companies often sell the copiers and printers at a loss and then aim to make their profits on the cartridges, spares and accessories.
- **Psychological pricing** – this occurs when products are sold at prices intended to create a particular impression of the product. For example, selling a product at £49.99 instead of £50 makes customers think of it as 'less than £50', which may encourage them to buy it. Firms also use tactics that involve marking down prices, for example 'was £60, now £49.99', to encourage people to buy on the basis that it is a bargain. Alternatively, a firm may set a high price to convey quality – people often assume that a higher-priced item must be better than a lower-priced one.

Business in Focus

Business in focus: Easycinema

When the Easygroup moved into the cinema business it adopted a low-price approach. The Easycinema opened in Milton Keynes and, typical of the Easygroup, it adopted a no-frills approach to help keep prices down. There was no box office – you could only book online or by phone. The earlier you reserved your seats, the cheaper it was. However, despite its low prices the business struggled because the main film distributors did not want to let Easycinema show its blockbusters. These firms make their money from earning a percentage of the ticket price, and so did not want lower prices. Some Easycinema tickets were selling at 20 pence and so the distributors were not making any profit, especially as customers could have gone to other cinemas where they would have been paying higher prices.

If you ran a cinema, what prices would you set for films? Why? Would you change the prices for different films, days or times? Why?

Examiner's advice

You need to understand the many different factors that can influence the price, and the different pricing strategies and tactics. You need to be able to discuss the factors that determine the right price in any situation.

To make a business more effective managers need to select a price that makes customers feel that they are receiving excellent value for money. The price must be reviewed and changed as market conditions and external factors change.

Summary

The price set by a business will determine whether or not a product is affordable and whether the customer regards it as value for money. The price that is set by a business will depend on many factors, such as the costs, the prices of substitutes, the likely demand and the firm's own profit targets. Pricing strategies include price skimming and penetration pricing. Pricing tactics include psychological pricing and loss leaders. Effective marketing involves the right marketing mix: this includes setting the right price for the marketing conditions and the other elements of the mix.

Quick questions

1 Price is one element of the marketing mix. State three others.
2 Why might changes in costs affect the price of a product?
3 State two factors apart from cost that might affect the price of a product.
4 What is meant by a price penetration strategy?
5 When would a price skimming strategy be appropriate?
6 What is meant by a loss leader?
7 What is meant by psychological pricing?
8 Why must the price of a product fit with the rest of the marketing mix?

Issues for analysis

- The factors determining price.
- The relationship between price and sales.

Issues for evaluation

- What determines the relative importance of the price compared to other elements of the marketing mix?
- Is price the most important factor?
- What are the most important influences on price.

Analysis and evaluation questions

1 'I knew we had developed an electric toothbrush that was significantly better than anything else on the market – that was the easy bit. Marketing it was the difficult part,' says John Davies, managing director of a small business he set up himself to produce this new product.

a Analyse the factors that are likely to determine the price set by John for this new product b To what extent will the price determine the success of this new product?

2 Eve Sinner runs a growing chain of clothes stores across south-east England. 'We use a range of pricing tactics to boost sales when things are flagging in a particular store. When we open a new store in an area we usually use penetration pricing.'

a Analyse the pricing tactics that Eve might use in an existing store to try to boost sales.

b Discuss the case for and against Eve using penetration pricing when opening a new store in an area.

Assessment

Case study

In the early 1990s, Dean Hoyle was selling greetings cards from the back of his van in his home town of Wakefield. By 1997, he and his wife Janet had set up the Card Factory company, a retail card shop, with the aim of selling quality cards at low prices. Today, the company has 300 shops, 20 of which came from the acquisition of Celebration Cards in January 2006.

Case study questions

30 marks; 40 minutes

1 Explain two possible segments within the greetings cards market. (6 marks)
2 Analyse the factors that might determine the price that Dean sets for his firm's greetings cards. (9 marks)
3 To what extent is the price a key element of the marketing of greetings cards? (15 marks)

29 Understanding and using the price elasticity of demand

One of the main factors influencing demand is the price of a product. In this chapter we examine the extent to which demand changes when the price is changed. This is measured by the price elasticity of demand. An understanding of price elasticity of demand is essential to effective marketing.
What you need to know by the end of this chapter:
• the meaning of the price elasticity of demand
• the factors that influence the price elasticity of demand
• the difference between a price elastic and price inelastic demand
• the impact of a price change on total revenue.

Demand

The demand for a product measures the amount that customers are willing and able to purchase. This can be influenced by many factors, including:

• the income of customers, because this determines what they can afford
• the price and benefits that rivals offer, because this determines whether customers will regard the product as value for money and will switch to them or not
• the effectiveness of a firm's marketing, because this determines the perceived value of what you offer
• external factors such as the weather can influence whether customers want products (e.g. barbecue sets).

Every business is interested in what affects demand for its products and services. What is it that makes its sales go up, or down? Will sales alter if it changes the price, or if incomes change? What is the strength of the relationship between, for example, price and sales? If the price is cut by 10 per cent, will sales go up by 5 per cent, or 50 per cent? Similarly, if average consumer income levels rise by 5 per cent, what impact will this have on demand for the firm's products?

The relationship between changes in demand and changes in factors such as price and income is measured by the elasticity of demand. There are several types of elasticity but one of the most important to businesses is the price elasticity of demand. This specifically measures the sensitivity of demand to a change in price. A business can change its price, but before it does so, it will want to know the possible impact on the demand for its products.

Effective marketing involves an understanding of what influences demand and how sensitive demand is to different factors: this inevitably requires an understanding of the concept of elasticity.

Why does the price elasticity matter?

By calculating the price elasticity of demand, a firm can identify how changes in price may affect the quantity of its sales and, therefore, revenue. This is important for its marketing planning. If, for example, a firm is planning a price cut, it will want to estimate how much sales are likely to increase. This allows a business to ensure it has sufficient stocks or capacity to meet demand. It may also have implications in terms of employing people. For example, the firm may need to hire extra people or get staff to work overtime to meet orders. The business will also want to calculate whether the price cut is worthwhile financially. Will the price cut lead to higher profits, or not? An understanding of price elasticity should, therefore, lead to better pricing decisions.

Price elasticity of demand

The price elasticity of demand is measured by:

$$\frac{\text{Percentage change in quantity demanded}}{\text{Percentage change in price}}$$

The answer for the price elasticity of demand is negative. This is because the quantity demanded falls when price increases and vice versa. With one variable going up and one falling the overall response is negative. However when discussing the size of the price elasticity we ignore the sign and focus on the number itself. –2, for example, means that the percentage change in quantity demanded is twice than of the percentage change in price. The negative sign simply shows one falls when the other increases. When discussing –2 we ignore the negative sign (which shows us the direction of the movements) and concentrate on the 2 which shows us the strength of the relationship.

Price elastic demand

Demand is said to be price elastic if the value of the price elasticity of demand is greater than 1 (ignoring the negative sign), i.e. every 1% change in price brings about a more than 1% change in quantity demanded.

For example, if demand rises by 20% when the price is cut by 10%, the price elasticity of demand will equal +20/–10 = –2. This is said to be bigger than one because we ignore the sign and focus on the number, 2.

The value of 2 shows that for every 1% change in price, the quantity demanded changes by 2%, i.e. by twice as much. The negative sign simply shows that the price and quantity demanded move in different directions. If price goes down, quantity demanded rises, and if prices rises, quantity demanded falls.

Similarly –3 or –5 would be regarded as bigger than one because it is the value of the number, ignoring the sign, that we focus on.

Price inelastic demand

Demand is said to be price inelastic if the value of the price elasticity is less than 1, i.e. a 1% change in price leads to a less than 1% change in quantity demanded. (As ever we ignore the negative sign.)

For example, a price cut of 10%, leading to an increase in demand of only 5%, will have a price elasticity of demand of +5%/–10% = –0.5.

The negative sign shows that as price goes down, quantity demanded rises (i.e. they move in opposite directions). The 0.5 (which is less than 1) shows that every 1% change in price leads to a 0.5% change in quantity demanded. This means that demand is not very sensitive to price changes i.e. demand is price inelastic. Similarly –0.1 or –0.8 are both less than 1 (ignoring the sign) and are therefore price inelastic.

> **Key term**
> The **price elasticity of demand** measures the sensitivity of demand to a change in price.

Figure 29.2 Factors influencing the price elasticity of demand

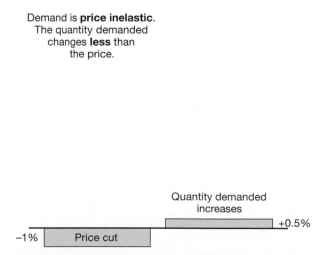

Figure 29.1 Price elastic and price inelastic demand

What determines the value of the price elasticity of demand?

The price elasticity of demand for a product will be affected by a number of factors, such as:

- The **availability of similar products**. If a consumer can switch easily from one product to another, its demand is likely to be quite sensitive to price changes (i.e. demand will be price elastic). When buying bin liners, for example, most customers do not care what brand they buy – faced with two types, they are likely to buy the cheaper one. Demand would therefore be price elastic.

  Many businesses attempt to differentiate their products so that consumers do not switch to competitors' offerings (i.e. the firms try to make demand for their products price inelastic). Coca Cola, for example, has worked hard to distinguish its products from other cola drinks. Coca Cola hopes that relatively few consumers will switch brands even if its price is higher. Successful branding should, therefore, reduce a product's price elasticity of demand and make demand price inelastic.

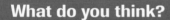

What do you think?

Is:

- Intel the same as AMD?
- McDonald's the same as Burger King?
- BBC the same as ITV?
- Facebook the same as MySpace?
- TopShop the same as Next?

If not, why not?

- **Time**. In the short term, customers are often loyal to their existing provider (for example, their credit card company, their bank or their insurance company). This may be because they can't be bothered to look for alternatives or because they think that changing isn't worth it in the short run as conditions might change again and so any advantage a competitor has may be temporary. However, over time, if customers feel they are getting a bad deal, this will act as an incentive to switch. They also have more time to explore their options. This means demand will become more price sensitive (i.e. more price elastic) over time.
- **The type of product**. When buying convenience products, such as a pint of milk, purchasers tend

to go to the nearest shop. Consumers do not spend much money on each item and are not too concerned about price. Demand for this type of product is likely to be price inelastic. In comparison, shopping goods such as clothes are likely to be much more sensitive to price (i.e. more price elastic): this is because customers spend time comparing their options.

- **The proportion of income spent on the product**. If you only spend a small proportion of your income on a product you may not be very sensitive to price changes because they will have a limited impact on your spending. However, if you spend a high proportion of your income on something (such as housing) then a given percentage change will have a more noticeable effect and demand is likely to be more price sensitive.
- **Demand for the brand versus demand for the product**. Demand for petrol is likely to be very price inelastic – most consumers would find it difficult or inconvenient to do without their cars. However, demand for one company's petrol is likely to be more price elastic than demand for petrol in general, as it is fairly easy to switch to another garage. Demand for a particular brand is therefore likely to be more price elastic than demand for the whole product category.

What do you think?

Do you think the demand for the following is likely to be price elastic or price inelastic? Why?
- MOT test for your car
- The car insurance offered by one company
- Your mobile phone contract
- A new dishwasher
- Tickets to a Chelsea match
- Sky TV.

Price elasticity, total revenue and profits

a. a price cut and price elastic demand

If demand for a product is price elastic, a business can increase its revenue by lowering the price. Although it earns less for each item, its overall income increases because it is selling so many more products.

Imagine that a firm sells 10,000 units at £5; its total revenue is 5 × 10,000 = £50,000. If the price is cut to £4 and sales jump to 15,000 the new total revenue will be £4 × 15,000= £60,000. A 20 per cent price cut increases sales by 50 per cent and revenue increases.

What do you think?

What is the value of the price elasticity of demand if a 20 per cent price cut increases demand by 50 per cent?

Whether this increase in revenue also means an increase in profit depends on what happens to the costs when the firm produces and sells more. If, for example, a firm has to increase capacity, it may incur significant additional costs and so, although it is earning more, profits may fall. On the other hand, if revenue increases more than costs, profits will rise.

Key term
The **total revenue** is the income generated from sales. It is also called 'turnover' or 'sales'.

b. a price cut and price inelastic demand
If demand for a product is price inelastic, the revenue will fall when the price is cut. This is because the increase in sales is not big enough to compensate for the fact that each item is selling for less.

Imagine that a firm sells 10,000 units at £5; its total revenue is 5 × 10,000 = £50,000. If the price is cut to £4 and sales increase to 11,000 the new total revenue will be £4 × 11,000= £44,000. A 20 per cent price cut increases sales by only 10 per cent and revenue falls.

What do you think?

What is the value of price elasticity of demand if a 20 per cent price cut increases demand by 10 per cent?

In this situation, when demand is price inelastic the business could earn more by putting the price up. Although it would lose some customers, the fact that

it is charging more per unit means its overall income will increase.

Imagine that a firm sells 10,000 units at £5; its total revenue is 5 × 10,000 = £50,000. If the price is increased to £6 and sales fall to 9,000, the new total revenue will be £6 × 9,000 = £54,000. A 20 per cent price increase cuts sales by only 10 per cent and revenue increases.

Key terms
A **price inelastic demand** means that the impact of a change in price leads to a smaller change in the quantity demanded (in percentages).

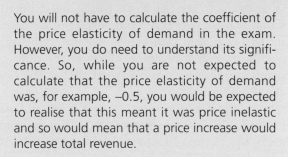

Examiner's advice

You will not have to calculate the coefficient of the price elasticity of demand in the exam. However, you do need to understand its significance. So, while you are not expected to calculate that the price elasticity of demand was, for example, −0.5, you would be expected to realise that this meant it was price inelastic and so would mean that a price increase would increase total revenue.

Problems with the price elasticity of demand concept

It is important to remember that the value of price elasticity of demand at any moment is an estimate (you will never know exactly how sensitive demand is to price until you actually change the price and see what happens). Therefore, a specific value of price elasticity of demand needs to be treated with some caution. This is especially true because markets keep changing and this will affect the price elasticity of demand. New products, changes in consumer tastes, developments in distribution and competitors' marketing campaigns will all affect the demand for a product. This can make it difficult to know exactly what caused a change in sales following a price change. Was it the price change? Or was it government policies, or consumer confidence?

	Price decrease	Price increase
Price elastic demand	Revenue increases	Revenue decreases
Price inelastic demand	Revenue decreases	Revenue increases

Table 29.1 Summary table : price elasticity and revenue

While it may appear that a price cut of 1 per cent increased sales by 2 per cent, suggesting a price elasticity of –2, in reality the sales may have gone up for completely different reasons.

Having said this, with experience, by asking experts or by analysing the results from a test market, managers are likely to have some idea of approximately how sensitive demand is to price and may feel confident to base pricing decisions on this. Even if they do not know the exact value, an understanding of whether demand is price elastic or inelastic is useful when it comes to setting and changing prices.

One step further: price discrimination

You will sometimes find that demand conditions for the same product can vary. For example, demand for pubic transport around 8 am is very heavy, as people want to get to work for 9 am. Similarly, demand is busy between 5 pm and 6 pm, as people want to get home. Demand is less heavy at other times of day. If a business can identify different demand conditions it may want to change the price in the different markets.

The demand for transport before 9 am and after 5.30 pm is likely to be price inelastic: it is not sensitive to price because people have to get to and from work. At these times a transport business may increase price to increase revenue. At other times of day demand may be more price elastic (i.e. sensitive to price) because there is not the same pressure on people to travel; they can always delay their journey or not go at all. To raise revenue at these times the business may decrease price.

The result is that you pay different prices for the same journey at different times of day. This is known as 'price discrimination'.

Price discrimination may occur when firms charge different prices:

- at different times of day e.g. taxi fares may be higher after midnight
- to different age groups e.g. lower fares on the bus for children and pensioners
- to different customer groups e.g. discounts for members.

Another step further: Other types of elasticity of demand

Firms are not only interested in how price influences demand; they also want to analyse the relationship between other variables and demand. Another common measure of elasticity is the income elasticity of demand: this is analysed below.

Income elasticity of demand

The amount that demand changes in relation to changes in income can be measured by the income elasticity of demand.

$$\text{Income elasticity of demand} = \frac{\text{percentage change in quantity demanded}}{\text{percentage change in income}}$$

For example, if demand increases by 20 per cent when income rises by 10 per cent, then:

$$\text{Income elasticity} = \frac{+20}{+10} = +2$$

This product is income elastic because the demand has changed by more than the percentage change in income. These are 'luxury' products such as health clubs.

Alternatively, if demand increases by 5 per cent when income rises by 10 per cent then:

$$\text{Income elasticity} = \frac{+5}{+10} = +0.5$$

This product is income inelastic, because the demand has changed by less than the percentage change in income.

In both the above cases. demand increased when income increased. These are called 'normal products' and have a positive income elasticity of demand.

If demand *falls* as income rises, the product is known as an 'inferior' product. This leads to a negative income elasticity of demand.

For example, if the quantity demanded falls by 2 per cent when income rises by 6 per cent, then:

$$\text{Income elasticity of demand} = \frac{-2}{+6} = -0.33$$

Products such as basic own label items may be perceived as inferior products; with higher levels of income customers switch to other items that are perceived as better.

Other types of elasticity that it would be possible to calculate include:

- **Cross-price elasticity of demand**. This shows how much demand for one product (A) changes when the price of another product B changes:

$$\frac{\text{Percentage change in quantity demanded of A}}{\text{Percentage change in price of B}}$$

This can show the nature of the relationship between the two products. With substitutes, customers will buy more of A when the price of B increases (switching from B to A), and the cross-price elasticity will be positive. With complements, customers will buy less of A when the price of B increases (e.g. high-priced computer consoles reduces sales of consoles and of computer games, so the games and consoles are complements), so the cross-price elasticity is negative. The size of the cross-price elasticity of demand will show the strength of the relationship between the products (e.g. the extent to which they are close substitutes).

- **Advertising elasticity of demand**. This will show the sensitivity of demand in relation to changes in advertising expenditure:

$$\frac{\text{Percentage change in quantity demanded}}{\text{Percentage change in advertising expenditure}}$$

- **Weather elasticity of demand**. This shows the sensitivity of demand in relation to changes in factors such as the temperature or rainfall:

$$\frac{\text{Percentage change in quantity demanded}}{\text{Percentage change in rainfall}}$$

Summary

The price is an important determinant of demand. An increase in price is likely to lead to a fall in sales – but how much will sales fall? This depends on the price elasticity of demand. If demand is price elastic, it means that a change in price leads to a bigger percentage change in demand. If demand is price inelastic, it means that a change in price leads to a less than proportionate change in demand. If managers know the price elasticity of demand for their products, they can change their pricing approaches accordingly. To increase revenue, they could lower the price when demand is price elastic, or increase the price when demand is price inelastic. Effective marketing therefore requires an understanding of the price elasticity of demand.

Examiner's advice

It is important to understand the difference between price elastic and price inelastic demand and the significance of this in terms of changing the price. You should understand the relationship between price changes, price elasticity of demand and revenue.

A good understanding and awareness of the price elasticity should enable firms to set the right price to achieve their revenue and/or their volume objectives.

Quick questions

1. What is meant by the price elasticity of demand?
2. Why would managers want to know the price elasticity of demand for their products?
3. If demand is price elastic, would a price fall or a price increase lead to an increase in revenue?
4. State two factors that influence the price elasticity of demand for a product.
5. If the price elasticity of demand is –2, what would the effect on demand be if a business cut price by 10 per cent?
6. Over time is demand for a product likely to get more or less price elastic? Why?
7. Price is one factor affecting demand. State two others.
8. If the price elasticity of demand is –0.8, would a price increase lead to a fall or increase in revenue?

Issues for analysis

- The relationship between price, price elasticity and revenue.
- The factors determining the price elasticity of demand.

Issues for evaluation

- How useful is the concept of price elasticity of demand when setting the price?

Analysis and evaluation questions

1. 'We had charged an £80 basic fee per job for a couple of years and were averaging about 50 jobs a week. Eventually we realised that demand was likely to be price inelastic and so increased price' says Bob Pipes, the owner of a plumbing business.

a. Analyse the likely effects of a price increase by Bob on the firm's sales and revenue.

b. Discuss the factors that might make demand for Bob's business price inelastic

2. 'The last time we cut the price it seemed to work really well and sales jumped. That's why we reduced the price again recently. This time we ended up selling about the same amount for less – we could have kicked ourselves! I'm beginning to wonder whether

it actually was the price that boosted sales last time.' Megan Chiller, Marketing Director of Luscious, a luxury ice cream business.

a   Analyse the other factors that might influence demand for ice creams.

b   Discuss the value of the concept of the price elasticity of demand to a manager such as Megan when setting the price of a product.

Assessment

Case study

Sir Richard Branson, the founder of Virgin, has set up a company to take passengers into space. He is having five 'Spaceliners' built in the USA by the team behind the SpaceShipOne vehicle. The California-based rocket plane became the first privately developed carrier to go above 100km in 2007. The estimated price is around £100,000 to go on a 'Virgin Galactic' Spaceliner, and the first flights should begin around 2010. Branson says 'If it is a success, we want to move into orbital flights and then, possibly, even get a hotel up there.' He thinks there are about 3,000 people who would want to do this. The spaceship will have space for five passengers and a week's pre-flight training will be needed before the three-hour trip.

(Source: Adapted from http://news.bbc.co.uk/go/pr/fr/-/1/hi/sci/tech/3693020.stm)

Case study questions

(30 marks; 40 minutes)

1   Outline two elements of the marketing mix of the 'Virgin Galactic' Spaceliner other than the price. (6 marks)

2   Analyse the ways in which Sir Richard Branson might have estimated demand for the Virgin Spaceliner. (9 marks)

3   Discuss whether the demand for the Virgin Spaceliner is likely to be price inelastic or price elastic. (15 marks)

30 Using the marketing mix – place

Using the right distribution channels is an important element of effective marketing. The distribution of a product determines where it is available to customers and how easy it is to access it. It also affects costs and the overall buying experience. In this chapter we examine different approaches to distribution and the factors that influence the choice of distribution channel.

What you need to know by the end of this chapter:

- the importance of distribution
- the different types of distribution channels
- the factors that influence the choice of appropriate outlets/distributors.

Distribution

The distribution of a good or service refers to the way in which the ownership of it passes from the producer to the consumer. In some cases, the product goes directly to the end customer from the producer: for example, Dell computers supplies its customers direct, without intermediaries, as does Avon cosmetics. Services such as insurance, healthcare and education tend to be provided directly to the end customers.

In other cases, producers use intermediaries: most producers of electrical goods, such as Sony and Phillips, have intermediaries between the producer and the final seller. These intermediaries include:

- retailers (such as Currys and PC World), which are the final stage in the distribution chain. Many goods are sold through retailers rather than direct to the customer.

- wholesalers. These buy products in bulk from producers and sell these on to retailers, who then sell direct to the final consumer. Retailers use wholesalers because they offer a range of products and it is easier than dealing direct with them than with many different individual manufacturers.

> **Key terms**
> The **distribution channel** describes how the ownership of a product moves from the producer to the customer.

The different distribution channels can be described in terms of the number of levels involved in the process:

- In a zero-level channel, the good or service passes directly from producer to consumer without any intermediaries. For example, dentists, accountants and plumbers have zero-level channels.

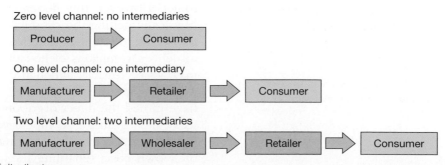

Figure 30.1 Levels of distribution

- A one-level channel has one intermediary. For example, a retailer buys the product from the manufacturer and sells it to the consumer.
- A two-level channel has two intermediaries. For example, a wholesaler buys the product from the manufacturer and sells it on to retailers, who sell to the final customers.

The distribution strategy will vary considerably from product to product. In the case of milk, newspapers and chewing gum, for example, the aim is usually to generate as wide a distribution as possible. These types of goods are called convenience items because consumers are not willing to travel far to buy them – they need them to be easily accessible. To get to as broad a market as possible, several intermediaries may be used.

With products such as personal computers, vacuum cleaners, microwaves, and so on, consumers usually want to compare the features and prices of different brands. Manufacturers of these products need to get them distributed to certain stores where customers expect to go to find them. These shopping goods do not need to be distributed to as many outlets as convenience items, but the firm may have to fight hard to get intermediaries to stock them. Although with the growth of online shopping manufacturers now sell directly to customers, many sales are still through retailers.

More exclusive (or speciality) products, such as Rolex, Porsche, Bang and Olufsen and Bose have even fewer outlets, but the nature of these outlets is very important. They must reinforce the nature of the brand and so a great deal of time is spent ensuring they are well maintained and suitably exclusive. In some cases, the manufacturer owns the outlet to ensure it presents its products in a way that is appropriate to the brand.

Products that are sold to other businesses (i.e. using business-to-business marketing) rather than the final consumer are called industrial goods (rather than consumer goods). These tend to be distributed directly. This might include machinery, office equipment and specialised computer software.

> **Key terms**
> **Industrial goods** are sold from one business to another; they are used in the production of the final product.

> **What do you think?**
>
> How far do you think you would travel to buy the following:
> - a ticket to concert by your favourite band?
> - batteries?
> - a new pair of trousers?
> - a bar of chocolate?
> - a pad of paper?
> - a new car?

Choosing a distribution channel

The choice of distribution channel will depend on factors such as:

- **Access to markets**. If the target number of customers is relatively small (e.g. you are targeting a few large companies) then it may be possible to distribute directly. If, however, you have a mass-market consumer product, it is not realistic to try to distribute individually to all your customers – you will want to use intermediaries to help get your products to the market. Heinz could not distribute its baked beans to every individual household in the UK: it has to sell via wholesalers and retailers.
- **The desired degree of control**. If a producer sells its products to other intermediaries then it hands over control of the way they are marketed. The new owner can change the price, the way it is described relative to its competitors and where it is displayed in the market. Concern over the impact of such decisions on the brand may mean that a producer decides to sell directly or only via its own outlets.
- **Costs**. It may be cheaper to sell a product direct to the customer. If the product goes through various intermediaries, all of whom add on their own profit margin, the final price will probably be higher than if the business sold direct to a customer. However, this depends on the costs of physically getting the products to customers. If they come to you it is more feasible. If you have to deliver to millions of households directly this may not be feasible, although companies such as Amazon.com, Direct Line and lastminute.com have turned the direct distribution of their services into a major competitive weapon. By distributing directly to the customer, they have cut their own costs (enabling them to offer better value) and provide a more convenient service for

customers. You can now order your weekly shopping, buy your books, check your bank account and book your holiday from home. The internet allows many firms (even very small firms) to deal directly with their customers on a global basis.

Choosing the right distribution channel is therefore, an important (and often underestimated) part of the marketing mix. It can have a big impact on the success of the business in terms of factors such as:

- market coverage
- costs
- control over the way the product is promoted and marketed in store.

Getting the right distribution outlet

Of course, the nature of the distribution outlet itself can have an impact on the buying experience. The layout of the stores, the décor, the availability of staff and changing rooms, the in-store displays all leave an impression and influence your view of a product. This is particularly important for speciality items such as luxury cars, jewellery or sophisticated technology. Visit a Mercedes dealership, a Gucci outlet or an Apple store and you immediately get a sense of the brand values.

If producers of such products are selling through stores (theirs or anyone else's) the store design and the way their products are displayed is very important. Ikea, the Swedish furniture retailer, is renowned for its highly effective store design. Its stores are very large and are placed out of town. This makes it cheaper for the company to offer a large number of parking spaces. The stores are relatively easy to get to for car drivers, which is important because the items bought are often big and bulky. Once customers get there, the stores are designed in such a way that they have to walk through all the displays to get to the tills – you cannot nip in and buy one thing. This tends to mean that customers end up buying more than they had planned.

Business in Focus

Lakeland

Figure 30.2 Lakeland head office

'The Lakeland story began in 1963. Alan Rayner, an agricultural feed salesman, had the idea of providing local farmers with polythene bags for packing poultry. He set up a mail-order business with his wife Dorothy, supplying agricultural plastics and home-freezing products from the garage of their Windermere home in the Lake District.

Demand for kitchen accessories soon outweighed everything else. In 1974, Alan retired and handed the business over to his three sons Martin, Sam and Julian, marking the beginning of Lakeland Plastics.

The range of products grew to include wooden, glass, ceramic and stainless steel kitchenware, as well as a range of specialist foods. The Lakeland Plastics name wasn't quite right any more, so the name was changed to Lakeland Limited in 1997. Now based in large, modern, purpose-built premises in both Windermere and Kendal, Lakeland has around 4,000 products in its range and produces around 18 catalogues each year – these are sent to over one million households around the world! The mail order business has grown from a few parcels sent out from the local post office to over 6,000 parcels despatched from our Kendal Despatch Centre every day.

The number of retail outlets has also expanded. There are now 35 thriving Lakeland stores – with more on the way – from as far north as Aberdeen, all the way down to the tip of Cornwall in Truro.'

Discuss the advantages and disadvantages of selling via mail order.

Should Lakeland concentrate of opening more retail outlets or developing the website?

Business in Focus

Betterware

'From our humble roots in East London in the 1920s, Betterware has gone from strength to strength and has evolved into the progressive market leading company you see today. Building on the reputation of our core kitchen-ware and cleaning products, Betterware now offers a wide range of contemporary, creative and problem solving homeware products. It's safe to say that very few people have ever picked up a Betterware catalogue without exclaiming "That's a good idea, I must get one of those!" '

With a team of over 7,000 distributors (who go door to door), the company now operates from its own purpose-built office and ware-housing complex in the Midlands; handling over 7 million customer orders every year. Customers can order products through a network of dis-tributors, online, by post or over the phone to Betterware's call centre in Birmingham.

(Source: Adapted from www.betterware.co.uk)

What other products can you think of that are sold door to door?

Why do you think Betterware does not sell its products through other retailers?

What do you think?

How would you describe the layout and décor of the following high street stores:

- Accessorise?
- Marks and Spencer?
- Primark?
- Next?

What do the stores tell you about the business?

Business in Focus

Dell Computers

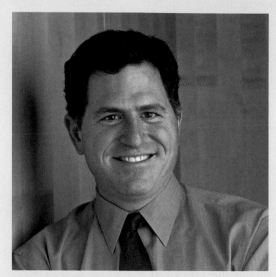

Figure 30.3 Michael Dell

Michael Dell revolutionised the personal com-puter industry by missing out intermediaries and selling directly to the customer. He also inno-vated the way PCs were produced by developing a process to mass-produce individually made-to-order computers. Customers select from a variety of options what type of monitor, what memory, what base unit and so on. These are selected and then the computer you 'built' is produced for you. You can make these choices and order your computer online without having to speak to anyone.

Michael Dell was in born February 1965 and started his business in his University of Texas room in 1984 with just $1,000 and an idea to provide affordable personal computers to col-lege students. He went on to become the youngest CEO ever to earn a ranking on the Fortune 500.

Michael Dell is the author of *Direct from Dell: Strategies That Revolutionized an Industry*. The book includes the story about his rise to the top and also his business philosophy.

The design and layout of a store can have a big influence on its sales. In supermarkets, for example, all kinds of techniques are used to make you buy more:

- The width of the aisles and the music being played affects the speed that you walk around the store.
- You will usually be greeted by the fresh fruit displays when you walk in; this creates an impression in your mind that all their products are fresh.
- The aroma in the store is likely to be fresh bread (many now have bakeries on site but even if they do not they can create the smell of fresh bread): this tends to create positive, warm feelings within us.
- You will usually enter on the left-hand side of a store because we tend to like to walk in and turn right.
- The basic items such as bread and milk will usually be at the back of the store so that you have to pass many other items to find them and hopefully buy other things along the way.
- Key items on promotion will be placed in display bins at the end of aisles so you see them when you turn, or by the tills: these are to prompt impulse items.
- Complementary items such as soft drinks and crisps will usually be placed near each other: buying one may prompt the buying of the other.

Store designers have become very aware of the effect that the décor and layout can have and have therefore become much more sophisticated in their designs.

What do you think?

How important do you think store design is when opening a shop?

Which store do you most like visiting? Why?

Business in Focus

Hotel du Chocolat

Angus Thirlwell, managing director of the upmarket chocolate chain Hotel du Chocolat, started an online chocolate business 10 years ago but has found greater success with a conventional high-street presence.

He has put careful thought into the design of the stores, the first of which opened in Watford in October 2005, two years after the internet site launched.

'We chose dark walnut wood interiors and porcelain tiles. We've also used long counters like a hotel reception desk and made them spacious so that people can wander around, like in a hotel lobby,' he says. Whereas fast delivery was the sales pitch of the internet website, quality is the selling point of the stores.

The internet company out of which Hotel du Chocolat grew was funded with £5,000 each from Angus Thirlwell and his business partner, Peter Harris. It now has a turnover of more than £40m a year.

Why do you think Hotel du Chocolat was more successful when it opened stores than it was when it was just operating online?

Distribution targets

When developing a distribution strategy, firms often set themselves distribution targets. These might be in terms of the sales they hope to achieve in different areas or through different types of store. To achieve these targets, businesses may need to convince intermediaries to take their products or promote their services. This is often the job of the sales force. They meet with intermediaries, to persuade them to buy the firm's products.

Examiner's advice

You need to think about the factors that influence a company's choice of distribution channel and the effect this has on its costs and the quality of service it provides.

A business may improve its effectiveness by reviewing its distribution, as this may influence its market coverage, the level of service provided and its costs.

Summary

Distribution is an important part of a firm's marketing mix. Choosing distribution channels will affect a firm's costs, its ability to get its products to customers and the control that a firm retains over the marketing of its products. Effective marketing therefore involves the right choice of distribution channels.

Quick questions

1 What is meant by a distribution channel?
2 What is meant by a one-level distribution channel?
3 Explain two factors that might influence a firm's choice of distribution channel.
4 What is meant by the term 'wholesaler'?
5 In what ways does the choice of distribution channel relate to the rest of the marketing mix?
6 What is the difference between an industrial and a consumer product?
7 In what way can the choice of distribution channel affect the competitiveness of a business?
8 How has the internet influenced the choice of distribution channel by firms?

Issues for analysis

- What affects the relationship between distribution channel and costs.
- The relationship between distribution channel and market coverage.

Issues for evaluation

- What affects the relative importance of distribution in the marketing mix.
- Is distribution the most important element of the marketing mix?
- Does effective distribution guarantee the success of a product?

Assessment

- Does the internet mean that all firms will end up selling directly to customers?

Analysis and evaluation questions

1 'At the moment we sell mainly through chain stores and our relationship with different stores can have a big impact on sales. However, online demand is growing and I am considering switching to selling only through this form of direct order.' (Tracey Trafford, managing director of Pulsar, a producer of digital radios.)

a Analyse the ways in which the relationship between Pulsar and the chain stores might affect the company's sales.
b Discuss the factors that Tracey Trafford should consider before switching to online sales only.

2 'We must get our product stocked and sold by more wholesalers and retailers. Distribution is probably the most important part of our marketing mix. At the moment we only have about 30 stores taking our product. We need some deals with wholesalers.' (Julius Octavia, the marketing director of O2toU ,a bottled water.)

a Analyse the benefits to O2toU of using wholesalers.
b 'Distribution is probably the most important part of our marketing mix.' To what extent do you agree with Julius' view?

Case study

While still at Liverpool University, Robert Williams and Jason Tavaria used their credit cards and £1,500 of their own money to set up a company that sells musical equipment by mail order and over the internet. Today, Dolphin Music sells products from 300 different suppliers such as Yamaha and Shure to home users, professionals and the education sector. In 2004, the company added sales through eBay and last year opened a shop in Liverpool specialising in rare guitars from the likes of Gibson, Fender and Rickenbacker.

Case study questions

(30 marks; 40 minutes)
1 Outline two other sources of finance that Robert and Jason might have used to start their business. (6 marks)
2 Analyse the factors Robert Williams and Jason Tavaria might have considered before opening their shop in Liverpool. (9 marks)
3 Discuss the factors that Robert and Jason might have to consider before opening more shops. (15 marks)

31 Using the marketing mix – promotional mix

A business has to communicate the benefits of its products to its customers. It has to let them know the product exists, what it does and why they should buy it. In this chapter we examine the importance of the promotional mix in marketing. Managing the way that a business communicates with its customers about its products is vital to its success.
What you need to know by the end of this chapter:
• the different elements of the promotional mix
• influences on the choice of the promotional mix.

What it promotion?

The promotion of a product involves communicating about it to existing or potential customers. These messages may be intended to:

• inform customers (e.g. tell them about modifications to the product, promotional offers or new releases)
• persuade them (e.g. highlighting your product's benefits compared with the competitors)
• reassure buyers they did the right thing by buying the product in the first place.

The promotional mix

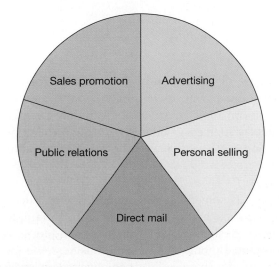

Figure 31.1 The promotional mix

The promotional mix refers to the combination of ways in which a business can communicate with its customers. The choice of promotional mix influences the effectiveness of the way in which the business is communicating: this in turn influences the effectiveness of the firm's marketing.

The elements of the promotional mix include the following.

Advertising

Advertising is a paid for means of communication. Advertising is often used as a long-term strategy to build brand loyalty. There are, of course, many different media available in terms of advertising, such as newspapers, radio, television and billboards. Managers must determine the most appropriate media to use. This depends on the resources available, the target group and their lifestyles, the likely sales (which influences how much can be spent) and the nature of the product. Mass-market products such as cars may be able to justify television advertising, for example, whereas a local decorator may advertise in shop windows or the Yellow Pages. The difficulty with advertising is that many consumers are bombarded by different adverts and so getting a message through to your target group that they actually pay attention to can be difficult. With the growth of digital television and radio, as well as the internet, the volume of messages aimed at consumers is increasing all the time and this can reduce the effectiveness of some advertising. Advertisers therefore have to think carefully about what messages to deliver, what media to use and when to advertise.

Having said this advertising can be very effective. For example, heavy investment in advertising built the Magner's cider brand so well that sales in 2006 rose by 225 per cent! Effective advertising targets the customer cost effectively and communicates the key messages successfully.

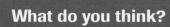

What do you think?

Think of an advert you have seen recently. What message was it trying to communicate? How was it trying to do this? How effective do you think it is? Why? What are the best media to use to advertise to you? What about to your parents?

Sales promotions

Sales promotions are attempts to boost sales using techniques such as promotional offers, competitions and price cuts. Offers can include 10 per cent extra free and 'buy one, get one free' (called 'BOGOF'). Sales promotions may be used as a means of boosting sales in the short term. When undertaking a promotional campaign a firm must consider:

- What will it cost?
- What will it do to the brand image?
- To what extent will the offer be effective (e.g. the type of offer you would give as a sportswear company is different from a wine or perfume business)?
- What is the likely impact on sales?

Personal selling

Personal selling is based on face-to-face contact with customers. This may be used by manufacturers to get distributors to take their products or in industrial markets and the service sector, to increase sales directly to the customer. Financial services, such as pensions, insurance and mortgages, are often sold in this way. Similarly, the sale of products, such as photocopiers, often takes place through a salesforce. If a product is sold in low volumes, and/or is technical and complex and needs explaining to customers then a salesforce is likely to be an effective promotional method. The salesteam can be absolutely essential in some markets; in the tobacco market for example advertising cigarettes is prohibited in the UK. This means manufacturers must work through the retailers; the tobacco

companies sales teams compete very aggressively to get their products displayed in the best way to get their promotions highlighted in the stores.

Public relations (PR)

Public relations activities involve contact with the media and the various groups that the firm deals with. It attempts to send out particular messages about the firm or its products. Whereas with advertising you pay for an advert to be run in the media with public relations you are creating a story or event to attract attention that you do not have to pay for. Public relations might involve press releases to the media, handling customer complaints and organising events to promote particular messages.

Sponsorship is a common form of public relations activity. A business will sponsor an individual or event to raise its profile. You will often find major sports competitions are sponsored by businesses.

> ### Key terms
> The **promotional mix** refers to the combination of ways in which the business communicates about its products

What do you think?

Can you think of any organisations that sponsor events? Why do you think they chose that particular event? How do you think the sponsorship helps the business and its image? How might a business measure the effectiveness of its sponsorship?

Direct mail

This type of promotion involves sending mailshots to customers. With increasingly sophisticated database information, these can be carefully targeted to particular segments within the market. This type of targeting is also now happening via emails and texts.

Branding

A brand is something that identifies a product and distinguishes it from competitors; for example, a name or design. In some markets branding is very important. By building a brand, businesses hope to make customers more loyal. This may allow them to charge more for items, by making demand price inelastic. It may also make it easier to introduce new products under the same brand name as customers

Business in Focus

Richard Branson

Figure 31.2 Richard Branson

Richard Branson was born in 1950 and educated at Stowe School. He went into business at 16, publishing *Student* magazine. As a young entrepreneur it was clear he had a real flair for publicity. Having originally founded Virgin as a mail-order record company he later opened his first store, in London's Oxford Street. The Virgin Records music label was formed in 1972. Mike Oldfield's *Tubular Bells*, recorded in Virgin's first recording studio – an Oxfordshire barn – and released in 1973, was a best-seller. When punk rock came along, Virgin signed the Sex Pistols, even though other record companies refused to touch them. This proved to be a marketing success. Many other stars were signed up including Genesis, Peter Gabriel, Simple Minds and The Rolling Stones, making Virgin Records a major player in the international music business. Since then, the Virgin brand has been expanded into air and rail travel, mobile phones, finance, weddings, wines, retail, drinks, hotels and gymnasiums. It now has around 200 companies in over 30 countries employing more than 25,000 people.

One of Branson's strengths has been his ability to get free publicity for the business. He has had his picture taken in a wedding dress, as well as with Pamela Anderson, with Diana, Princess of Wales and Nelson Mandela. In 1985, Sir Richard set out from New York to beat the record for crossing the Atlantic by boat, but barely a hundred miles from home the boat hit some floating driftwood and sank. In 2004, he set the record for the fastest crossing of the English Channel by an amphibious vehicle to mark the 20th anniversary of Virgin Atlantic.

(Source: Adapted from news.bbc.co.uk/go/pr/fr/-/1/hi/business/5368602.stm)

Questions:

What other products do you think the Virgin brand could be extended to? What would it not be suitable to offer under this brand?

If you were asked to describe the Virgin brand what would you say?

---

may feel reassured and be more willing to try it. If customers recognise a brand they can associate with all of its values and this in itself can provide a benefit – people may feel more secure driving a Volvo, more fashionable using an Apple Mac and smarter wearing Prada. Increasingly, some people want to identify with a brand and the lifestyle that is associated with it. Brand loyalty is very important because it is easier and cheaper for a business to sell more to an existing customer than it is to generate a new customer.

However, a brand has to be protected and managers have to be careful that it does not become associated with the wrong things. For example, if a company has a problem with one of its products, as Cadbury's did in 2007, when some of its chocolate contained salmonella, then this can affect the sales of all its products because they also carry the name Cadbury's, even though it is an established company with a very long track record of high quality. Managers need to respond effectively to the situation to rebuild the brand image.

Key term

A brand is a name, design, logo, symbol or indeed anything that makes a product recognisable and distinguishes it from the competition in the eyes of the customer.

Business in Focus

Jo Malone

Figure 31.3 Jo Malone products

The Jo Malone story began over twenty years ago when Jo first designed her facial treatment for a select group of clients. Clients appreciated Jo's personal touch and the hand-mixed products, tailored specifically for their individual skin. Word of mouth about her personal technique spread quickly and before long there were over 2,000 clients vying for the facial appointments and skin-care secrets.

The first fragrance Jo designed was the Nutmeg & Ginger Bath Oil, created as a thank-you gift and given to the original facial clients. One client ordered a further 100 bottles to give as gifts to her party guests and from these 100, 86 guests called to place their own orders. At this point, the Jo Malone brand was born.

News of the Jo Malone products quickly spread among the private clients. As demand grew Jo and her husband realised they could no longer cope with production at home. In 1994 the first Jo Malone store was opened in London, selling a capsule Skin Care collection, nine personal fragrances and a selection of scented candles.

Beautiful packaging and thoughtful presentation is synonymous with the Jo Malone brand:
'From the first moment the iconic gift bag with signature bow is received, a sensorial journey begins. A Jo Malone gift is the perfect pleasure, a luxurious way to create a lasting memory.'

(Source: adapted from www.jomalone.co.uk)

Business in Focus

The Conservative Party

When David Cameron became leader of the Conservative party he wanted it to be 'different'. He wanted it to be interactive, open to new ideas and new directions. To show this change he commissioned a new logo.

The green in the new logo was intended to show a shift from the traditional Conservative blue (although note that Conservative blue was still there in the roots of the picture) highlighting a move towards more environmentally friendly policies. The choice of a tree suggests growth, knowledge and solidity, all of which are meant to be characteristics of the revitalized party. The logo was therefore a way of expressing and communicating the values of the revived party and marking a change with the past.

Figure 31.4 The old and new Conservative Party logos

How important do you think a logo is to the success of an organisation?

Merchandising

Merchandising refers to marketing activities that use a brand image or name on a range of other items. Bands will sell CDs but also T-shirts, posters, mugs, toys and so on. Universities will sell tracksuits, files and scarves with their name, colours and logo. The brand is being extended via merchandising. Merchandising also includes the various methods used to promote in-store sales, such as point-of-purchase displays (POPs).

Each of the different methods of promotion has its own advantages and disadvantages, as shown in Table 31.1.

For example, personal selling is obviously quite labour intensive and therefore expensive, but the firm gets immediate feedback from its customers.

Other forms of promotion

As well as the methods discussed above there are many other ways of promoting products such as celebrity endorsements and exhibitions. Firms are always looking for new ways of promoting their products. Recent trends include 'buzz' or 'viral promotion' (often via the internet) where the buyers are targeted with messages to get them talking to their friends about a film, song, television programme, computer game, or other product. Buzz marketing relies on person to person communication about a product generating interest as more and more people talk about it.

The promotional mix

Businesses use a combination of promotional methods to communicate to potential customers about their products.

The composition of the promotional mix depends on numerous factors:

- The nature of the product – consumer durable products, such as televisions and washing machines, are likely to be advertised to the final customer. Firms usually use a sales team to deal

Business in Focus

Swatch

The Swatch Group manufactures and sells finished watches, jewellery, watch movements and components. Its brands include:

Tissot, Swatch, Flik Flak, Blamian, Brecquet, Omega, Rado, Calvin Klein. These brands target different groups and have different price points.

Figure 31.5 Swatch watches

Why do think a firm such as Swatch operates with different brand names?

Table 31.1 A comparison of promotional methods

Method of promotion	Advantages	Disadvantages
advertising	wide coverage control of the message can be used to build brand loyalty	can be expensive, e.g. TV advertising
public relations	can be relatively cheap	Cannot control the way the story is covered by the media
direct mail	relatively cheap	may not get read
sales promotions	can entertain and interest the consumer	often short-term effects can encourage brand switching
personal selling	two-way communication; can answer customer enquiries	can be expensive can only reach a limited number of customers

with wholesalers and retailers but use advertising to get customers to demand the product in the stores. By raising awareness of the brand, customers will recognise it when they go to buy a product. Similarly, companies producing shampoos and household cleaners often advertise on television. By comparison, sales of heavy construction equipment are usually made direct to the customer and rely on the sales force. There are relatively few customers in this case, the product is expensive and sold in low volumes and there are many technical details that need explaining. A sales force is likely to be much more effective than, say, an advert in a brochure.

Business in Focus

Red Bull

Red Bull is an 'energy drink' that originated in Thailand and is sold to combat mental and physical fatigue. The marketing of the product has been highly successful and includes a number of unusual promotional methods. For example:

- Selected students (students are a key market) are given free cases of Red Bull if they throw a party; others are given a car with a model Red Bull on the top to drive around and be noticed by others. This is known as 'viral marketing'. It relies on a few key trendsetters spreading the word about a product and leading to others wanting to be associated with it.
- Sales teams identify key bars and clubs and promote heavily via merchandise such as branded coolers and POP displays
- Heavy investment in brand building including promoting the slogan 'Red Bull gives you wings'.
- Red Bull sponsors many extreme sports events including cliff diving, BMX and skiing. Red Bull also sponsors the Red Bull Flugtag ('flight day' in German), a competition where entrants launch themselves off a 30-foot ramp in homemade 'flying machines' into a body of water.
- In recent years mainstream advertising such as television has also been used.

Web link

Weblink: for more information on Red Bull visit www.redbull.com/

What other types of events do you think it would make sense for Red Bull to sponsor?

- **The marketing expenditure budget** – inevitably, the budget acts as a constraint on all firms' promotional activities because it limits the amount of money available to spend in this area. Faced with a small marketing budget, for example, a firm cannot even consider television advertising and may have to rely on local newspaper advertising instead.
- **The available options**. Technological developments are creating new possibilities, such as internet advertising and text advertising. Legal changes also influence what is possible e.g. what products can be advertised and how they can promote themselves. For example, there are strong restrictions on the promotion of alcohol and tobacco.

Improvements in the promotional mix may:

- reduce costs as cheaper ways of communicating are adopted
- boost sales as better ways of communicating are used to communicate more effectively and to more people.

Key term

The **marketing expenditure budget** is the amount of money a business allocates to spend on marketing activities such as promotion.

Examiner's advice

You need to be able to understand the different elements of the promotional mix and how these will be changed for different products and different situations.

To make its promotion more effective, a business might alter the total amount spent on it or review the promotional mix. As customers habits change, the mix might need to alter as well (e.g. switching to more internet advertising).

Summary

Effective marketing relies on effective communication. Businesses need to inform customers about their products and persuade them that their products are better value than others. This communication can take many forms, such as advertising, sales promotion, branding, a sales force and public relations.

The nature of the promotional mix will depend on a variety of factors such as the product itself and the finances available.

Quick questions

1 What is meant by the promotional mix?

2 What is meant by a brand?

3 What is the value of building a brand?

4 What is meant by public relations?

5 What is one advantage of using a sales force rather than advertising?

6 Explain what is meant by sales promotion.

7 Explain how the promotional mix might be affected by the nature of the product.

8 Explain the ways in which you might promote a new book.

Issues for analysis

- The impact of promotion on demand.
- The factors influencing the choice of promotional methods.

Issues for evaluation

- Is promotion the most important element of the marketing mix?
- Is advertising the most important element of the promotional mix?

Assessment

Analysis and evaluation questions

1 James and Carol Worthing are about to open their first business. They are great golf fans and have decided to set up a golf range. Customers can come and pay for one of the 10 'stalls' where they get a bucket of balls and can practise their golfing shots.

a Analyse the possible benefits of promotion to James and Carol.

b Discuss the best ways for James and Carol of promoting their new business.

2 'Our sales team are essential to everything we do. They visit the schools, meet the teachers and explain what books we have coming out and why they should choose them. We support this with publicity materials and have a website as well, but the sales team is very important.' So says Tony Guy, the marketing director of Boxwood Books. Boxwood is a specialist publisher of GCSE and A level textbooks. Among its portfolio it has some well-established brands such as QuickFix (intensive revision guides) and its 'All you need to know about...' series.

a Examine the ways in which having an established brand might benefit Boxwood Books.

b Discuss the possible advantages to Boxwood Books of using a sales team compared to other forms of promotion.

Case study

'The initial concept for our Really Useful Boxes came from our owner, who as an accountant at a plastics company wanted a transparent, strong, stacking storage box to store his archive records. After exhaustive searches he was unable to locate such a product so in good old-fashioned tradition, created it himself. We have now evolved this concept into archival storage for CDs, VHS tapes, DVDs and LPs. We can now proudly claim to have the world's largest range of transparent, strong, stacking storage boxes.

We were established in 1999 to develop a range of innovative plastic storage boxes. As far as we can understand it was the first time that a plastic storage box was created from a users' viewpoint. We had no previous container experience. The product does contain a great deal of original thought and we have applied for a patent. Most people who see our product are impressed by both its simplicity and ability to live up to its name of 'Really Useful Box'. The concept is one of those obvious products that should have been available years ago.

From 1999 it took a year before we had a repeatable product that passed our vigorous quality requirements. We were fortunate that this coincided with both Staples UK and Makro UK committing to initial promotional trials. We subsequently introduced new sizes and new related products. These new products have been customer driven.

We have now significantly expanded our customer base and supply to companies like W.H. Smiths, Ryman's, Partners, Maplins and in mail-order, Viking Direct. Customer satisfaction is our overriding aim.

We are a customer driven organisation.'

Web link

To find out more, visit www.reallyusefulproducts.co.uk

Case study questions

1 Explain what is meant by Really Useful Box being a 'customer driven organisation'. (6 marks)
2 Analyse the possible benefits of having a patent to the Really Useful Box company. (9 marks)
3 Discuss the key elements of a successful promotional strategy for Really Useful Box. (15 marks)

32

Marketing and competitiveness

The success of a business will be influenced by many external factors, including the conditions of the market in which it operates. For example, how many other firms are there? Is it easy for other firms to enter the market? How powerful are suppliers or buyers? The nature of these conditions will affect how a business competes. As these conditions change, so will the activities of the business. This chapter examines the nature and importance of market conditions in determining business success. It also consider how a business can increase its competitiveness within a market.

What you need to know by the end of this chapter:

- the possible impact of market conditions on business behaviour
- the effect of different degrees of competition
- the meaning and significance of competitivenes.
- how to improve competitiveness

Competitors

Firms do not operate in isolation. There will be other firms offering similar goods and services and these are their competitors. If they operate in the same industry, they are direct competitors, for example, Playstation and Wii, Facebook and MySpace. However, it may be that your parents are deciding between buying you a computer games console or paying for a ski trip: in this case the Playstation and the ski trip are competing for your parents' money and they are indirect competitors to each other. Although they are different types of products they represent possible alternatives to a customer and should therefore be seen as substitutes. Substantial changes in the skiing market, such as a lack of snow, may affect sales of Playstations. The degree of competition in a market and the overall structure of a market will naturally affect the decisions a firm makes.

Market structure

When examining the structure of a market we should consider both the number of firms in a market and their relative size and market shares.

The number of other direct competitors in a market varies considerably. Look online or in Yellow Pages and search for a plumber and you will find thousands in the UK. If you look for a company that

<aside>
Key terms
The **market size** is the total number of items sold (this is measuring volume) or the total value of sales.
The **market share** of a business measures its sales as a percentage of the total market sales.
</aside>

refines sugar, you might only find a couple. Of course, when measuring the number of competitors you need to define the market carefully. The number of competitors in the European retail market is greater than the number in the UK. There may be many cinemas in the UK but only a couple of cinemas in your town.

Deciding where to draw the line to measure the market can be difficult – in part, it depends on how customers behave. If households are only willing to drive 15 minutes to go shopping you might measure the number of competitors within this radius. If they will travel up to 40 minutes to go to the cinema then the relevant 'catchment' area might be bigger. With online shopping many retailers have found their competitors can now come from anywhere in the UK (if not the world). A shop selling bicycle parts may be the only one for miles around and therefore have felt relatively safe from competition in the past: now we can find providers online easily, which means that competition is fiercer and so the appropriate definition of the market has probably changed.

If there are relatively few competitors there may be less pressure on a business to maintain the quality of it service. It may become complacent because it is not competing so much to win and maintain customers. In a market with many more competitors, customers have choice and the pressure is on to meet customers' needs more fully or lose their business to others.

The size of competitors is also important, because there can be a big difference between a market with four equal-sized firms and a market with one large firm and three much smaller ones in terms of how those firms behave in relation to each other. If one firm dominates a market, it is likely to have more power over suppliers and distributors and therefore may have lower costs (for example it may bargain with suppliers and get a lower input price). This can mean that the smaller firms have to cooperate and collaborate with the larger firm because it could always undercut them if it wanted. For example, the smaller firms may be price-takers and follow the price set by the larger firms. If the firms are of a similar size they may end up trying to cooperate and will certainly watch each others' moves very closely. If one firm dominates a market it is known as a 'monopoly'. If a few firms dominate a market it is known as an 'oligopoly'.

What do you think?

Which of the following markets do you think are dominated by a few firms and which have many competitors in them?

Advertising
Banking
Taxi firms
Car production
Airlines
Hairdressing

Why do think such differences in markets exist and what do you think are the consequences of this?

Entry threat

The way a business behaves will not only be affected by the existing number of competitors in the market. It will also depend on how likely it is that other firms will enter the market in the future.

This in turn depends on the existence of barriers to entry. Barriers to entry are factors that make it difficult to enter a market. For example:

- Entry costs. Heavy investment may be required to set up the business because of specialist equipment or facilities needed. You can imagine that setting up a hotel or leisure complex could require quite large sums of money. This will automatically make it difficult for some entrepreneurs to enter the market.
- Brand loyalty. If the established firms have a high level of brand loyalty then it will be more difficult for others to enter the market because of the problems gaining sufficient market share to break even. Loyalty to Nike sportswear, Twinings tea and Wrigley's chewing gum make entry into these markets quite tough (though not impossible as we saw when Cadbury's launched Trident gum).
- Legal restrictions. If the existing provider has a patent this means you cannot imitate the invention without permission (and usually paying a licensing fee).

High barriers to entry mean that the firms already in the market are 'safe' from competition, at least for a while. This means that the competitive pressure is reduced and this may affect the quality of the service. On the other hand, if entering a market is very simple then it is very competitive, forcing better service. For example, setting up a sandwich shop is not particularly expensive or difficult and so there is enormous pressure in terms of the prices charged and quality of food and service provided. There are always shops closing and opening and new forms of food emerging because of the very high level of competition. This is good for customers but not so good for the entrepreneurs who have to remain very responsive to market requirements to survive.

Business in Focus

Business in focus: Directory Enquiries

For many years 192 was the only number you could call for directory enquiries. It received around 600 million calls each year. In 2003 the government changed the law so that other firms could compete. This led to many other businesses entering the market to offer directory enquiry services; their services began with the number 118. The provider of 192 improved its service by making sure you spoke to a person when you called, rather than a recorded number and providing additional services such as cinema listings and a TV guide.

It also developed a 'personal information hub', where customers can create address books and store individual information, such as bank account details, securely.

The fixed charge was also removed and replaced with a time-based fee.

How else might a directory enquiries service improve its service to compete?

Key term

A **barrier to entry** is something that makes entering a market more difficult for businesses such as the need for specialist skills.

Buyer/supplier power

The competitive environment in a market also depends on the power of buyers and suppliers. If you are reliant on a few key suppliers then they are likely to be able to charge you more and the level of service they have to provide may not be that high because you need them so much.

The power of suppliers depends on:

- the number of them and how similar their products are; if it is easy for you to switch suppliers then their power is less
- their size and the extent to which they depend on you. If the suppliers are small and rely on you then

you have power over them. If you only represent a small percentage of their business then they have more power because they are more likely to reject your requests if they don't like them.

Similarly, buyer power affects what happens in a market. If buyers have a lot of power they may be able to push the price down and insist that the product is amended to meet their requirements.

A buyer will have power if:

- there are relatively few buyers, so that the business relies on them heavily. For example, if a company makes very specialised technical equipment there will be a limited set of customers, so the business will need to retain those customers. On the other hand, the loss of one customer at a nightclub may not be that significant.
- they have many potential alternative suppliers so they can switch away from a business relatively easily if they need to. This puts a business in a weaker bargaining position. If you are the only firm that can produce a particular complex piece of equipment then you have a lot of bargaining power: if you are one of many possible suppliers of paperclips you are not in such a strong position.

Actions to change the competitive environment

Businesses try to make the competitive environment more favourable. This means that to increase their own chances of success they would want:

- a high barrier to entry so that other businesses will not enter the market: this would remove a competitive threat
- few competitors and substitutes, so that customers could not easily find alternatives
- low supplier power so that they have power over suppliers, This might mean that they can demand a low price and do not have to pay quickly for the items (and so can hold on to the money and earn interest in the bank for longer).
- low buyer-power, so that buyers are dependent on their products. This should make demand more price inelastic and so they may be able to charge more for them.

Michael Porter

Some of the analysis in this chapter is based on the work of business writer Michael Porter and his 'five forces' analysis.

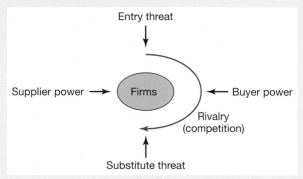

Figure 32.1 Porter's five forces

According to Porter, you could assess the likely profitability within an industry by examining the five forces. Businesses are likely to make more profit if:

- barriers to entry are high
- there are not many competitors
- there are not many substitutes
- suppliers are not powerful
- buyers are not powerful.

Businesses will want to change the five forces to make the industry more favourable. For example they might:

- join together in an industry association to have more buying power over suppliers
- buy competitors' companies to reduce the degree of competition in the market
- develop USPs to reduce the ability of customers to find substitutes.

Can you think of other ways in which firms might try to influence the five forces to make the industry a more favourable environment to operate in?

Competitiveness

A firm's competitiveness refers to its ability to offer better value to customers than its rivals. Being competitive is vital to a firm's survival and growth.

A firm may increase its competitiveness by:

- **offering similar benefits to competitors at a lower price**. This means that its operations must be more efficient in some way to enable the firm to match competitors' offerings but undercut on price. When the budget airlines started operating from local airports rather than the hugely expensive Heathrow and Gatwick airports it enabled them to cut prices. At the IKEA home store, customers choose what goods they want and put them on their own trolleys and take them to their own cars. This cuts staffing costs and enables competitive pricing. At Yo! Sushi restaurants customers sit around a moving track and choose their own food. This removes the need for waiters and waitresses, making the business cheaper to run. Primark has very basic stores without much

investment in displays in order to reduce costs. Michael Porter refers to this approach to improving competitiveness as 'cost leadership'.

- **offering more benefits than rivals**. This means that a firm provides a combination of benefits that are greater than the competition: this means they can charge a higher price. This is called a differentiation strategy. Oswald Boateng suits, Jimmy Choo shoes, and Versace dresses have a unique design and brand name that customers are willing to pay high prices for. Their products are sufficiently differentiated to make the customer pay more and still believe that they provide good value.

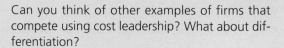

What do you think?

Can you think of other examples of firms that compete using cost leadership? What about differentiation?

Business in Focus

Dualit

Figure 32.2 Dualit toaster

Dualit is a UK manufacturer of catering equipment. It is most famous for the toasters it makes. These are instantly recognisable, thanks to a distinctive design. As the company says: 'For over fifty years, Dualit toasters have reflected an attitude that's fundamentally British. Dualit toasters can turn out hundreds of crisp, golden slices per hour. They are gleaming, sturdy and tough as old boots. And as much a part of British life as toast itself. Today, Dualit toasters are recognised as the best in the world. Part of a range of hard-working products they are designed to a standard that remains unsurpassed.'

Dualit toasters are not the cheapest on the market by any means but the brand, design and quality justify the price for many customers.

What other products do you think have a very distinctive design? Is this reflected in a high price?

Web link

To find out more, visit www.dualit.com

Key term

The **value** of a product depends on the benefits it offers to customers relative to its price.

Competitiveness is a dynamic concept. What you need to do to be competitive changes over time. At one time, manufacturing firms in the UK could compete on price, but such firms have generally lost this competitive advantage. Firms locating in countries such as China and India can significantly undercut UK producers because the wage costs are so much lower. To remain competitive, UK manufacturers have had to move into more exclusive products and focus on the design aspects. They have switched from competing on price to competing through benefits.

Improving competitiveness

Whichever approach is chosen, there are implications for all the functions of the business. For example, to fight via lower prices the business may:

- focus on reducing wastage in the transformation process (e.g. recycling materials and finding ways of re-using inputs). This has implications for operations.
- find cost-effective means of communication (e.g. public relations rather than advertising). This has implications for marketing.
- find ways of helping employees become more productive (e.g. different ways of organising the work). This has HRM implications.
- find cheaper sources of finance. This has implications for the finance function.

Similarly, a decision to focus on additional benefits affects all the different functions. For example, the business may:

- invest in more training and a more skilled workforce
- invest in new more sophisticated equipment to help improve the quality of the product
- invest in building a brand (e.g. undertake a major promotional campaign)
- borrow more in order to finance investment programmes.

Of course, marketing is fundamental here, as companies need to understand exactly what customers want, and what would really add value for them.

The competitiveness of a business does not just depend on what you are doing, but also on what your competitors are doing. Your offer to deliver products within 24 hours may differentiate you at the beginning, but is likely to be imitated fairly soon afterwards and you may need to deliver with 20 hours to stay competitive and ahead of your rivals. Similarly, your new fashion designs may be imitated within days by other retailers. The business world is dynamic and you need to keep looking for ways of improving what you do.

Examiner's advice

You need to be aware of the importance of a company's ability to compete. Being competitive is essential for business survival. Marketing is one way in which businesses can compete. They may also compete by improving the way they manage their people, their operations and their finances.

To increase effectiveness, a business might try to change the market forces to make them more favourable (e.g. by increasing the barriers to entry).

One step further: market structures

A market where one firm dominates is called a 'monopoly'. Technically, under UK law this is a business that has more than 25 per cent of the market share. A monopoly firm has power over the market and may well make high profits. As there is little choice for customers, the monopoly firm may be able to charge high prices, There may also be little incentive to innovate and therefore the quality of service may reduce. Having said this, to remain a monopoly a firm may have to be innovative to stay ahead of the competition.

In many markets there are a few large firms that dominate the market rather than just one. This is called an 'oligopoly market'. For example, in the UK there are a few large banks, a few large supermarkets and a few large electricity providers. These are all oligopolistic markets. In this kind of market, the big firms will watch each others' movements and decisions very closely. There is a high degree of interdependence. This may lead to high degrees of competition as the dominant firms fight it out. This is often via promotional campaigns (just think of the numerous offers from banks and supermarkets to attract your business). However, it can also be via the way they do business. For example, does the bank have lots of branches? Can you do online banking? Does it offer insurance and investment advice? Is there a small business adviser?

Oligopolies may also lead to collusion. This means that the firms combine to work together and act as a monopolist. This can lead to higher prices and less choice for consumers. A few years ago several private schools were accused of setting their fees in line with each other. Parents choosing private education were faced with high fees from a whole group of schools. Other markets are more competitive because they have far more firms of a similar size. This means that customers can choose between the alternatives and switch between them. In most towns there are several hairdressers, pubs, taxi firms and coffee shops. A customer can walk from one to the other if she does not like the service or price. This competitive pressure should lead to better value for money for customers. Firms may till try to differentiate what they do by building a brand, or by developing their offering, but the greater the choice for customers the greater the pressure on firms to meet their needs in order to stay in business.

Summary

The decisions that managers make to ensure a business is competitive will be influenced by the market structure. The market structure depends on the number of firms in the market and the relative size of these firms. Other important factors in the competitive environment include the power of suppliers and buyers, the likelihood of new entrants into the market and the availability of substitutes.

Quick questions

1. How might the number of firms in an industry affect a company's behaviour?
2. Why is it important to consider the likelihood of other firms entering the market?
3. What are barriers to entry?
4. Why might the power of suppliers influence the success of a business?
5. Why might the power of buyers influence the success of a business?
6. What actions can a firm take to make the market conditions more favourable?
7. What is meant by competitiveness?
8. How can a firm increase its competitiveness?

Issues for analysis

- The links between market structure and firms' behaviour.
- The importance of competitiveness.

Issues for evaluation

- How important is competition in improving service for customers?
- Is competition good or bad for firms?

Analysis and evaluation questions

1 'We had quite a nice living here until Marks and Spencer's opened across the road and Costa Coffee opened up next door. Suddenly the game had changed.' (Mark Mowab, who owns a small café in Leicester.)

a Analyse the possible impact on Mark Mowab's shop of the two other stores opening up nearby.

b Discuss the ways in which Mark Mowab might respond to the opening up of these two stores nearby.

2 'I wanted to set up a nightclub in the centre of London but it just proved too difficult to enter that market and be successful. So instead I went into something completely different and went into the lava lamp business. However, even here it is proving very difficult to be competitive.' (Don Aisworth, Managing Director of Light up your Life Ltd.)

a Analyse the possible reasons why it might have been difficult for Don to set up a successful nightclub in the centre of London.

b Discuss the ways Don might improve the competitiveness of his love lamp business.

Assessment of Section 5: Marketing and the competitive environment

Case study

Harry Potter

Harry Potter features in a series of seven children's books by J.K. Rowling. The story is mostly set at Hogwarts School of Witchcraft and Wizardry, a school for young wizards and witches, and focuses on Harry Potter's fight against the evil wizard Lord Voldemort, who killed Harry's parents as part of his plan to take over the wizarding world.

The first novel, *Harry Potter and the Philosopher's Stone*, was published in 1997. Since its launch the books have gained immense popularity and commercial success worldwide, also leading to films, video games and various merchandise: from 'Quidditch' chess sets to 'HufflePuff' wall hangings, 'Goblet of Fire' candle holders to 'Hedwig' pillowcases.

Altogether, the books have sold well over 350 million copies and have been translated into more than 63 languages. The success of the novels has made Rowling the highest-earning novelist in literary history.

Although Rowling did not have any age group in mind when she wrote them, the publisher initially targeted young children, aged nine to eleven. Rowling, whose first name is Joanne, was asked to use her initials rather than her first name because it was thought that young boys would not be interested reading a book by a woman.

Word-of-mouth reviews, especially amongst young males, have been an important part of the books' success. Rowling's publishers were able to capitalise on this buzz by the rapid, successive releases of the first four books, which maintained interest in the brand. The books have also gained many adult fans, leading to two editions of each Harry Potter book being released in the UK, identical in text but with one edition's cover artwork aimed at children and the other aimed at adults.

The launch of a new Harry Potter book was a great event, with long queues forming outside the books shops and some stores opening at midnight to sell the first copies.

Case study questions

(30 marks; 40 minutes)

1 Explain how market research might have been used to help the marketing of Harry Potter books. (6 marks)

2 Analyse the ways in which the marketing mix has been used to maintain sales of Harry Potter. (9 marks)

3 No more Harry Potter books will be written. To what extent does this mean that sales of Harry Potter must inevitably decline? (15 marks)

33 Making operational decisions

There are four main functions within a business. These are: marketing, finance, human resource management and operations management. These functions are all interrelated, as decisions in one area affect the other three, and are affected by their resources. In this chapter we consider what is meant by operations management and its significance in terms of managing the business effectively and efficiently.

What you need to know by the end of the chapter:
• how to identify operations issues
• the importance of adapting the mix of resources to meet changing circumstances
• the impact of different levels of capacity utilisation
• the importance of productivity
• the issues involved dealing with non-standard orders.

The nature of operations

The process of transforming inputs into outputs is the responsibility of operations managers. They are there to make sure that the process occurs in the way that the business wants and that particular operations targets are met. For example, operations managers may be concerned with achieving a particular level of quality and ensuring that costs are not too high. The effectiveness of a business depends a great deal on the quality and cost of the operations process. If managers can improve the operations of the business, they can make it more efficient, increase the volume of output and improve quality.

The precise nature of operations will vary from business to business. If you are running a hotel, for example, operations management involves making sure the rooms are ready, the kitchens meet health and safety requirements, the televisions, kettles and trouser presses in the rooms work, the towels are washed and dried and there is enough food to feed the guests. If you are running a tyre and exhaust centre, operations management involves making sure you have enough spares in stock so that you can fix a customer's car quickly and safely, the equipment you have is suitable and working, and you can generate the bill accurately. If you are running a clothes shop it involves making sure you have the right number and mix of clothes on display, the store layout is appropriate, the queues are not too long and there is a security system to prevent theft.

What do you think?

What do you think are important operational issues if you are running a nightclub?

Operational decisions and targets

Effective operations management involves planning, organising and coordinating the firm's resources to provide the goods and services required in an efficient and appropriate way to meet customer needs and the firm's own objectives. Operations managers have to:

- design the transformation process
- manage the operations process
- improve the operations process.

Key term
The **transformation process** describes how inputs are converted into outputs

To do this effectively, managers must ensure that:

- the required inputs are there when they are needed – for example, that they have the components, materials and parts with the specifications and features you need as and when they need them
- the most effective method of production is used to provide quality products at minimum cost. For example, making sure they have found the best way of providing a service. An online music business, for example, must make sure that it has a good selection of music available, the download speed is fast and that it is protected against viruses. Decisions will have to be made about how to produce effectively, for example how to organise the work and the appropriate mix of people and equipment to use
- the firm can produce an appropriate range of goods and services: for example, decisions must be made about the number of items to stock in a shop, the range of equipment and facilities in the health club or the range of menus offered by a party catering service
- the goods are produced in an appropriate time for the customer. Quite what is the right time may vary from business to business. We might expect an online supermarket shopping order to be delivered within 48 hours but be willing to wait much longer than that for an extension to the house to be built.

Operations management therefore involves managers making decisions about:

- how to produce products
- what people, equipment and machinery are required
- the level, type and quality of materials and components the firm needs to have available at any given moment.
- whether to accept an order and if so how to produce in time and at the right quality
- the maximum level the firm needs to be able to produce. This is known as the capacity.

These decisions will be crucial to the success of the business.

What do you think?

Why do you think operations decisions are so important to the success of the business?

Key term
Capacity measures the maximum amount of output a firm can produce at a given moment with its existing resources.

Typical operations targets focus on:

- the volume of output that needs to be provided (e.g. the ability to process 2,000 insurance claims a day, or to serve 300 customers a day in your shop)
- the quality levels that need to be achieved (e.g. to process all claims within 3 days)
- the unit cost to be achieved (e.g. to keep processing costs down to 2 per cent of revenue).

Capacity and capacity utilisation

The capacity of is the maximum amount a business can produce given its existing resources. The capacity of a business depends on the number and quality of its resources. What is the amount and what is the standard of equipment available? How many staff does the business have and how well trained are they? How efficient is its transformation process? Over time, the capacity can be increased with more investment, but at any one moment that will be a maximum number of orders that a business can cope with. The capacity of a bus company might be measured by how many passengers it can carry. The capacity of a restaurant is how many meals it can serve. The capacity of a school is how many students it can accept.

Capacity utilisation measures the existing output relative to the maximum. It can be calculated using:

$$\frac{\text{Existing output over a given time period}}{\text{Maximum possible output over a given time period}} \times 100 = \text{capacity utiliation (\%)}$$

For example:

Existing output 300 units a week, maximum output 500 units a week.

Capacity utilisation = (300/500) × 100 = 60 per cent

Existing output 400 units a week, maximum output 500 units a week.

Capacity utilisation = (400/500) × 100 = 80 per cent

Imagine a gig where the stadium is completely sold out, with 30,000 in the audience; this means that capacity utilisation is 100%, which is good for the promoter of the event. But what if you have a theatre that is half full? This means that its capacity utilisation is only 50 per cent.

What do you think?

What do you think the capacity utilisation would be if the existing output was 200 units a week and the maximum output was 500 units a week? What would the output be if the capacity was still 500 units a week and capacity utilisation was 15 per cent?

If capacity utilisation is low, it means that the existing output is relatively low compared to the amount that can be produced. This is inefficient because resources are not being fully utilised. The business could be producing more and, assuming the demand was there, earning more revenue and profit. The train could have more passengers, the health club could have more members, the sandwich business could be making more sandwiches. A business will, therefore, usually want a high level of capacity utilisation.

Higher levels of capacity utilisation are desirable because they spread the fixed costs of a business over more units. This helps reduce the unit cost and therefore increase profit margins. Imagine you were renting a market stall for £500 and you sold 250 items. Each item would have to earn £2 simply to cover the

rental costs. If you sold 1,000 items each one would only have to earn 50 pence to cover the fixed costs: this is because as your output increases the fixed cost per unit falls. This is very significant because it means there are cost advantages of having higher capacity utilisation. A business with low capacity utilisation not only wastes resources but has high unit costs. This will reduce profit margins if the price stays the same. If the firm tries to increase price to cover the higher unit costs it may find that sales fall and the situation becomes even worse.

Improving the position of the business may therefore involve increasing the capacity utilisation, either by boosting demand (which may be through marketing activities – see Chapters 25 to 32) or reducing the capacity of the business if some of it is no longer needed.

What do you think?

For many businesses the level of capacity utilisation varies at different times of the day or week or year. Can you think of examples of this? What could organisations do about this?

Capacity under-utilisation

Capacity is under-utilised (i.e. capacity utilisation is low) if demand is not matching the level of output you are able to provide. If a cinema can seat 400 people but there are only 80 watching the film this is 20 per cent capacity utilisation. If a café with 40 tables has only 4 occupied this is 10 per cent capacity utilisation. Capacity under-utilisation therefore occurs when demand is too low.

In this situation the business may:

- do nothing. If this is seen as a temporary issue the business may accept underutilisation for a short time (for example when a World Cup football match is on television the number of high street shoppers falls; capacity utilisation in restaurants is usually lower during the week compared to the week-end).
- renew its marketing activities to boost demand. For example, changes in the promotional strategy may be made, new offers, increased efforts by the sales team or more advertising may help increase sales.
- reduce the level of capacity. If, over time, demand is lower than capacity the business may rationalise. This means it may reduce its capacity levels. For

example, it may reduce the number of staff, sell off some of its production equipment if it is not needed or sell off some land if this is not required. Of course, changing capacity levels may be easier in some businesses than others. If you run a taxi or delivery business you could reduce the number of vehicles you operate fairly easily, However, if you run a cinema it is not easy to split the cinema in half to reduce the capacity. If you have a café you cannot easily sell off a quarter of it. In general, it is easier to reduce the labour input by making people redundant or asking them to go part time. Reducing the land and capital input can be more difficult.

- subcontract. If you do have excess capacity you may offer your resources to other firms and produce on their behalf. Some shops may rent out part of their space to other businesses, for example, a food business may offer to produce for someone else and put the other firm's brand name on the products.

Key terms

Rationalisation occurs when a business reduces the scale of its operations and reduces it capacity level.
Capacity under-utilisation occurs when a business is producing less than the maximum amount it can produce, given its existing resources.

Capacity shortage

If demand is too high for the firm's capacity, there is a capacity shortage (e.g. there are more people wanting tickets for a gig than there are places, there are queues outside the nightclub, or there is a waiting list for a product).

In this situation a business may:

- do nothing. You may think that the fact that the product is in short supply relative to demand adds to its appeal. Some nightclubs might want to build on the image that they are difficult to get into. Morgan sports cars used to have a waiting list of several years but simply saw this as evidence of the appeal of its cars – the company did not want to increase their output. You may also think that the excess demand is temporary and so not want to make any major changes, given that it may not last, (e.g. it may be the latest fashion trend to wear a certain brand of sunglasses or T

shirt or it may just be a particularly busy day or night). In this situation people will simply have to wait. A business may start a waiting list or limit the number any one person can buy .

- expand capacity. If you believe demand is likely to remain high then you may increase capacity. This will require investment (for example, you may need more people, more equipment and bigger premises) but may well be worthwhile due to the extra sales you can generate.

- subcontract. If you cannot meet all the demand yourself you may use other producers to produce for you. This increases the amount you can supply but you need to be careful that quality does not suffer and because the other producers will want to make a profit, your own profits may be less on the units they make, compared to you making them yourself.

- increase the price. If demand is too high relative to supply, a business may increase the price to bring it down to the 'right' level. This is what happens in many markets. If demand for a particular company's shares increases there is only a certain number available and so the owners of these can increase the price. If you have a house in an area that becomes very desirable then, given the higher levels of demand compared to supply, you can increase the price. The price can therefore, act as a rationing mechanism to reduce the demand (and at the same time this increases the profit margin per item).

Business in Focus

Magners

Magners cider was one of the great successes in 2006. In fact, boosted by heavy investment in the promotional mix demand rose rapidly and supply could not keep pace. In September 2006 the owner of the brand invested over £100 million in a new cider- making facility in an attempt to double capacity within 18 months.

What factors would the company have considered before making this investment decision
  How would the company decide how much capacity to aim for?

Matching supply and demand

The whole issue of capacity utilisation is related to the level that a business can supply at and the level of demand. In an ideal world, a business could forecast exactly what demand would be, this would be stable and the firm could then plan accordingly. It could invest in the right size premises, the right level of equipment and the right staffing levels.

In reality:

- demand levels are not always easy to predict. Just think of how changes in the weather (which are notoriously difficult to anticipate) can change demand. An improvement in the weather in the summer may see demand for sun cream, sunglasses, barbecue sets, barbecue food and beer suddenly increase. A spell of snow may increase demand for roadside assistance, de-icing fluid and whisky.
- demand can fluctuate on particular days of the week (e.g. busy Saturday shopping) and at particular times of year. A café in a seaside resort may be overwhelmed with customers during a good sunny summer and is likely to have very few customers during the rainy winters.

Matching supply to demand is therefore a key element of operational planning and an important part of managing a business effectively. Imagine you are a builder and decorator – you may well find there are certain weeks when you have no work at all and other weeks when you have several people wanting work done on their houses. Somehow you need to juggle what you can offer with the demand available.

The key is to try and keep your supply flexible so you can increase or decrease it at will. This may be possible by:

- using overtime so that when an extra order arrives you can get people to work later or at the weekends to produce it. However, you usually have to pay more to get people to work overtime and so your unit costs increase. Also you may not want to rely on overtime for significant periods of time or your workforce may become exhausted.
- using part-time and temporary staff (see Chapter 11). This allows you to change your labour input more easily than having full-time employees. You may hire more staff to cover the busy seasons in a theme park or hotel, for example.
- sub-contracting. As we have already seen, you may use other people to produce for you when demand is high (this is common in the building trade) or try to work for others when demand is low.
- changing stock levels. If you anticipate an increase in demand and produce tangible products (rather than services) you may build up stocks in advance. You may, for example, produce Easter eggs all year round to meet the demand in a few weeks. Cadbury's crème egg factory produces 400 million eggs over the year (70,000 an hour) but sales are mainly concentrated into a few weeks. Similarly, if demand is lower than expected, you may simply stockpile the products and hope and plan for increase in demand in the future.
- changing capacity levels if you believe the increase or decrease in demand is permanent.

The ability of a business to change its supply to meet demand will vary considerably. A language school offering English courses in the summer to international visitors and using local families as accommodation can be quite flexible. With more demand you employ more teachers (or make the class sizes bigger) and recruit more families to rent out rooms. A manufacturer of sofas may not be as flexible – it cannot suddenly increase the scale of its production facilities. A café cannot suddenly fit in more tables; a hotel cannot create more rooms. Similarly, if demand falls, many businesses cannot rationalise quickly or easily.

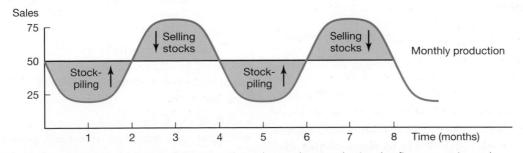

Figure 33.1 When sales are below production stock increase; when sales are above production the firm uses up its stock

Stock levels

Managing the level of stocks is another important aspect of operations management. A fall in demand may lead to an unplanned increase in stock levels, but managers must decide on the planned level as well.

There are different types of stocks, including:

- general supplies such as light bulbs, paper, pens, cartridges
- components and materials
- works in progress (e.g. a design that is not yet finished or a manufactured item that is yet to be completed)
- finished goods – in the case of tangible items you can have stocks of the complete product.

Any stocks you hold represent an opportunity cost. There is money tied up in producing and holding them (e.g. security costs and storage costs). This money could be sitting in the bank earning you interest. There is also the danger that any stocks you have may get stolen, damaged or go out of date and become obsolete. On the other hand, you need some stocks in order to keep production going, to meet demand and in some cases to give customers the chance to look at your range. When you go shopping for a mobile phone you want to look at your options, try some out and if you decide on buying one you expect to take it away there and then. Therefore the store has to hold some stocks. The aim of the operations manager will be to hold the right amount to meet customer needs without holding too much in terms of increasing costs. To do this she will work with the marketing function and look at past and predicted data to anticipate sales. They will also work closely with suppliers to try to ensure they are also flexible, so that when the retailer orders more phones they arrive promptly. The quicker and more reliable the suppliers are when it comes to delivery the less stock a business has to hold.

> **Key term**
> **Opportunity cost** refers to benefits that are given up (e.g. in the case of stocks, the opportunity cost is the benefits that could be gained if the money was not tied up in these items).

In general, there has been a move in business towards reducing stock levels as much as possible and trying to respond more quickly to changes in consumer demand rather than having to hold lots of stocks just in case the demand is there. Improvements in information technology enable firms to have a better idea of what is happening in terms of sales at any moment so they can spot a trend emerging; it also provides better links with suppliers, enabling a faster response from them (see Chapter 36). Also, the increase in online shopping reduces the need for retailers to hold stock; when you order something they can produce and deliver but they do not have to hold large stocks for you to see and try out.

Of course, the significance of stock management varies a great deal from business to business, In retailing it is critically important: thousands of pounds are tied up in the goods on display but at the same time it is vital to have a good range of products for customers to look at. In other businesses, such as hairdressing or taxi driving, stocks are not so important.

> **What do you think?**
>
> What products would you be happy to buy online? What products would you would want to visit a store and see? Why is there a difference?

Productivity and operations management

A business's level of output is the total amount it produces. The success of operations management depends not just on the total output produced but also on the value and quantity of inputs used up in the production process. There is little point using up £2,000 of resources to produce £500 worth of output, for example.

The aim of operations managers is to use as few resources as possible to produce a given output. At the same time, managers seek to maintain a given level of quality. An important element of managing resources effectively is the level of productivity that can be achieved.

A business's productivity measures the output produced in relation to the inputs it has used. There are actually many different measures of productivity, such as:

- output per hour
- output per machine per time period (capital productivity).

The most commonly used measure is labour productivity (output per worker).

Labour productivity measures the output of the firm in relation to the number of employees. For example, if 50 units are produced by 10 employees each week, their productivity is 5 units each. The higher the labour productivity, the more is produced per person per time period.

$$\text{Labour productivity} = \frac{\text{Total output in a given period}}{\text{Number of employees}}$$

Productivity is a crucial concept in operations management because it can have a significant effect on the costs of producing a unit. The higher the labour productivity, the more units each worker is making and, if wages are unchanged, the labour cost per unit will be cheaper. As a result, managers are constantly seeking ways of improving labour productivity because this means the firm will either make more profit per unit, can reduce the price to become more competitive or can produce more. Improving the effectiveness of the business may therefore be directly related to improving the productivity of its resources. Imagine a juice drinks business where employees are squeezing the fruit by hand; if they bought a juicer, productivity would increase so that more customers could be served or less staff may be required.

> **Key terms**
> The **output** of a business is the total amount produced in a given time period.
> **Productivity** measures the output per hour, per person or per machine.

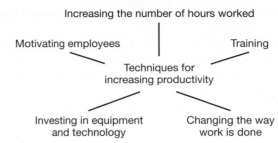

Figure 33.2 How to increase productivity

How can productivity be increased?

Productivity may be increased by using a variety of techniques:

- **Increasing the number of hours worked**. If employees work more hours or more days each week, this could increase their output. However, this is not necessarily a long-term means of increasing employees' productivity because they are likely to get tired and stressed, and may therefore become less productive in the long term. Also, there is a limit to how many extra hours can be worked.
- **Training**. This is a very important way of increasing productivity. Training can increase employees' output by helping them to gain more skills and to learn new and better ways of doing things.
- **Investment in equipment and technology**. If employees have modern and more efficient machinery, they should be able to make more output than their colleagues who are using outdated equipment. As the UK government says when commenting on the low productivity in the UK compared with many other countries: 'A worker can be 100 per cent efficient with a shovel

What do you think?

Complete the table below. (Assume that employees are paid £200 each per week.)

Number of employees	Weekly wage bill (£)	Output (number of units)	Productivity (output/number of workers)	Labour cost per unit (weekly wage bill/number of units)
100	£20 000	1000	10	£20
100	?	2000	?	?
50	?	1000	?	?
?	?	2000	40	?

Table 33.1 Calculating productivity

but it won't count if his international counterpart is equipped with a JCB!'

- **Changing the way the work is done**. If the way in which a product is made is changed this can affect the speed and the effectiveness of the production process. Many firms have implemented team working in recent years, resulting in improved productivity levels. If activities in the process can be combined and undertaken simultaneously rather than in sequence, this speeds up production and enables higher productivity.

- **Motivating employees**. If employees can be motivated (perhaps by offering more rewards or by giving people more responsibility – see Chapter 24) effort and productivity may increase.

At any moment managers will have to consider which of the above options are available given the firm's resources, and which will work best when it comes to boosting productivity. In one business the issue might be motivation; in another it might be a lack of modern equipment. If managers can boost productivity they will be improving the performance of the business.

Employee resistance to higher productivity

While managers might be eager to increase productivity, employees may resist such efforts, because:

- they do not want to work longer or harder
- they do not want to learn new skills
- they fear that higher productivity levels may lead to job losses because if each worker produces more, fewer workers will be needed
- they feel it is unfair that they are producing more unless they receive higher rewards.

> **Key term**
> **Labour productivity** measures the output per employee.

> ## What do you think?
>
> What motivates you to work? What would make you work harder in your studies?

Operations management and competitiveness

The competitiveness of a firm depends on its ability to offer customers better value for money than its rivals. This means it must offer more benefits than the competition and/or produce goods at a lower price. For a firm to be successful, customers must think its products or services offer good value for money and are worth buying.

Operations management can improve a firm's competitiveness in several ways:

- by reducing the cost per unit so the firm is able to lower its prices. This may be achieved through selecting different suppliers (see Chapter 36) or increasing labour productivity reducing the labour cost per unit
- by providing better quality goods which meet the needs of customers more effectively than other firms (see Chapter 34 on quality)
- by producing more reliable goods with fewer faults than competitors
- by producing goods faster than the competition so they can get them to the customer more quickly
- by developing new products quickly so that customers are offered new models or new varieties ahead of the competition
- by providing a better range of products than the competition.

> ## What do you think?
>
> Being able to do something quickly is often an important operational target. Being able to deliver a pizza in 40 minutes, produce a new pair glasses in a couple of hours or develop someone's photos in an hour are all ways of competing. Can you think of any other businesses that compete by using time effectively?

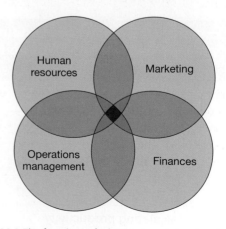

Figure 33.3 The functions of a business are interrelated

Operations management and other functions of the business

Operations managers have to work closely with the other functions of the firm.

Marketing
The marketing function focuses on customer needs and determines what needs to be produced and when it needs to be produced by. It also influences the amount a firm can afford to spend on producing the item, because it knows how much customers are prepared to pay for the goods or services. This will affect the choice of materials used and how the item is produced. Marketing, therefore, influences the design of the product, the required output levels and the timing of production.

Human Resources
The human resource function is important because a business needs the right number of employees with the correct skills in order to meet its production targets. Planning to ensure the firm has the appropriate workforce is a vital support to operations management.

Finances
Operations management has an impact on the firm's finances. A business may need to raise money to buy stocks of raw materials, to build a new factory or move into new offices. Production costs are likely to have a significant effect on profits.

Of course, the relationship between operations and the other functions is two way. Specialist skills in the workforce or a labour shortage may determine what is produced and how much is produced. The availability of finance may determine what transformation process is affordable and what scale the business can produce on. The capacity level of the business will influence the sales target that marketing needs to achieve.

The operations manager must coordinate the production plans with the other functions. If this does not happen, the firm may find that:

- it is producing goods even though there is not enough demand for them
- it does not have the right number of employees or workers with the right skills to provide the goods and services it wishes

- it does not have the money it needs to buy in supplies
- it is offering products that are not profitable.

Examiner's advice

Operations management affects the costs, quality and volume produced. This is an essential element of a firm's competitiveness. You should be aware of the types of decisions operations management makes to affect these factors.

To improve the effectiveness of the business, managers may seek to increase productivity, improve coordination with the other functions and use operations to add value through lower costs and/or better quality.

One step further: Problems measuring productivity

Measuring productivity is fairly easy if there is a physical product. It is easy to calculate the number of mobile telephones produced per employee or the number of pairs of jeans made by each worker.

Measuring productivity is more difficult in the service sector – it may not be so obvious what to measure. For example, how might the productivity of a doctor be measured? Also, there is a real danger that if doctors strive to see more patients (which might be seen as an increase in productivity) they spend less time with each one and the quality of service may suffer. Similar problems exist when trying to measure and increase the productivity of teachers, firefighters or shop assistants. Teaching bigger classes may increase the productivity of a teacher but the students may suffer. Having to put out fewer fires is more desirable than putting out more fires. The sales of a shop assistant may not be under their control – it depends in part on how many people enter the shop.

Another step further: UK productivity

Productivity is a key issue facing the UK because our levels are generally low compared to that of our European competitors. Although we do have some outstanding firms, we also have many firms that perform poorly. This causes concern because, if productivity is low, the cost of producing a unit is likely to be higher. This means that UK firms will either have to charge more or make lower profit margins. If UK firms want to continue to win orders abroad, and thereby provide jobs and incomes, they may have to significantly improve their productivity in the next decade.

Figure 33.4 shows that the difference between UK labour productivity and that of France, Germany and the USA is getting smaller, but it is still below these other countries.

Productivity in France, for example, is around 20 per cent higher than in the UK.

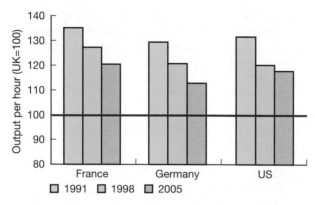

Figure 33.4 This chart shows productivity abroad in percentages compared to the UK (the red line). For example in 1991 France's productivity was around 35% higher than the UKs; in 2005 it was around 20% higher.

(Source: 'Policy Analysis: UK Productivity during the Blair Era', Centre for Economic Performance, London School of Economics, June 2006 http://cep.lse.ac.uk/pubs/download/pa009.pdf)

Summary

Operations management is responsible for managing the transformation process. This means it must select the right inputs and the right way of transforming these into outputs. Effective operations management must be linked to the other functions of a business. Typical operational targets relate to unit costs, volume and quality.

Quick questions

1. What is meant by operations management?
2. How can operations management make a business more competitive?
3. In what ways is operations management dependent on the other functions of the business?

4. What is meant by an operational target?
5. Why does the level of unit costs matter to a business?
6. Why does the level of quality matter to a business?
7. What is meant by capacity?
8. If the capacity utilisation of a business is 40 per cent and the capacity is 1600 units a week, what is the present level of output?

Issues for analysis

- The link between productivity and unit costs.
- The importance of capacity utilisation.
- The effects of under capacity utilisation.
- The ways in which firms might react to under-utilisation.

Issues for evaluation

- How important is operations management in determining competitiveness.

Analysis and evaluation questions

1. Malcolm runs a medium-sized business producing bean bags. He distributes these all over the country. His staff have been with the firm for many years and he respects them. However, he believes has to get productivity up or the business will not survive.

   a. Analyse the impact increasing productivity might have on Malcolm's costs and profits.
   b. Discuss the ways in which Malcolm might increase the productivity of his workforce.

2. 'We have ten coaches, each of which can take 50 passengers. At the moment the average demand is for two coaches a day. This is a problem and we cannot continue as we are. We are operating way below capacity.' Hannah de Betz, managing director of Traveller Coaches.

   a. Analyse the possible problems caused for Hannah's business by the under-utilisation of capacity.
   b. Discuss the ways in which Hannah might react to the present situation with the business operating under capacity.

Assessment

Case study

After leaving school at 18, Clive Beecham studied business at the London School of Economics. After graduating he went to work for Unilever in its Birds Eye group. That gave him an insight into large companies and made him realise that this sort of career was not for him. At age 25, with no ties and £10,000 worth of savings, he decided to set up his own business with the help of a partner called Andrew Sellers. He called the business Kinnerton Confectionery. The business idea was to produce chocolate figures such as chocolate Father Christmases or chocolate cartoon characters. Clive invested in a car and borrowed office space from his brother. He then approached chocolate manufacturers and offered to provide the design and packaging if they provided the chocolate figure.

The first order for his figures was from Woolworth's and was for £100,000. After that, other big orders followed. Eventually, Clive decided he should move the business into actually manufacturing the chocolate. He was worried that if he did not do this the chocolate companies would start producing products like his for themselves and compete directly with him.

So, 11 years after starting up Kinnerton, Clive bought a factory in Norfolk. This allowed the business to develop its product range further (adding in Disney characters, Teletubbies, Thomas the Tank and Barbie for example). One of the company's USPs is that its products are all produced in a nut-free zone and are completely nut-free. Its slogan is 'Chocolate with character!'

Web link

To find out more, visit www.kinnerton.com

Case study questions

(30 marks 40 minutes)

1 Explain the possible benefits to Kinnerton of having a USP (6 marks)
2 Analyse possible operational targets that Kinnerton would set (9 marks)
3 Discuss the factors Kinnerton would have considered when deciding whether to manufacture the chocolates itself. (15 marks)

34 Developing effective operations – quality

As we saw in Chapter 33, the operations targets of a business usually include quality. Managers have to decide what level of quality they want to achieve and how to achieve it. In this chapter we examine the meaning of quality, consider how firms set out to achieve and improve it, and discuss its impact on the effectiveness of a business.

What you need to know by the end of this chapter:

- the meaning and importance of quality
- the distinction between quality control and quality assurance
- systems of quality assurance and quality standards
- the issues involved in introducing and managing quality systems.

What is quality?

An important aspect of operations management is making sure that the goods and services produced are of a suitable quality. A quality product is one that meets the specifications that the firm has set out and, in turn, meets the customers' needs. As famous management writer Peter Drucker says' 'Quality in a product or service is not what the supplier puts in. It is what the customer gets out and is willing to pay for. A product is not quality because it is hard to make and costs a lot of money, as manufacturers typically believe. This is incompetence. Customers pay only for what is of use to them and gives them value. Nothing else constitutes quality.' What is and what is not quality therefore depends on the customers' views.

Quality has been defined as 'fitness for use' by Juran (1981) and 'conformance to requirement' by Crosby (1979). A pad of paper priced at £1 or a light bulb priced at 75p can both be quality products, provided they do what consumers expect them to do. By comparison a £1m house or a £400 suit may be poor quality if they do not meet consumers' expectations. The fact that these products are expensive does not mean they are necessarily of good quality. To improve the effectiveness of the business, managers must make sure that what they are producing consistently meets customers' requirements. This in turn means that to produce good quality

products, a firm must identify exactly what customers are looking for. The firm must then specify exactly what the product has to do and make sure that these specifications are achieved every time.

By improving the quality of their products, managers should improve customer satisfaction and lead to repeat business.

What do you think?

What would you say has been your 'best buy' recently? What is an example of good service you have received recently? What made the good you bought or service you received so special?

Key term

A **quality** product is one that meets customer requirements.

Quality targets

The nature of the quality targets set will depend on the type of business.

A hotel might set targets involving:

- customer satisfaction levels
- accurate billing
- speed of response, for example, by reception and in the restaurant.

A manufacturing business might consider:

- the proportion of products with defects
- the amount of waste produced in the process
- the proportion of returned goods.

A hospital might consider:

- the time taken to see patients
- the average length of time spent by patients in hospital
- the recovery rates for different types of operation
- patient satisfaction rates.

Business in Focus

The Cadbury Bubbly plant produces bars with such precision that the tiny air bubbles in the chocolate are within 0.2–0.3 mm of each other.

Why might the size of the air bubbles in a chocolate bar matter?

These targets will not be fixed forever. Once a target is achieved managers should look to make it even more challenging or find another area that needs focusing on and thereby improve the business further.

Why does quality matter?

Poor quality leads to mistakes that have to be put right or fixed. Goods may have to be thrown away. Items may be returned and have to be replaced. In a worst-case situation you may even be sued for failing to deliver the products promised. You may also lose customer goodwill and loyalty. The effects of poor quality are therefore expensive. Crosby, a management writer in this area, believes that between 20 and 35 per cent of firms' revenues can be spent putting right all the consequences of poor quality. He argues that investing to prevent mistakes occurring is far cheaper than putting things right later on. Improving quality can not only improve customer satisfaction; it can also save money.

What do you think?

How do you think a business can stop poor quality occurring?

Quality control and quality assurance

The traditional approach to improving the quality of a firm's products is to put resources into inspecting the finished products to find any faults that exist and remove them. The logic behind this approach is that, if all the goods and services with defects can be found, the customer will only receive perfect products. As a result, quality will be improved. This is known as a quality control system and it relies on the inspection of products.

In recent years, many managers have questioned whether quality control is the best approach. One problem is that quality control assumes that defects are inevitable. The task is to make sure that they are discovered before the customer receives the product. In effect, this is saying to some elements of the production team that it is acceptable for them to make mistakes, because the quality control department will find them later. This may mean that employees do not take sufficient care in their work.

The quality assurance approach puts more emphasis on preventing mistakes. If the process can be designed in a way which ensures defects do not happen (and in which employees produce correct work every time), inspection at the end of the production process is less important. This approach to quality focuses more on prevention, not just inspection. It stresses the need for employees to get it right first time.

An important part of this approach is that employees check their own work rather than rely on someone else to check it for them at the end of the process. This is known as 'self-checking'.

Under this approach, employees also have the right to reject any work of an unacceptable standard, whoever produced it. Previously, employees often accepted poor quality items as they did not feel responsible for the finished product or that they had the authority to reject poor work. Faulty products were simply passed along the production line until

Figure 34.1 Quality is based on customers' needs and expectations

the quality control department found the mistakes at the end. Under a quality assurance system, employees are held responsible for their own work; if they find faulty work from other employees they need to communicate with colleagues to sort it out, or report it.

Ensuring that they produce quality work is now seen as a part of everyone's job. At General Motors, for example, employees are told, 'don't accept errors, don't build errors and don't pass them on'. This is a very different view from the past, when quality was seen as something undertaken only by the quality control department.

Quality assurance requires training so that individuals can carry out their tasks effectively. It also involves choosing the right suppliers so that they deliver products without any defects. You will not check their products because you assume that they are correct; the responsibility for any problems caused later will be with the suppliers, which therefore puts pressure on them to get it right.

Figure 34.2 Elements of a quality assurance system

Total Quality Management (TQM)

Total Quality Management (TQM) is an approach to quality involving all the employees in the organisation. This quality assurance system appreciates that everyone within the firm contributes to the overall quality of the product or service.

TQM recognises that all employees are of equal importance, including the factory floor, the office staff, the cleaners, the maintenance staff and the delivery drivers in that they all contribute to the quality of the transformation process. The way in which customers are dealt with when they ring up, the accuracy of invoices sent out and the reliability of the deliveries all have an impact on how customers view the firm. It is not just the people who directly make or provide the product who matter.

It is very important that all employees think about the work they do and whether it is of a suitable quality. This means that they need to think of who their customers are. These customers may be the people who actually buy the product, but include anyone for whom work is produced.

Customers are not just external (the people from outside the business who buy the product); they are also internal. Employees need to think of the requirements of all the people they produce work for and ensure they are providing exactly what is required.

Business in Focus

Edwards Deming was an American quality expert who went to Japan and helped many companies there improve their approach to quality. He was later recognised by American firms as something of a 'guru' when it came to quality.

Deming encouraged the Japanese to adopt a systematic approach to problem solving, which later became known as the Deming or Plan-Do-Study-Act (PDSA) Cycle. He highlighted that meeting and exceeding customers' requirements is the task that everyone within an organisation needs to accomplish. Furthermore, the management system has to enable everyone to be responsible for the quality of his or her output to 'internal customers' (people they work for within the business).

According to Deming, you must plan what needs to be done to achieve your quality targets and then implement these activities. The next stage is to study the results to see what is working and what is not. You must then take action to remedy any problems. Once these have been fixed you must plan to improve and set more demanding targets. Notice that this is an ongoing process – you are always striving to improve.

Figure 34.3 The PDSA cycle

Imagine that you produce bottles of perfume and the amount in the bottles varies by + or − 0.5 per cent. Once you have made sure the variation lies within these limits, you then try to reduce the variation to + or − 0.4 per cent, and so on. Notice that the process relies on targets and measurement; a quality process is driven by data.

(Source: *The New Economics for Industry, Government Education*, 2nd Edition, by W. Edwards Deming, MIT Press, 2000)

For example, the warehouse staff have to load materials onto the van for delivery, so the delivery drivers are the internal customers of the warehouse staff. Under the TQM approach everyone has to think about their customers' needs: what they want, what standard they want it to meet and when they need it by.

The TQM approach considers that employees should always aim to improve the quality of what they do. It is tempting to assume that what you are doing is good enough and, if profits are reasonable, it is easy to become complacent. Such complacency is dangerous because markets and conditions can change incredibly rapidly. To succeed, firms must be continually trying to improve what they do to ensure that they actively delight customers. Under TQM, quality is seen as a dynamic process: it is a journey, not a destination. If managers improve the quality of the firm's operations this should improve its competitiveness.

Why might employees resist a TQM approach?

Some employees may resist the introduction of a TQM approach. This could be because they see quality as the job of a separate quality control department and do not see why they should check their own work. They may think it will lead to the redundancies of colleagues in quality control if they actually manage to prevent all mistakes and so do not want to do this. They may also be reluctant to take on additional tasks. If they adopt TQM they must first be willing to reject any work which is passed to them that is not satisfactory; that may involve telling colleagues and friends to do something again which can be difficult to do on a personal level. Also they must check their own work before passing it on and they may not see why they should do this. Some employees may also resist a TQM approach because they:

- don't see why it is necessary.
- don't want to have to undertake additional training.
- prefer to carry on doing things in the same old way.

Given that TQM involves a change in responsibilities and duties, managers must make sure:

- They explain why it is necessary.
- Provide the necessary training and support so employees feel capable and reassured.
- Provide appropriate rewards so employees feel they are treated fairly for taking on extra responsibilities.

Quality standards

A quality standard is a recognition that certain targets have been achieved and that a system is in place to monitor the level of achievement and take action if required. There are various quality standards but one of the most well known is ISO 9000.

ISO 9000 is a quality award available to organisations in the EU. In the UK it is sometimes known as BS 5750. These awards are gained by firms which are able to show that they have a system whereby quality is regularly measured and in which action is taken if quality levels fall below the set targets.

To achieve ISO 9000, firms must:

- set quality targets
- examine their production process to ensure that these are achieved
- measure the actual results and take action if what actually happens is different from what the firm wants to happen.

Quality targets might involve:

- the speed with which the firm responds to enquiries
- the delivery time of goods
- customer satisfaction ratings.

ISO 9000 does not, in itself, mean that a product or service is good quality. This is because it is not based on what the actual targets are – it focuses on whether the firm has a process of quality. If the firm sets standards that are relatively easy to achieve, it is still possible to achieve the award, provided it has the procedures in place to ensure it meets the targets on an ongoing basis. The award, therefore, rewards a system of quality. Does the firm have targets? Does it measure whether these are being achieved? Does it take action if targets are not met? If so, it may qualify for ISO 9000.

In reality, a business that aims for the ISO 9000 award is likely to be very focused on improving its quality and likely to set demanding targets. An organisation that sets out to achieve ISO 9000 is therefore likely to have a culture of improving quality.

> **Key terms**
> **ISO 9000** is a quality standard which recognises businesses that have a system of quality.
> The **culture** of a business refers to the values, attitudes and behaviours of its employees.

What do you think?

What quality targets might you set for your school or college?

The value of the ISO 9000 awards

Organisations that set out to gain ISO 9000 must develop a whole set of procedures to set and achieve quality targets. This type of process is likely to lead to less wastage and greater focus on customer requirements. This can lead to higher revenues, lower costs and more profits. Achieving ISO 9000 can therefore be a means of driving change and becoming more competitive.

Organisations achieving ISO 9000 are also able to use them in their marketing. This might be one way in which they can differentiate from their competitor, improve their competitiveness and win more customers. Several leading manufacturers, for example, are more likely to use suppliers who have ISO 9000.

However, introducing such a system may be met with resistance from some staff who do not want to change. It also involves a system of record-keeping which can seem bureaucratic and will require investment in training and possibly equipment to ensure quality errors are identified, and action taken to put them right and prevent them happening again. These difficulties can make some firms reluctant to introduce a quality system in any systematic way.

Designing the product

The process of improving quality begins with a good understanding of what internal and external customers want. This involves effective market research and use of information. The better the understanding of customers needs (including your own staff, your operations department) the more likely it is that a firm will produce something that meets their needs precisely.

The aim is to design a product to meet customers' requirements and a means of producing a product that enables the business to make an appropriate amount of profit. The design stage is absolutely critical to the success of a product and to achieving good quality. Effective planning before production begins means that the firm will produce something that customers want and that it is produced in an efficient way. The way the process is laid out, the equipment used, the level of technology involved and the way in which work is organised all have a major impact on the final quality of the goods or services.

Most companies would benefit from investing more at the design stage. If the initial design of the product and process is wrong, it is very expensive to put things right later. Unfortunately, in the rush to put products on the market, firms are willing to accept products and processes that are only adequate, rather than excellent. This is all part of a very common approach that is often more expensive in the long run. According to the UK government, 'Many senior managers (in the UK) still consider the design function a necessary evil, a costly and non-productive unit which often delays the introduction of a new product.'

Examiner's advice

You need to be aware of the importance of quality and the difference between quality control and quality assurance. You should be able to discuss the benefits of better quality, the ways this can be achieved and difficulties achieving it.

To increase its effectiveness, a business may try to improve its quality and prevent mistakes occurring.

Improving quality

Quality is an important element of a firm's success. Not surprisingly then, managers should always be looking to improve the quality of their goods and services. If managers want the business to improve its quality they must make it clear that it is a priority and develop appropriate systems to make sure that employees are always trying to improve quality. Bringing about better quality involves:

- defining clearly the needs of your internal and external customers in order to set appropriate quality targets
- introducing a Total Quality Management approach and ensuring that aiming for zero defects and getting it right first time is seen as an important element of everyone's job
- ensuring that the resources are available to enable quality targets to be achieved (e.g. sufficient training so staff can check their own work). This may cost money at first but should save money in the long term.

- working closely with suppliers to ensure they can meet your needs quickly and reliably
- ensuring that there is an on-going programme of target setting and measuring – once targets are consistently achieved more demanding targets can then be set
- ensuring that your reward systems recognise those who achieve better quality.

One step further: Philip Crosby's Four absolutes

Philip Crosby's name is best known for his writings on the concepts of 'Do It Right First Time'. He considers traditional quality control, the idea of acceptable quality limits (i.e. accepting a certain level of defects as acceptable) to represent failure rather than an assurance of success. In his view, firms must aim for 'zero defects' rather than 'an acceptable level of defects'. Of course having a 'zero defects' approach will not prevent people from making mistakes, but it will encourage everyone to improve continuously.

The ultimate goal is to train all the staff and give them the tools for quality improvement and to help them to prevent mistakes occurring.

Crosby's Four Absolutes of Quality Management are:

1 Quality is defined as conformance to requirements, not as 'goodness' or 'elegance'. (i.e. quality is defined by the customers, not by you!)
2 The system for causing quality is prevention, not appraisal. (i.e. don't fix it later– get it right first time).
3 The performance standard must be zero defects, not 'that's close enough' (i.e. don't accept mistakes).
4 The measurement of quality is the price of non-conformance (i.e. quality saves you money because it saves you all the costs of fixing the mistakes and having to rework items).

Summary

A quality product is one that meets its customer requirements. To ensure this happens businesses may develop a Total Quality Management approach; this means that everyone within the organisation seeks to prevent mistakes occurring. This is different from an approach which seeks to find mistakes that have already occurred. By managing effectively and improving quality, a business can increase its competitiveness. To improve quality, managers must decide what needs to be improved, how much it needs to be improved and how best to improve it.

Quick questions

1 What do we mean by 'quality'?
2 What is meant by quality assurance?
3 What is meant by quality control?
4 What is a quality standard?
5 What is Total Quality Management?
6 Why might employees resist the introduction of Total Quality Management?
7 Why might a business want to achieve a quality standard?
8 How does better quality help a business to be competitive?

Issues for analysis

- The links between better quality and sales.
- The links between better quality and lower costs.

Issues for evaluation

- How important is Total Quality Management to the success of a business?

Analysis and evaluation questions

1 'If we can improve quality, our profits will rise. But to do that we have to change the way we do things and not just rely on quality control.' So says Het Kurtman , managing director of Ezeenights, a manufacturer of beds.

a Analyse the ways in which improving quality might improve the profits of Ezeenights.
b Discuss the ways in which Ezeenights might improve the quality of their operations.

2 Wonderworld is a large theme park in the North of England. It employs over 200 staff and has recently hired a new chief executive, Julian Temple. Julian has worked in a large American entertainment business and wants to bring about change quickly to improve Wonderworld's performance. Within weeks of being there Julian has announced the introduction of a Total Quality Management approach. He has been surprised by the resistance from staff that he has received.

a Analyse the possible reasons why Julian wants to introduce a TQM approach.
b Discuss the possible reasons for the resistance to the introduction of TQM.

Assessment

Case study

In 2007, Cadbury recalled a million chocolate bars which may have been contaminated with a rare strain of salmonella. The company claimed the recall was precautionary and that the risk was low. However, government officials said that there was no safe level for salmonella in chocolate. The contamination was traced to a leaking pipe at a Cadbury's plant in Herefordshire. Samples were sent to an independent laboratory after the leak was discovered at the Marlbrook plant, and the *montevideo* strain of salmonella was identified. The factory at Marlbrook generates 97,000 tonnes of milk chocolate crumb every year. It processes 180 million litres of fresh milk, 56,000 tonnes of sugar and 13,000 tonnes of cocoa liquor annually in the production process. The crumb is transported to other sites at Bourneville, near Birmingham, and Somerdale, near Bristol, to be blended with cocoa butter and turned into milk chocolate.

Cadbury failed adequately to assess the risk of salmonella in its chocolate, according to the food standards inspectors.

The food manufacturer apparently used 'unreliable' methods which may have underestimated the level and likelihood of contamination.

Inspectors said 'Based on the information provided, Cadbury appears to have used methods for product testing which the committee considered would underestimate the level and likelihood of salmonella contamination.'

(Source: Adapted from http://news.bbc.co.uk/go/pr/fr/-/1/hi/uk/5110674.stm, 23/6/2006)

Case study questions

(30 marks; 40 minutes)

a Explain why the quality problems highlighted above might have occurred. (6 marks)

b Analyse the possible consequences of the above incident for Cadbury's. (9 marks)

c Discuss how Cadbury's can avoid such problems happening again. (15 marks)

35

Developing effective operations – customer service

Throughout this book we have stressed that meeting customer needs more effectively or efficiently than the competition is essential to be a successful business. An important element of meeting customer needs is good customer service. In this chapter we examine the meaning of good customer service and consider its significance in improving the effectiveness of a business. Managers must decide on the appropriate level of customer services, ensure that suitable systems are in place to reach this level and monitor whether it is being achieved.

What you need to know by the end of the chapter:
- the benefits of high levels of customer service
- how firms try to meet customer expectations
- ways in which firms monitor and improve customer service.

How important is good customer service?

One of the key factors that determines the quality of the buying experience for customers is the level of service they receive. Think of the following scenarios and you will appreciate how important good customer service is:

- You have been waiting in a long queue in a store for ten minutes while the shop assistant is chatting to his friends.
- You have asked the assistant about the differences between two mobile phones but she does not know very much about the products.
- You take the morning off work to go to the dentist and finds he has double booked and cannot see you after all!
- You ring up to book a table in a restaurant and the person taking the call is rude to you.

All of these are examples of poor customer service. Organisations that have poor levels of service are likely to lose customers to competitors who provide a better quality experience.

With rising standards of living, more choice and more information available to potential buyers, customer service is even more important now than in the past. What is regarded as good customer service ultimately depends on what customers expect. One of the biggest challenges facing businesses is that customers expect ever more, so to maintain good or excellent standards, businesses must look after their customers ever more successfully.

A recent survey by the Manchester Business School found that 77 per cent of customers had experienced problems caused by the products or services bought last year. Clearly then, there is some way to go in terms of improving the level of service offered in the UK. To make your business successful you must ensure good customer service and differentiate yourself from those who do not provide it. Given the ever-increasing competition, you must also try to improve your customer service all the time.

The essential elements of good customer service

Figure 35.1 Elements of good customer service

Good customer service involves:

- understanding what customers expect and providing this (or more than this) consistently. Customers tend to expect more over time, so businesses must keep improving.
- remembering that the customer buys the product and therefore pays the bills. The customer may be rude, impatient and ill-informed but even so, businesses must do their best to find out what they want and to provide it. No customers equals no business.

Business in Focus

The kitchenware business Lakeland has a simple promise: 'If you're not satisfied at any time, you receive your money back! This is our promise.' The company also has a Customer Ambassador to promote and protect the interests of customers.

Discuss the factors a business might consider before making a promise similar to Lakeland's.

- finding out the problem. The customer may not know exactly what they want. Your job is to understand what the problem is and then provide a solution.

- making sure you have well-trained employees who know about the business and the services they are providing. They need to have the skills and ability required to do the job properly. It is important for businesses to recognise the importance of service training and be prepared to invest in it. Employees need good interpersonal skills and the ability to be polite and helpful, even if customers are aggressive. Interpersonal skills include watching customers' body language. The way you sit, stand, the gestures you make and the expression on your face are telling the customer something – you need to be careful what messages you are conveying. A bored look on your face will not improve the customer's experience! Similarly, you need to be alert to the body language of the customer to try and understand how they are feeling. Good empathy is required in the service sector as employees need to understand how customers feel, what they want and how you can help them.
- focusing on long-term value rather than short term profit. Customer service can involve putting yourself out and being prepared to do more than is expected to make sure the customer is happy. Whether it is a refund if the customer is unhappy or a free return visit the aim is to build long term customer loyalty.
- making it easy for customers. Make it easy for customers to find what they want, find who they want, order what they want and to complain when necessary.
- delivering what you promise. A golden rule of customer service is that you do not over-promise. Customers will generally be happy if you deliver what you promise and delighted if you deliver more than you promise. They will be dissatisfied if you fail to provide what is expected. Imagine that you ask in a busy restaurant how long it will be until a table becomes free and are told 10 minutes but end up waiting 20 minutes. You are unlikely to be happy about it. However, if you are told the wait will be 25 minutes and are then offered a table after 20 minutes; you will probably feel quite positive about it. Better to under-promise than over-promise.

By improving the level of customer service managers increase the effectiveness of the business.

How do you achieve good customer service?

Figure 35.2 Elements necessary to achieve good customer service

To achieve better customer service a business may consider:

Market research

Good service happens when you understand what people want and don't want, when you find out what is irritating them and what they think of you compared to the competition. There are certain key variables you might want to measure to see whether your service is good. These include:

- Sales. Your sales figures will provide a good indicator of whether you are doing things correctly. If your sales are rising then this is a good sign; if they are falling this is not so good.
- Repeat business. If, for example, you own a café, restaurant, dentist's surgery, leisure centre or clothes shop and people are not coming back, you should worry.
- The proportion of business that is generated from customer recommendations – what proportion of customers are coming to you by word of mouth?

Research may involve asking customers directly what they think of the service. You will often find this at hotels and some stores where they ask you to fill in a card rating the service received.

When trying to measure customer service you may want to use quantitative and qualitative data. How many customers you have and what proportion return (quantitative data) may tell you something but you also what to know what they think of the service and why they think that (qualitative data).

open later than most other shops. He also pioneered the practice of discount retailing by buying wholesale goods from the lowest-priced supplier. This allowed him to pass on savings to his customers, which drove up his sales. Higher volumes allowed him to negotiate even lower purchase prices with the wholesaler on subsequent purchases. Another key factor was the location of the store. which was accessible to a wide range of customers.

Wal-Mart went on to grow and become the world's largest retailer. In 1998, Walton was included in Time Magazine's list of 100 most influential people of the twentieth century. Between 1985 and 1988 Walton was regularly listed as the world's richest man in the United States. The story of Wal-Mart is therefore clear evidence that you can start small but if you manage to provide great value for money along with superb customer service you can grow to become one of the largest businesses in the world.

From the very start, Walton's approach to business was very focused on customer service.

Figure 35.3 Sam Walton's original store now the Wal-Mart Visitor's Centre, Bentonville, Arkansas

He said:

'There is only one boss: the customer, and he can fire everyone in the company from the chairman and down, simply by spending their money somewhere else.'

'The two most important words I ever wrote were on that first Wal-Mart sign, 'Satisfaction Guaranteed'. They're still up there, and they have made all the difference.'

One of Sam's rules that he expected all his employees (called Associates) to follow was 'I want you to promise that whenever you come within 10 feet of a customer, you will look him in the eye, greet him, and ask him if you can help him.' Associates must also follow the 'Sundown rule'– this means that requests must be answered wherever possible by the close of business on the day they are received. Wal-Mart's focus on customer service remains one of its strengths.

Quality assurance and quality control

To ensure good customer service, a business must include this in its quality targets. It must then introduce a quality assurance process whereby each individual understands their role within the business and why it matters, understands their personal quality targets, feels responsible for the quality of what they do (and are held accountable for what they do) and understands the significance of meeting customer expectations. Essentially, it is about ensuring that everyone in the business appreciates the importance of customer service, monitors and measures what they do and is empowered to take action if quality is not satisfactory. Quality control may also be important to inspect what is being done and to report back on the quality being achieved. Some hotels and stores, for example, use mystery guests or mystery shoppers to provide an external check on the level of customer service. Aiming for and maintaining a quality standard such as ISO 9000 may be one way of formalising a quality approach that includes customer service. This would ensure a system of measuring the level of qulaity achieved and taking action if targets are not hit.

Choosing the right payment system

The way in which you reward your staff can have an impact on the level of and quality of customer service. If you pay your employees on commission based on sales you may find they try to push the customer into buying something that they don't really want. Although this generates a sale in the short term (and therefore increases earnings for the employee), the long-term effect may be customer dissatisfaction, returned goods and no repeat business.

You must also be careful about rewarding employees in a shop for the sales they make individually – this is because they might try to 'steal' a sale from their colleagues to boost their own earnings. You may find that nobody wants to clean out the stockroom or do the tidying because this does not generate commission. Instead, they fight over every customer because they can earn more money. Again, this can lead to a very pushy approach. A team bonus system is likely to work better.

To avoid some of these problems, some businesses pay a bonus based on the level of customer satisfaction. Richer Sounds, the consumer electronics shop, asks each customer to rate their service, and bonuses are paid on this rather than on sales. (According to the *Guinness Book of Records* Richer Sounds has the largest sales per square foot of any retailer in the world.)

Training

Listening to customers, treating them politely, going out of your way to solve their problems, dressing smartly, talking confidently about products, seeing things from customers' points of view and not losing your temper even if your customers do, are all important skills. They do not always come naturally, so training is important. Employees need to be trained in a whole range of areas such as interpersonal skills, anger management and presentational skills as well as knowing all about the products and having appropriate technical information. Training needs to be on-going because there will always be changes to the products being offered, the terms and conditions of sales, the special offers and the business itself. Employees need to be up to date on these developments.

Business in Focus

A number of DIY stores have told their staff to stop asking customers what they want and instead to ask them to describe the problem they have. This is because customers are often amateur builders and often what they think they want is the wrong thing! This means they go home with the wrong product and have to return to change it, or do a bad job. The stores believe customers will be better served if they describe the problem and then staff can work out what they need.

When you go into a store, do you prefer assistants to come up to you or leave you alone to browse? Why?

Poor customer service

Figure 35.4 Possible causes of poor customer service

Poor customer service can occur due to:

- A **lack of training** (possibly because firms want to keep costs low or simply do not appreciate how important training can be). This means employees do not know enough about the business, its products or how to deal with customers.
- A **failure to realise the importance of customer service**. Sometimes, owners do not realise the need to provide good customer service. They believe that if the tangible product is good then customers will automatically buy it. This ignores the importance of customer service as part of the overall buying experience. In some cases, managers may not see customer service as important because they do not really regard the users of their services as 'customers'. Schools, universities, hospitals and libraries, for example, have been guilty in the past of expecting 'customers' to appreciate what they are given, rather than trying to meet their needs more successfully. When industries are owned and protected by the government, this can remove the incentive to provide a good service: the greater the degree of competition the more pressure there is to serve the customer excellently to retain their business.
- **Poor recruitment**. Firms may hire the wrong people – for example who do not have good interpersonal skills or who are not motivated by their work (although this could also be due to the design of the job or the rewards offered).

Some businesses may get away with poor customer service in the short term, but over time customers will switch to competitors who provide better service. The proportion of customers switching providers in many markets such as telephones, gas, electricity, water and banks has increased by 52 per cent in the last five years, according to the National Consumer Council.

Web link

To find out more about the role of the National Consumer Council, visit www.ncc.com

What do you think?

Can you think of a time when you have received poor customer service? What impact do you think this will have on the success of that business in the long term?

Business in Focus

According to the National Consumer Council, the five main ways that businesses get customer service wrong are:

- inflated expectations and broken promises. Customers get irritated when promises are broken and you fail to deliver.
- trying too hard to sell even if the product is not right for the customer. Customers do not like pushy salespeople.
- dishonesty. Customers do not like it if companies try to mislead them or use confusing marketing tactics such as complex pricing structures.
- impersonal service that does not seem to listen to what the customer is saying or respond to their needs
- incompetence. Customers do not like firms that respond slowly, appear to patronise them or seem incapable of doing the simplest thing.

Could you add to this list? What would you add?

Examiner's advice

The way in which customers are treated is an important part of their overall experience and the value provided by a business. You need to be aware of what good customer service involves and how businesses can improve customer service.

To increase effectiveness a business will try to increase the level of customer service and always seek to exceed customer expectations.

Summary

Customers have an increasing amount of choice and have increasing expectations of what a business should do for them. This means that customer service is becoming ever more important if businesses want to keep hold of customers and gain new ones. Effective businesses provide excellent service. Being able to exceed customer expectations is a very important competitive weapon.

Quick questions

1 Give one example of good customer service you have experienced recently.
2 Give one example of poor customer service you have experienced recently.
3 Explain why good customer service is important to a business.
4 Explain two actions a business might take to improve its customer service.
5 Explain one possible reason for poor customer service.
6 What sorts of skills are needed to provide good customer service?
7 Do you think the need for good customer service is increasing or decreasing? Why?
8 Why is market research important for good customer service?

Issues for analysis

- The links between customer service and sales.
- The ways in which customer service can be improved.
- The link between customer service and competitiveness.

Issues for evaluation

- How important is good customer service to the success of a business?

Analysis and evaluation questions

1 Following disappointing results at the Yum Yum fast-food chain, marketing manager Vera, undertook primary market research. The results did not surprise her: customer service was regarded as very poor.

a Analyse the possible effects on Yum Yum of having very poor customer service.
b Discuss the actions which Vera might take to improve customer service.

2 'Long queues and rude, scruffy and ignorant staff who know nothing about the products they are supposed to be selling apart from how much commission they get.' So said one customer of Phone Today, a chain of mobile phone shops.

a   Analyse the possible reasons why customer service at Phone Today might be so poor.

b   To what extent does it matter whether customer service at Phone Today is perceived by this customer as poor?

Assessment

Case study

David Reibstein at the Wharton Business School found that dissatisfied Starbucks customers visited the chain for one year, made 47 visits that year and spent a total of $200. By contrast, a highly satisfied Starbucks customer visited the chain for 8 years, made 86 visits a year and spent more than $3,000 during that time. So the difference between satisfaction and dissatisfaction is about $2,800, simply for people buying coffee. The lifetime value of a satisfied BMW customer is likely to be $143,500.

(Source: The Stupid Company, at www.ncc.com)

Case study questions

(30 marks; 40 minutes)

a   Explain two factors that might affect the demand for Starbucks products. (6 marks)

b   Analyse the possible benefits to Starbucks of having satisfied customers. (9 marks)

c   To what extent is the satisfaction of customers at Starbucks likely to depend on the price of the products? (15 marks)

36 Working with suppliers

A business relies on its suppliers. The quality and cost of a firm's inputs affects the price and quality of the final product. In this chapter we examine the importance of the relationship between a business and its suppliers. We consider the way in which suppliers are managed can influence the effectiveness of the business.

What you need to know by the end of this chapter:
- the importance of suppliers
- the factors involved in choosing effective suppliers.

Why are suppliers important?

The quality of a firm's products will depend in part on the quality of the suppliers it uses. The choice of suppliers and the relationship with them is therefore a crucial part of any organisation. If you think about how many thousands of different components that go into making a car, you can imagine how complex the process of managing suppliers can be for a car manufacturer.

Organisations tend to work with some suppliers on an on-going basis; for example, a school will have regular deliveries of photocopying paper and a delicatessen will have regular deliveries of food. Other suppliers may be used for specific tasks, such as using a marketing company for a rebranding exercise. Some supplies may be vital to a business, for example, the computer systems for an online business. Other suppliers may be less significant to the overall success of a business, such as the supplier of milk or tea bags for the staffroom of a school.

Types of supplies

Types of supplies include:

- **accessories**. These are relatively inexpensive items that are bought regularly, such as office supplies. Firms may choose them from brochures or online, and may not spend that long on making the decision. There will be many possible suppliers of accessories and switching to another supplier is likely to be easy.

- **capital items**. These include spending on equipment, machinery and premises and may involve major investments. Such spending may not be on a regular basis and firms will investigate the options thoroughly. They are likely to examine the specifications, compatibility, features and financial implications in some detail before selecting the item.

- **Components and supplies**. These are the general inputs into the transformation process, such as materials. Firms will be very interested in factors such as the quality and the reliability of supply.

Business in Focus

Antonio Carluccio was born in the province of Salerno in Italy. After a spell in the Navy, Antonio worked as a correspondent for the newspaper *La Stampa* in Turin. He moved to Vienna, studying languages and learning about café society, and then to Germany where he became a wine merchant, which was also his occupation when he moved to London. The experience of observing many restaurants led in 1981 to his being asked by his brother-in-law to run his Neal Street Restaurant in Covent Garden.

In 1983 Antonio made his first appearance on BBC2 and at the same time was asked to write his first book, *An Invitation to Italian Cooking*. He has since written twelve books, published worldwide. During the 1980s he contributed to numerous 'food and drink' programmes, including a twelve-part series about the regions of Italy.

In 1991, Antonio and his wife Priscilla opened the Carluccio's food shop, which then led to the opening of a chain of highly successful Italian-style shops and restaurants. He has received the Commendatore Omri for service to Italian gastronomy and in January 2007, an honorary OBE.

The company says: 'The aim of Carluccio's Caffès is to provide great quality, authentic Italian food at sensible prices; to allow informal but excellent service to our customers.

The success of Carluccio's Caffès is based on carefully selected fresh Italian produce and the creation of a happy, bustling restaurant environment combined with a shop.'

What do you think are the essential ingredients of a successful restaurant?

The importance of suppliers

The choice of suppliers can affect the effectiveness of a business and its sales. It can affect:

- the **costs of inputs** and therefore the overall costs of the business and its profit margins
- the **flexibility of the business**. If suppliers can deliver quickly and to order, the business itself can be more responsive to customer requests. This may be an important source of competitive advantage.
- the **quality of the overall product**. If a garment is faulty (e.g. the zip breaks or the buttons crack) this affects your impression of the final product and the producer, even though it may originally be a supplier fault.
- **image and customer confidence**. When choosing a computer, for example, people may look at the processor (Intel v AMD) within it. You may prefer food products that use British or local ingredients, only organic ingredients.

The choice of suppliers

The choice of suppliers may depend on:

- **the price they charge and the payment terms**. For example, how much credit is given? This will affect your cash flow; the longer you have to pay them the longer you can hold on to your money and earn interest or the more credit you can give to your own customers (which may attract more sales)

- **the ability of the supplier to meet your precise specifications** in terms of design or delivery
- **the ability of the supplier to cope with the quantity of work** involved and meet the agreed deadlines. When choosing a supplier you will be interested in its overall capacity and its present capacity utilisation
- **the reliability of the supplier** when it comes to meeting specifications. When choosing suppliers you might ask for samples of their work and speak to previous clients to assess their quality. You may also insist that the supplier has achieved specific quality standards such as ISO 9000 (see Chapter 35).

> **Key term**
> The **capacity** of a business measures the maximum it can produce at a given moment, according to its existing resources.

Choosing suppliers is therefore a combination of many different factors. Choosing the right suppliers can influence your own costs and quality: better suppliers should improve your own performance.

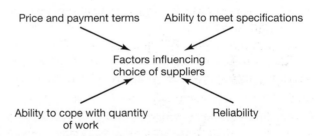

Figure 36.1 Factors influencing choice of suppliers

Contracts and service level agreements

When you have chosen a supplier you will probably want to formalise the arrangement through some form of contract or service level agreement (SLA). This should set out the standards that have to be met and the responsibilities of either side. For example, it might cover details of:

- the service that has to be provided and the desired level of quality
- the timetable for delivery and penalties if these are not met
- the responsibilities of either side (e.g. what happens if you decide to change your mind about some of the features of the product or delivery date)

- payment terms
- confidentiality agreements (because you might not want your suppliers telling your competitors what you are working on).

Relationship with suppliers: the partnership approach

The relationship between a business and its suppliers can vary considerably. At one extreme, a business may regard its suppliers as partners. It may seek to develop a long-standing, trusting relationship with its suppliers. This may involve:

- keeping suppliers well informed about future plans and requirements, giving the supplier time to change its plans accordingly
- paying the supplier a fair price and not trying to beat the price down
- paying the supplier promptly
- asking the supplier for advice on how to make your two systems more compatible
- trying to coordinate requirements to fit in with suppliers' other commitments
- passing on leads for other business to them and recommending them to others.

In some cases, suppliers may even invest in a business and/or vice versa to make the relationship even closer and to highlight the shared interests of the two organisations.

The benefits of collaborating with suppliers and adopting a partnership approach are that suppliers may:

- try harder to meet your needs e.g. if you have a special or rush order they may be willing to put themselves out to get it completed
- offer more favourable terms because they know that in the long term they will benefit from more orders
- work with you on new projects to find the best way of doing it e.g. they may advise you on the right materials to use to do the job properly.

Relationship with suppliers: the non-partnership approach

Rather than seeing suppliers as partners you may try and bully them to force the best short-term deal out of them and always put your interests ahead of theirs. This might involve:

- delaying payment so that you can keep the money you owe in your own bank account for longer
- arguing over the price and using whatever power you have to push it down

- threatening to switch suppliers if you get a better short-term offer, even if this gives little notice to your existing suppliers.

In this case, suppliers may offer you good deals because they are afraid of what you will do otherwise. However, this does not build long-term loyalty and when given the opportunity to work with other firms, your suppliers may well switch away from you. When they can they will also seek to take advantage of you.

Which is the right approach to suppliers?

This depends in part on your whole approach to business. If you like to collaborate and work with others then you are likely to adopt the partnership approach. If you see yourself as out for what you can get, you will probably not collaborate well with suppliers.

It may also depend on how much you need suppliers and what you think they can do for you: the more essential they are to you, the more you may try to work with them as partners.

A final factor may be your own experience and the experience of others in your sector. If collaboration has been shown to work in the past, you are more likely to adopt this approach in the future.

Examiner's advice

Businesses rely heavily on their suppliers. You need to be aware of the factors that determine which suppliers a business works with, how suppliers help a firm to compete and the approach a business adopts towards its suppliers.

To improve its effectiveness, a business can develop a relationship with suppliers that leads to a better quality product; for example, the transformation process may be cheaper, more differentiated, more flexible or faster.

Summary

The choice of, and the relationship with suppliers can affect a firm's costs and the quality of its transformation process. The way in which a business manages its relationship with its suppliers can, therefore influence its effectiveness. Good suppliers will deliver products in the right quantity, at the right quality, on time, and be flexible to your requirements.

Quick questions

1 Distinguish between two different types of supplies.
2 Explain two factors that might influence your choice of supplier.
3 Explain two ways in which the actions of a supplier might affect a firm's performance.
4 Why might a firm want to delay payment to a supplier?
5 How might the choice of supplier affect your marketing?
6 Why might you want two suppliers for the same component?
7 Explain two benefits of adopting the partnership approach to suppliers.
8 Explain one reason not to adopt the partnership approach to suppliers.

Issues for analysis

- The impact of suppliers on a firm's quality.
- The factors influencing the choice of supplier.

Issues for evaluation

- How important are suppliers to the success of a business?
- Should firms adopt a partnership approach when dealing with their suppliers?

Assessment

Analysis and evaluation questions

1 Awesome Organics started as a sandwich store using only organic ingredients. It was set up by Chuck Handle in 1990. The business has grown reasonably fast and Chuck now has 15 shops in the UK. The company promotes 'healthy, fresh, local, organic food'.

a Analyse the possible importance of suppliers to the success of Awesome Organics.
b Discuss the factors that Chuck might take into account when choosing a new supplier for an ingredient to be sold in one of his stores.

2 Clemency Watts runs a business making engines sold to various boat manufacturers. Although the business has done reasonably well, Clemency would like it to grow faster and make more profits. She is determined that the business should aim for the ISO 9000 award. She has also instructed her own buyers to pay their suppliers later and try to push the price paid down wherever they can.

a Analyse the possible effects of Clemency's instructions to her buyers.
b Discuss the possible importance to Clemency Watts' business of gaining ISO 9000.

Case study

Ros Lee is the administration director for a publishing company McMillan-Scott. When she joined the business, one of her first challenges was to rethink the way suppliers were managed.

At that time the company did not have an official purchasing policy. All staff were still ordering supplies on an individual basis.

The first thing Ros did was to list all the firm's suppliers and calculate the current spending on everything from stationery to company cars. Once the information was stored in a central database, she could look at areas for improvement. It was clear that there was scope to cut costs by centralising all purchasing, rationalising the supplier base and negotiating better deals with key suppliers. The

next step was to consult with existing suppliers and investigate alternatives. Even where there were cheaper options, Ros did not dismiss existing suppliers out of hand. She talked to them face-to-face to explain the new purchasing policy. She wanted to give them a chance to compete with the other suppliers she was considering.

She also made sure new suppliers understood the firm's needs and that she understood the way they operated. According to Ros, developing good relationships from the outset is important. She believes that if you help your suppliers, then they will be more willing to help you.

Ros felt it was essential to put an end to individual buying decisions, so the new policy was immediately circulated to all staff. There was some initial resistance, but by talking to them and listening to their concerns this was overcome. One major staff worry was that product quality would decline, making their jobs harder. Ros was careful therefore to provide a product sample for testing whenever a substitution was planned.

Some savings were apparent straight away. For example, changing the stationery supplier resulted in an immediate 20 per cent cost reduction, while limiting supplier choice for company cars led to an average 15 per cent discount on prices.

The ultimate goal of a purchasing policy is to control costs. But good supplier relationships are based on more than just money and Ros learnt this in the early stages.

For example, she initially decided to switch telephone suppliers to gain a huge cost saving. Unfortunately, the service levels did not meet the company's needs and the business suffered temporarily. Before long, Ros reverted to the original supplier. Now, every decision she makes to retain a supplier or take on a new one involves careful analysis of the service levels they provide.

Case study questions

(30 marks; 40 minutes)

1 Explain how Ros overcame resistance to her proposal for central purchasing. (6 marks)
2 Analyse the benefits to the business of buying all supplies centrally. (9 marks)
3 'The lowest cost supplier is the one to choose.' To what extent do you agree? (15 marks)

37 Using technology in operations

Operations management commonly has targets relating to costs, volume and quality. The achievement of these targets can be helped considerably by the use of technology in the transformation process. In this chapter we examine the role of technology in operations and consider how the way in which technology is managed can influence the effectiveness of the business.
What you need to know by the end of this chapter:
• the different types of technology used in operations management
• the issues involved in introducing and updating technology.

Technological developments

The way in which inputs are transformed into outputs is continually being improved, thanks to developments in technology. Technological developments occur due to improvements in science and engineering. Unbelievably, the internet did not exist until the 1990s, and yet it is now an essential part of how business is conducted. Technology is developing all the time, improving the way business provides goods and services and the customer experience.

Technological developments improve the way we communicate, the way we store, access and use information and the physical way in which we produce. Just look at the way shopping has changed in the last few years. First, scanning equipment became common, then some stores introduced a system where you scanned your own products as you went around the store and now many shops have self-scanning by the checkouts. Businesses must anticipate and react to changes to remain competitive. Better use of technology can improve the effectiveness of many aspects of a business.

> **Key term**
> **Technological developments** refers to improvements in a product or a process due to improvements in science and engineering.

Using technology to improve performance

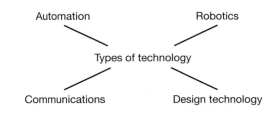

Figure 37.1 Types of technology

There are many ways in which technology is used in a business to improve its operations.

Robotics

Robots are machines used to undertake a range of tasks, such as moving, lifting, turning and cutting. You can see robots when you visit factories such as car plants. They will be lifting cars from one place to another or undertaking activities such as welding.

Businesses use robots because they can improve quality, lower costs and make production more flexible. Using robots also takes away some difficult and tough jobs from employees who can then concentrate on other tasks. Robots are particularly useful when:

• a high level of precision and accuracy is required
• the task involves a high level of repeatability.

Key terms

A **robot** 'is a reprogrammable device designed to both manipulate and transport parts, tools or specialised manufacturing implements through variable programmed motions for the performance of specific manufacturing tasks.' (British Robots Association)

Figure 37.2 Robots in action

Automation

This occurs when tasks are undertaken automatically by a machine. For example, when stock levels reach a certain point a new order for suppliers might be placed by computer without anyone having to check each time. Automated stock control is now quite common in stores. As items are scanned using an Electronic Point of Sale (EPOS) system the sale is automatically recorded and the stock level adjusted accordingly.

Other automated tasks may include packing, wrapping and labelling.

Web link

To find out more about robots and automation, visit the British Robots Association at http://www.bara.org.uk/

While robotics and automation have many benefits, it is important to remember that:

- there are costs involved in their purchase and installation
- the type of tasks they can carry out is still relatively limited. The importance of human skills should not be ignored. Unlike machines, employees have the ability to learn and be creative in coming up with a solution. Robots and automated systems therefore work well for some jobs, but not others.

What do you think?

Can you think of jobs that would not be suitable for a robot?
Can you think of a job that a robot would do better than an employee?

Communications

Communications have also been revolutionised by technology. Developments in information technology have radically cut the costs of communicating and improved the ease of doing so. This means that managers can keep in contact with employees more easily, as well as with suppliers and other important groups. We now live in a 24-hour world, where communicating electronically is much more affordable and efficient. Whether it be email, mobile phones, texting, Skype or video conferencing, it should be possible to get a message to the people when you need to. Management of operations is more effective, because you can find out what you want when you want. Using mobile phones enables people to talk on the move and thereby increases productivity. Networking computers enable individuals to share best practice and resources. Plans are coordinated better, and less time and resources are wasted through mistakes.

Sharing information with suppliers, ideally in real time, allows you to forecast your requirements better and ensure that they can provide what you want when you want. Some firms have introduced enterprise resource planning (ERP) systems. These link their purchasing information and ordering systems directly with suppliers. You receive an order, an order is sent for the relevant parts to the supplier and you can track at each stage where the supplier is in the process. It also enables the supplier to issue an invoice automatically. This highlights the value of integrating your systems with partners. A key issue in the effective use of technology in operations is making sure that all the different systems internally and in relation to suppliers and distributors are linked effectively. Otherwise you end up with 'islands of technology' not working together.

Even if you are not linked directly to a supplier, communications technology can be very useful in relation to suppliers. Using the internet you can search out supplies more easily and compare prices and features. Online buying should lead to lower prices by shopping around, greater efficiency, as you can avoid a lot of the paper involved in traditional buying systems, and faster ordering as you can buy any time you want.

> **Key term**
> **Information technology** involves the hardware and software used to store, retrieve and manipulate information.

Real-life Business

Facebook was started in 2004 by Mark Zuckerberg, a student at Harvard who was 19 at the time, along with two friends.

The site requires users to provide their real names and email addresses and then links them with current and former friends and colleagues. Each Facebook entry is accompanied by information on the user, photos, gossip and messages. There has been talk of selling shares to the general public, although for the time being Mr Zuckerberg seems more interested in changing the world. He looks like a student (with his Adidas sandals, jeans and fleece sweaters) but he is the owner of a rapidly growing, billion dollar global business.

What do you think is the appeal of Facebook?

Design technology

Design technology helps firms develop products more efficiently than they could manually. It includes Computer Aided Design (CAD), which enables firms to design a new product and test it on screen without actually having to build a physical prototype.

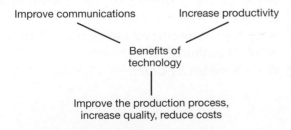

Figure 37.3 Benefits of technology

The benefits of technology

Using technology can:

- improve communications and the flow of information between customer, business and suppliers. This can lead to a faster response time and fewer mistakes being made.
- improve the transformation process by making it more flexible, cheaper as well as having less defects, being more accurate and more consistent. Fewer errors reduces the amount of waste in terms of materials and time. This improves quality and reduces costs.
- help employees to do their jobs better and more quickly: this increases productivity.

All of these effects should improve the effectiveness and competitiveness of a business.

> **Key term**
> **Labour productivity** measures the output per employee over a given period of time (see Chapter 33).

However, not every firm needs all the technology available, nor could they afford it. Therefore a business must consider:

- what technology would most add value and cover the costs of investment. Often with investment decisions businesses have to prioritise – what is essential to buy in the short term? What is desirable over the long term?
- how to introduce technology to maximise its effectiveness (e.g. in terms of links with other systems inside and outside the business and providing the necessary training for employees).

Reviews need to be frequent, because with the rate of change in technology, equipment and systems can become out of date quite rapidly. Managers then face the decision of whether to update or scrap the existing system and start again. Look around your school or college and think about the developments in technology and how it is helping you learn. Faster internet access, flat screens, wireless connections, interactive white boards and online study resources are all improving operations in education. However they all require investment.

What do you think?

How might developments in technology further improve the teaching and learning process in the future?

Problems of introducing technology in operations

Despite the many benefits of technology there are also some potential problems. For example:

- **the cost of purchasing and maintaining it**. The costs may vary from a few pounds for a mobile phone to thousands of pounds for a robot but firms must consider the amount spent relative to the potential benefits.
- **the reaction of employees**. Much new technology improves the working lives of employees; it enables them to do their work more easily and more efficiently. However, in some cases it may lead to redundancies. With greater labour productivity through new technology fewer people will be needed for the same output. Redundancies may be resisted by employees. Also, new technology may require training. This is another cost and while training may be welcomed by some as an opportunity to develop their skills, others may not want to learn how to do things differently.

- **the adjustment period**. Introducing technology can be disruptive as one system is changed to another. It can lead to a 'down time' when things are not working properly due to the handover: this may affect the service provided. Sometimes, both systems need to be running parallel to check the new one works before giving up the old one. However, this may not be feasible. For example, space may be too limited in the case of production equipment. For the introduction to work properly everyone needs to know what has to be done at each stage and the implementation needs to be monitored.

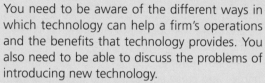

Summary

New technology can help a business to be more effective by improving its flexibility, reducing costs and improving quality. However, when introducing technology, care must be taken that service does not suffer during the changeover period, that employees understand why it is being introduced and that they receive the necessary training. Effective use of technology will improve a firm's performance.

Quick questions

1. How can robots help a business?
2. What are the problems of introducing new technology into a business?
3. How can technology help communications within a business?
4. What is meant by CAD?

5 What are the benefits of introducing new technology into a business?

6 State two factors a business might consider before deciding whether to introduce new technology

7 State two ways a business might finance new technology

8 What is meant by productivity?

Issues for analysis

- The link between technology and competitiveness.
- The impact of technology on costs.
- The impact of technology on flexibility.
- The impact of technology on quality.

Issues for evaluation

- How useful is technology in terms of a firm's competitiveness?
- Is better or more technology the key to a firm's success nowadays?

Analysis and evaluation questions

1 Valeria Sergeeva is the managing director of a business producing computers. The business is fairly automated already but Valeria thinks there are even more opportunities to automate further.

a Analyse the possible problems for Valeria of introducing automation in her business.

b Discuss the factors that Valeria might consider before automating more of the firm's operations.

2 Gheeta Bandari has linked her chain of city centre clothes stores with many of their suppliers using computer links.

a Analyse the possible benefits to Gheeta's business of having computer links with suppliers.

b To what extent can such links guarantee the success of Gheeta's business?

Assessment

Case study

MGM Ltd is a Newcastle-based building restoration and renovation business that has introduced technology into many of its day-to-day operations to help streamline processes and manage costs.

One of its managers says:

'I talked to our accountants as I wanted to use an IT system that would easily integrate with theirs. I also discussed workloads with staff. We decided that the most efficient way of progressing was to take on someone who had already worked on accounting packages. This would save time and cost on training, and we simply didn't have enough people in the office to handle the extra workload.

First, we introduced an accounting package, so we could invoice customers and make and receive payments through BACS. This is the automated clearance system where you can transfer money directly into recipients' accounts, rather than write cheques and have to wait for them to clear. This made our financial control much tighter so we didn't miss any payments 'We then put the payroll onto the accounts system to pay staff monthly

salaries direct into their bank accounts. This has cut down on paperwork and reduced manual errors. Next we introduced programming of workloads so we could guarantee that the right people are in the right place, doing the right work, at the right time. This has greatly increased customer satisfaction.

The latest change is the introduction of a tracker system in each of our 21 vehicles. I researched the available systems on the market and opted for the one best suited to our needs. I explained to everyone that the tracker system would streamline our efficiency as we would be able to plan routes more effectively. This meant they arrived to jobs on time, and had an easy-to-follow, reasonable schedule every day. The tracker system has resulted in a number of cost savings, including reducing our insurance premiums and petrol costs.

It's only during 2004 that we've finally networked all our technology together. It's made a huge difference to our efficiency. We can all see the same IT files and can access information as soon as we need to. We can keep our invoicing up to date and respond to customer queries immediately.

▶

Now we have our monthly management accounts, we can control the business better, knowing what our profitability is at regular intervals, and making adjustments if needed.'

The managing director's tips to other businesses include:

• 'Embrace technology - don't be afraid of it just because it's something different and makes you work in different ways.'

• 'Back up everything – technology's great, but if you lose all your data and information, you're stuck.'

(Source: Adapted from www.businesslink.gov.uk)

Case study questions

(30 marks; 40 minutes)

1 Explain why some employees at MGM Ltd might not want to embrace technological change. (6 marks)

2 Analyse the benefits to MGM Ltd of investing in technology. (9 marks)

3 IT has worked well for MGM Ltd. Discuss the possible reasons why its introduction was so successful. (15 marks)

Unit Two Assessment

Question One: Any Junk?

Any Junk? was set up by Jason Mohr a former city banker. Jason Mohr quit his well-paid career in London to set up a junk clearance firm, removing a wide range of rubbish.

An extract from the company's website explains the service the business offers.

> 'Our waste collection service covers the clearance, loading and disposal of all types of waste from anywhere on the premises. Friendly, uniformed drivers in smart, shiny removal trucks specially designed and equipped to collect and remove waste fast. Our website removal rates include all labour and disposal fees. We turn up when we say we will, we guarantee all waste is disposed of properly. So don't waste time, call us and get your waste removal problem sorted today.'

Any Junk? prides itself on offering a high quality and professional service. It has well trained staff who receive hourly pay plus bonuses and its contacts all its customers after providing a service to check on customer satisfaction. The company does take any junk (except hazardous waste) that households (and businesses) generate and is fully licensed to do so. The company charges only for the amount of rubbish that is removes, unlike in the case of skips where a standard charge is levied. It charges from £20 for the removal of the equivalent of six bin bags to £282 for taking away two skips of rubbish.

Any Junk? is proud of its green credentials. It uses local charities and recycling centres to reuse junk wherever possible. In this way the company helps to protect the environment as well as reducing its own costs of disposal. The company claims that this allows it to offer more competitive prices to customers.

Recent developments at the firm have seen it implement expansion plans to offers its services in Bristol and Bath as well as London. As a result of the expansion Jason's brother Luke, 27, has left his job as an accountant to run the service in Bristol and their home city of Bath.

Source: Any Junk? website (www.anyjunk.co.uk)

Questions

a Explain one way in which Any Junk? might measure the performance of its workforce? (4 marks)

b Analyse two ways in which the company might improve its service by altering its organisational structure as it expands to Bristol and Bath. (9 marks)

c Discuss whether reducing costs should be the company's major operational target as it strives to improve the performance of the business. (12 marks)

d Is Any Junk? a competitive company because it offers a competitive price? Justify your view. (15 marks)

▶

Question Two: Seeds of Success Ltd

Jayne Turner has made some progress in breaking into the UK's snack market, although she acknowledges that it is a tough challenge. Jayne has launched a range of products called 'Healthy Nibbles'. These are made from a selection of seeds including sunflower, sesame and pumpkin which are mixed with a sauce and roasted. They offer her a USP over traditional snacks of crisps and biscuits.

After two months trading she is experiencing more severe cash problems than she imagined. She needed to offer 30 days' trade credit to persuade a small retail chain to stock her products though so far this arrangement has not been entirely successful.

She has suffered in other ways. She has used several different firms to supply her seeds and has had limited contact with any of them. They did, however, demand cash on delivery and she was disappointed when one firm delayed delivery of an order.

Jayne's primary market research indicated that her products were popular and that a niche market existed for them. However, she has encountered production problems. Shortages of certain supplies and low levels of productivity amongst her seven production line workers have led to delays in orders being sent out and complaints from customers.

Jayne has opted to pay her workers a bonus for meeting deadlines and has supervised the whole production process herself. This has led to her working very long hours to complete the essential management tasks of running the company.

However there is some good news. Her accountant has told her that the profit margin on sales is 30% and that she should make a small profit in her first year of trading.

Questions

a Complete Jayne's cash flow for May & June by completing the columns for actual figures. (6 marks)

b Analyse the two ways in which Jayne's suppliers could determine the success of her business. (8 marks)

c Discuss whether Jayne's decision to use money as a motivator for the workforce was a wise one in these circumstances? (12 marks)

d To what extent is the future of Seeds of Success Ltd dependent upon Jayne managing her cash flow more effectively? (14 marks)

	May Budget	May Actual	June Budget	June Actual
Cash in				
Cash sales	21750	24500	22025	25765
Credit sales	0	0	4500	?
Total cash inflow	21750	?	26525	25765
Cash out				
Wages	6500	7125	6780	7400
Raw materials	12580	13000	13435	13970
Marketing costs	950	450	300	250
Other costs	6500	9050	5800	7240
Total cash outflow	26530	?	26315	28860
Net monthly cash flow	−4780	−5125	210	?
Opening balance	1000	?	−3780	−4125
Closing balance	−3780	−4125	−3570	?

Jayne's cash flow

Index

Notes: Page numbers in **bold** refer to Key Terms, page numbers in *italics* refer to diagrams or tables